WHAT'S GOING ON?

The Holy Spirit in Christian History, Black Theology, and the Economy of God's Love

by
Darvin Anton Adams

ISBN: 978-1-960853-64-6

Liberation's Publishing LLC
Columbus - Mississippi

Previous Works

The Mythology of Kobe Bryant: Theology and the Culture of Sport
Cowritten with Lewis Brogdon
(2022)

Inner-City Blues: Black Theology and Black Poverty in the United States **(2023)**

Darvin Anton Adams

Table of Contents

Darvin Adams's new book, *What's Going On?* is groundbreaking in positive proof that every meaningful, relevant Black liberation theology must always be inherently biographical. Like the unimpeachable giants in theology, from Paul Tillich, Gary Dorrien, and Cornel West to Stephen Ray, and James Cone, Dr. Adams refuses to talk about the God of the oppressed without embracing the daunting challenge of communing with and talking to his dearly departed mother and his ebony ancestors on the chocolate covered 'Eastside' of his hometown, Hopkinsville, KY. *What's Going On?* is not just a cry of dereliction and despair; it is a theological testament of genuine Christian hope in the liberating work of the Holy Spirit. Dr. Adams's book is grounded in the prophetic insight of the theological affirmation that his Black liberation theology is rooted in divine revelation, results in Black liberation, and culminates in eschatological healing and salvation of mind and body, heart and soul, economy and ecology, human beings and the whole world.

Rev. Zachary W. Royal, B.S., MDiv, MTS
PhD Candidate, Union Theological Seminary
New York City, New York

First with *Inner City Blues: Black Theology and Black Poverty in the United States* (2023), and now with *What's Going On: The Holy Spirit, Black Theology, and the Economy of God's Love* (2024), Adams continues to pursue new paths in Black Theology for others to follow. Thank you for pushing the boundaries and expanding our imagination about the Spirit's liberating work in the world.

-- **Dr. Lewis Brogdon**
Executive Director, The Institute for Black Church Studies and
Associate Professor of Preaching and Black Church Studies
BSK Theological Seminary - Offices in Lexington and Louisville
Kentucky

In *What's Going On? The Holy Spirit in Christian History, Black Theology, and the Economy of God's Love*, Dr. Darvin Adams expertly challenges readers to reexamine, reframe and reinterpret their views on ecclesiology and pneumatology through a comprehensive examination of the role of the Holy Spirit in addressing economic evils, particularly the historical and present dilemmas of Black poverty in America. Adams leaves no stone unturned in addressing the pressing issues in contemporary society regarding the impacts of vulture capitalism and those who suffer the most under its survival of the fittest modality. Drawing on the prophetic and sacred discourse as a foundational axis for understanding the concept of revelation, Adams asserts that the voice of the Holy Spirit, reflected through the prophets, encourages spiritual awakening and communal responsibility. He emphasizes that true prophetic insight is both spiritual and deeply incarnational, revealing God's call for humanity to care for one another and for creation. This book not only invites reflection on what it means to embody the Holy Spirit but also offers practical pathways for applying these revelations to urban challenges, making it an essential read for anyone seeking to understand the intersections of black theology, community, and justice.

--Eric M. Betts, PhD
Assistant Professor, Hampton University School of Religion
Religious Activities Coordinator and Lecturer, Center for Religion,
Leadership and Culture Athens State University
Author *of Good Cop, Bad Cop, a Sociological and Historical Study of the Black Church and the Black Muslim Movement.*

Essential to a Christocentric understanding of the epistemological and ontological work of the Holy Spirit is what Adams asserts as Black liberative freedom, the healing power of the Holy Spirit of God, resistant, and in the battle for the holistic liberation reflective of the womanist energy associated with 'Mama'." Pivotal to this work is the inclusion of the Upanishads of Hinduism expressing the unborn, eternal, everlasting, ancient Spirit. He also includes tenets of the pneumatology of the Nation of Islam through the teaching and advocacy of El-Hajj Malik El-Jabaz, Malcolm X who embodies a "creative enough, productive enough" Spirit that births a Black cultural-spiritual perspective in community and society liberating mind, body, culture, and resources. In this, Adams adds to a very distinctive and crucial body of work, a dialogical trinitarian pneumatology conversant with strict monotheistic and non-theistic spirituality. He then challenges us to examine the Spirit in Blackness, not as an anthropomorphic identity but as in praxis justice and freedom.

--**Dr. Kai Horn El-Amin**, Lane College

As one who is currently intersecting Black Theology with Ontology while utilizing Existentialism in critique of black oppression in the United States and the world abroad, I am certain that Dr. Adams's new book *What's Going On?* is the greatest and most complete theology book on Pneumatology ever written. Constructive, cultural, descriptive, exciting, honest, historical, and prophetic, this new Holy Spirit book is unprecedented. I thought *Inner-City Blues* was an all-time great book. *What's Going On?* ascends to an even higher level. Black theology is blessed to have Dr. Adams in the writing fold. Such a great piece of writing.

–**Rev. Shea Thompson**, B.S., MTS from Boston University.

Dedication

To my all-world Momma Carolyn
Mack Adams of Hopkinsville,
Kentucky:
May your eternal nap be peaceful and
serene. Dad, Delvin, and I will forever
cherish you, love you, and miss you.
Thank you for being the guiding light
of all our lives. You did good.
Abundant blessings to you Momma
until we see you again in Heaven.

Malachi 4:2
But for you who fear My name, the
sun of righteousness will rise with
healing in its wings.

Revelation 21:4
He will wipe every tear from their
eyes. There will be no more death or
mourning or crying or pain, for the
older things have passed away.

Preface

God Healing My Momma of Cancer and The Apostles' Creed

Whether they speak of the Holy Spirit or not, every book should have a spiritual perspective. This new theology book begins with a personal one. As I research and write this new volume on the liberating work of the Holy Spirit, my mother continues to suffer from a Stage 4 metastatic breast and lung cancer diagnosis. Her name is Carolyn Mack Adams. Cancer has spread from the breast and lungs to her bones, liver, and parts of her brain. My family and I are not giving up hope. We often time weep, but we do not weep as one who does not have any hope (Rom. 12:15; 1 Thess. 4:13). Even though at times it seems like we are approaching the transitionary phase of my mother's illness, I am still holding fast to my faith in the hope that the Holy Spirit will heal my mother of her sickness. And she can live a little longer in the presence of her husband and her twin sons. The Holy Spirit is a healer and a liberator. The Holy Spirit has healed me and liberated me in so many ways throughout the course of my life. In the same way, I believe the Holy Spirit can heal and liberate my Momma from the bondage of her illness.

To say that God is a healer is to say that the Holy Spirit heals the hurting body, the lost mind, and the sin-sick soul. Healing is a form of liberation (Exo. 15:26, Jer. 30:17 and 33:6, Isa. 41:10 and 53:5, Ps. 10:32-33 and 41:3, Matt. 4:24, 9:35, 14:14, 15:30, and 18:16-17, Mk. 10:52; Lk. 4:18, 9:11, 10:9, 17:19; Acts 4:30, 10:38; Jas. 5:14-15; 3 Jn. 1:2; Rev. 21:4). And liberation is the work of the Holy Spirit.

Speaking on Luke 4:18, Trinity Funmi Akinwale proclaims that "We are invited to a holistic transformation through Christ Jesus. This transformation goes beyond physical healing to encompass liberation, divine visitation, and spiritual renewal. The Lord's healing power brings freedom and redemption to our lives. God urges us to spread the good news to the world and ensure all people receive their healing."[1] Theologically, the major purpose for writing this new pneumatology book is to engage, experience and explore the world-changing power of the Holy Spirit within the realms of liberation, healing, and transformational love.

Mayowa Sanusi confesses:

> As I learn more about the teachings of Black feminists like bell hooks[2] and Audre Lorde, I see the importance of healing to the liberation — freedom of oppression and constant presence of self-determination — of Black and other persecuted peoples. I define healing in the Black liberatory context *as the intentional process of reconciling internalized trauma and conflict to position oneself physically, mentally, and spiritually to address continuing challenges in daily life, especially those brought on by varying forms of oppression.* Healing is also a liberatory political practice — the politics of emancipation, self-determination, dignity, participation, and equality — for all. Lastly, healing can happen in solitude or community. In the Black community, healing is something that is talked about, sometimes, but infrequently put into practice. We talk about the constant trauma that we face on a physical, mental, and spiritual level, but not often enough do we make time to seek out healing and peace. I think this is largely because we never have an opportunity to heal. We are

---

[1] Trinity Funmi Akinwale, "23 Powerful Biblical Scriptures," Para. 20-21.
[2] Like myself, Dr. bell hooks was born and raised in Hopkinsville, Kentucky. In different generations, we grew up in the same inner-city neighborhood—Eastside Hopkinsville. Dr. hooks was a valued friend of the family. She attended our annual 4th July family cookouts, and she was my Aunt Ehrai's (Adams) best friend. They were extremely close. The Spirit led Dr. hooks to me a few sacred occasions where she shared with me the importance of authoring my story for the purpose of publishing my theology to the world. Each time I conversed with Dr. hooks in private, I could feel the power of the Holy Spirit in her presence and in her encouraging words. She was a source of literary knowledge, spiritual wisdom, and cultural understanding. My Aunt Ehrai and her siblings, my Dad included, knew Dr. hooks by her birthname Gloria Jean Watkins.

constantly having to function in "survival mode" because of the constant obstacles we face in society.[3]

With the words of Akinwale and Sanusi in mind, I recognize that my Momma is just as great of a Black woman as anybody I have ever encountered; famous or not. And as a believer in God, I have the faith needed to activate my Momma's healing. I know that God heals people through the faith of other people. I know that faith in Jesus Christ is the work of the Holy Spirit. I know that grace is the work of the Holy Spirit. I know that hope is the work of the Holy Spirit. I also know that love is the work of the Holy Spirit. And in my prayers, I consistently ask the Holy Spirit to heal my Momma of her sickness. As the only preacher in my immediate family, I am sure the Holy Spirit hears and would hear my prayers and grant me the desires of my broken heart. If anyone could heal my mother of cancer, God in Jesus Christ by power of the Holy Spirit could do it. And if anyone had the human power and strength to pull through this exceedingly difficult paralysis, it would be my Momma. The strength that "believing" Black women have always had is remarkably indescribable. To be sure, my Momma is a remarkable human being.

At the church I pastor, the Lane Tabernacle CME Church in Hopkinsville, Kentucky, we have three different members who were diagnosed with some form of cancer. These three women, my mother included, are always at the top of the prayer list. Every Sunday before the church prayed together, we would always recite the Apostles' Creed. As one who loves the Cardinal doctrine of pneumatology or the study of the Holy Spirit, the most fulfilling part of the Apostles' Creed was when the church says "I BELIEVE IN THE HOLY SPIRIT." The beginning portion of the Creed says that *"I believe in God the Father Almighty. The maker of Heaven and earth. And in Jesus Christ the only Son our Lord. Who was conceived by the Holy Spirit. Born of the virgin Mary. Suffered under Pontius Pilate. Was crucified, dead and buried. On the third day, He arose from the dead. He ascended into Heaven and sitteth at the right hand of God the Father Almighty. From this He will come to judge the quick and the dead."*

Productively, the Apostles discussed the third person of the

---

[3] Mayowa Sanusi, "Healing is Essential to Liberation," Para. 1.

Triune God in two contexts. First, the Holy Spirit is one that the Christian church must believe in. The Bible teaches that the Holy Spirit comes to those who believe. Second, the Apostles presents the Holy Spirit as one who conceived Jesus Christ. Matthew 1:18-21: *[18]Now the birth of Jesus the [a]Messiah was as follows: when His mother Mary had been [b]betrothed to Joseph, before they came together she was found to be pregnant by the Holy Spirit. [19]And her husband Joseph, since he was a righteous man and did not want to disgrace her, planned to [c]send her away secretly. [20]But when he had thought this over, behold, an angel of the Lord appeared to him in a dream, saying, "Joseph, son of David, do not be afraid to take Mary as your wife; for [d]the Child who has been conceived in her is of the Holy Spirit.*

The biblical text and the Apostles Creed give us reasons to be believe in the Holy Spirit; especially where faith in Jesus Christ is concerned. In his splendid book, *A History of Christianity*, Kenneth Scott Latourette suggests that

> By emphasizing the belief that Christ, the Son of the Father, is to be judge, the creed is repudiating, either deliberately or without that view explicitly in mind, the Marcionite contention that it is the Demiurge, not the Father or the Son, is to be judge. Of the concluding phrases [I believe] "in the Holy Spirit, and the resurrection of the flesh (dead)," the first was not in controversy and so was not amplified, but the second, and addition to the primitive formula, seems to have been intended as a protest against the view which counted flesh as evil.[4]

As a trained theologian in pneumatology, economic poverty, Black culture, and the Black religious experiences, I always look forward to the reciting the Apostles' Creed. Because I know the sufferings of Black people. However, at this sacred time, I am thinking about my Momma's condition when the church says together that "I BELIEVE IN THE HOLY SPIRIT. But what is the spiritual connection between me asking God to heal my Momma's body and the theological taking serious of the Apostles' Creed? Put simply, when I am reciting the Apostles' Creed on those Sundays of my

---

[4] Kenneth S. Latourette, *A History of Christianity*, 136.

mother's enduring cancer, I am thinking deeply about my mother's physical healing when the church and I say we believe in the Holy Spirit. In other words, we believe in the Holy Spirit enough that the Spirit would heal my Momma's body of cancer in her breast and lungs. We also believed that the Holy Spirit would heal the body of the other two women diagnosed with cancer.

1 Corinthians 12: 4, 9, and 11 reveal that there are diverse kinds of gifts, but the same Spirit distributes them. To another faith by the same Spirit, to another gifts of healing by that one Spirit. These gifts are the work of the Spirit, and the Spirit distributes them to each one, just as the Spirit determines. Even as I ask the Holy Spirit to heal my Momma's body by way of prolonging her years of life, I understand that the Spirit heals in a great many ways. One way that the Holy Spirit heals is by way of transitioning the sick away from and out of the suffering within their painful bodies. It is not up to us to decide how the Spirit heals our bodies or the bodies of our loved ones.

Here, I am reminded of what THE UPANISHADS (c. 900-600 BCE) say about the Holy Spirit: Spirit is not born, nor deceases ever, has not come from any, or from it any. This Unborn, Eternal and Everlasting Ancient is not slain, be it slain the body.[5] With the deceased body of my Momma in mind, I also reflect upon Gabriel Horn's description of the eternal return of the Spirit: "When we are born, it's like taking a cup of spirit out of the gene pool of life that the Mystery provides. We must pour that cup back when we die, like a drop of rain that falls back into the ocean where it originated, except that the drop of spirit we take into this world.[6] Horn is a contemporary Native American writer.

When I recite the Apostles' Creed on those Sundays of my mother's debilitating cancer, I was not being selfish, but rather I am trying to be affectionately spiritual. This is my way of loving on my Momma when I am not in her physical presence. In saying that I believe in the Holy Spirit, I am publicly expressing my love for God and my Momma. As a lifelong member of the Christian Methodist Episcopal Church, I understand the Apostles Creed to be "an expression of what was taught by the apostles, and the designation

---

[5] Frederic Brussat and Mary Ann Brussat, *Spiritual Literacy*, 231.
[6] Ibid, 407.

"Apostles Creed" is not an accident or a mistake. Moreover, in those few words, "Father, Son, and Holy Spirit," is succinctly summarized the heart of the Christian Gospel—God Who is Father, Who once in history revealed Himself in one who was at once God and man and Who because of that continues to operate in the lives of men through His Spirit. In this is the uniqueness of Christianity."[7] Latourette confers that "At Alexandria, it will be noted, the question of the Holy Spirit became more prominent than at Nicaea. At Alexandria it was made clear that the approved belief that the Holy Spirit is not a creature but is inseparable from the Father and the Son."[8]

The Holy Spirit is also referred to as the Lord and Giver of Life in the Nicene Creed. He is the Creator Spirit, present before the creation of the universe and through his power everything was made in Jesus Christ, by God the Father. The Holy Spirit is the One who empowers the followers of Jesus with spiritual gifts and power that enables the proclamation of Jesus Christ, and the power that brings conviction of faith and the liberation of the oppressed.

After a 14-month battle with breast and lung cancer, my mother made the ultimate transition to her place of eternal residence on Thursday December 16, 2022, at 2:33 A.M. I heard the loud heaviness of my Momma's death rattle. The sound of my momma's last breaths gave human shape to an incomparable love. As one who did not know what to do or say, I was both scared and at peace in my spirit. But not at the same time. I was not mad at God. I was angry at my Momma's cancer. While I continue to suffer in my mourning and grieving the physical loss of my Momma, I am convinced that her spiritual transitioning was the work of the Holy Spirit. While the Holy Spirit did not answer my prayers of healing my Momma in the way that I had hoped, the truth is that the Holy Spirit answered my prayers and healed my Momma of her bodily pain and suffering. This form of healing was also a form of liberation. I can hear my Momma telling myself and my older twin brother Delvin: "Boys, you just keep on living." Here the motherly wisdom was that she wanted her twin boys to keep on living and keep on believing that God in Jesus Christ by the power of the Holy Spirit will always make a way. After the members of Lane Tabernacle and I would say collectively, "I

---

[7] Kenneth S. Latourette, *A History of Christianity,* 136.
[8] Ibid, 161.

BELIEVE IN THE HOLY SPIRIT," the remaining portion of the Apostles' Creed reads: *the holy catholic church, the communion of saints, the forgiveness of sins, the resurrection of the body and life everlasting. Amen.*

In answering the earlier question of God's presence in the life of those who are physically sick, healing is the liberating work of the Holy Spirit. As the Spirit of Christ, the anointing of the Holy Spirit heals the brokenhearted, announces freedom for prisoners and captives; all the while comforting those that mourn those difficult moments in life. Why didn't the Holy Spirit heal my Momma according to my faith in Jesus Christ? The answer is the Holy Spirit did, in fact, heal my Momma. I say that because healing comes in diverse ways. And "grief takes time, and grief is work."[9] Grief is also the work of the Holy Spirit. The Holy Spirit is our Comforter, and one of the ways the Spirit comforts us is by helping us to grieve and process our grief. Grief is a natural response to loss, and the Holy Spirit helps us work through our grief by providing comfort, strength, hope, and peace. When we grieve, the Holy Spirit is present to help us process our most difficult emotions and find God's healing. Somewhere between people taking care of their emotional needs and their physical needs, the point is stressed for the bereaved to take diligent care of their spiritual selves.

In his book, *A Time to Grieve*, Kenneth C. Hauck writes:

If you are one of those people who has other family members depending on you—your spouse, siblings, children, or a remaining parent—you may find it easy to focus all your energy on those others while neglecting your own needs. Remember that one of the most important ways to take care of those who depend on you is to take good care of yourself. If you are attending to your own needs in healthy ways, you will be much more capable of meeting their needs as well.[10]

To the right side of this powerful quote, Hauck places Psalm 147:3: He heals the brokenhearted and binds up their wounds. No question about it. Healing is the liberating work of the Holy Spirit. Is the psalmist speaking of the Holy Spirit when he lists the two things

---

[9] Kenneth C. Hauck, *A Time to Grieve*, 24.
[10] Ibid., 25.

God does well? I believe so. The context of Psalm 147 is that the LORD builds up Jerusalem. He gathers the outcasts of Israel. The psalmist describes the goodness and greatness of God so he and others would have reasons to worship and praise God. The first reason is God's active care for Jerusalem, a reference to its restoration after the exile. Here, the implication is that God heals through Jesus Christ by the power of the Holy Spirit.

In her provocative article, "Groans Too Deep: The Holy Spirit and Suffering," Andrea Hollinsworth talks about what it means to discern the Spirit's role in suffering. As we have observed, the Spirit of God plays quite different roles in relation to human suffering—at times generating it, at times providing solace in the midst of it, and at times actively opposing it.[11] Hollinsworth believes that "When the suffering is connected to illness, grief, or loss, there may be cause to affirm the presence of the Holy Comforter (The Spirit Attends Suffering). And when the suffering is linked with the painful effects of social sin and injustice, there may be cause to affirm the presence of the Holy Liberator (The Spirit Contests Suffering)."[12] Throughout the course of human history, Black people of all groups, cultures and races have, in some way and for some reason, mourned and grieved the loss of their loved ones. And the Holy Spirit heard their faintest cries, comforted their spirits, healed their broken hearts, and bound up their painful wounds. It is important to keep in mind that because situations that give rise to human suffering are complex (and because God's ways are mysterious), the Spirit may be working in more than one way in any given circumstance.[13]

The pertinent questions are: Are we truly liberated if healing does not accompany liberation? Can we maintain the fight for liberation without experiencing God's healing? My answer would be no. And the sooner we view healing as an act of resistance *and* a part of the battle for holistic liberation, the sooner the Black oppressed can walk around the earth and claim, without consequence, that they are free. The work of the Holy Trinity is spiritually sympatico in that all three persons work cohesively together and individually within. God heals the broken heart in Isaiah 61:1-3, "The Lord has chosen

---

[11] Andrea Hollingsworth, "Groans Too Deep: The Holy Spirit and Suffering," Para. 32.
[12] Ibid., Para. 34.
[13] Ibid., Para. 35.

and sent me to tell the oppressed the good news, to heal the brokenhearted, and to announce freedom for prisoners and captives...the Lord has sent me to comfort those who mourn. He sent me to give them flowers in place of their sorrow." It was the Spirit of the Lord, the Holy Spirit, who was upon the prophet Isaiah choosing him and sending him to do the work of Jesus Christ. As she was committed to taking my twin brother and I to church on Sunday mornings, it was my Momma who assured her twin boys of the fact that healing and liberation are works of God in Jesus Christ by the power of the Holy Spirit. Because of her faith in God, my Momma was not afraid to die. As a result, God has healed my Momma and set her free by the power and work of the Holy Spirit.

Darvin Anton Adams

Introduction

The Holy Spirit in Paul Ricoeur's Biblical Hermeneutics

Holy Spirit, speak comfort to my soul. Holy Spirit, let your joys unfold. LORD of the highest. Spirit of Glory. Voice of the law. Breathe on me.[14]

The moral sense of a scriptural text does not mean to extract moral lessons from the text. It rather means to relate the ancient text of the Scripture, which is historically separated from the reader, to her/his here and now. The text is not simply a written document. It is also a mirror. Accordingly, hermeneutics is not simply exegesis. It is also seeing oneself in a mirror. In other words, the reader does not simply try to understand what the text says. She/he rather makes it speak to him/her personal and tries to understand his/her existence through understanding the text. She/he actualizes the spiritual meaning of the text by interiorizing it, i.e., by making it speak to her/his inner self. This is the "mutual interpretation of Scripture and existence."[15]

Even in the critical practice of interpreting scripture, the spiritual life is inside out and not outside in.[16] The only way Christian believers can actualize the spiritual meaning of the biblical text for the purposes of interpreting, living, preaching, and teaching the truth of God is by the illumination of the Holy Spirit. The Holy Spirit is what makes all things spiritual. In distinct ways, the moral sense is the spiritual sense. Put another way, to be moral is to be spiritual. With the spiritual idea

---

[14] https://www.songlyrics.com/new-jersey-mass-choir/holy-spirit-lyrics/

[15] Ricoeur, *Conflict on Interpretations*, 384.

[16] Frank A. Thomas. *The Choice*, 94.

of holistic discovery in mind, Paul Ricoeur reads the biblical text from an ontological rather than an epistemological perspective. Much like Paul Tillich, Ricoeur wishes to view hermeneutic philosophy from an ontological rather than epistemological platform, whereby "understanding" becomes a "way of being and a way of relating to beings and to being."[17] Using ontology as the philosophical starting point, Ricoeur distinguished between a 'hermeneutics of tradition' where the inquirer listens closely to a text in order to access the hidden message and to gain insight into a deeper, more substantive understanding of the biblical text.

Indebted to psychoanalysis as well as to the tradition of French semiotics, Ricoeur intends to demonstrate that there is no unbridgeable gap between ontological and critical hermeneutics. Although the differences between the two are legitimate, Ricoeur proposes an alternative that aims at unifying the most convincing aspects of both perspectives. Ricoeur agrees with Habermas and Apel that the hermeneutical act must always be accompanied by critical reflection. Yet, he does not find that this requires a leaving behind of the field of tradition and historical texts. Thus, Ricoeur emphasizes how the text itself may open up a space of existential and political possibilities. This dynamic, productive power of the text undermines the idea of reality as a fixed, unyielding network of authoritative patterns of interpretations.[18]

Using the critical tools developed by Sigmund Freud for interpreting dreams, Ricoeur applies his hermeneutic of interpreting myths, symbols, metaphors, and other multi-layered texts to his thoughts about Scripture. He adds another philosophical dimension to the understanding of the biblical text. In writing of the role of symbol and myth, particularly in understanding evil, Ricoeur argues that biblical hermeneutics must free itself from three historicist myths—the mind of the author, the original reader, and the original meaning.[19] Ricoeur's visionary insight about a particular text "grows in 'surplus of meaning' as it moves through the history of interpretation, and that the text's career escapes the finite horizon of

---

[17] Paul Ricoeur, *Hermeneutics Human Sciences*, 44.
[18] Stanford Encyclopedia of Philosophy-Hermeneutics.plato.stanford.edu /entries/ hermeneutics
[19] Ibid.

its author and now means more than what the author meant, are valid."[20]   In his theological hermeneutic, Ricoeur, like Friedrich Daniel Ernst Schleiermacher, philosophically searches for new language to talk about the unique relationship between God and humanity. In the biblical record, God reveals information about himself and inspired reports of how people responded to him. God also reveals himself to humanity through Jesus Christ and Holy Spirit, the second and third persons of the Holy Trinity. Hermeneutically, Ricoeur refers to this revelation as prophetic discourse. Ricoeur asks the question and gives the answer:

> Which of the biblical forms of discourse should be taken as the basic referent for a meditation on the idea of revelation? It seems legitimate to begin by taking prophetic discourse as our basic axis of inquiry. Indeed, this is the discourse which declares itself to be pronounced in the name of... and exegetes have rightly pointed out the importance of its introductory formula: "The word of Yahweh came to me, saying, 'Go and proclaim in the hearing of Jerusalem, . . .'"(Jet. 2:1). Here is the original nucleus of the traditional idea of revelation. The prophet presents himself as not speaking in his own name, but in the name of another, in the name of Yahweh. So here the idea of revelation appears as identified with the idea of a double author of speech and writing. Revelation is the speech of another behind the speech of the prophet. The prophetic genre's central position is so decisive that the third article of the Nicene creed, devoted to the Holy Spirit, declares: "We believe in the Holy Spirit...who spoke through the prophets." Yet if we separate the prophetic mode of discourse from its context, and especially if we separate it from that narrative discourse that is so important for the constituting of Israel's faith, as well as for the faith of the early church, we risk imprisoning the idea of revelation in too narrow a concept, the concept of the speech of another.[21]

The connection between the Holy Spirit and the words of the prophets is clear and obvious. The Spirit spoke through the prophets for the purpose of spiritual revelation to the people who needed

---

[20] Ibid.
[21] Paul Ricoeur, "Toward a Hermeneutic of Revelation," Para. 19.

God's correction. I would argue that for one to be prophetic, he or she must be innately spiritual. Only by the person, power and work of the Holy Spirit are we spiritual. True revelations from God come from the Holy Spirit. Revelation, for Ricoeur, is one way of explaining the relationship between God and humanity, God breathes God's spirit into humanity in a way that separates humans from animals and God's other creation, which God speaks into existence. What this means is that humanity has a role in the will of God in that

> God's unique role for humanity also sets us apart from the rest of creation. God gave humanity a role in God's creation. Humanity is caretaker of God's world. According to Psalm 8:3-9, God placed humanity slightly lower than God's self in the created world. Relationship another way in which humanity is unique among God's creation is that God determined humans had the need for relationship (Genesis 2:18-22). God in God's self is a relational being. God exists as the Trinity- Father, Son, and Holy Spirit. God created humanity in God's image, therefore God created humanity as relational beings as God is relational. Humanity was created first to relate to God and secondly to relate to one another.[22]

The hermeneutical revelation of the Spirit is that the Holy Spirit collaborates with all human beings. The Bible says that the Spirit has an ensuing ministry toward humanity which is God's creation.

With the notions of the Holy Spirit and creation in mind, the hermeneutical problem which Ricoeur seeks to address is how human discourse is equivalent to text. For Ricoeur, "human discourse and action both depend on and are independent of the context: they are meaningful only against the background of the context."[23] Ricoeur affirms that the context might give our religious performances in preaching, teaching, and writing unintended meanings. As a result, he wants to expand the boundaries of what defines "text" and consequently the nature of the knowledge that a text can yield will also change. In Ricoeur's work, there exist a rule of spiritual judgment through observation that is systematically relative to the individuals and situations involved; with regards to interpretation of Scripture,

---

[22] "Foundations for holistic ministry lesson two – icreation," Para. 7-8.
[23] Internet Encyclopedia of Philosophy Iep.utm.edu

this approach can be challenging to the traditional way of looking at the biblical text. As a result, and with the idea of biblical hope, Ricoeur desires to give great attention to *what is said* in and by the writing of the text—and not necessarily the writer of the text. By way of giving great attention to the message and not the messenger, Ricoeur seems to be leaning toward the Holy Spirit, and not the bible writer, as the one who helps believers to accurately interpret the text. I say this because the Holy Spirit is holistically involved in the writing of Scripture.

> When extended to all the other forms of biblical discourse we are going to consider, this concept of revelation, taken as a synonym for revelation in general, leads to the idea of scripture as dictated, as something whispered in someone's ear. The idea of revelation is then confused with the idea of a double author of sacred texts, and any access to a less subjective manner of understanding revelation is prematurely cut off. In turn, the very idea of inspiration, as arising from meditation on the Holy Spirit, is deprived of the enrichment it might receive from those forms of discourse which are less easily interpreted in terms of a voice behind a voice or of a double author of scripture.

Lewis S. Mudge suggests that "Instead of beginning with an image derived from prophetic discourse, that of another voice behind the prophet's voice, and extending it by analogy to narration, prescriptive saying, wisdom literature, hymnic composition, and so on, we are delivered from psychologizing interpretations of revelation to a particular sensitivity to the sense of the text, to the world-reference it opens up before it."[24] Here, Ricoeur's hermeneutic philosophy opens up the interpreter to possibilities; to a new way of seeing and being. Along the same lines, Werner G. Jeanrond claims that "Ricoeur helps us to acknowledge that any serious reading of literary or religious texts may result in challenging us to review our present mode of being in the light of the mode of being in the world disclosed by the text in the act of reading."[25] In our reading of the Bible, the Holy Spirit is credited with inspiring believers all the sacred scripture and leads prophets both in Old Testament and New Testament. Because the

---

[24] Lewis S. Mudge, "Essays on Biblical Interpretation by Paul Ricoeur," Para. 66.
[25] Werner G. Jeanrond, "Hermeneutics and Christian Praxis," 174.

Holy Spirit is the author of Scripture, the Spirit of God helps believers to read the Word of God with a new way of seeing God and being a child of God. Says Jeanrond:

> For this reflection the author of the narration comes to the fore and appears to be related to his writing as the prophet is to his words. The narrator, in turn, may by analogy be said to speak in the name of. . ., and then he is a prophet, and the Spirit speaks through him (or her). But this absorption of narration into prophecy runs the risk of voiding the specific feature of the narrative confession — its aiming at God's trace in the event. If we do not see the analogical bond between the other forms of religious discourse and prophetic discourse, we generalize in univocal fashion the concept of inspiration derived from the prophetic genre and assume that God spoke to the redactors of the sacred books just as he spoke to the prophets.[26]

> The Scriptures are then said to have been written by the Holy Spirit and we are inclined to construct a uniform theology of the double divine and human author where God is posited as the formal cause and the writer is posited as the instrumental cause of these texts. We over-psychologize revelation if we fall back on the notion of scripture as dictated in a literal fashion. Rather it is the force of what is said that moves the writer. The objective dimension of the revelations of the Holy Spirit is one of liberation and salvation. The two biblical doctrines contribute greatly to a non-psychologizing theology of the Holy Spirit.[27]

According to Collin Angell, Ricoeur believes that

No biblical hermeneutic would be complete without a developed concept of revelation. Revelation, in this thesis refers to how God reveals himself, whether through Scripture or elsewhere. This is a mountain of a question that could fill libraries with exposition and reflection, but this thesis maintains that a proper understanding of biblical modes of discourse such as narrative, prophecy, wisdom, and hymns

---

[26] Ibid.
[27] Ibid.

constitute a holistic framework for understanding revelation. Furthermore, a more complete understanding of the inspiration of the Holy Spirit the writers of Scripture were moved by also requires a proper understanding of the biblical modes of discourse. This thesis opposes a prevailing notion of inspiration that asserts that the Holy Spirit dictated Scripture to the authors, mainly because of its lack of coherence. A proper understanding of inspiration is essential to an adequate biblical hermeneutic, so a concept of inspiration that corresponds with how God reveals himself in the various modes of biblical discourse is preferrable.[28]

Out of the spiritual flows of the Holy Spirit's liberation, emancipation and salvation come faith, grace, healing, prophetic ministry, and sanctification. In the same scriptural flow, the Spirit helps believers to discover the spiritual objective dimension of revelation in the Bible and in the life that human beings are called to live. In theological consideration of Ricoeur's hermeneutical work, the thought that comes to mind is creative inspiration. In the words of Angell,

> Therefore, envisioning David, for example, lamenting to God in Psalms 22 using exactly the words that God told him to say undermines the significance of the lament. How could David's words to God have any real 43 meaning if David did not conceive of them himself? A better conception of inspiration, in this case, conceives David as being genuinely frustrated with God, with his words guided by the Holy Spirit in such a way that it leads David to the proper conclusion, resulting in an authentic piece of writing that is still worthy of being enshrined as the Word of God.[29]

Theologically, Ricoeur is moving toward the spiritual objective of the Holy Spirit's work within Biblical hermeneutics and properly interpreting the Bible. David Jasper writes that, Ricoeur we see, in a sense stretches back beyond the Reformation, to earlier modes of Christian hermeneutics characteristic of Augustine, the church fathers, and the medieval theologians, who saw many levels in the biblical texts all working together."[30] For example, in *Time and*

---

[28] Collin Angell, "Paul Ricoeur and Biblical Hermeneutics," 17.
[29] Ibid, 43.
[30] David Jasper, *Introduction To Hermeneutics*, 110.

Narrative, Ricoeur's theory of narrative is played out within its own context. Because Ricoeur's narrative theory presents a way of understanding the self through the activity of emplotment[31] or mimesis as part of interpreting cultural texts, the configuration of this story (narrative) is the activity of emplotment.[32] Not only does Ricoeur offer a cultural and social extension to creative human knowledge, but Ricoeur's referential theory of narrative emplotment supports an emphasis on "story" as narrative in phenomenological therapy. Ricoeur achieves the goal of "story" by arguing that a speaker is someone who seeks to bring to language a new experience. Further, the speaker seeks to share this new experience with someone else.

As a result, a text, being a series of sentences, refers to a world beyond itself and "narration then illuminates human action and makes manifest its temporality."[33] In this vein of thought, narration, in and of itself, is the liberating work of the Holy Spirit. Going back to the words of Pastor Roy Buck, "Biblical illumination is the process by which the Holy Spirit helps a person to understand the truth of God's Word. Illumination is often discussed alongside related concepts of biblical inspiration and interpretation involves how God has revealed spiritual truth; Illumination involves our understanding of spiritual truth and involves both the Scriptures and the influence of the Holy Spirit."[34] In other words, the Holy Spirit illumines the reader to the interpretive truth of God's Word.

According to Ricoeur, "Biblical illumination brings about inspiration conceived as the direct speaking of God through a vessel in the case of prophetic discourse, the response of the Holy Spirit in conversation in the case of hymnic discourse, and the source of prayerful reflection in the case of wisdom discourse."[35] Within the conversation of inspiration, it is understood that the Spirit illuminates the believer's ability to accurately interpret the biblical text. There is no illumination of the Holy Spirit without the Spirit's internal involvement in the life and spirit of the believing reader. Is not the distance between the believing reader and the Bible covered by the

---

[31] The word emplotment is defined as the assembly of a series of historical events into a narrative with a plot. (*historiography*)
[32] "A View from Nowhere Moral selves," Para. 4-5.
[33] Ibid.
[34] "What is Biblical Illumination?" Para. 1.
[35] Collin Angell, "Paul Ricoeur and Biblical Hermeneutics," 44.

presence of the Holy Spirit? In accordance with whatever type of distance or break the reader decides to take away from the biblical text, is that process or ritual the domain of the Holy Spirit? I believe so.

Consequently, as text, a speaker's discourse or narration of a new experience is confronted by the limits of literal predication and must be rescued from semantic impertinence by the metaphorical process. This referential power of the metaphorical statement has its analogy in the horizon of possibilities for experience disclosed by narrative discourse. The effacement of the text's literal predication becomes "the negative condition for freeing a more radical power of reference to those aspects of our being-in-the-world that cannot be talked about directly."[36] In essence, an accurate explanation of narrative emplotment creates a powerful interpretive tool for the liberation theologian seeking to proclaim central doctrines of the Christian faith. These actions and processes could very well be the work of the Spirit. To be sure, the study of the Holy Spirit (pneumatology) is a Cardinal doctrine of Christian theology.

If we are willing to listen with the heart of God, the Holy Spirit will inform believers about what is going on in the church, in society and in the world. The Spirit will lead us and guide us into what needs to be done regarding what is going on. Creatively and otherwise. If the Holy Spirit tells the believer what to say and what to pray for, then the Spirit can illumine the believing reader's mind toward the proper biblical interpretation. Here, the Holy Spirit reveals to the believers what is going on because the Spirit knows the mind of God. When it comes to interpreting the Bible, the Holy Spirit is the center of all theological hermeneutics.

Further, Ricoeur admits that his "biblical faith" and the rooted convictions lie at the heart of summarizing "the task of the contemporary Christian hermeneut."[37] Jasper states that "At the same time, "textual interpretation" demands a rigorous discipline, which involves, as far as possible, the suspension of the prejudices and preconceptions inherent in any uncritical "faith."[38] *Oneself as Another*, as a rigorous investigation into philosophical questions must

---

[36] Paul Ricoeur, *Time and Narrative*, 80.
[37] David Jasper, *Introduction to Hermeneutics*, 111.
[38] Ibid.

"bracket out" the requirements of his convictions about the Bible and indeed his discussion of God while at same time these convictions actually lie at the secret heart of his whole endeavor.[39] Assuming the Holy Spirit did not write chaotically and randomly, isolated texts are now seen in a pattern and signify something else, something creative and sacred beyond the pale of what the church has always believed. Because grace is also the work of the Holy Spirit, the Holy Spirit is sufficient in leading believers into the proper biblical interpretation.

In critiquing and exploring the hermeneutic framework of Ricoeur, Richard Topping argues that "God disclosure and salvific initiative is generative of inscriptured witness to the Gospel of Jesus Christ, which by the illuminative work of the Holy Spirit constitutes and sustains the Christian church."[40] The implication is that the witness and power of the Spirit is sufficient for the Christian church's interpretation of the Bible. Beyond Ricoeur's notion of structuralism and reading the text is the ideal that the text has a diverse myriad of meanings. Uniformly, the Bible teaches that Jesus lives inside every believer through the person of the Holy Spirit. The love that we receive through the presence of the Holy Spirit is the most precious gifts God has given to humanity.

According to the Apostle Paul, our body is the temple of the Holy Spirit. The Holy Spirit dwells in the heart of the believer. The Spirit of God dwells in us and lives inside us. In other words, there is a hermeneutical role of the Holy Spirit in the life of the believer. The biblical role of the Holy Spirit is the hermeneutical role of the Holy Spirit. Both inspires and enables the believer to interpret the text in a disciplined fashion. As believers in the Holy Spirit, the hermeneutical task calls upon the interpreters of Scripture to be confessors and witnesses to the life-changing power of Jesus Christ. Ricoeur explains his philosophy in two ways:

> The "confessional" kernel of testimony is certainly the center around which the rest gravitates. The confession that Jesus is the Christ constitutes testimony par excellence. Here again the witness is sent, and his testimony does not belong to him: "It is not for you to know times or seasons which the Father

---

[39] Ibid.
[40] Richard R. Topping, *Revelation, Scripture and Church*, 4.

has fixed by his own authority. But you shall receive power when the Holy Spirit has come upon you; and you shall be my witnesses in Jerusalem and in all Judea and Samaria and to the end of the earth" (Acts 1:7-8), says the Christ of the ascension. But if testimony is confessional in its kernel of meaning, it is not a simple confession of faith. All the traits of the ordinary meaning are resumed, assumed, and transmuted by contact with this confessional "kernel."[41]

With Luke, the witness is witness of things seen and heard; he is witness of the teaching, the miracles, the passion and the resurrection: "You are witnesses of these things," says the resurrected Lord in Luke 24:48. To be sure, the fact is inseparable from its meaning, but the meaning is recorded in history; it has taken place, it has happened. Of all that you are witnesses. The affirmation of the apostles appearing before the Sanhedrin echoes this fact: "And we are witnesses to these things, and so is the Holy Spirit whom God has given to those who obey him" (Acts 5:32). The two faces of the notion are here inseparable. On the one side, only the one sent — the apostle — is witness. Of that the Spirit alone is guarantor; but he is witness of things seen. The moment of the immediacy of the manifestation (I will return later to this expression which is Johannine before being Hegelian) is essential to the constitution of testimony as testimony. It is principally about the essential confession — that of the resurrection — that the dialectic of meaning and fact and confession and narration is played out for Luke. Everything indicates that the "appearances" have played the decisive role in that they prolonged the manifestation beyond death. The different sermons that the Acts of the Apostles reports return to this *Leitmotiv:* "This Jesus God raised up, and of that we all are witnesses" (Acts 2:32; cf. 3:15). The preaching of Paul is the same: "But God raised him from the dead; and for many days he appeared to those who came up with him from Galilee to Jerusalem, who are now his witnesses to the

---

[41] Paul Ricoeur, "Essays on Biblical Interpretation," Para. 46.

people" (Acts 13:30, 31).[42]

In *Time and Narrative and Oneself as Another* and for the sake of demonstrating a critical hermeneutic, Ricoeur, the philosopher, seems to be moving beyond a rhetorical (metaphorical) theology to a narrative (contextual) theology. The theological move from rhetorical-metaphorical to narrative-contextual is important because Ricoeur believes that the historical-critical reading of Scripture has closed us off from reading the text in a way that expands our horizons to the possibilities inherent in God's future. Ricoeur, following Hans Gadamer, insists on a "fusion of horizons" whereby we connect "our horizon of assumptions, culture, and traditions to the horizon of the text," so that an understanding of the text emerges only through understanding our own horizon. Along the same lines, the result of the Holy Spirit coming at Pentecost was fusions of spiritual horizons.

The first fusion of spiritual horizon came in the form of believers being together in one place. The second fusion of spiritual horizon came in the form of a sudden sound like the blowing of a violent wind coming from heaven and filling the whole house. The third fusion of spiritual horizon came in the form of them filled with the Holy Spirit and beginning to speak in other tongues as the Spirit enabled them. The concept of what it means to be together in one place (unity), to experience a violent wind coming from heaven that fills the whole house where the Church was sitting together (worship) and to be filled with the Holy Spirit and speak in other tongues, languages and cultures gives room for a hermeneutic of interpretation in the contemporary context. In turn, these fusions of spiritual horizon open the possibility of conversation and further understanding with people who bring to the text other experiential horizons.

Ricoeur writes that "The testimony that the witness has in himself is nothing other than the testimony of the Holy Spirit, a notion that indicates the extreme point of internalization of testimony: "But when the Counselor comes, whom I shall send to you from the Father, even the Spirit of truth, who proceeds from the Father, he will bear witness to me; and you also are witnesses, because *you* have been with me from the beginning" (Jn 15:26-27)."[43] The testimony of the Holy Spirit

---

[42] Ibid., Para. 48.

[43] Ibid., Para. 52.

as Counselor gives witness to the Spirit of Truth. Because the Spirit is truth, the Holy Spirit as Paraclete counsels and convinces the world of the Spirit's truth.

> The internal testimony of the Holy Spirit derives all its meaning in the struggle which is waged between the Christ and the world before the court of history. The first epistle of John evokes the "dramatics" of testimony and trial. "Who is it that overcomes the world but he who believes that Jesus is the Son of God? This is he who came by water and blood, Jesus Christ, not with the water only but with the water and the blood. And the Spirit is witness because the Spirit is the truth. There are three witnesses, the Spirit, the water, and the blood; and these three agree" (I John 5:5-8). The water and the blood here designate the punishment of the Cross, the Passion. If we do not link the testimony of the Spirit to the eschatological trial, we would hardly understand why he is called the Paraclete when the Counselor comes John 15:26-27). The Paraclete is the figure who is the counterpart of the accuser. The same Paraclete who "will convince the world of sin and of righteousness and of judgment" (John 16:8) will be the counselor to the believers when Satan will have become the accuser.[44]

Ricoeur criticizes Gadamer for setting up a false antimony between truth and method.[45] The distanciation of the written discourse from an author's intended sense results in the production of the world of a text. This world is uncovered by the structuralist method. The reader then is confronted by the world of the text, and a distanciation between its truth and horizon of the reader results. Distanciation is

---

[44] Ibid., Para. 58.

[45] According to Barry D. Smith's article on Érudit, Ricoeur was certain that "This first distanciation, in turn, gives rise to a second, namely, the distanciation between the reader and what the text is about, i.e., the truth of the text. It is in this second sense that Gadamer understands distanciation. Further, Ricoeur postulates that the distanciation of the written discourse from an author's intended sense results in the production of the world of a text. This world is what is uncovered by the structuralist method." (pgs. 215-216) While Gadamer's hermeneutics mostly focuses on construction, i.e., forging or building understanding within a community or forging the very community itself through a fusion of horizons, Ricoeur believed that Gadamer's approach to hermeneutics was too focused on the tradition of the community and that it failed to account for the role of the individual in the interpretive process.

overcome in interpretation. For Ricoeur, truth and method, therefore, are really two stages in the interpretation of a text, corresponding to two late related types of distanciation.

Is distanciation the work of the Holy Spirit or is he the one that works between the truth of God and the horizon of multiple possibilities within one's reading of the biblical text? My understanding is that "if appropriation happens through distanciation, the distance between the different horizons must be generated and preserved and not surpassed.[46] Ricoeur was in an intense dialogue with the biblical scholars working in these different fields.

> Yet "how shall they call upon him in whom they have not believed? Or how shall they believe without a *preacher?* And they shall praise the Lord that seek him, "for that they *seek* him find him, and *finding* him they shall *praise* him. Lord, let me seek you by *calling* upon you, and let me call upon you by *believing* in you, for you have been *preached* to us. Lord, my faith calls upon you...[47]

The Apostle Paul's words bring us to the biblical and hermeneutical fact that the Holy Spirit comes to those who believe in Jesus Christ and are willing to know him. If anyone knows what's going on in the world, in the church, and in society, it would be the Holy Spirit. I say that because as an equally contributing member of the Holy Trinity, the Holy Spirit knows the mind of God and the hearts of human beings. Now the questions are: Does the people of God know and believe in the Holy Spirit? Does the people of God feel the love and power of the Holy Spirit? What's going on in the world and in the societies of which God's people inhabit?

A Contextual Suspicion Within the Spiritual Idiom

Both my spiritual intuitions and my neighborhood memories of cultural embracing led me to the discovery that

> 'What's Going on?' is an idiomatic expression either used as an informal greeting or as an expression of concern awaiting an explanation. There are also some alternate uses for the expression in various cultures. The meaning of 'What's Going On?' is equivalent to asking what are you doing? By way of a

---

[46] Pierre Buhler, "Ricoeur's concept of distanciation," 162.
[47] Romans 10:14

> verbal questioning or a mental inquiry, asking 'What is Going On?' is an informal way of greeting people and situations. Usually among friends this line of questioning is a way to find out what is happening in one's life, in society, in religion or in the world. 'What's Going On?' could come in the form of "How's it going? Or What's up?" It is an expression of concern and awaiting an explanation about a situation.[48]

This descriptive statement is true of Black religion and Black culture (and other cultures too) when two or more people are in the process of greeting one another in good spirits (Matthew 18:20). Put another way, What is 'G\going on?' is natural to inquiry about what is going on when your body has been in a specific mode for a while, with no other activity to reference or be involved in. What has happened or is currently happening? To be sure, "What's going on?" is an idiom of human curiosity. It is one of the most used expressions in English writings. "What's going on?" represents an expression of concern or asking for an explanation. It is also a phrase used to express one's confusion while requesting an explanation for an unfamiliar situation.[49] Another way of asking what is going on? is what could the Spirit be up to or what is the Holy Spirit doing during these difficult and tumultuous times?

Concomitantly, the question of 'What's going on?' presupposes the curious inquiry of 'What is the theological hermeneutic or the hermeneutic of suspicion that the believer experiences as he or she reads the biblical text? In this vein of thought, 'What's Going on?' comes across as a spiritual idiom in that the inquiry itself presupposes the spiritual commentary within the personal story and the human experience. I believe that by examining the various nuances of one's narrative (story) and context (human experiences) with God, we can better understand why he or she uses a certain type of hermeneutical approach for interpreting Scripture. In terms of appropriating the biblical text in contextual light of the experiences and cultures of a particular people, one must consider the "story" of the same people as a way of gauging their reflections upon both God and God's word. As a theologically concerned pastor of 22 years in the Christian

---

[48] https://www.bing.com/search?q='What's+Going+on%3F+is+an+idiomatic+ Expression+either+used+as+an+inform…
[49] Ibid.

Methodist Episcopal Church tradition, my hermeneutic of suspicion begins with the belief that the Holy Spirit perfectly inspires Scripture; yet Scripture was imperfectly written by sinful human beings.

As a result, I read and interpret the Bible through the lens of the oppressed who are holistically in need of a liberator God who culturally identifies with the blatant suffering of God's people. The reason my hermeneutic of suspicion presupposes the questions of who has benefited, who is benefiting and who will benefit economically and financially from a particular interpretation of Scripture is simple. A sizable number of twenty-first century, Black churches has embraced a postmodern turn backwards (slavery amnesia) by emulating the capitalistic economy and psychologically oppressing its people with the 'name it and claim it' religion that affirms that God in Jesus Christ is both our Lord and Savior and our money tree solution to the problem of human suffering. Now in survival mode (due to the COVID-19 pandemic and the growing residuals of embracing an economically oppressive theology) and in some regions, on the brink of extinction, the historical, mainline Black church has taken society's postmodern marching orders and transformed the Church into an invisible, economic institution. All the while deciding not to publicly critique the social, political, and economic systems that victimizes a sizable number of their people.

How has the Black church, micro and macro, become excessively colonial and imperial in its way of doing God's economic business? One way is through using a watered-down biblical interpretation that speaks to the psychological condition of the people and calling it a move of the "*Spirit of God upon your life.*" Once the people are convinced that what they are feeling is, in fact, inspired by God, then the action of giving beyond their means becomes the slave command; it becomes easy. The colonial part of the process is that prosperity theology comes from the mouths of people who know that the sizable amount of Black people are dirt poor. Often, that city-slick, jive-time, shakedown, offering time theology of theoretical materialism embedded in a sizable number of Black Christian churches leads to a worsening economic and spiritual condition amongst Black Americans. It also leads to a misunderstanding of what the Bible teaches about giving. On the other side of the economic coin, it is true that White Americans and other groups, races, and cultures of people are materially poor as well.

Holistic Transformation, Marvin Gaye, and the Deep Spiritual Rivers

My central guiding principle for interpreting Scripture is the Holy Spirit's holistic transformation in Jesus' revealing God's liberating love for all people through his work on the cross. Liberation is part of God Almighty's plan of unconditional love for God's creation. Even as a child attending church on a regular basis, I understood that Jesus loved me only when I felt the power of the Holy Spirit. But the love of God's Spirit did not fully resonate with me until I realized that Jesus loves everybody; not just me. For me, interpreting the Bible is not about how I can inherit eternal life per say, but it is more about God's plan of spiritual and social salvation for the world and the role of the Holy Spirit in God's redeeming quality.

I agree with such scholars as Cheryl Anderson, Brad Braxton, Bishop Thomas L. Hoyt Jr., Wonhee Anne Joh, K. K. Leo, and Fernando F. Segovia in that we must embrace and respect other biblical interpretations—for the sake of *our own* liberation. Our own liberations are dependent upon our commitment to unconditionally loving and respecting those of diverse groups, races, and cultures. As a product of the Black church, the Spirit has guided my feet into participating in interdenominational worship experiences, interreligious discussions, intercultural festivals, interracial conversations, and interdisciplinary studies. The one common thread in all these initiatives is the presence of the Holy Spirit. Will we ever listen to what the Spirit is telling us?

When I talk about the Holy Spirit in Christian theology, I am referring to a particular theological perspective of the Holy Spirit's power and work. I define the Holy Spirit as the Spirit of Jesus Christ, the giver of life, the worker of grace, hope and salvation, and the liberator of the oppressed. Certainly, the Holy Spirit does even more wonderful things in the life of the believer... the ministries of healing and sanctification included. I could go on and on about the works of the Holy Spirit, but the truth of this study on Ricoeur's hermeneutic philosophy lacks an approximation for Christian teaching on the role of the Holy Spirit, a role taken by what Ricoeur calls the "creative imagination" or by imaginative approximation. But that does not mean that the Black church cannot preach and teach the doctrine of the Holy Spirit with both a creative imagination and a vision of holistic liberation. Because they can.

J. Deotis Roberts believes that "The Bible is a source book for theology, but it must be interpreted under the guidance of the Holy Spirit, who leads us into truth. As we read the Bible, it is the Spirit that broods over the chaos of our minds and spirits to teach, illumine, and guide."[50] When Marvin Gaye began the song, "What's Going On," by stating "Father, father", I am led to believe that he was praying to the Spirit of God about the disastrous situation of the United States and people of color—in spiritual hopes that God would either intervene in our oppressive situations or change the hearts of those who are in charge. Either way, Gaye's socially conscious music represented his journey of theological discoveries and greater distanciation experiences with God, Jesus Christ, and the Holy Spirit. These were the moments that helped to define the historical year of 1971 and the musical legacy of Marvin Gaye.

Theologically, the United States and the world abroad are the spiritual better for our experiencing and hearing Gaye's transcendent music. If anyone knew what was going on in 1971, it is the person of the Holy Spirit (Jn. 14:26, 16:13; Acts 1:8; Rom. 8:26-28; 1 Cor. 2:11; 2 Tim. 3:16-17). Whereas we consider the theological conversations of good, evil and the question of revelation, Ricoeur gives us clues as to how the Holy Spirit helps us to accurately interpret cultural texts. Social ethicist Riggins Earl reminds us that, "Paul Ricoeur says that the paradox of the religious philosophical principle of both consent and hope manifest itself when we have "consent[ed] as much as possible, but hope[d] to be delivered of the terrible at the end of time to enjoy the new body and a new nature granted to freedom."[51]

In lieu of human freedom, Rhema is a Greek word translated "word;" it means "when words leave one's lips." The Spirit's voice in our hearts is one example of *rhema,* while verses leaping off the pages of Scripture and into our hearts is another example. God's voice sounds like flowing, spontaneous thoughts that light upon our mind. Here, the Holy Spirit is sensed as a river of God's living water which flows within (Jn 7:31-39). Verses 37-39 declares: "Now on the last day, the great day of the feast, Jesus stood and cried out, saying, "If anyone

---

[50] J. Deotis Roberts, *A Black Political Theology*, 37.
[51] Paul Ricoeur, *Freedom and Nature*, 480.

is thirsty, let him come to Me and drink. He who believes in Me, as the Scripture said, 'From his innermost being will flow rivers of living water.'" But this He spoke of the Spirit, whom those who believed in Him were to receive; for the Spirit was not yet given, because Jesus was not yet glorified." Says the writer of the famous slave spiritual "Deep River":

Deep river, my home is over Jordan.
Deep river, Lord, I want to cross over into campground.
Oh, don't you want to go to that Gospel-feast?
That Promised Land, where all is peace?[52]

There is no life in the Spirit without a creative imagination and a proclamation of spiritual faith to go with it. In viewing the Holy Spirit as the deep rivers and living waters of one's spiritual life, Doris Grumbach says that "Water to me is saving grace. As a child I forgot my anger at my parents or camp counselors or teachers if I went to a swimming pool, or to a lake...Water was freedom, an element in which I believed I had perfect control. Lake and pool waters were calm enough to provide that (spiritual) illusion. I moved through the water in a kind of ecstasy, cut away from the rules of the land, social requirements, limitations, disappointments. Water was action, more effective than prayer. When I swam, I believed in God."[53] Grumbach's words paint a liberating picture of what it feels like to swim in the living waters of the Holy Spirit (Jn 7:37-39).

Describing Other Spiritual Mediums and Introducing Black Theology

Scott R. Sanders creatively traces the liberating work of the Holy Spirit through the mediums of water, air, and fire.

Water is the formless potential out of which creation emerged. It is the ocean of unconsciousness enveloping the islands of consciousness. Water bathes us at birth and again at death, and in between it washes away sin. It is by turns the elixir of life or the renewing rain or the devastating flood. Air is the wind that blows wherever it wills. It is the voice sounding in the depths of matter, the word made flesh. It is breadth,

---

[52] Odetta, "Deep River," https://www.lyrics.com
[53] Frederic Brussat and Mary Ann Brussat, *Spiritual Literacy*, 525.

which the Romans called *spiritus,* a divine thread drawn through every living creature. And Fire is the transformer, cooking meat, frightening beasts, warming huts, forging tools, melting, shaping.[54]

Sanders also references the power of the Spirit in such existential realities as birth, life, the blood of Jesus, spiritual renewal, scripture, breath, and transformation.

The deep rivers and sounding waters of the Holy Spirit know what is going on because as the third person of the Holy Trinity and an active member of the Triune God, the Holy Spirit knows the mind of God (1 Cor. 11-13). This spiritual knowing is creative enough in community and productive enough in culture to confirm Black people's safe place in the Kingdom of God. Some religionists refer to this vainglorious place as Heaven, over Jordan and the Promised Land. Martin Luther King's last public words in April 1968 that "We as a people will get to the Promised Land" were the work of the Holy Spirit. King's poignant words and the words of other brave soldiers of human emancipation and Black liberation ring true in the ears of those who have yet to see the coming of the salvific Glory of the Lord.

Or even Malcolm X's spiritual proclamation "By any means necessary"[55] where one of the greatest Black prophets in history talked about what it meant to be inspired by the Holy Spirit—to be encouraged and inspired enough to take positive action toward a progressive and protective equality of all people in the bond of sisterhood and brotherhood across the globe. As a reminder of the Spirit, if God's people of faith in all generations, genders, cultures, and races are not willing to unite in Spirit, in love, and in action "then we will always be a part of the problem rather than the solution to the

---

[54] Ibid., 136. See Scott Russell Sanders's book *Writing from the Center*

[55] While political pundits and cultural critics believe that Malcolm X was attempting to promote physical violence amongst the Black oppressed and the white oppressors, I am certain that X's visionary statement was one of holistic and spiritual affirmation. By any means necessary included Black people's right to protect themselves against the attempted racial brutality of physical harm and the spiritual provision of God the Creator. Theologically, I believe the statement of 'by any means necessary' brings to light the liberating work of the Holy Spirit in the life of oppressed people. This liberating work is holistically prioritized as a protective covering for Black people, white people, and all other oppressed groups, races, and cultures of people.

spiritual famine plaguing America [56]today. Certainly, the person, power and work of the Holy Spirit can help us in our active pursuit of emancipation and liberation. The work of the Holy Spirit is the solution to the spiritual famines of the United States and the world abroad.

Black theology, then, in partnership with all church denominations, remains committed to working in partnership with God in order that God's creation be redeemed, transformed, and liberated through the life, death, and resurrection of Jesus, and in the regenerative power of the Holy Spirit. Black people in Methodism have played an important part in that development and continue to do so.[57] The oppressions of Black people that arose during the era of institutional slavery is revisualized today in the material poverty and structural marginalization of Black people across the globe. Black theology, then, is also an academic discipline, spiritual protest within cultural creations, and a form of community faith-based practice. With the power of the Holy Spirit, Black theologians, religious scholars, church leaders, laypeople, and politicians alike must intentionally address the social, political, economic, educational ills of Black people in the United States and all over the world. Black theology affirms a blackness of the Spirit that symbolically references "skin color and oppression than can be applied to all persons of color who have a history of oppression,"[58] Black theology begins with the liberating work and transcendent power of the Holy Spirit in the real-life experiences of those who are dehumanized, marginalized, and oppressed.

This new book chronicles the person, power and work of the Holy Spirit in the Bible, the history of Christian experience, Black/African theology, white European theology, Economics, Race, Black religion, social progressive movements, Civil and human rights, Black culture, Black spirituality, African slavery, theology Black, Black history; and in my own narratives, stories and testimonies of what it means for normal mojo human beings to hear and respond to the voice of the Holy Ghost moving in their lives. In highlighting the ways the Holy Spirit gives life to the dying and the oppressed, *What's*

---

[56] Marian W. Edelman, *Guide My Feet*, 93.
[57] Anthony G. Reddie, *Black Theology*, 81.
[58] Anthony B. Bradley, "The Marxist roots Black liberation theology," Para. 4.

Going On? presents an ultra-exciting smorgasbord of liberating perspectives on the Holy Spirit. Chapter 1 describes the Holy Spirit in Christian History through the theological lens of Saint Basil the Great, Saint Augustine of Hippo, Martin Luther, John Calvin, Huldrych Zwingli, John Wesley and others. The opening chapter also speaks to the spiritual intricacies of the Protestant Reformation and Pentecostalism as powerful movements developed and inspired by the work of the Holy Spirit.

Chapter 2 describes the liberating work of the Holy Spirit in the Bible, in Black cultural identities, and in instances and moments of Black darkness. In discussing how the Holy Spirit works in the light of Black people's darkness, Chapter 2 also introduces a new term in the Black liberation theology conversation: theology Black. Theology Black intricately describes the liberating work of the Holy Spirit in the religious, cultural, and existential experiences of Black people and other oppressed groups of people. As a form of Black theology, theology Black intentionally presents the Holy Spirit as a Black person/person of color working within the flow of the Spirit of Blackness and love. Black theologians James H. Cone, Kelly Brown Douglass, and Major J. Jones lead the constructive way in describing the how and why each person of the Holy Trinity is Black for the Black cultural, existential, human, and religious experiences.

Chapter 3 presents the power and work of the Holy Spirit in Black theology as a way of beginning to understand economics. In unpacking the early moments of what it could mean to talk about the Holy Spirit within the conversation of economic poverty, this chapter describes instances, images and other types of theological reflections that center on the description of the Holy Spirit's liberating work in Black theology, Womanist theology, and other important facets of Black religion. This chapter also begins the pneumonic argument that Black human experiences in the United States and the world abroad are more pneumatological than Christological. In unpacking the transformative interactions of the Holy Spirit with Black theology and Black religion, this chapter represents the centerpiece of the new book by citing sources that help to construct and describe a Black pneumatology for the contemporary context. Chapter 3 represents the theological middle ground between the Holy Spirit in Christian history (Chapters 1-2 and Chapter 4) and the love of the Holy Spirit in theology and economics.

Chapter 4 unpacks the love of God in Jesus Christ by the power of the Holy Spirit as the primary interlocutor between the study of theology and the science of economics. Within the growing academic conversation of theology and economics, this chapter is the most balanced chapter in the book in that it nuances the liberating work of the Holy Spirit in the life of the poor with the substantive arguments of renowned economists and economic theologians. In referencing the work of white and European theologians, Chapter 4 also speaks briefly to the ministry work of the Black church in the presence of those deprived of economic resources. In addition to arguing that theologians and religious leaders would be more effective in their familiarity with the reading of economics, this chapter brings to light poor people's need for both the love of God's Spirit and the love of their fellow human beings.

Chapter 5 focuses on how the Bible talks about the Holy Spirit giving life explicitly and implicitly to those in need. In doing so, this chapter also speaks to the work of the Holy Spirit within the important theological conversations of liberation, compassion, memory, and hope. In presenting the Fruits of the Spirit, the 7 Gifts of the Spirit, and the 9 Gifts of the Spirit as the implicit works of the Holy Spirit in the life of believers, this portion of the new text descriptively transitions the conversation from biblical descriptions of religious proportions to the real-life experiences of Black people and other oppressed people who struggle spiritually and otherwise. This chapter also reveals descriptive elements of theology Black and details how this theological perspective liberates through the person, power, and work of the Holy Spirit.

Chapter 6 represents one of its most important arguments in the new book. The ways and means that the Holy Spirit resists and contests the demonic in society and the world symbolizes the liberating work of the Holy Spirit in the life of those who believe but are yet hegemonized. Chapter 6 describes the liberating work of the Holy Spirit in Black cultural identity and social movements. 1971 proved to be a landmark year for Black people in general and for the United States in particular. Through the inspirational work of the Holy Spirit, the culture of Black people in social organizations within grassroots movements expanded in socially conscious music, secular music, election politics, and sports entertainment. This cultural narration exists in the creation of justice-minded social movements and the faithful presence of the Holy Spirit working in the most despondent of situations. One notable example of this spiritually freeing work is the African slaves' experience with the Liberator Spirit. Freedom and liberation are direct results of Spirit resisting and contesting the demonic outreaches of Satan.

Chapter 7 and the final reflections provide an academically-ladened synopsis of various academic books, cultural conversations, theological analyses—all of which are relevant to the work of the Holy Spirit in creating and producing theological responses to the oppressive issues of racism, and poverty. These chapters speak about the role of the Holy Spirit in the development of Black existential thought, Black spirituality, Black cultural texts, and Black religious thought in slave narratives. Within the conversation on Christian eschatological hope and the various nuances of Black liberation, these chapters help to theologically distinguish J. Deotis Roberts from Jurgen Moltmann, give considerable attention to what it means to be spiritual due to the transformational presence of the Holy Spirit, reveal the African slaves' desperate need for the Holy Spirit in their lives as a way defining what it means for Black people to be a naturally-religious people, unpack the contours of what an apophatic theology looks like in the context of Black theology, describe the true meaning of liberation, affirm the Godliness of the darker-skinned human being, and lastly, give the critical thoughts of prominent thinkers W.E.B. Du Bois, Dwight N. Hopkins, Lewis O. Brogdon, George C. Cummings, Riggins Earl, Anthony G. Reddie, Andrea Hollingsworth, and Sonya Renee Taylor.

Chapter One

The Holy Spirit in Christian and World History

Come, Holy Spirit, fill the hearts of Thy faithful and enkindle in them the fire of Thy love. Send forth Thy Spirit and they shall be created. And Thou shalt renew the face of the earth.[59]

Saint Basil the Great

Saint Basil the Great's theological legacy rests upon his providing a powerful defense of how the Holy Spirit partakes the fullness of divinity. As one of the Cappadocian Fathers, Saint Basil writes in response to the Arian controversy of those who had reservations about the divinity of Holy Spirit. By way of seeing varying degrees of divinity in the Father, Son, and Holy Spirit respectively, the more radical Arians had staked their claim to which persons were divine. After concluding that the Son shared in the Father's divinity, the debate then moved to the status of the Holy Spirit. Basil answered the *pneumatomachoi* by using the authority of the Bible. By referencing the Holy Scriptures Saint Basil demonstrated that the Holy Spirit was called Lord and thus ranked no less than the Father and the Son.[60] For Saint Basil, Scripture answers all questions regarding the Holy Spirit's divine status amongst the Father and the Son. Saint Basil's

---

[59] https://www.catholic.org/prayers/prayer.php?p=331
[60] St. Basil the Great: *On the Holy Spirit* (trans. David Anderson; Crestwood, NY: St. Vladimir's Seminary Press, 1997), summary of pg. 6-12, 17 and 29. Most of the Basil's description of the Holy Spirit are referenced on pages 6-10. Basil takes biblical names seriously in that the Holy Spirit was termed as Lord, which are names that are also given to the Father and the Son.

orthodox thinking led him into the conversation of the divinity of Christ over against the divinity of the Spirit. With Nicene Orthodoxy claiming Christian baptism in the name of (God) the Father, Son and Holy Spirit, Basil taught that God in 3 persons makes up the Holy Trinity. Here, the Spirit proceeds from the Father...F → **HS** ← S →...through the Son; remarkably like Saint Augustine's construction of the Holy Trinity. The Holy Spirit belongs to the Holy Trinity in both equality and dignity. Surprisingly, Saint Basil never refers to the Holy Spirit as God. However, Saint Basil's hesitancy did not deter him from affirming the divinity of the Holy Spirit. Basil confidently theologized God the Father and God the Son as agents of inseparable union with the Holy Spirit. With the idea of inseparable union in mind, Basil wrote *On the Holy Spirit,* during the latter part of the Trinitarian controversies of the fourth century. Saint Basil's doctrine of the Holy Trinity put in motion the contrast and the communionship of the divine Persons.

In Chapter 17 of *On the Holy Spirit,* Saint Basil writes that "On the other hand (against those who say that the Holy Spirit must be numbered with the Father and the Son, but under them[61]), if you limit subordination to the Spirit alone, you must learn once and for all that the Lord speaks of the Spirit and the Father in exactly the same way: "In the name of the Father, and of the Son, and of the Holy Spirit."[62] In his book, *The Spirit of Early Christian Thought*, Robert Louis Wilken affirms that through his theology of the Holy Spirit, "Basil appeals directly to the formula used in baptism, "in the name of the Father and of the Son and of the Holy Spirit," as support for his argument that the Spirit is to be ranked with the Son and the Father."[63] Here, Saint Basil's theology lifts up the individuality of the Holy Spirit over "against those who say it is not right to rank the Holy Spirit with the Father and the Son."[64] Basil explains:

> How could Father, Son, and Spirit testify to their union and fellowship, let them explain to us why we should agree with their opinion. How could Father, Son and Spirit be united in a different or more suitable way? If indeed the Lord did

---

[61] Ibid., 68.
[62] Ibid., 70.
[63] Robert L. Wilken, *Early Christian Thought*, 103.
[64] St. Basil the Great, *On the Holy Spirit*, 45.

not speak of Himself, the Father, and the Spirit as being united in baptism, then let our opponents blame us for having invented this doctrine. But no one is so shameless that he will deny the obvious meaning of the words which clearly say the Spirit *is* one with the Father and the Son.[65]

Saint Basil's text, *On the Human Condition,* distinguishes between that which is according to the image, the rationality and free choice that humans always have, and that which is according to the likeness, the deiform virtues that we can acquire through participation in Christ by using our freedom to cooperate with the Holy Spirit. Saint Basil notes that God has honored humans by enabling them to become fashioners of the divine likeness within themselves.[66] Thus, "the purpose of human existence and participation in the divine image is fulfilled in knowledge and vision of God, likeness to God and union with him.[67] Saint Basil's theology of the human condition stressed the importance of oneness in and with the Holy Spirit. He writes that, "But as for that good and pleasant condition (the human condition), the dwelling of brothers in one place, which the Holy Spirit compares myrrh emitting a fragrance from the high priest's head [Psalm 133.1-2], how, when dwelling in solitude, will this be accomplished? Thus, it is an arena for struggle, a fragrance of progress, and continuous training and practice of the Lord's commandments when brothers dwell in one place."[68] For Saint Basil, this one place to experience the fragrance, training and practice of God's commandments was the church.

Nevertheless, in community life the activity of the Holy Spirit in one person must pass to everyone together. So the one living by himself perhaps has one gift, and he makes it useless because it is uncultivated, buried in the earth within himself.[69] And if indeed we all, who share in the one hope of our calling [Eph 4.4], are one body, having Christ as head, and are each members of another [1 Cor 12.12], if we are not fitted together in the Holy Spirit to join in concord into one body, but each of us chooses the solitary life, we will

---

[65] Ibid.
[66] Saint Basil the Great, *The Human Condition*, 9.
[67] Ibid., 20.
[68] Ibid., 122.
[69] Ibid., 121.

not serve the common good with coordinated planning according to God's good pleasure, but fulfill our own passion for self-indulgence.[70] Connectionally, Saint Basil viewed love as one of the teachings of the Holy Spirit. He writes "And as he wished to arouse our soul toward this commandment (love one another), he did not demand in return as proof from the disciples' miracles and extraordinary powers, though indeed he also enable them to do these things in the Holy Spirit."[71]

In *The Fathers Speak: St Basil the Great, St Gregory Nazianzus and St Gregory of Nyssa,* Basil writes that "For he who says that the Father, the Son, and the Holy Spirit are one single reality under several person and profess only one hypostasis common to the three, what else does he do but deny the pre-existence of the Only Begotten before all ages? He rejects also His sojourn and conversing with men, the descent into Hades, the Resurrection, the Judgment, and he denies the distinctive operation of the Spirit."[72] Saint Basil believes that "Whatever your mind suggests on the mode of being of the Father, even though your mind cannot fix itself on a distinct concept because we believe that the Father's being is beyond any conception, you shall think the same of the Son, and also of the Holy Spirit. The notion of "uncreated" and "uncomprehensible" is one and the same for the Father and for the Son and for the Holy Spirit, since it is impossible that one be more uncreated or more incomprehensible and that another be less. We must have a clear conception of the Trinity by means of proper signs."[73] For Saint Basil, these proper signs suggest a clear understanding of the divinity of Jesus Christ.

When discussing the blaspheming of the Only Begotten Jesus Christ, Saint Basil writes that "The Holy Spirit is rejected, and anyone who could refute the impious is exiled. Polytheism has prevailed. There is among those people a great god and a lesser god; they do not regard "the Son" as the proper noun of the nature, but as the proper noun. The Holy Spirit does not close the circle of the Holy Trinity for them; it partakes not of the divine and blessed nature, but it is added to the Father and the Son, perchance and haphazardly, as

---

[70] Ibid., 120.
[71] Ibid., 117-118.
[72] Georges Barrois, *The Fathers Speak*, 119.
[73] Ibid., 124.

something from the world of creatures."[74]

Saint Basil records that

The Holy Spirit is counted together with the Father and the Son because it is also above the creature, and it ranks third, as we learned when the Lord said to the Gospel: "Go, baptize in the name of the Father, and of the Son, and of the Holy Spirit" [Matthew 28:19]. Therefore he who places the Holy Spirit before the Son or says that it is more ancient than the Father, contradicts the divine order and strays from sound faith because he does not keep the right mode of glorification, but imagines for himself a new way of speaking, in order to please men: for if the Spirit is above God, it is not from God, and yet it is written: "The Spirit is from God" [1 Corinthians 2:12]. But if is from God, how can it be more ancient than He from whom it is? What is the folly to say that there is one Holy Spirit above the only begotten Son, when is only one unbegotten? The Holy Spirit is neither before God's only Son nor something between the Son and the Father.[75]

Saint Basil warns against the spiritual attempt to place the personhood of the Holy Spirit somewhere between (above) the creatures and (below) the Father and the Son. Being called by the Holy Spirit means that because of the Holy Spirit's holiness, creatures are made holy. Saint Basil believes that this process of being made holy presupposes sanctification. In the mind of Basil, only the Spirit can sanctify. Creatures cannot sanctify other creatures. If the Spirit sanctifies creatures, then the Holy Spirit must be divine. Only God as Trinity is divine by nature. For Saint Basil, rejecting the divinity of the Holy Spirit is the equivalent to rejecting the Spirit's work in faith, renewal, and sanctification, which leads to salvation. Because God is present through the son and in the Spirit, no one can say that Jesus is Lord, but by the Holy Spirit. In claiming that the Spirit gives life to the earth's face, Saint Basil believed that one can tell who the Spirit is by what the Spirit does.

According to Saint Basil, "the Holy Spirit is the name of "the corporeal, most simple there is." We are admonished not to think

---

[74] Ibid., 88.
[75] Ibid., 128.

when we say Spirit "of a limited nature, subject to change and variation." The union of the Holy Spirit with God." To be truly spiritual is to put nature ruthlessly underfoot as the enemy, to be free from flesh."[76] Lastly, Saint Basil affirmed the distinct persons of the Holy Trinity: The Father as unoriginated, the Son as Begotten of the Father, and the Holy Spirit as proceeding from the Father and through the Son. In this process, the Holy Spirit undertakes full divinity amongst the Father and the Son. The formulation of the position that clearly distinguished between *ousia* and *hypostasis* and said that in God there is only one *ousia*, in which Father, Son, and Holy Spirit share, but that there are three *hypostases*, Father, Son, and Holy Spirit, was largely the work of what are often called the three great Cappadocians, Gregory of Nazianzus, Basil of Caesarea, and Gregory of Nyssa.[77] While I do not consider any of these theologians to be prophets, there is something distinguished and profound about thinkers who are willing share what God has given to them through the person, power and work of the Holy Spirit.

> It may be that *The Revelation of John* was viewed with suspicion and the other writings of Christian prophets did not find a permanent place in the canon because of the distrust with which those prophets claiming to be the mouthpieces of the Holy Spirit were viewed by the bishops and their clergy. There was no place for John's reflections on the Holy Trinity in the book Revelation. The Montanists, with their assertion that Spirit-inspired prophets continued to arise in the Christian community, were a challenge to the administrative regularity represented by the bishops, and their rejection of the Catholic Church may have accentuated the distrust for the prophets and their writings. Certainly, prophets, accorded a place in the early Church next to apostles, were no longer granted recognition by the Catholic Church. Inspiration through prophets was supposed to have ceased with the apostolic age.[78]

In other words, the Canon in the New Testament was determined by the inspiration of the Holy Spirit within the religious context of the

---

[76] Blair Reynolds, *Toward a Process Pneumatology*, 116.
[77] Kenneth S. Latourette, *A History of Christianity*, 161-162.
[78] Ibid., 134.

prophets still having inspirational influence beyond the apostolic age. Due to the way the incarnate Christ shows forth throughout the New Testament (the Holy Spirit is the Spirit of Christ), it can be argued that the New Testament is both the work of the Holy Spirit and prophetic in nature. Inspiration wise, the New Testament contains prophetic literature that has been inspired by the power of the Holy Spirit.

Wisdom dwelt in the prophets but was uniquely in Christ as in the temple. Jesus was a man but was sinless from his birth. The Holy Spirit was in him, he was united in will with God, by his struggles and sufferings he overcame the sin of Adam, and he grew in his intimacy with God.[79] Sabellius held that the Father, Son, and Holy Spirit are three modes or aspects of God, much as the sun is bright, hot and round.[80] Tertullian declared that in his *sunstantia*, or substance, God is one. Father, Son, and Holy Spirit, so Tertullian seemed to have in mind the use of that word in Roman law, where it meant a party in a legal action. These personae, or persons have their place in the economy, or the administrative activity of God.[81]

To define the Holy Trinity of God, Yale historian, Kenneth S. Latourette, confesses:

A problem which long vexed the Church, and which even now has not been solved to the satisfaction of all who bear the Christian name, is that of the Trinity. As we hinted in an earlier chapter, through their deepest experiences the first Christians were confronted with the fact of Christ and of the Holy Spirit. How were Christ and the Holy Spirit related to God? The Christians were that God is one. Most of them were also convinced that some unique way in Christ was both man and God and that the Holy Spirit was from God and is God. How could one hold to a belief in one God and make room for what had become known of Christ and of the Holy Spirit. The phases of the questions which most engaged the attention Christians were the relation of Christ to God and the work of Christ, which in essence is the work of the Holy

---

[79] Ibid., 144.
[80] Ibid.
[81] Ibid., 145.

Spirit.[82]

To be sure, John 3:16 says that God so loved the world that he gave us he gave us his only begotten Son that whoever so believeth shall not perish but have eternal life. The Holy Spirit is a part of the love that God has for the world. The Spirit also inspires believership among the faithful. Many theologians argue that the Holy Spirit plays a significant role in one's salvation.

Saint Augustine of Hippo

In his text, *Saint Augustine of Hippo: Selections from Confessions and Other Essential Writings Annotated and Explained,* Joseph T. Kelley writes that "Augustine's theology of the Holy Spirit can be summed up in two words: gift and love."[83] For Saint Augustine, the Holy Spirit as gift and love included the spiritual realities of experiencing the love of God and human beings, loving God and those in the world around us. Saint Augustine believes that the reason God is the only anything that should be enjoyed in this life is because charity (love) is the gift of God the Holy Spirit. Saint Augustine declares that the nature of God is love and in recognizing God's intentional love for humanity, God's love represents the subjective and unifying standard which Scripture is taught. In other words, the imperfect reality of enjoying the love of God should push or catapult the interpreters of Scripture into a more intimate relationship with the God of three persons.

If we desire to accurately interpret the Scriptures in a way that is pleasing to God, Saint Augustine believes that we should take seriously the task of comprehending God in the interpretation of Scripture; while enjoying all that the Triune God has to offer to those who believe. Saint Augustine puts his biblical philosophy this way: "The things which are to be enjoyed are the Father, the Son, and the Holy Spirit, a single Trinity, a certain supreme thing common to all who enjoy it, if, indeed, it is a thing and not rather the cause of all things, or both a thing and a cause."[84] Using love as a theological category, Saint Augustine teaches that anyone who claims to understand the Scriptures but does not interpret the scriptures in the

---

[82] Ibid., 140.
[83] Joseph T. Kelley, *Saint Augustine Hippo*, 90.
[84] Saint Augustine, *On Christian Doctrine*, I.5.

light of God's love does not understand what he or she is attempting to interpret. Only the Holy Spirit can give believers the spiritual understanding they need to accurately interpret Scripture.

Within the life of the One Triune God, the Spirit is the Eternal Love between Father and Son. Since that shared divine love is perfect, infinite, and eternal, it is itself a Divine Person, coequal with Father and Son.[85] Robert L. Wilken says that

> Augustine believes that in Romans 5:5, Acts 2 and John 4:13, there is something unique about the character of the Holy Spirit, namely, "that the Spirit can make us abide in God and him in us." And because we can abide in God only through love, one can say that love is the proper term to depict what is distinctive of the Spirit. It follows then that the Holy Spirit is the "gift of God who is love." What is given enters into the life of the recipient and becomes his or her own and turns the recipient toward the giver. Gift and love, as used in Scriptures, are relational terms and have built into them reciprocity and mutuality.[86]

In his classic text, *The Trinity*, Saint Augustine writes that "Now we are able to speak about the Holy Spirit, insofar as God the Giver shall permit. According to Sacred Scriptures, this Holy Spirit is neither the Spirit of the Father alone, nor the Son alone, but the Spirit is both, and therefore, He insinuates to us the common love by which the common love by which the Father and Son mutually love each other."[87] Saint Augustine posits that, "If then we seek anything above the nature, and truly, then it is God, namely, a nature that is not created but creates. We must now show whether this is the Trinity, not only to believers by the authority of the divine Scriptures, but also to those who seek to understand by some kind reason, if we are able."[88] "Thus, he says, let us enter together on the path of charity in search of Him of whom it is said: 'Seek his face evermore.'"[89] These two statements are fundamental to Augustine's Trinitarian theology. For Saint Augustine, the Holy Trinity represents the Triune God, the

---

[85] Joseph T. Kelley, *Saint Augustine Hippo,* 90.
[86] Robert L. Wilken, *Early Christian Thought,* 107.
[87] Saint Augustine, *The Trinity,* 491.
[88] Ibid., 451.
[89] Ibid., 8.

Godhead whereby God is distinctly, yet mutually present in three persons—working on behalf of creation and inspiring humanity to do the same for the sake of God's glory. This notion of the Triune God—that the Spirit is the love shared between Father and Son, is one of the triadic analogies that Augustine develops in *The Trinity*.[90]

In his text, *On Christian Doctrine*, Saint Augustine speaks of the Holy Spirit as an equal person within the Trinity. Saint Augustine explains his Trinitarian doctrine:

> It is easy to find a name that will suitably express so great an excellence unless it is better to speak in this way: the Trinity, one God, of whom are all things, through whom are all things, in who are all things. Thus, the Father and the Son and the Holy Spirit, and each of these by Himself, is God, and at the same time they are all one God; and each of them by Himself is a complete substance, and yet they are all one substance. The Father is not the Son nor the Holy Spirit; the Son is not the Father nor the Holy Spirit; the Holy Spirit is not the Father nor the Son: but the Father is only Father, the Son is only Son, and the Holy Spirit is only Holy Spirit. To all three belong the same eternity, the same unchangeableness, the same majesty, the same power. In the Father is unity, in the Son equality, in the Holy Spirit the harmony of unity and equality. And these three attributes are all one because of the Father, all equal because of the Son, and all harmonious because of the Holy Spirit.[91]

Augustine puts his biblical philosophy this way: "The things which are to be enjoyed are the Father, the Son, and the Holy Spirit, a single Trinity, a certain supreme thing common to all who enjoy it, if, indeed, it is a thing and not rather the cause of all things, or both a thing and a cause."[3] The most enjoyable things in life are revealers of truth. Christian truth is eloquent in all its ways. Eloquence leads to the experience of Christian truth. Eloquence and truth are dependent on the creative presence of the Holy Spirit. Here Augustine is successful at showing how the preacher can use precepts from classical rhetoric to teach the truth of the Scriptures. In this context Augustine uses

---

[90] Joseph T. Kelley, *Saint Augustine Hippo*, 90.
[91] Saint Augustine, *On Christian Doctrine*, I.V.5.

rhetoric as a way of convincing the reader that rhetorical charm, by way of logic, can do serious harm to those who diligently seek to know the truth of *Scripture.* The Holy Spirit helped me in understanding Augustine's hermeneutic of biblical interpretation to be a hermeneutic of order. I use the word *order* affectionately because I am not referring to an order of rationalization as in the keynote preacher setting the ecclesial environment in order by way of rationalization through honoring God and referencing those who are the highest positions of episcopal power—so on and so forth. Rather, I am speaking of an order of coherence whereby the through the power of God's Holy Spirit, which is poured into those who believe, the person who is attempting to interpret the Scriptures understands that in the sacred act of interpreting the Word of God, God lovingly possesses our very being.

Augustine believed that interpreting the scriptures in an accurate manner is the work of the Holy Spirit. At the very moment we begin to formulate what God wants us to get out of a particular text, God informs us that we have our very presence, our hearts, our souls, our minds, our talents, our gifts, our knowledge, our ministries, our families, and our contexts in God. And because God's intellect is not to be tapped into or fully understood, like Augustine, believers must take the time to work at interpreting Scripture. Whatever hermeneutic believers decide to use, it must be done in the quest for the unconditional love of God that unites the fabrics that continue to hold our worlds together—the Holy Spirit of God. But even from the spiritual perspective of interpreting scripture, the question of the Holy Spirit having material consequences and implications within God's creation is still up for debate.

In his *Confessions,* Augustine seems reluctant to disavow a materialist concept of Spirit. In 7. 1, he views the Spirit as a wind or material breath in the manner of the Stoic materialists. In *City of God,* the dynamic office of the Holy Spirit in creation is represented by a materialist manifestation of God, the breach.[92] Here, Augustine acknowledges that he was unable to conceive of an immaterial substance and that he held a purely materialistic concept of the Spirit prior to his conversion. In seeking to ensure the oneness or unity of Spirit and matter, he seems to evoke something analogous to the

---

[92] Blair Reynolds, *Toward a Process Pneumatology,* 121.

substance attribute dichotomy as a concession to the conflict between the monopolar tenets and the dynamic, physical aspects of the Spirit.[93] With regard to Saint Augustine, Blair Reynolds asks the critical questions:

> Must the Spirit be incarnate or possess a physical aspect to be truly relevant in us? If matter is eliminated from the nature of the Spirit, is not its relationship to the material order seriously constructed, rendered remote and unintelligible? These are, of course, questions posed by process theology, not by Augustine. However, it does seem fair to say that he at least implies an affirmative answer, although he is not cogent concerning exactly in what sense the Spirit is incarnate. He evidences some appreciation of the fact that the concept of a wholly disembodied entity is too different from our most fundamental experiences of reality to be tenable.[94]

Regarding God's relationship with humankind, Saint Augustine teaches that the Spirit of God is God's gift to us, drawing us into union with Christ, and through Christ with the Eternal God.[95] In addition to making references to Genesis 1:2, which describes the Spirit of God hovering (or dancing, as some scholars would translate the Hebrew) above the cosmic, primeval waters out of which life emerges, Augustine understands why the Holy Spirit should be identified as both God and the Gift of God. God's "supereminent Love" hovers and dances above and throughout the created universe[96] and inspires the acts of love that are continuous acts of divine creation. For Saint Augustine, "The Spirit infuses our minds and hearts and draws us into the life of the Eternal God. This is Saint Augustine's astonishing claim: we humans, individually and together, are destined to share in the dynamic, inner life of God. This is the Gift of God."[97] Kelly brings out Saint Augustine even more:

> When we love, we have begun to live the very life of God. The Gift that is the Holy Spirit is no more and no less love, love for each other that binds ever more closely to the Love

---

[93] Ibid.
[94] Ibid.
[95] Joseph T. Kelley, *Saint Augustine Hippo*, 90.
[96] Saint Augustine, *The Confessions*, XIII.7.8.
[97] Joseph T. Kelley, *Saint Augustine Hippo*, 90.

that is God. In the end, Augustine's theology of God is simple and profound: God is **Love**. When we love each other (and by "we" Augustine would mean any human being who absolutely loves), we live and move and have our being in the **Love** of God. The Spirit of God *is* the act of **love**, according to Peter Lombard, one of the very early commentators on Augustine's theology.[98]

Saint Augustine believes that the Holy Spirit helps human beings to overcome the evil of sin by steering us toward the Godly work of love. In addition to the Holy Spirit's light of love possessing enough power to defeat light of sin, Augustine, like St Basil the Great, views baptism as a visible sign of the Spirit. A considerable portion of Saint Augustine's theologizing the work of the Holy Spirit focuses on the connection between Jesus Christ and the Holy Spirit. Because the Holy Spirit comes through Christ our eternal God (1 Cor.), He or She draws human beings into an eternal union with Jesus Christ. Saint Augustine believes that Jesus Christ is born of the Holy Spirit as a form of God's grace.

The Holy Spirit in Other Religions and the Paraclete

Saint Augustine's view of the Holy Spirit working in other religions is found throughout his *De Trinitate*. However, in juxtaposing the work of the Holy Spirit as a form of grace, Saint Augustine believes that the Holy Spirit gives life by way of lifting our sunken nature from the gates of death (1 Pet. 3:18; Rom. 8:2,10). This teaching is a critical part of what Saint Augustine affirmed in the Holy Spirit. In addition to giving life in the context of death, the Holy Spirit suffices for all of God's creation and is representative of the Holy Church. By way of responding to one of the taboo subjects regarding the work of the Holy Spirit, which is the question of the Spirit's presence in other religions, Kelly says that "Augustine directly answers this question about the Spirit of God dwelling in persons beyond the Christian community of the baptized. God's providence is not limited by historical accidents of time or space. The indwelling of God's own Spirit in human beings is "ineffable and incomprehensible" and no person's or one religion's prerogative."[99]

---

[98] Ibid.
[99] Joseph T. Kelley, *Saint Augustine Hippo*, 92.

In his important journal article, "The Spirit in Modern Black Theology and Religion," Kurt Buhring argues that an area of Black theology that might be enriched by deeper engagement with non-Christian resources is the idea of the Spirit. Though the Spirit is alive and well in Black churches, Buhring contends that the idea has been underdeveloped within especially the first-generation of black theology. In Abrahamic religions, the Holy Spirit is an aspect or agent of God, by means of which God communicates with people or acts on them. In Judaism, the Holy Spirit refers to the divine force, quality, and influence of God over the universe or over his creatures. In Christianity, the Holy Spirit is the third person of the Trinity. In Islam, the Holy Spirit acts as an agent of divine action or communication. For Muslims, this holy spirit is not a divine person. The holy spirit refers to the Angel Gabriel. In the Baha'i Faith, the Holy Spirit is seen as the intermediary between God and man and "the outpouring grace of God and the effulgent rays that emanate from His Manifestation." The Hebrew Bible contains the term "spirit of God" (ruach hakodesh) which by Jews is interpreted in the sense of the might of a unitary God. In religions which recognize a divine spark within every human being, all personal interactions can be seen as encounters with the holy. In Christianity, the concept of the Trinity—often phrased as Father, Son, and Holy Spirit—envisions the sacred as being relational. In the moral code of Confucianism, the health of the society derives from the maintenance of proper relationships with family, friends, and community.[100] Central to the Christian faith is the belief that God is with us now in the Holy Spirit. Holy Spirit, however, in some form, is a feature of religious belief and experience common to all faiths.[101]

On my read and watch of the Holy Spirit outside Christianity, most religions would agree that God is a Spirit, and the Spirit liberates. Other descriptions of the Holy Spirit in philosophy and scripture read as such:

MARY BAKER EDDY (1821-1910)
Spirit is
the real and eternal; matter is the unreal and temporal.

[100] Frederic Brussat and Mary Ann Brussat, *Spiritual Literacy*, 419.
[101] Henry P. Van Dusen, *Spirit, Son and Father*, 25.

Science and Health, with Key to the Scriptures[102]

NEW TESTAMENT
Be strengthened with might by [God's] Spirit in the inner man.
Ephesians 3:16

The fruit of the Spirit is **love**, joy, peace, longsuffering, gentleness, goodness, faith, Meekness, temperance.
Galatians 5:22-23

It is the Spirit that gives life, the flesh is of no avail.
John 6:63

RAMANA MAHARSHI
(1879-1950)
That inner Self, as the primeval Spirit, eternal, ever effulgent, full and infinite Bliss, single, indivisible, whole and living, shines in everyone as the witnessing awareness. That Self is its splendour, shining in the cavity of the heart. Collected Works, Arthur Osborne[103]

SAINT AUGUSTINE
(354-430)
A good conscience is the palace of Christ; the temple of the Holy Ghost; the paradise of delight, the standing Sabbath of the saints.
Confessions[104]

In view of what other religions believe about the Holy Spirit, what can the Christian church say about the Holy Spirit (Paraclete)? We can say the Holy Spirit is the Helper. We can say that the Holy Spirit convicts the world of sin. We can also say that the Holy Spirit convinces the world of righteousness and judgment. In John 16:1-15, the disciples were grief-stricken. All they knew was that they were going to lose Jesus. But he told them that in the end this was all for the best, because, when we went away, the Holy Spirit, the Helper, would come. When he was in the body, he could not be everywhere

---

[102] Frederic Brussat and Mary Ann Brussat, *Spiritual Literacy*, 237.
[103] Ibid., 238.
[104] Ibid., 227.

with them; it was always a case of greetings and farewells. When he was in the body, he could not reach the minds and hearts and consciences of humanity everywhere; he was confined by the limitations of place and time. But there are no limitations in the Spirit. Everywhere a person goes, the Spirit is with them. The Holy Spirit's ministry is revealing Jesus to us, to bear testimony of Jesus (John 15:26). The Holy Spirit uses diverse ways and different gifts to accomplish this, but the purpose is always the same: to reveal Jesus. One of the Holy Spirit's main purposes is to unveil Jesus' true likeness, to paint his in divine colors. Thus, John presents Jesus as saying that "he [Paraclete] will glorify me," making Jesus' cosmic meaning known to John's group.

The Holy Spirit in the Protestant Reformation

The Protestant Reformation was a movement in Europe that commenced with Martin Luther's activities in 1517. With roots and precursors[105] dating back into the 14th and 15th centuries, the purpose of the Protestant Reformation was to reform the Roman Catholic church while helping members of the Christian church to better understand the Bible and the biblical implications for one's understanding of God, faith, and the church. Western Christians were not pleased with what they saw as false doctrines and blatant malpractices within the Roman Catholic Church; particularly involving the teaching and selling of indulgences. Other points of contention were the practice of buying and selling church positions and the corruption found within the hierarchy of the church. According to scholars of the Reformation, the corruption was systematic at the time; even reaching the position of the Pope.

On October 31, 1517, in Saxony (now Germany), Martin Luther nailed his *Ninety-Five Theses* to the door of the Wittenberg Castle Church, which served as a notice board for university-related announcements. The *Ninety-Five Theses* represented specific points for debate that criticized the actions of the Roman Catholic Church

---

[105] Precursors to the Protestant Reformation were Catholic church corruption, the emergence of the Muslim jihad, the invention of the printing press, books given to the public and Bibles printed in the native language of the laity. The Renaissance era ushered in an increase in one's understanding of the true nature of Christianity and signaled the return to a Bible-based church. Also, personal, and political greed founded in one's quest for power preceded the biblical self-discovery of disgruntled Catholics.

and the Pope. In addition to the practice of selling indulgences, the Church's policy on purgatory were the main points of controversy. According to the Roman Catholic doctrine, purgatory is an immediate state after physical death in which those destined for heaven "undergo purification, so as to achieve the holiness necessary to enter the joy of heaven." Luther believed purgatory to be something different. Luther argued that purgatory was not the Catholic Church's dogma. For Luther, one's refusal to believe in purgatory does not make him or her a heretic. Even though he believed that purgatory exists, Luther's understanding of doctrine led him to believe that he could not force purgatory on any human being.

The Protestant Reformation was just as much a pneumatological (spiritual) movement as it was a religious one. The theological principles that caused the Reformers to depart from the Roman Catholic Church were Sole authority of Scripture, Justification by faith alone, and Priesthood of the believer. Sola Scriptura (by Scripture alone) was one of the code words of the Reformation. This doctrine maintains that Scripture is the only authority for the Christian in matters of salvation and practice. The doctrine of the church is to be completely dependent upon the Scriptures. Sola Fide (by faith alone) was the other code word of the Reformation. This teaching maintains that God justifies us by faith alone. The early Reformers affirmed that Sola Fide incorrectly understood until it became anchored in the broader principle of Sola Gratia (*by grace alone).*

Hence, the Reformers were calling the church back to the basic teaching of Scripture where the Apostle Paul writes that as believers, we are saved by grace through faith and that not of ourselves, it is the gift of God (Eph. 2:8). The last theological principle of the Reformation was the priesthood of all believers. According to 1 Peter 2:5, "Believers are a "holy priesthood." All believers are priests before God through our great high priest, Lord, and Savior Jesus Christ. 1 Timothy 2:5 reads: "There is one God and one mediator between God and man, the man Christ Jesus." As believers, we have a direct connection to God through Jesus Christ, our divine mediator.

In answering the question of *where is the Church in history,* John Briggs speaks of how "modern Protestants have sometimes been guilty of neglecting tradition altogether."[106] According to Briggs, this historical neglecting of tradition is "the opposite error of the Roman church since the Council of Trent to magnify the authority of tradition, independent of the authority of the Bible."[107] Synonymous to the errors of inclusion and exclusion, Briggs claims that "it is dangerous to suggest that the Holy Spirit was inactive in a particular period"[108] within history. Protestant historians of the nineteenth century preferred not to admit that the Spirit was at work in the mainstream of the Catholic faith and devotion. Despite the obvious signs of the Spirit's presence throughout the history of the church and society, theologians and church leaders alike fail to reference the fullness of the Spirit within the Christian tradition. They attempted to trace the work of the Holy Spirit from the time of Constantine to the Reformation in an 'apostolic succession' of heresies; some of them we would regard as reform movements, but others were heretical by any standard.[109]

Writing from a historical context, Briggs is clear in his assessment of how Protestants have been neglectful in their treatment of the tradition. But just like with most examples of theological neglect in world history, there has been modern deviations in recording the history of Christian experience. For Briggs, the claims of a number of modern deviations from Christianity (for example, the Mormons and the Jehovah's Witnesses) that they, in later years, have received a special revelation that promotes their supporters to the numbers of the elect, but excludes all others, must be rejected.[110] As a trained historian, Briggs claims that denying the Spirit's activity throughout world history is an error that must be corrected. The same is true with the Christian church. To accurately interpret the history of the Christian church, one must be able to follow the moves of the Holy Spirit within the life and witness of the church.

According to Briggs, too many Protestants have adopted an unnecessary negative attitude to tradition and have therefore failed to inform their faith by the study of the story of the church. It is said that

---

[106] Tim Dowley, *History of Christianity*, 18.
[107] Ibid.
[108] Ibid.
[109] Ibid.
[110] Ibid., 19.

the Acts of the Apostles are more correctly described as the 'Acts of the Holy Spirit'.[111] For Briggs, all of church history should be recognized as the act(s) of the Holy Spirit. Any Christian movement which neglects this story (of the Spirit) loses the dimension of solidarity with Christ's church in all ages.[112] Here, Briggs stresses the work and presence of the Holy Spirit throughout the entirety of Christian history and not just specific parts of it. Briggs summarizes: "The slogan 'Back to the New Testament!' represents only part of the truth. 'Onwards with the Spirit!' is the other half of this truth; together they make up the authority of the Reformers—which was always that of 'Word and Spirit'. It is the same Spirit who inspired the Bible who is alive in the church, creating the tradition and bringing afresh to every age the authority of the once-given Word."[113]

In his important text, *The Holy Spirit: The Holy Spirit in the Bible, the History of Christian Thought and Recent Theology*, Alasdair I. C. Heron expounds further on the connection between the Holy Spirit and the Reformation. Even as mainstream Protestant theology was able to maintain and establish Western doctrine and at the same time, concentrate with a new intensity on what the Spirit *enables* and *performs*[114], Heron believes that the Reformation precipitated a shift in pneumatological interest fully as dramatic as that ushered in by Augustine.[115] Heron also believes that there is a good heal of justice in the claim of the Princeton theologian, B. B. Warfield: 'The developed doctrine of the work of the Holy Spirit is an exclusively Reformation doctrine.'[116] Contrasting the Reformers work in the area of pneumatology with that of the medieval period, Warfield is convinced that the true understanding of the Spirit's activity is a critical and innovative part of Reformed theology. In summary, Heron writes that "The new note is sounded by many writers; typical of is the seventeenth century English Puritan Richard Baxter, who on this point at least well expresses the conviction of the great Reformers of the century before:... to believe in the Holy Ghost is to take him for Christ's Agent or Advocate with our souls, and for

---

[111] Ibid.
[112] Ibid.
[113] Ibid.
[114] Alasdair I. C. Heron, *The Holy Spirit*, 99.
[115] Ibid.
[116] Ibid.

our Guide, Sanctifier, and Comforter, and not to believe that He is the third Person in the Trinity."[117]

While most Church historians claim that the Reformation was primarily about "the rectifications of abuses in the church, the battle-cry of justification by faith alone, the uniqueness of Jesus Christ as Redeemer and Savior and the authority of Scripture,"[118] it is possible that the Reformers themselves would disagree. Aware that faith, redemption by Christ, justification by faith, the authority of Scripture was all necessarily bound up with the Holy Spirit,[119] the Reformers undertook pneumatology as the guiding force behind their theological affirmations. According to Jane Dempsey Douglas, "historians all too seldom turn their attention to the Reformers' understanding of the Holy Spirit, yet something profoundly significant happened to the doctrine of the Holy Spirit in the Reformation. Theologians like Luther and Calvin, though quite traditional in their view of the person of the Holy Spirit—because they found the tradition biblical—nonetheless reframed the understanding of the Holy Spirit's work in the church and the world, giving the Spirit a new immediacy in the lives of believers.[120]

Martin Luther

According to Danish Lutheran priest and theologian Regin Prenter, "The concept of the Holy Spirit completely dominates Luther's theology. In every decisive matter, whether it be the study of Luther's doctrine of justification, his doctrine of the sacraments, his ethics, or any other fundamental teaching, we are forced to take into consideration his concept of the Holy Spirit."[121] Prenter's historical text, *Spiritus Creator: Luther's Concept of the Holy Spirit*, is divided into two parts: Luther's concept of the Holy Spirit prior to his encounters with the enthusiasts and Luther's defense of his concept of the Holy Spirit in the presence of the enthusiasts. Luther's thinking regarding the work of the Holy Spirit evolved from its traditional forms to one of ecclesial and evangelical relevance. Following the lead of Augustine, Luther embraced the Holy Spirit as gift and love.

---

[117] Ibid.
[118] Ibid., 100.
[119] Ibid.
[120] Jane D. Douglass, "The Lively Work of the Spirit in the Reformation," 121.
[121] Regin Prenter, *Spiritus Creator*, xi.

Luther believed that the Holy Spirit represents "God's overflowing self-giving"[122] as a form of God's unconditional love. Prenter recalls that, "In Luther's lectures of the Epistle to the Romans during 1515-16, we read in the notes on Romans 2:15: "From this I believe that sentence 'let the law be written in their heart' says the same thing as 'Love is infused into the heart through the Holy Spirit.' It is the same sense in both the law of Christ and the fulfillment of the law of Moses."[123] Prenter clarifies:

> This is the young Luther's fundamental formula for the understanding of the work of the Spirit. It is in complete accordance with the traditional way of expression, especially in the Augustinian sense. When the young Luther speaks of the works of the Holy Spirit, he very often uses Augustinian terminology, and he often quotes Augustine directly. The work of the Spirit is to infuse into the heart the true love of God so that obedience to the command of the law is brought about not by fear of punishment but because of a free and happy love to God.[124]

Luther believes that God gives creation the gift of the Holy Spirit as a way of demonstrating God's love to creation, which is comprised of nature, human beings, and the Church. Luther believed that the Holy Spirit works in the life of all creation. Not only was the Spirit active in creation, but Luther posits that the Spirit made creation alive. As a creation of God, individual beings did not become human beings until the Spirit breathed life into them in the moment of creation. The Spirit in creation confirms God's satisfaction with God's creation. Along these lines, Luther's creative analogies of the Spirit are nuanced in the realms of movement, motion or being brooded which signals the Spirit's work of making God's creation alive. The sending of the Spirit implies the visible coming of the world because sending means coming. In the mind of Luther, one cannot come to Christ without the Spirit calling, gathering, and creating. By way of connecting the Son and the Spirit, Luther believed that both have an image corresponding to their inner essence. Whereas the incarnational side to the work of the Spirit reveals that the work of Spirit parallels that

---

[122] Veli Matti Karkkainen, *The Holy Spirit in Ecumenical*, 53.
[123] Regin Prenter, *Spiritus Creator*, 3.
[124] Ibid.

of the Son, Luther claims that the Holy Spirit points to Christ's work in us.

Prenter writes that "With this understanding of love as the work of the Spirit must also be understood differently. The Spirit can no longer be understood as a transcendent cause the sublimated idealism, but it must be understood as a direct presence of God, a sphere of life wherein the will of man can be and remain *Odium sui*."[125] Instead of seeing the work of the Spirit as one of dejection within the will of the human being, Luther believed the Holy Spirit to be an active agent of new life and a new will in God. How Luther conceives of the direct presence of the Spirit as a new sphere of life, in which something so impossible as *Odium sui* can be the most natural of all, we all shall be able to learn on when we follow Luther a few steps further in his new understanding of the meaning of *caritas*.[126]

Luther views the work of the Spirit in *caritas* as a transforming work that brings into a life of faith. Because "the Holy Spirit is the creator of the new life,"[127] Luther believes that He should be the desired category under which we want to place the concept of the experience of faith.[128] For Luther, "the experience of faith is part of the new life. It is the realization of faith in reality. This too, is the new life, and so Luther at times designates the new life as the creation of the Holy Spirit and at times as the effect of faith. To the extent that the experience of faith belongs to the new life, it is a work of the Holy Spirit. But new life is a reality."[129] Luther affirms that, "There are a variety of ways faith comes to us—we are experiential beings. Buy the way we can be certain of our faith is that the Spirit calls us to faith "through the Gospel" –the good news of Jesus Christ in his life, death, resurrection and new life promised among us. Just as Jesus called the disciples to "follow" our daily call points us to the word that is Christ himself."[130]

Further naming the work of the Spirit, Luther believed that the

---

[125] Ibid., 8.
[126] Ibid.
[127] Walter Von Loewenich, *Luther's Theology of the Cross*, 110.
[128] Ibid.
[129] Ibid.
[130] Ibid.

Spirit could strengthen and encourage Christians in need. The Spirit also works in the community for the purpose of helping those who cannot help themselves. The Spirit also acts through material signs at any given point and time. Here, Luther believed that within the framework of the Trinity, the Spirit is the indivisible work. Even as all three persons of the Trinity have roles to play, the Spirit is material and bodily in that the Spirit's sending refers to his relationship to the Creator. The symbols of Confession in Christ's faith are God, the Son who was born in flesh and the Spirit who proceeded in a material bodily way. Within the relationship between the Spirit and the Creator, Luther related the inward works of the Spirit with the outward works of the Spirit. The Holy Spirit is sanctifier and justifier in that sanctification and justification are works of the Spirit. In affirming that the Spirit proceeds from the Father and the Son, Luther sees a distinction between the Spirit as a person and Spirit as gift. In other words, there is a difference between the Spirit's Godhead and the Spirit's Personhood.

Most important, Luther believed that the Spirit comes through the Word. Even as Luther did not devalue Scripture or solely put his reliance upon the Holy Scripture, he did speak biblically about the Holy Spirit in his Pentecostal sermons. In terms of referencing what we have already highlighted about Luther's theology of the Holy Spirit, these are excerpts from Luther's sermons:

6. This, we say, is portraying the Holy Spirit in the most friendly and comforting way. We are not to look upon him otherwise than as a kind and friendly comforter and helper, and we are to know that he was sent from God the Father and from Christ for that purpose; that he will certainly prove himself such through the Word, by showing us the pure grace, love and goodness of God. He shall assure our hearts that God, both the Father and the Son, is not angry with us nor does he condemn us, nor desire us to be filled with fear. The Holy Spirit was sent by the Father and Son to be a comforter and has been commanded not to declare anything but what he has heard, as we have learned in the preceding Gospel.[131]

---

[131] John N. Lenker, ed. Translated by John Nicholas Lenker and others--*Sermons by Martin Luther: Volume 3 For Pentecost* **martinluthersermons**.com/ **Luther_** Lenker_**Vol_3**.pdf, *pg. 275.*

6. Thus, reason takes offense at the Spirit, imagines unreality, and conceives of this new birth. Therefore, Christ proceeds, explaining this birth to clear his understanding, and says: "Verily, verily I say unto thee, except one be born of water and the Spirit, he cannot enter the Kingdom of God.

7. In other words: The new birth of which speak must be otherwise explained. I do not abolish the natural birth, but I speak of a birth which is of water and the Spirit. Then he continues: "That which is born of the flesh is flesh; and that which borne of the Spirit is spirit."

8. These words cannot be grasped by reason, which seeks to explain the words "Spirit" and "water," speculating how such birth may be. Here, it sees nothing in the nature of a birth and therefore plays the part of the fool by saying: How earl a man be born of water and the Spirit? Indeed, such a source would produce but water bubbles.[132]

44. In the second place, this parable aptly shows that Christianity is not bound up in external affairs, places, persons, garments, and other things, such as the outward holiness of Jews required. As a Christian is set up in the liberty of the Spirit, rid of the Law and all its bonds. He cannot be bound and made captive by any sorts of laws, rules or works that may be proposed to him with a view of his becoming righteous through their efficacy in the sight of God. (We are not speaking now of his outward life, in which he may keep all laws, provided, however, it is done without injury and damage to his spiritual liberty of mind and conscience.) Hence, by faith in the Word and his baptism he remains a free man, superior to all laws, because he has through Christ forgives of sin, the grace of God and the Holy Spirit, and governs his entire life accordingly. Through the Holy Spirit, who operates in his heart, he is now become righteous, and has been quickened to life, and, except as the Holy Spirit by the Word guides and directs him, he does not look for other teaching regarding works of holiness.[133]

---

[132] Ibid., 380.
[133] Ibid., 406-407.

45. Hence, as Christ states, Christianity is like the wind, which is blows where it will, and yet no one sees or knows whence it comes and whither it goes, through what distance or extent it passes. In like manner, the Spirit in a Christian cannot be confined by rules and teachings, nor can it be determined by reason, but it must be untutored and unjudged by everybody, as St. Paul states in 1 Corinthians 2:15. It is not felt, heard or manifested outwardly except in the Word and in its proclamation, by which everybody must be governed, without regard to the persons of men who preach it, no matter how great and holy they are; the only requirement is that they exercise the office and Word aright.[134]

Upon reading Luther's sermons in completion, one will find that his reflections on the presence, power and work of the Holy Spirit are in Scripture. Often when Luther speaks of the Spirit in his preaching, he is illuminating what the Bible says about the Holy Spirit. Here Luther's sermons possess a pneumatological bent in the way he presents certain contexts and situations that calls for the Spirit to be of help to those who need God. Luther preaches about the Holy Spirit that works within and beyond the Church. Whether the need is because one's lifeless situation or one's misunderstanding of the Spirit's work, Luther affirms a life-giving Spirit as referenced in biblical doctrine. One can argue that Luther was at his preaching best when he expounded on the work of the Holy Spirit.

In conclusion, Luther believes that the work of the Holy Spirit focuses on keeping believers on track, focused on Jesus, as we go out into the world. Lest we think the Spirit is just out there and unknowable; the Spirit shows us a glimpse of the world to come as we go out and serve others through our daily vocations and roles we play in the world. For Luther, the Holy Spirit keeps believers on track by way of connecting them to one another and Scripture. Karl Barth explains:

If we are assured of this fellowship between God and us by the miracle of the Spirit, then we can hazard the further thought that was so much a concern for Luther and that we found already in the *Institutes.* As the Spirit speaks in the sign

---

[134] Ibid., 407.

to our spirits, Christ is present to us, and truly no less so than if we could see him with our eyes and touch him with our hands, indeed, with such power and efficacy that he not only gives the hope of eternal life to our spirits but makes us certain of the immortality of our flesh.[135]

John Calvin

The third book of the *Institutes* (1559) gives great attention to the person and work of the Holy Spirit, who according to Calvin, resurrected the body, mind and spirit of Christ from the dead and proceeds from the Father and the Son to produce a greater, more perfect union of the Spirit in the Church and the world through our belief in Jesus Christ. Calvin, a French theologian, and pastor is the premier theologian of the Holy Spirit. More so than any of the reformed thinkers, Calvin undertook the most systematic exploration of the Spirit's work.[136] Calvin sets out to explore and unfold their (Luther and himself) implications and to map out the dynamics of life in Christ as empowered by the Spirit.[137] As a way of connecting Christ to the Spirit, Calvin believes that the Spirit unites us to Christ himself. For Calvin, the Spirit leads us to Christ because the work of the Spirit is the work of Christ. In other words, the Holy Spirit *is* the Spirit of Christ.

Calvin believed that God speaks through the Holy Spirit by means of Scripture. In other words, the Bible was the "school of the Holy Spirit." Its writers were instruments, organs, amanuenses of the Holy Spirit.[138] Accordingly, without the illumination of the Holy Spirit, the Word can do nothing.[139] Calvin also believed that God's Spirit spoke through the prophets. For Calvin, the words of the prophets penetrate the hearts of those living in all generations. Because the Spirit is the author of Scripture, the Spirit bears witness to the Word in such a way that the believers' trusting, as the result of the Spirit's

[135] Karl Barth, *Theology of John Calvin*, 282.
[136] Regin Prenter, *Spirit Creatorus*, 102.
[137] Ibid., 103.
[138] Institutes, 4.8.9; OS 5: 141: "Illi fuerunt certi et authentici Spiritus sancti amanuenses:et ideo eorum scripta pro Dei oraculis habenda sunt."
[139] John Calvin, *Institutes of the Christian Religion*, translated from the 1559 Latin ed. Ford Lewis Battles, 2 volumes in Library of Christian Classics, Book Three. *The Way in Which We Receive the Grace of Christ* (Philadelphia, PA: The Westminster Press, 1960), 3.2.33 (1:580). www.foundationrt.org/outlines/Calvin_Institutes_III.pdf.

presence, comes from reading Scripture. Calvin believed that because the Spirit dictated the words to the Bible writers, Scripture is efficient for the reality of God's love and love of neighbor. More importantly, God's Spirit illumines believers to the fact that Scripture is God's word. Because the Holy Spirit is the truest form of holy or holiness, Scripture does not become the Holy Scriptures without the illumination of the Holy Spirit. Here, the interpretive work of the Bible is taken up by the Holy Spirit. For Calvin, only the Spirit leads us to Christ.[140] "Indeed the Word of God is like the sun, shining upon all those to whom it is proclaimed, but with no effect among the blind. Now, all of us are blind by nature in this respect. Accordingly, it cannot penetrate into our minds unless the Spirit, as the inner teacher, through his illumination makes entry for it."[141]

Calvin believed that "faith is the principal work of the Holy Spirit. The Spirit is the inner teacher by whose effort the promise of salvation penetrates our minds, a promise that otherwise would only strike the air or beat upon our ears. Faith itself has no other source than the Spirit. Perfect salvation is found in the person of Christ; we may become partakers of it as he baptizes us in Holy Spirit and Fire.[142] Calvin proclaimed that, "As long as Christ was outside us and separate from us, his sufferings were of no value to us. To share with us what he received from the Father, Christ comes and dwells with us. We obtain this by faith, to grow into one body with him. It is by the Spirit that we come to enjoy Christ and all his benefits. Three witnesses in heaven, Father, Son and Holy Spirit; so, three on earth—water, blood, spirit. "The Holy Spirit is the bond which Christ effectually unites us to himself."[143] The Holy Spirit unites human beings to Christ when Christ is apprehended through faith in the promises of Scripture.

According to Calvin, without the Holy Spirit, saving faith is impossible. In Christ, the Holy Spirit is always conjoined to the word, for "there is a permanent relation between faith and the word." Christ came endowed with the Holy Spirit in a special way, to separate us from the world and to gather us unto hope of the eternal inheritance. Hence, he is called the "Spirit of sanctification." Further, Son is to be

---

[140] Ibid., (1:581).
[141] Ibid., 3.2.34 (1:582).
[142] Ibid., (1:541).
[143] Ibid., (1:537).

minister and steward of the Father's liberality in bestowing him with the whole fullness of the Spirit. He arouses a hope of full renewal. He is Mediator, the second Adam.[144]

The union between Christ and human beings lies at the heart of Calvin's theology. Calvin believes that one comes into union with Christ through the work of the Holy Spirit and not by human effort. Because the Holy Spirit binds us to Christ by faith, Calvin believes that our minds must be intent upon the Spirit; so that when the Holy Spirit reveals faith to our minds and seals this same faith upon our heart, we can understand the process as one of salvific importance. For Calvin, faith entails assurance. "Where there is no assurance of faith there is no faith (Romans 8:16). Since faith is the entire work of the Holy Spirit, then the Holy Spirit imparts assurance only by imparting faith in Christ, which faith brings assurance with it. For Calvin, this spiritual assurance creates an arousal. According to Calvin, "we must be aroused (by our assurance of Jesus Christ) to be aroused to seek Christ; also, the invisible Father is to be sought solely in this image."[145]

The twin doctrines of the headship of Christ and our union with him by the Spirit lead to Calvin's detailed account of the Spirit's work and of the Christian life as a sharing with Christ in his life, death and resurrection for us.[146] Because the work of the Spirit unites us with Christ, this work also manifests itself in affecting one's individual life. The Holy Spirit works on us by making us look more like Christ. The Holy Spirit conforms us to the image of Christ. As a way of expounding on what it means to look more like Christ, Calvin views the vivification of the Spirit as a work of the Spirit. For Calvin, vivification is the Holy Spirit bringing to life a new creation as the Spirit works upon us as we experience repentance. Repentance, regeneration, and forgiveness alike include the vivification of the Spirit. Further, vivification means a coming alive to Christ in the power of the Spirit—a consolation that comes specifically from having faith. "Faith rests upon the knowledge of Christ." "Christ cannot be known apart from the sanctification of his Spirit." "It follows that faith

---

[144] Ibid., (1:538).
[145] Ibid., (1:542).
[146] Regin Prenter, *Spirit Creatorus*, 104.

can in no wise be separated from devout disposition."[147]

For Calvin, however, this knowledge and instruction are the most vital and direct and supreme things that God can now do for us here and now. For the knowledge and instruction come about through the Spirit. Is there anything stronger or more direct and divine than the Spirit for us who are human and not God?[148] For Calvin there is no belittling or conjuring away of the mystery. His concern was to put the mystery in the right place where it is unambiguously not just any mystery but *the* mystery of the relation between God and us, the mystery of the *Spirit*. If Christ has gone up to heaven and left this dwelling on the earth in which we still find ourselves to be pilgrims, even so no distance can take away his ability to quicken his own people by what is his. The reference is to the Spirit, to the *Spirit*, to the supreme Spirit, to the Spirit of God.[149] Again, without the Spirit man is inescapable of faith.[150] Calvin affirms that, "Now we shall possess a right definitions of faith if we call it a firm and certain knowledge of God's benevolence towards us, founded upon the truth of the freely given promise in Christ, both revealed to our minds and sealed upon our hearts through the Holy Spirit."[151]

> It now remains to pour into the heart itself what the mind has absorbed. For the Word of God is not received by faith if it flits about in the top of the brain, but when it takes root in the depth of the heart that it may be an invincible defense to withstand and drive off all the stratagems of temptation...The Spirit accordingly serves as a seal, to seal up in our hearts those very promises the certainty of which it has previously impressed upon our minds.[152]

For Calvin,

Faith is much higher than human understanding. And it will

---

[147] John Calvin, *Institutes of the Christian Religion*, translated from the 1559 Latin ed. Ford Lewis Battles, 2 volumes in Library of Christian Classics, Book Three. The Way in Which We Receive the Grace of Christ (Philadelphia, PA: The Westminster Press, 1960), 3.2.33 (1:551). www.foundationrt.org/outlines/Calvin_Institutes_III.pdf
[148] Karl Barth, *Theology of John Calvin*, 282.
[149] Ibid.
[150] John Calvin, *Institutes of the Christian Religion*, translated from the 1559 Latin ed. Ford Lewis Battles, 2 volumes in Library of Christian Classics, Book Three, (1:582).
[151] Ibid., 3.2.7 (1:551).
[152] Ibid., 3.2.36 (1:583-584).

not be enough for the mind to be illumined by the Spirit of God unless the heart is also strengthened by his or her power.[153] Put another way, faith goes beyond bare assent. Faith is the singular gift of God, both in the mind of humans are purged to be able to taste the truth of God and in that his heart is established therein. For the Spirit is not only the initiator of faith but increases it by degrees.[154]

Because one trusts God through faith, one is enabled by the Spirit's power to rise, take heart, regain courage, and return from death to life. Here, Calvin stresses that "faith rests upon the knowledge of Christ. Christ cannot be known apart from the sanctification of his Spirit. It follows that faith can in no wise be separated from a devout disposition."[155]

Further, the power of the Spirit at work in us creates a reciprocal relationship (move) between God and human beings. Like Luther, Calvin believes that the Spirit is at work for us for the purpose of salvation. The Spirit also penetrates and transforms our hearts by inflaming the individual heart with the love of God. While being active in all people, the Spirit comes to those who believe in Jesus Christ as their Lord and Savior. According to Calvin, without the Spirit, sin will lead us astray. In consideration of faith as the work of the Spirit, Calvin writes that, "Christ when he illumines us into faith by the power of his Spirit, at the same time so engraft us into his body that we become partakers of every good."[156] With this sense of God goodness in mind, Calvin gave titles to the Holy Spirit as he found the Spirit active in Scripture. Those titles are Spirit of Adoption, Guarantee and seal of our inheritance, free benevolence of God embracing us, Life because of righteousness, water making us fruitful to righteousness, oil and anointing regarding of vigor of life, Fire boiling away inordinate desires, Spring whence all heavenly riches flow forth to us, Hand of God exercising his might, Christ unites himself to us by the Spirit alone. By grace and power of the same Spirit we are made members, to keep us under himself and in turn to

---

[153] Ibid., 3.2.33 (1:581).
[154] Ibid. (1:581)
[155] Ibid., (1:551).
[156] Ibid., (1:582).

possess him.[157]

Unlike Augustine and Luther, Calvin does not dismiss the physical component of poverty by spiritualizing the term "poor."[158] Knowing that the Church needs encouragement in its time of persecution, Calvin, instead, challenges his readers to search the Scriptures for themselves, so that they might learn from the struggles in the past—that "they might realize that the Church has always overcome by suffering."[159] With this encouragement, Calvin affirms that God's Spirit can "revive the godly" when they groan "under the severest hardships." In addition to affirming the Holy Spirit as the "True Splendor" of the Church (Isa 49:18), the source of "seasonal aid" and the inspirational power of the Holy Sacraments,"[160] Calvin theologizes the experience of poverty as one of cross bearing and spirituality-building. Pattison summarizes the thoughts of Calvin:

> Cross bearing, in Calvin's thought, is a theological description for the way poverty and affliction benefit a believer's spirituality. It pertains to the manner in which a believer endures the experiences of hardship. The experience of poverty and affliction for the Christian is consecrated in the life and death of Christ in such a way that these experiences are now essential instruments for divine grace and blessing. Believers can experience God's grace in the midst of their troubles because poverty challenges the kind of self-confidence which hinders self-doubt and humility. This revelation of a true knowledge of self allows the Holy Spirit to work, driving believers to flee to Christ where they can receive aid for the ailing consciences in the grace of his cross.[161]

Huldrych Zwingli

Chronologically placed between the pneumatological work of Luther and Calvin, the theology of Huldrych Zwingli was a major force in the Protestant Reformation that swept through Europe in the 16th century. While Zwingli's insistence that the Bible, not the Church, was the source of Christian truth made him unpopular with the

---

[157] Ibid., (1:540).
[158] Ibid., 194.
[159] Ibid.
[160] Ibid., 195.
[161] Ibid., 351-352.

Catholic church, his theological convictions aligned with those of Luther and Calvin. "The principles that guide Zwingli's interpretation derive primarily from his humanist education and his reformed understanding of the Bible and the Christian faith. Fundamental, however, is the sense that scripture is from the Spirit and can be understood only where the Spirit gives understanding. Here, the Spirit plays an important role in Zwingli's theology."[162] Zwingli asserts:

> Before I say anything or listen to the teaching of man, I will first consult the mind of the Spirit of God (Ps 85): 'I will hear what God the Lord will speak.' Then you should reverently ask God for his grace, that he may give you his mind and Spirit, so that you will not lay hold of your own opinion but of his. And have a firm trust that he will teach you a right understanding, for all wisdom is of God and Lord. And then go to the written word of the gospel. ...You must be theodidacti, that is, taught of God, not men: that is what the Truth itself said (Jn 6), and it cannot lie.[163]

For Zwingli, "it is not that the Spirit is enough without scripture, nor that it is by the Spirit that the scripture is tested; it is rather that the Spirit is indispensable for the understanding of scripture and must be sought before we turn to it."[164] Zwingli believed that "there is one way to receive this spiritual insight—from God himself. The same Spirit who inspired the prophets and apostles to write the Scriptures must be present to confirm and persuade from the truth. In other words, Scripture is self-authenticating. The Holy Spirit enlightens the text of the Bible in such a way that we know and confess it to be the Word of God.

In this sense Zwingli could speak of the "prevenient clarity" of Holy Scripture. Also, for this reason Zwingli could dispense with the official channels of approved interpretation—the pope, the councils, the schoolmen, and Fathers. "God's word can be understood by a man without any human direction."[165] Zwingli thus brought together two affirmations that would be even more closely cojoined by Calvin: the supremacy of Holy Scripture over human tradition and the inward

---

[162] W. P. Stephens, *The Theology of Huldrych Zwingli*, 59.
[163] Ibid., 60.
[164] Ibid.
[165] Timothy George, *Theology of the Reformers*, 132.

illumination of the individual believer by the Holy Spirit. Hence, Zwingli could say, "understand Scripture only in the way that it interprets itself by the Spirit of God. It does not require any human opinion."[166]

For Zwingli, the believer is faithful in his or her actions through the Spirit of God.

> Now where God is, there the good always increased and grows. And when we see some people who believe in the word of God and yet do not mend their ways, then it happens that either they are not believing and are play-acting before people as if they were believing, or they are still immature in faith, but will increase and grow until the acquire the perfect maturity according to the strength of Christ described in Ephesians 4:13. To put it in a few words: where the love of God is, its efficaciousness is not less than that of lustful bodily love.[167]

In other words, if Christian believers are to take seriously the inspired Word of God, then our lives should demonstrate that personal growth and spiritual evolving. Zwingli believed that baptism with the Spirit, not water baptism, was how individuals were drawn into the orbit of divine salvation. The Spirit was not bound to external signs: "God baptizes with the Spirit how, whom, and when he will."[168] Baptism was an ecclesial event. Zwingli also believed the purpose of baptism was to inform the whole church rather than oneself of the faith that had been inwardly wrought by the baptism of the Holy Spirit.[169]

Theologically, Zwingli is remembered for his view of the Lord's Supper, which he interpreted as a memorial or symbolic remembrance of Christ's sacrifice. This not only distinguished him from the Roman doctrine of transubstantiation, but also from the Lutheran view (consubstantiation) in which Christ was regarded as spirituality present "in with and under" the elements of bread and wine.[170] Timothy George writes that "If "This is my body" was Luther's favorite text, Zwingli had one of his own, John 6:63: "It is the spirit

---

[166] Ibid., 132-133.
[167] Huldrych Zwingli, *Selected Writings of Huldrych Zwingli: Volume Two*, 60.
[168] Timothy George, *Theology of the Reformers*, 143.
[169] Ibid., 144.
[170] Hugh T. Kerr, *Readings in Christian Thought*, 172.

gives life, the flesh is of no avail." The text supported Zwingli's emphasis on the direct, unmediated impartation of salvation by the Holy Spirit, and his disparagement of the "husks of externals." It became the centerpiece of his attack on Luther's doctrine of the corporeal presence of Christ in the Lord's Supper."[171]

Zwingli agreed with Calvin in affirming that "Christ was locally present at the right hand of the Father in heaven and should not be thought of as "attached to the element of the bread," to be touched by the hands, chewed by teeth, and swallowed by the mouth (*Inst.* 4.17.10-11)."[172] Calvin asks the question: How can Christ be at once at the Father's right hand and present at the "spiritual banquet" of Communion? Zwingli agrees with Calvin's response. Calvin writes that, "What our mind does not comprehend, let faith conceive: that the Spirit truly unites things separated in space" (*Inst.* 4. 17. 10). So important was the Supper as spiritual nourishment for the church that Calvin advocated its weekly celebration."[173] Zwingli writes about the Sacraments in the document entitled Reckoning of the Faith of Ulrich Zwingli to Emperor Charles V, Augsburg, 1530: 7-8. Sacraments: I believe, yea, I know, that all the sacraments are so far from conferring grace that they do not even convey or distribute it. For as grace is produced or given by the Divine Spirit, so this gift pertains to the Spirit alone.[174]

> Moreover, a channel or vehicle is not necessarily to the Spirit, for He Himself is the virtue and energy whereby all things are borne, and has no need of being borne; neither do we read in the Holy Scriptures that perceptible things, as are the sacraments, bear certainly with them the Spirit, but if perceptible things have ever been borne with the Spirit, it has been the Spirit, and not perceptible things, that has borne them...The sacraments are given as a public testimony of that grace which is previously present to every individual.[175]

Appropriately, Zwingli fully supported Calvin's theological emphasis on the role of the Holy Spirit in the Eucharist, on the lifting up of our

[171] Timothy George, *Theology of the Reformers*, 156.
[172] Ibid., 247.
[173] Ibid., 247-248.
[174] Clyde L. Manschreck, *A History of Christianity*, 72.
[175] Ibid.

hearts in adoration, praise, and worship to God.

In terms of being initiated and identified by God in the baptismal moment, we have seen that for Zwingli faith was the gift of the Holy Spirit and had no intrinsic connection with water baptism.[176] When and how the Spirit chose to impart faith to the individual being baptized was irrelevant to the rite itself.[177] Zwingli strongly emphasized the role of faith in the Christian life and never allowed the work of the Holy Spirit to be compromised by reliance on external means of grace.[178] In his text, *Zwingli*, G. R. Potter describes the Swiss reformer this way:

> A man of prayer and supremely God-fearing, he humbly sought the guidance of the Holy Spirit through God's word in the Scriptures or directly from above. Biblical quotations, texts, phrases permeate every page of his letters and treatises. He was a renowned scholar, and he had devout friends and disciples. His faith was irresistible, unclouded by doubt, utterly submissive to the Divine will. He seriously believed that Pope and Emperor could be overthrown and a new era, almost a reign of the saints, begin. In Switzerland, united and a great power, men would show by hard work, by contentment with a life of agriculture and cattle rearing, and by lives in which religion was predominant, what Christians could offer the world.[179]

John Wesley and Pentecostalism in Brief

The influence of the Protestant Reformers is heavily visible in John Wesley's views on justification and the atonement. While liberal Methodist scholars have attacked the penal substitution theory of atonement, Collins reminds us that the substitutionary death of Christ was central to Methodist theology, just as it was for the Reformers. In his book, *John Wesley: Holy Love and the Shape of Grace*, Kenneth J. Collins notes that "Drawing the relation between the suffering servant of Isaiah 53 and Christ, Wesley reveals that at Calvary, the lamb of God bore 'those punishments by which our peace, our

---

[176] Timothy George, *Theology of the Reformers,* 146.
[177] Ibid., 147.
[178] Ibid., 165.
[179] G. R. Potter, *Zwingli,* 418.

reconciliation to God, was to be purchased."'[180]

Wesley's views on justifying faith mirrored Martin Luther and John Calvin. Wesley's new birth experience occurred at Aldersgate in 1738 while listening to a reading of Luther's preface of the Epistle to the Romans. This is where Wesley proclaimed that his heart became strangely warm in the presence of the Holy Spirit. In his agreement with Calvin on justification, Wesley declared, "I do not differ from him a hair's breadth." Collins goes on to state, "Wesley believed that this teaching was also expressed in the ancient authors; especially in Origen, St. Cyprian, St. Chrysostom, Hilary, St. Basil, St. Ambrose, and St. Augustine.[181]

While justification and the new birth offered a measure of assurance, there was a greater assurance in the witness of the Holy Spirit to the life of the believer. For Wesley, the doctrine of assurance, the direct witness in particular, was so vital to the Christian faith that he not only referred to it as 'one grand part of the testimony which God have given to [the Methodists] to bear to all mankind,' but also considered it to be an important element of the proper Christian faith," says Collins.[182] Wesley himself declared: By "the testimony of the Holy Spirit" I mean an inward impression of the soul, whereby the Spirit of God immediately and directly witnesses to my human spirit that I am a child of God, that Jesus Christ hath loved me, and given himself for me; that all my sins are blotted out, and I, even I, am reconciled to God.[183] Within the ecclesiastical contexts of church ministry, Christian theology and social justice awareness, John Wesley's intellectual gift was his unique ability to connect the power of the Holy Spirit or what the Bible says about the work of the Holy Spirit in the presence of those who were hurting and oppressed.

In stressing the worldwide agency of the Holy Spirit, Wesley connected the work of the Holy Spirit to what human beings were experiencing on a day-to-day basis. A Trinitarian thinker, Wesley believed that the Holy Spirit works in all means of grace available.

---

[180] Ray Nothstine, "The theology of John Wesley," Para. 3.
[181] Ibid., Para. 4.
[182] Ibid., Para. 5.
[183] John Wesley, *A Plain Account of Christian Perfection*, quoted by M. James Sawyer, "The Witness of the Spirit in the Protestant Tradition," Bible.org.

Wesley lifted the Holy Spirit's role in grace because he believed that the Holy Spirit *is* the grace of God working within the individual believer. Here, the Holy Spirit pours divine grace into the human soul for the purpose of creating prevenient grace. In the mind of Wesley, prevenient grace is that grace that comes before the deep healing of the body, mind (spirit) and soul. The Holy Spirit produces prevenient grace, which signals and appropriates the conscience of the individual as the immediate action or as the part of the human spirit that feels convicted in sin. In other words, conscience is a form of prevenient grace; one in which moves the hearts of people toward the love of God and vision of Christ by way of the Holy Spirit.

Another important part of Wesley's theology of the Holy Spirit is that of witness. According to Wesley, God gives believers the witness of the Spirit. In the same vein, the Holy Spirit bears witness to the human spirit confirming that we are children of God. Referencing Romans 8:16, Wesley writes that, "I contend not; seeing so many other texts, with the experience of all real Christians, sufficiently evince, that there is in every believer, both the testimony of God's Spirit, and the testimony of his own, that he is a child of God."[184] Putting great emphasis on what he terms the testimony of God's Spirit, Wesley confesses that "It is hard to find words in the language of men to explain "the deep things of God." "Indeed," Wesley confides, there are none (words) that will adequately express what the children of God experience. But one might say, (desiring any who are taught of God to correct, to soften or strengthen the expression.)

For Wesley, the testimony of the Spirit is an inward impression on the soul, whereby the Spirit of God directly witnesses to my spirit, that I am a child of God; that Jesus is hath loved me, and given himself for me; and that all my sins are blotted out, and I, even I, am reconciled to God..."[185] What this means is that the witness of the Holy Spirit adjoins with the witness of the human spirit for the purposes of love, faith, hope and grace. Wesley writes: Then, and not till then, --when the Spirit of God beareth that witness to our spirit, "hath loved thee, and hath washed thee from thy sins in his blood,"— "we love God, because he first loved us"; and, for his sake, we love

---

[184] John Wesley, "The Witness of the Spirit: Sermon 10 [text from the 1872 edition]," Para. 6.
[185] John Wesley, "The Witness of the Spirit: Sermon 11" SPIRIT DISCOURSE II, Para. 6.

God and keep his commandments; and "hereby also know that we are of God."[186]

Wesley's discussion on salvation includes the doctrine of the Holy Spirit. Wesley's pneumatology (the study of the Holy Spirit as the third person of the Triune God) traces back in its Patristic roots in Eastern Christian tradition, particularly from Macarius, a Syrian mystic. Wesley's spirituality and practical theology focuses on the transforming power of the Holy Spirit. Life in the Spirit directly connects to Christian perfection and spiritual holiness. Here, the sanctified life of the Christian believer is set apart by and through the Holy Spirit. The Holy Spirit is the immediate cause of holiness. Holiness is the work of God through the power of the Holy Spirit. Wesley's theme of sanctification relates to "deification" (theosis) of Eastern Orthodox spirituality, which means that the life of God in the human soul is participation of the divine nature. Holiness as the work of the Holy Spirit is sanctifying and perfecting the creation.

For Wesley, perfection is experiencing the pure perfect love of God. Perfection is the dynamic goal by which the fullness of love comes through the transforming power of the Holy Spirit. The believer is "indwelt and led by the Spirit rather than possessed by the Spirit as if some irresistible force controls the believer."[187] The doctrine of perfection/holiness is perfecting perfection, which means is a process of growth and maturity in the life of the Spirit. Wesley believes that to be perfect means to be perfect in love. To be perfect in love is to be perfect in God's love. We can be perfect in God's love if God works in us. God works in us through the power of the Holy Spirit. This happens when the believer lives his or her life within the life of the Spirit. Living in the Spirit means life in union with the life of God, which is participation in the divine nature in the perfect love of God. Because the witness of the Holy Spirit is utterly dependable, the Spirit's witness produces gifts of the Spirit.

In addition to spiritual implications, the witness of the Holy Spirit also has social consequences in that it can serve as a leveler of social classes. Spiritual excellence in ministry and worship means being

---

[186] John Wesley, "The Witness of the Spirit: Sermon 10 [text from the 1872 edition]," Para. 14.
[187] Randy L. Maddox, *Rethinking Wesley's Theology for Contemporary Methodism*, 205.

filled with the Holy Spirit. Here, Wesley believed that the work of the Holy Spirit comes from God for the purposes of healing and deliverance. In his own life, the Holy Spirit inspired and moved Wesley to a deep sense of personal acceptance and deliverance from evil. What Wesley was getting at was that the work of the Holy Spirit awakens us to living a life that is pleasing to God. Put another way, the Holy Spirit works in our wills and hearts with the purpose of helping us to turn to God. Not only does the working of the Holy Spirit bring about a new birth, but it also quickens or brings alive the love of God; communicating to the individual believer that he or she is alive through Jesus Christ. Through our identification as believers, the Holy Spirit gives us integrity and puts us back in line with the original plan of Jesus Christ.

In his handbook, *Wesley for Armchair Theologians*, William J. Abraham says

> Looking back at the big picture, we can see that Wesley provided a unique vision of the Christian life that is worthy of admiration. He was Lutheran insofar as he insisted on justification as foundational; he was Reformed insofar as he believed that we shall be fighting sin to our dying day; he was Anglican in that he expected God to work objectively in the sacraments to mediate grace; he was Roman Catholic in that he held that conspicuous sanctity or goodness really was possible; he was Pentecostal in that he stressed the pivotal role of explicit experience of the Holy Spirit in our lives.[188]

Pentecostalism In Brief

In believing that Pentecost is the explicit role of the Holy Spirit in our lives, Wesley took seriously the biblical books of Joel (Joel 25) and Acts (Acts 2) where the Holy Spirit comes as one that falls upon all human flesh (God's creation) for the purpose of embodying the ministry of Jesus Christ. Here the theological implication is that the Holy Spirit is the Spirit of Christ. From Wesley, the grandchild Pentecostals received an emphasis on holiness and sanctification, sometimes called the "second blessing" or "baptism of the Spirit." Pentecost is the explicit role of the Holy Spirit in our lives. What this means is that God's Spirit has an inner voice that works in the

---

[188] William J. Abraham, *Wesley for Armchair Theologians*, 38.

metaphysical and spiritual lives of believers in Jesus Christ. Wesley writes about the work of the Spirit in his sermon......:" We allow that the state of a justified person inexpressibly great and glorious. He is born again, "not of blood, nor of the flesh, nor of the will of man, but of God" [...] His very body is a 'temple of the Holy Ghost,' and an 'habitation of God through the Spirit.' He is 'created anew in Christ Jesus....'[189]

What some scholars consider to be the grandchild of Methodism, Pentecostalism derives its name from the event of Pentecost, the coming of the Holy Spirit when Jesus' disciples were gathered in Jerusalem. Pentecostalism also believes that, once received, the Holy Spirit is God working through the recipient to perform the gifts of the Spirit. These gifts are in 1 Corinthians chapter 12. The Pentecostal movement places special emphasis on the work of the Holy Spirit, especially the gift of speaking in tongues. Many Pentecostals hold that the "baptism of the Holy Spirit" is a distinct form of the Christian regeneration, separate from the "born-again" experience of conversion or water baptism.[190] Many church denominations believe that "Holy Spirit baptism is a necessary element in salvation."[191] An early baptismal formula, in accordance with the command in the closing words of Matthew 28 "in the name of the Father and of the Son and of the Holy Ghost."

Even in theological consideration of what the Bible says about the baptism of the Holy Spirit, it can be said that Pentecost is more than church folk "engaging in extended episodes of "shouting" or paroxysmal dancing under the influence of the Holy Spirit that only ended when they "fell out" or fainted and lay prostrate on the floor in a semiconscious state."[192] At its core, Pentecostalism is the spiritual way of living out the *biblical* testimony of Acts 2. Like those who attended the Azusa Street Revival in 1904, Pentecostals believe they are "saved, sanctified, and filled with the Holy Ghost" in reference to the three works of grace of Holiness Pentecostals, the original branch

---

[189] Wesley, edited by Thomas Jackson. Global Ministries of the United Methodist Church. http://www.umcmission.org/Find-Resources/Global-Worship-and-Spiritual-Growth/John-Wesley-Sermons/ Sermon-13-On-Sin-in-Believers
[190] Wikipedia: Pentecostalism
[191] "Holy Spirit in Christian Denominational Variations," Para. 6.
[192] Timothy J. Nelson, *Every Time I Feel the Spirit*, 5.

of Pentecostalism.

When Pentecostals mention the name Holy Ghost, they are talking about the Holy Spirit. Darryl Lawson explains the nature and sanction of the Holy Spirit in this manner: "The Holy Ghost is what the Bible teaches. It's a comforter, it's a guide, it's a keeper, it's more than three in one. And the Holy Ghost is something that—say for instance that you make me mad, real mad. Ordinarily, I didn't have the Holy Ghost, I'd jump on you and kill you. But because of the Holy Ghost teaching, it would be teaching me, "Vengeance is not yours." It would bring the Word back to your remembrance to keep you from getting in trouble."[193] Put another way, "the Holy Ghost will be a teacher or a guide to tell you [God's will]."[194] Ronald Manigault discusses the Holy Spirit as the internal voice of conscience, but also, like Darryl Lawson, emphasizes that the Spirit doesn't override the believer's free will—one has to choose to follow the Holy Ghost's leading.[195] [A]fter you [become saved], then you receive the Holy Ghost. The Holy Ghost will basically come to lead and guide you, will speak to you and tell you what to do.[196]

Malaysian American Amos Yong is the most prolific Pentecostal theologian of the contemporary era. In his study on the Holy Spirit's work within and beyond the Christian church institution, Yong stands as one who both affirms Pentecostal piety and the full intellectualization of the Pentecostal movement. Scholars and theologians would be hard pressed to find a relevant conversation on the Holy Spirit away from Yong's in-depth scholarship. A considerable portion of Yong's work[197] in pneumatology centers on the witness of the Holy Spirit. Yong's theology calls for the Spirit to come with a new Pentecost for the present age of believers. In their co-edited book, *Afro-Pentecostalism: Black Pentecostalism and*

---

[193] Ibid., 64.
[194] Ibid., 65.
[195] Ibid.
[196] Ibid.
[197] Amongst Yong's many works, four of his published books in particular help to inform my theology of the Holy Spirit as Supreme Liberator: *The Spirit of Love: A Trinitarian Theology of Grace* (2012), *The Missiological Spirit: Christian Mission Theology in the Third Global Context* (2014), *The Spirit Poured Out On All Flesh: Pentecostalism and the Possibility of Global Theology* (2005) and *Discerning the Spirit(s): A Pentecostal Charismatic Contribution in Christian Theology of Religions* (2019).

Charismatic Christianity in History and Culture (2011), Yong and Estrelda Alexander positively theologize the far-reaching "diversity of the Pentecostal movement interface with social ethics, economic justice, gender equality, and other contemporary issues."[198] Inclusive to the histo-cultural diversity of the Pentecostal movement is the Black religious experiences in the United States and many other places around the world. Pneumatology as the study of the Holy Spirit has helped to make room for Black human, Black existential, and Black cultural experiences. These experiences are construed as multiple Black religious experiences; and not just one singular religious experience. Theologically, this is because the Holy Spirit works explicitly and implicitly in a diversity of contexts.

Afro-Pentecostalism provides powerful insights from a vast array of interdisciplinary scholars from different facets of the Pentecostal movement. Yong and Alexander's text provides historical and theological perspectives on Black Pentecostalism, which are inclusive to their missiological foci, their interdenominational commitments, their theological connections to secular and popular cultures, and the important conversations surrounding race and gender. Yong and Alexander's important volume helpful in explaining how the work of the Holy Spirit is liberating for all groups, races, and cultures of Black religionists. In carefully unpacking the Pentecostal movement's distinctive theology, *Afro-Pentecostalism* strategically draws upon the exploratory thoughts of scholars and theologians from a wide array of backgrounds and contexts. Overall, *Afro-Pentecostalism* succeeds in describing how Black Christians have been integrally involved in every aspect of the Pentecostal movement since its inception and have made significant contributions to its founding as well as "the evolution of Pentecostal/charismatic styles of worship, preaching, music, engagement of social issues, and theology."[199] Juan Floyd-Thomas summarizes:

> Undeniably, the most significant growth within the Black Church tradition was the Holiness and Pentecostal

---

[198] Kenneth L. Waters, "Afro-Pentecostalism: Black Pentecostal and Charismatic Christianity in History and Culture," Para. 2.

[199] Amazon book description of *Afro-Pentecostalism: Black Pentecostal and Charismatic Christianity in History and Culture (Religion, Race, and Ethnicity)* by Amos Yong and Estrelda Alexander.

movements. The Holiness movement and the advent of the Pentecostal church movement greatly affected Baptist and Methodist congregations. Partly in reaction to the elite domination and stiff authority of white Methodism, the Holiness movement gained foothold among white people and then spilled over among Black Southerners. Holiness churches ordained women such as Neely Terry to lead them. Holiness clergy preached the Wesleyan notion of sanctification, an ideal that allowed a Christian to receive a "second blessing" and to feel the "perfect love of Christ" through the anointing of the Holy Spirit. Believers thus achieved an emotional reaffirmation and a new state of grace.[200]

Randy Woodley adds to the narrative of God's plan for an American Pentecost:

During its initial two-year surge, it was common for the Azusa revival to hold meetings from early morning till midnight. By 1908 hundreds of ministries had been formed around the world as a result of the thousands touched by the Holy Spirit at Azusa. In Mau 1908 *The Apostolic Faith* newspaper reported the following spin-off, under the heading[201] "Italians and Indians Receive the Holy Ghost"

Truly the latter rain appears to be falling on every kindred, tongue and nation. While I was a way, a number of Indians from the reserve, about 200 miles north, heard of the work in Winnipeg and came in the city. Five of them received the baptism and others were saved and sanctified. Since they returned home, we have heard that other Indians have been saved. While the Indians were at the meetings in the city, two of the Saints, under the power of the Spirit, spoke in other languages, which were understood by the Indians and one of the interpretations was, "Jesus was coming soon."[202]

---

[200] Juan M. Floyd-Thomas, *Liberating Black Church History*, 84.
[201] Randy Woodley, *Living in Color: Embracing God's Passion*, 31-32.
[202] Azusa Street Online website: www.dunami.com/brightspot/azusa/html>.

According to Kenneth L. Waters, "A doctrine of the Holy Spirit has always been implicit in African American discourse on salvation and worship, and little to no distinction was made between the presence of Christ and the Spirit. In the Spirit, enslaved Africans experience liberation from sin, and this by extension made the sin of slavery and slave master more intolerable."[203] In theological consideration of how the Spirit saves and why believers worship God in Spirit, therein lies a metaphysical connection between the indistinctive work of Jesus Christ and the Holy Spirit and the slaves' experience of spiritual liberation. Along the same lines, Carmichael D. Crutchfield believes that the metaphysical connection is founded in "how the Holy Spirit's ministry is revealing Jesus to us, to bear testimony of Jesus (John 15:26). The Holy Spirit uses many different gifts to accomplish this, but the purpose is always the same: to reveal Jesus."[204] In this way of thinking theologically, the ministry of Jesus Christ and the work of the Holy Spirit are inextricably tied together for sake of liberation, emancipation, and healing.

Christian theologians believe that the emancipatory ministry of Jesus Christ and the liberating work of the Holy Spirit are one in the same. Pentecostalism is a Christian denomination that emphasizes the work of the Holy Spirit in the life of a believer. Pentecostal spirituality is abstracted around an encounter with the ministry of Jesus Christ as the center of the gospel message (Matthew, Mark, Luke, John), filtered through an emphasis on His work the cross and the resurrection of Christ's body. This Christological focus accentuates and confirms the work of the Holy Spirit as the most essential component of recognizing the life of Christ and, in turn, of living a Christ-like life. Concomitantly, through Jesus' work on the Cross and the resurrection, the Holy Spirit gives life to dead contexts and painful situations so that believers might tell others about goodness of God. The goal of experiencing the life-giving power of the Holy Spirit is for believers to be like Christ in the way they live their life.

Historian Kenneth S. Latourette says that "The coming of the Spirit brought about the circle who had been won by Jesus in the days

---

[203] Kenneth L. Waters, "Afro-Pentecostalism: Black Pentecostal and Charismatic Christianity in History and Culture," Para. 11.
[204] *Advent: Prophecy and Expectation*, 9.

of his flesh, were further strengthened and empowered by the fulfillment of a promise which had been given them by their risen Lord. On Pentecost, the Jewish feast which came fifty days after the second day of the Passover, there came upon the group in Jerusalem— a group which may numbered slightly above a hundred—what they called the Holy Spirit."[205] What this meant was that "The effects of the resurrection and the coming of the Holy Spirit upon the disciples were and are of major importance. From discouraged, disillusioned men and women who sadly looked up the days when they had hoped that Jesus "was he who should redeem Israel," they were made over into a company of enthusiastic witnesses."[206] At the baptism of the Holy Spirit moment, Montanus "spoke with tongues" and began prophesying, declaring that the Paraclete, the Holy Spirit, as promised in *the Gospel according to John*, was finding utterance through him (scripture). Two women, his disciples, were also believed to be prophets, mouthpieces of the Holy Spirit. The three taught the New Jerusalem would "come down out of heaven from God," as had been foretold in *The Revelation of John*, and that it would be fixed in in Phrygia.[207]

The Montanus movement played a key role in how theologians interpreted John 14:26 as he claimed to be the Paraclete (return of the Holy Spirit) prophesied in the Johannine text. The Montanist movement flourished in and around the region of Phrygia in contemporary Turkey and spread to other regions in the Roman Empire in the second and third centuries. Montanism, called the Cataphrygian heresy or New Prophecy, taught that the Holy Spirit was continuing to give new spiritual revelation through Montanus and his followers, and that Jesus would soon bring the New Jerusalem to a place in Phrygia. Followers of Montanism also claimed inspiration for themselves, saying that their words of revelation were as authoritative as anything in Scripture. Often, they could not even be understood. They were known for speaking in tongues, prattling, and chanting nonsense.[208]

In discussing the role of the Holy Spirit in how the Canon of the

---

[205] Kenneth S. Latourette, *A History of Christianity*, 59.
[206] Ibid.
[207] Ibid., 128.
[208] Ibid.

New Testament was determined, Latourette claims that,

> It may be that *The Revelation of John* was viewed with suspicion and the other writings of Christian prophets did not find a permanent place in the canon because of the distrust with which those prophets claiming to be the mouthpieces of the Holy Spirit were viewed by the bishops and their clergy. The Montanists, with their assertion that Spirit-inspired prophets continued to arise in the Christian community, were a challenge to the administrative regularity represented by the bishops, and their rejection of the Catholic Church may have accentuated the distrust for the prophets and their writings. Certainly, prophets, accorded a place in the early Church next to apostles, were no longer granted recognition by the Catholic Church. Inspiration through prophets were supposed to have ceased with the apostolic age.[209]

Either way we turn theologically, historically or within the contemporary context, Wesley's message is simple. The Spirit of God saves. The Holy Spirit positively affects the institution and through faith, the Holy Spirit indwells. Also, intellectual illumination depends on the work of the Holy Spirit. The Holy Trinity equals the love of God, neighbor, and self. As the third person of the Holy Trinity, the Holy Spirit is not enthusiastic by nature. On his death bed, Wesley affirmed that "The best of all is, the Spirit God is with us."[210] As one whose heart became strangely warm in sacred institutions and secular environments, I am certain that the Holy Spirit led Wesley to the important conclusion that the national disgrace of Slavery was not of God, but one of demonic actions. Under the influence of the Holy Spirit, John Wesley accepted Luther and Calvin's economic argument in the 18th Century.

Wesley's writing provides descriptive images of how the Spirit is concerned with social, economic, and political life within the believer's decision to serve God first and then bear good fruit in living the Christian life. Unsurprisingly, Wesley's theology of the Holy Spirit takes shape at the dawn of the modern industrial economy as poor people of all races descended to the bottom of humanity's well.

---

[209] Ibid., 134.
[210] "Best of all is God is with us (StF 610)" *Singing the Faith Plus*, The Methodist Church. Para. 5.

Wesley's doctrine was rounding into good theological shape just as capitalism was being theorized and practiced in his native Britain. Wesley was certain that the Holy Spirit rests on the body economic, presenting alternatives to a spirit of consumption and acquisition in the economy of gift. Wesley was not in favor of slavery of any kind in any place. Because the practice of slavery was a moral issue, he theologized the Holy Spirit as one who was not in favor of any form of oppression and dehumanization. As one who understood the atheological connection between capitalism and slavery, of Wesley's sermons have becomes hymns of the Methodist church. He laments the harmful spirit of consumption that pervades economic life and employs an economy of gift.

HOLY Ghost! My Comforter!

> Now from highest heaven appear,
>> Shed they gracious radiance here.
>> Come to them who suffer death,
>> With thy gifts of priceless worth,
>> Lighten all who dwell on earth!
> Thou the heart's most precious guest,
>> Thou of comforters the best,
>> Give to us, the o'er-laden, rest
> Come! In thee our toil is sweet,
>> Shelter from the noon-day heat,
>> From whom sorrow flieth feet.
> Blessed Sun of grace! o'er all
>> Faithful hearts who on thee call
> Let thy light and solace fall.[211]

Spirit Sermon

This is a revised sermon that I preached in 2008 while I was pursuing my Master of Divinity degree at the Louisville Presbyterian Theological Seminary. It was an occasion that the seminary community observed and celebrated Black History Month. The location was the historic Caldwell Chapel in Louisville, Kentucky.

---

[211] https://hymnary.org/text/holy_ghost_my_comforter

The title of the sermon was "I Need the Spirit, We Need the Spirit!" The sermonic text was John 14:15-17.

April 4th of this year will mark the 40- year anniversary of the assassination of our beloved Dr. Martin Luther King Jr. in Memphis, Tennessee. And what is so amazing about the life and legacy of this African American man of God is that his *spirit* continues to live on in the communal realities of our diverse and multicultural contexts. More notably, I believe that Scripture, in particular John 14:15-17 speaks directly to the spirit of Dr. King in terms of what it means to be a follower of Jesus Christ while experiencing the regenerating power of God's Holy Spirit. Here, the Apostle John teaches us three biblical truths about the Holy Spirit—truths I believe speak to the philosophical and theological essence of prophetic leadership. The text teaches us that:

1. The Holy Spirit will be with us forever.
2. The world at large will not accept the Holy Spirit.
3. The Holy Spirit lives with us and in us.

Conservative Bible scholars have declared that the context of this section of the Gospel of John focuses on the church and not on Christians as individuals. Various commentaries quickly acknowledge that these verses are not interpreted as a mere 'subjunctive personal experience' of the Spirit by individuals, nor should the emphasis fall on a personal meaning for the word "in" for verse seventeen. Therefore, these passages should be viewed as a 'sociological defensive expression' of the church against the world.' It is understood that the social context to which John is addressing his Gospel is clearly that of a community pressured by the world. Because of the spread of Christianity, Judaism was left in a national and religious crisis that caused them to look for ways to continue their ritual and worship. The Jerusalem community was destructively divided, personally threatened, and spiritually dry.

But if we were to reflect on this context for a moment, were not America's communities, especially the deep Southeastern parts of the country, pressured by the world during the late 1960s? Were not our communities threatened, divided, and suffering from both a national and a religious crisis? Even today—in the twenty-first century, as we are amid fighting an unjustifiable war, dirty and dishonest politics, health care for a few and medical hell for the rest, covert racism, patriarchal sexism, rigid homophobia, church denominational economics, middle class poverty-which means lower class nihilism, the AIDS epidemic, homicide, global warming, and unequal public-school education—and other social evils as well. Are not our communities still pressured by the idolatries of the world? If the answer is yes, then somebody *ought to* say Amen.

And because these social issues continue to eat away at the interweaving fabrics of our society, our need for spiritual reformation is greater now than ever before. In other words, we need a divine presence to help us work out our systemic problems. Not because we deserve God's help, but because God's help is the transforming revealer of God's love. For those who have not yet been introduced to the main character of the message, it is my pleasure to introduce to you to the third person of the Holy Trinity, God the Holy Spirit; also known as the Paraclete. My brothers and sisters, it is important to recognize that God's gift of the Paraclete is not to be understood as some kind of 'merit based—binding agreement' between Jesus and his followers, as though the Wal-Mart exchange for the Holy Spirit is our obedience. We cannot earn the Holy Spirit any more than we can earn salvation. But in the process of responding to Jesus, we can discover that he has provided a divine agent for living in this world.

With there being confusion among Christians concerning the statement that the Paraclete is "with you and shall be in you," the Greek prepositions for "with" and "in" represent the words *para* and *en*. These translations help to provide a solution to the problem of individualistic interpretation. While this text is not about two ways the Spirit dwells "with and in" Christians like a two-stage salvation process, it does capture for us an individual way of reflectively processing what it means for the Spirit to "live with us and be in us" personally. The reason for the change from the stage processes to processing personally is because we, as followers of Christ, are no longer on the outside of the Christian reality looking in. We are now on the inside of the reality of community because the reality of the Spirit is now inside of us.

In the Johannine text, the Paraclete is given an initial identification as the Spirit of Truth. Among the most important attributes of Jesus for John, is that he speaks the truth and that he is the truth. Because Jesus is the truth, the work of the Paraclete is to keep the truth of Jesus present to the world after Jesus' departure. Jesus' promise to the disciples was that when he departed the earth, the Spirit of Truth would come and abide in them. That is to say that Jesus's promise to one Dr. Martin Luther King Jr., also a follower of Jesus Christ, was that the Spirit of Truth would come continue to abide in him throughout his life and ministry. King says in his sermon *Pilgrimage to Nonviolence*:

> Like the Apostle Paul, I can humbly, yet proudly say I bear in my body the marks of the Lord Jesus. The agonizing moments through which I have passed during the last few years have drawn me closer to God. True, I have always believed in the personality of God. But in the past the idea of a personal God was little more than a metaphysical category that I found theologically and philosophically satisfying. Now it is a living reality that has been validated in the experiences of everyday life. God has been profoundly good to me in recent years. Amid lonely days and dreary nights, I have heard an inner voice saying, "Lo, I will be with you." When the chains of fear and the manacles of frustration have all but stymied my efforts, I have felt the power of God transforming the fatigue of despair into the buoyancy of hope in Jesus Christ.[212]

Here, the testimony of God counseling us and doing constructive work on the inside of believers should teach us that whether it is me, you, they, we, the church, the community, the disciples, or King himself, as ministers, preachers, teachers, administrators, employees, and servants, we all need the Spirit of God in our lives. I need the Spirit so God can help me to become a better person, a better servant, a better leader, a better citizen, and a better student. We need the Spirit of God to help us to spiritually construct our Seminary community, to minister to the needs of the Louisville community, to speak life into those who have been overlooked and left for dead, to help us to deal with this universal issue of poverty, to make contributions to the up building of our struggling country and to help us change ourselves so that we can change the world. The inner voice King heard during his suffering was that of the Holy Spirit. For King, the Holy Spirit is the personal God. In response to the question of

---

[212] https://kinginstitute.stanford.edu/king-papers/documents/suffering-and-faith

'what's going on in society and in the world,' King says that "In a dark, confused world the spirit of God may yet reign supreme.[213]

Furthermore, I believe that while spiritual reformation begins with God, social transformation begins with God and the individual, who may or may not be a member of the Christian church. Because of our embedded theologies, it is possible for the Spirit of Truth to touchdown on the church and the community, and not even affect, influence, or change the heart of the individual. Once the heart of the individual changes through the inspiration of the Holy Spirit, then and only then can believers respond to Jesus and become followers. When the transforming process begins, the Counselor, the Spirit of Truth, will dwell with those individuals who obey Jesus and be within them as someone they knew in a way that the world cannot. Yet, the focus of verses 16-17 is not on those who receive the spirit and those who do not; rather the focus is on the assurance that the Paraclete is the Holy Spirit's abiding presence with the believing community. However, I believe that the spiritual effectiveness of the Paraclete's relationship with the believing community is highly contingent upon the Holy Spirit abiding in the individual believer.

This notion of the individual relationship with God through faith in Jesus Christ by the power and might of the Spirit is what makes Dr. King such a phenomenal human being. I believe that King's idea of love, this agape-filled-radical in your face-peacefully standing for justice and equality-while protesting injustice-sacrificial discipleship-understanding collective evil-love ethic of Jesus-speaking up for poor people-preaching political, economic, and social liberation-kind of love was inspired by guiding influence of the Spirit of Truth. After struggling to deal with the death threats and the human reality of fear, (I am still thinking about the disciples in John 14 where their hearts were troubled by the notion that Jesus was going to leave them), King lay awake at night and prayed earnestly to God for direction. He asked God what he should do about fearing for his life and leaving the movement. At the same time King did not want to be a coward. He stated in his sermon, *Our God is Able*:

> At that moment I experienced the presence of the Divine as
> I had never before experienced God before. It seemed as

---

[213] Martin Luther King, Jr. "Pilgrimage to Nonviolence" Para. 19.

though I could hear the quiet assurance of an inner voice, saying, "Stand up for righteousness, stand for truth. God will be at your side forever." Almost at once my fears began to pass from me. My uncertainty disappeared. I was ready to face anything. The outer situation remained the same, but God had given me an inner calm.[214]

The inner voice and inner calm that King heard and received came in the form of the Holy Spirit's comforting strength. King's words reminded me that God did not give us the spirit of fear. But God gave us the spirit of power, love, and self-discipline (2 Tim 1:7).

In combining the two chief aspects of the Spirit's work—being God's nearness and aiming us at God's goal of perfection, Major J. Jones claims that Martin Luther King, Jr. connected Holy subjectivity with the human subjectivity of Black people, as follows:[215] Says King:

Let us realize that as we struggle for justice and freedom, we have cosmic companionship.... The God we worship... is an ever-living God who forever works throughout history for the establishment of his kingdom.... The cross is the eternal expression of the length to which God will go in order to restore broken community. The resurrection is a symbol of God's triumph over all the forces that seek to block community. The Holy Spirit is the continuing of created reality that moves through history.[216]

King knew that liberation was the primary work of the Holy Spirit in the life of oppressed Black people. Poor white people too. He had come to the realization that the Spirit would see him through the exceedingly difficult days that lay ahead. Meanwhile, Jones's language of cosmic companionship accentuates Black people's struggle for justice and freedom as most prominent thinkers do not define liberation as the collaborative work of the Spirit in freedom and justice.

In conclusion, I would like to say that the full-fledged, theological legitimacy of one Dr. Martin Luther King Jr. gives prophetic witness to his philosophical approaches to praxis. It is not so much what King

---

[214] Martin Luther King, Draft of Chapter VIII, "Our God Is Able," Para. 1 and 27.
[215] Major J. Jones, *The Color of God*, 103.
[216] Martin Luther King, "Prayer Pilgrimage for Freedom," 4.

did in his life—we know about the academic degrees, the awards, especially the 1964 Noble Peace Prize, the speeches, the interviews, and the audiences that he addressed. But rather, today's celebration is really about the things King *did not have to do.* African American New Testament scholar, Allan Dwight Callahan, says that "The Spirit of Truth remains with the followers of Jesus because of what they do, insofar as what they do is faithful to Jesus' words."[217] Callahan's description of John 14:17 provides great insight into the spiritual thesis of the message because King did not have to take the leadership role in the Civil Rights Movement.

- He did not have to take the role of president in the Southern Christian Leadership Conference.
- He did not have to march in Selma, Montgomery, Birmingham, Chicago, and Memphis.
- He did not have to be arrested three times for peacefully protesting racial discrimination.
- King did not have to write a letter from the Birmingham Jail, responding to the local clergymen.
- He did not have to take a knife to the chest in New York almost killing him.
- He did not have to eulogistically console the family of the four little girls who were killed in the Birmingham church bombing.
- He did not have to create the Poor People's Campaign for poor people of all races and cultures.
- King did not have to use the Ghanaian form of nonviolent resistance as a way of protesting racial injustice.
- He did not have to shake hands with Malcolm X in Washington D.C. for the sake of his people and history.
- He did not have to courageously assist America in its long-awaited date with holistic destiny.
- He did not have to speak out on the war in Vietnam, going against the wishes of his supporters.
- King did not have to influence the signing of the Civil Rights Bill with President Johnson.

---

[217] Brian K. Blount, *True to Our Native Land*, 203.

- He did not have to go to Memphis to help underpaid and mistreated trash workers get a ten-cent raise.
- He did not have to come out of his hotel room on April 3rd in Memphis to preach his last sermon. On that night it was raining, it was dreary, and it was cold. The wind was blowing with great power, and King was suffering from a nasty cough.
- He did not have to take a fatal bullet to the left side of his upper cheek and neck at the Lorraine Motel. He saw the discombobulated body and face of Emmett Till in Chicago. He saw the clippings of President Kennedy's assassination in Dallas. He knew Medgar Evers was assassinated by a white nationalist sniper in Mississippi. He knew Malcolm X was assassinated execution style by his own people in New York. He knew thousands of African Americans in the South were physically assaulted, drowned, lynched, shot to death, burned, and kidnapped just for being Black.
- King did not have to die for what he believed in at the tender age of thirty-nine and with the heart of a 60-year-old man.
- He did not have to be the sacrifice for the advancement of humanity.

By in large, King, the Black liberation theologian, did what he did because a transcendent somebody was working inside of him caring for him, directing him, guiding him into truth, inspiring him, and giving him insights into future events—including his own death. Not something, but rather someone got a hold of him and enabled him to appropriate the power of the Holy Spirit. This somebody would not let him go. In other words, King always had this person with him and inside of him—teaching him and reminding him of Jesus' words. He was not by himself; somebody comforted and counseled him when he felt discouraged and lonely. In the missiological sense, the Spirit of Christ intoxicated King. In fulfilling the mission that God called him to, he was under the formidable influence of the Holy Spirit. The Spirit of blackness safely held him. King knew that the Spirit of God would see him past the fear of death and propel him to his destiny.

Our own Louisville Presbyterian Theological Seminary President, Dean Thompson, refers to King as America's Moses. I refer to King as a modern-day prophet who had the Spirit of God working inside of him. In this celebratory moment, the testimony of such a great man reminds me that I need the Spirit working in all areas of my life. But it is not just about me. This sermon should remind us that we all need the Holy Spirit working in our lives. I need the Spirit. We need the Spirit. To be a Christian theologian is to follow the directions of the Holy Spirit's presence in your life. As one who obediently followed the directions of the Holy Spirit, King was undeniably one of the greatest theologians in the twentieth century.

Chapter Two

The Holy Spirit in Theology Black and the Color of God

It was early one morning. Just about the break of day. Jesus came and He touched me, and He washed my sins away. I started running, I started shouting. I had no room to doubt him. Oh, but I found nothing but the Holy Ghost.[218]

Black identities that have been ensconced in a form of theological blackness have always been "diverse and complex."[219] Part of the reason why Black identities are complex and diverse is because of Black people's culturo-spiritual connection to the Holy Spirit. The person, power and work of the Holy Spirit defies any simplistic ways of categorizing human beings as people of God or people of the Spirit. Because the Holy Spirit is the Spirit of liberation, "Black theology seeks to liberate all people from multiple forms of political, social, economic, and religious subjugation and views Christian theology as a theology of liberation: "a rational study of the being of God in the world in light of the existential situation of an oppressed community, relating the forces of liberation to the essence of the Gospel, which is Jesus Christ"[220] and the Holy Spirit, the original advocate of the perspective. As led by the person, power and work of the Holy Spirit, Black theology mixes Christianity with questions of civil rights and other types of social movements such as Black Power and African American coalitions. By the person, power, and

---

[218] https://www.lyricsondemand.com/r/revmiltonbrunsonlyrics/theholyghostlyrics.html
[219] Anthony G. Reddie, "Black theology: an introduction," Para. 1.
[220] James H. Cone, *A Black Theology of Liberation*, Summary of pgs. 1-4.

work of the Holy Spirit within how the Spirit of God gives life to Black people's death situations, the diversity and complexity of Black show what fosters a more doctrinal understanding of Black theology. In this case, my doctrine of theological choice is pneumatology.

Introducing Theology Black

Theology Black is a new term of cultural competency and spiritual endearment given to me by the Holy Spirit as I drafted this new book. In defining the contours of a theology Black way of thinking theologically in the twenty-first century, we want to make sure that we avoid two traps and wrestle with 1. Nuancing and reducing God down to one group's ethnic identity; and 2. The idolatrous worship of one's group identity. Constructively, there is a way a group's identity and experience provide insight into who God is but do not reduce or confine God to one or any distinctions. In this way of thinking theologically, I first want to affirm theology Black as an exponential way of doing theology in predominantly Black churches, Black communities, Black neighborhoods, Black schools, secular places, and sacred spaces.

In terms of how the Holy Spirit gives life, theology that is done in Black contexts is a liberating theology that is articulated, described, and constructed in the face of Black oppression, dehumanization, and subjectification. Not only is theology in the Black a theology of the Holy Spirit's liberation of Black persons of all races and cultures throughout the world, but theology Black is also a theology that is hermeneutically profitable and spiritually beneficial to those who have physically felt the person, power, and work of the Holy Spirit because of their faith in Jesus Christ as Lord, Savior, Redeemer, Emancipator and Liberator. Because of the way the Holy Spirit works in theology Black, liberation can take place in all groups, races, and cultures of people.

Theology Black is a contemporary theology that has been historical and metaphysical when she elaborates on the person, power, and work of the Holy Spirit in the presence of death and evil. In stressing that the Holy Spirit gives life, theology Black is most effective when Scripture is the primary source of reference in theological reflection (1 Kgs. 18:45; Zech. 14:2; Matt. 5:1-12, 20:16; Lk. 14:11; Jn 3:16, 19:11; Rom 8:28; Phil.4:13; Gal 3:28, 5:14, 6:7). To operate holistically in theology Black is to participate in God-Talk within the spiritual blackness of the Holy Spirit. In this vein of biblical and cultural thought, theology Black looks face to face with Black theology in the faithful understanding that the Holy Spirit is Black for Black religious experiences (the Black church), Black cultural experiences (Black culture) and the Black existential experiences (Black existence) of all groups, races, and cultures of human beings. Here, the one unchangeable constant is that the Holy Spirit gives life to the circumstances, conditions, images and instances of the Black unconscious, Black mystery, and Black death. The person and power of the Holy Spirit works in the unconscious, in mystery and in death situations of Black people all over the world. According to Andrea Hollingsworth, "This notion that the Spirit's presence and action is tied closely to an individual's inward crisis holds weight not only theologically, but psychologically."[221] Christian psychologist Steven J. Sandage argues that transformations toward more salutary ways of being often involve times of stress, anxiety, and profound destabilization—what in the Christian tradition is often called the "dark night of the soul."[222]

According to world historians and political pundits, the color Black means cursed, unconscious, mystery, death, suffering, tainted, and oppressed. In that Black encompasses multiple colors, Black is also the absence of light within the very presence of the Holy Spirit. Black exists in nature without any light at all. Historically, the color Black that has been associated with the skin of Black human beings means evil, darkness, night, and despair. In other ways of thinking existentially, Black means protecting, banishing, grounding, and safety. Black is also the color of power and dynamism. The dynamic psychology of the color Black means authority, power, stability, strength, and intelligence. From the dualistic connotations of color, humanity, and psychology, comes theology Black for the spiritual purpose of connecting those descriptive images of Black folk, as children of God, to what the Bible says about person, power, and work of the Holy Spirit. Because Black theology has already affirmed that God is Black and Jesus Christ is the Black Christ, my theological claim is that the Holy Spirit is the third person of Holy Trinity—one

---

[221] Andrea Hollingsworth, "Groans Too Deep: The Holy Spirit and Suffering," Para. 13.
[222] F. LeRon Shults and Steven J. Sandage, *Transforming Spirituality: Integrating Theology and Psychology* (Grand Rapids, MI: Baker Academic, 2006).

that is Black for the Black religious experiences, the Black cultural experience, and the Black existential experience of the darker-skinned human being.

Black people's experiences with the Holy Spirit within and beyond the church building are different in scope. Black believers are comfortable and happy in the presence of the Holy Spirit. On the one hand, Black folk who love the Lord are appreciatively accepting of the Holy Spirit taking up productive space in their everyday life. Not only do they need the person, power, and work of the Holy Spirit in their lives, but they also have an expectation of spiritual growth that can only take place in the presence of the Holy Spirit. On the other hand, some may have a "fear of the Holy Spirit and the worship of Black churches whose focus upon summoning and responding to the Holy Spirit results in speaking in tongues and other intense manifestations of supernatural influence."[223] Even as the Bible teaches that God did not give us the Spirit of fear faith-wise, church-wise and otherwise, "the high expectation of call and response to the Spirit inadvertently, and sometimes ironically, forced the issue of equality and inclusion across the barriers of race, sex and age."[224] In these churches, it is unthinkable that the Holy Spirit would exclusively move men to preach, sing and shout, while forcing all the women to sit in silence. On the contrary, everyone is equally eligible to be moved by the Holy Spirit.[225]

These visions of human equality, cultural inclusion and divine inspiration represent the ways and means in which the Holy Spirit connects with and identifies with the lived (spiritual) experiences within Black Christians' oppression contexts. And other races and cultures of oppressed people too. The Holy Spirit is a person that is Black because she touches down into the life of Black folk for the purposes of equality, inclusion, and inspiration. Just when Black people need the LORD the most, the Spirit of Christ comes into their lives with healing power. The same can be said about all people of color; that the Holy Spirit is a person of color for their religious, cultural, and existential experiences. This is the most prevalent way the Holy Spirit identifies with the oppression experiences of Black

---

[223] Cheryl J. Sanders, "The Historiography Holy Spirit," Para. 2.
[224] Ibid., Para. 3.
[225] Ibid., Para. 4.

people and people of color.

As one who has physically felt the person, power and work of the Holy Spirit in my life, I understand the importance of ethicist Cheryl J. Sanders drawing from Henry Louis Gates, Jr.'s "illuminating parallels between misgivings about the excesses of Black religious worship and the "Frenzy," a term used by W.E.B. Du Bois more than a century ago to describe the exuberance of Black southern folk religion."[226] With the groundbreaking work of theologian Monica Coleman in view, I agree with Sanders in her opinion that "spirit possession should not be regarded as an exclusive or essential trait of African religion, but instead as a phenomenon that produces culturally distinctive manifestations among the many religions and peoples of the world."[227] But that is not to say that Spirit possession within the Black religious experiences is not particular to the experiences of Black folk in the United States, Africa, Brazil, Britain, or in the larger spheres of Black Christianity and world Christianity. Black people's experience with the Holy Spirit is always particular when the Holy Spirit saves them from death, pain and suffering for the first time. But the work of the Holy Spirit is also contextual and universal.

As a lifelong Methodist with Baptist church experience, this is precisely why the way Pentecostal churches address the issues of appearance, color, courtship, and womanhood is attractive. Most denominational and nondenominational Black churches will admit to experiencing a Pentecostal move of the Holy Spirit in their church meetings. Theologically, the Pentecostal move connects the church to the incarnation of Jesus. Just as the Incarnation – Jesus' historical presence in the world – shows that being flesh, being human and living in a particular time and space (a context) is important, so too does Pentecost. Pentecost shows that the Holy Spirit does not eradicate our differences; rather, the Spirit celebrates them.[228]

In John Burdick's journal article, "What Is the Color of the Holy Spirit? Pentecostalism and Black Identity in Brazil,"[229] he argues

---

[226] Ibid.

[227] Ibid., Para. 5.

[228] Anthony G. Reddie, "Black theology: an introduction," Para. 10.

[229] Brazilian theologians have diverse beliefs about the Holy Spirit. For instance, Leonardo Boff, a Brazilian theologian, in *Holy Trinity, Perfect Community*, emphasizes the social

that although evangelical Christianity involves a variety of beliefs that are incompatible with strong ethnic identity, this religion also includes a range of ideas and practices that nourishes rather than corrode black identity."[230] From the experiential intersections of faith and race in Black religious experiences all over the world, I affirm and declare that the Holy Spirit is a person who is Black. This is my way of practicing and nourishing Black identity in the evolving spheres of Black liberation theology and theology Black. The reason the late James Brown and other cultural figures affirm that Black is beautiful is because Black is created and nourished in the beauty of the Holy Spirit. Just like the Spirit of God moved upon the face of the dark earth for the purpose of giving life and light in Genesis 1, so too does the Holy Spirit move upon the blackness of Black people for the purpose of giving them life in the liberating light of God in Jesus Christ. Not as a people who are formless and void, but as a people who need the liberating work of the Holy Spirit in every area, level, and phase of their human and spiritual lives. Black people are a people who God loves as they are created in the image of God (Gen. 1:26).

In Jude 1:13 and 2 Pet 2:17, the authors speak of the sin and doom of Godless people with images of water both concluding that,

---

approach to the doctrine of the Trinity. He believes that God is relational, ecstatic, fecund, and alive as passionate love. Boff's social approach to the doctrine of the Trinity can help avoid errors in understanding the mystery of the triune God and embark on a whole new avenue for the theological exploration of God's mystery[1]. Brazilians believe that spirituality does not only come through the church. In identifying as culturally Christian, Brazilians do not confine their faith to the church. Discerning and questioning the actions and functions of the church are important aspects of understanding its influence in a nation and its people. In his most famous work, *The Spirits' Book*, Alan Kardec introduced the philosophy known as the Spiritist movement. While this book and others written by Kardec and his followers provide detailed descriptions of Spiritist principles, what is most essential to the movement is the belief that a spirit exists within each human body. This spirit reincarnates in a new body after death, ideally progressing towards spiritual perfection with each reincarnation. Beyond this, Spiritists also believe in the existence of other life forms in the universe, a God as the "Supreme Intelligence," and an afterlife that is physically close to planet Earth: (hence the colony of souls floating over Brazil). While I could not find where the Holy Spirit is active in the Spiritists movement, I noticed that the Spiritists play a role in the interpretation of art, culture, and class in Brazil. In his critical text, *The Holy Spirit and Liberation*, Brazilian theologian Jose Comblin argues that the primary function of the Holy Spirit is one of liberation. Here, the liberating action of the Spirit takes place in both the lives of the poor and in the history oppressed peoples.
[230] John Burdick, "What Is the Color of the Holy Spirit?" Para. 1.

"for whom the black (or blackest) darkness has been reserved forever." In Revelation 6:12 John speaks about the Seals when he writes that, "I looked when He broke the sixth seal, and there was a great earthquake; and the sun became black as sackcloth made of hair, and the whole moon became like blood;" The sackcloth was a course, dark cloth woven from the hair of goats or camels. The sackcloth was worn as a sign of mourning or penitence (Joel 1:13; Jn. 3:5-6; Matt. 11:21; see Gen. 37:34). Even as the Bible presents Black as a form of darkness that has no redeemable qualities, the truth is that Black is linked to such Godly actions as mourning, grieving, healing, miracles, the kingdom of God, being born of water and the Spirit and repentance. Biblically, not much good is said about the color and word Black, but the Holy works in all contextual realities—blackness included. The Holy Spirit brings life and gives life to those who believe; for the law of the Spirit of life in Christ Jesus has set you free from the law of sin and of death (Rom. 8:2). As the Spirit of Christ Jesus, the Holy Spirit has set Black believers (and other races and cultures of believers too) free from the law of sin and of death. Here, the Holy Spirit brings life and light to those who believe.

The Color of God in Black Theology

One of the key points of the new book is whoever God is or whatever God is to do, we believe that the work will align with and speak liberatingly to the oppression context of the Black human experiences. Here, the implication is that there is a distinct theological meaning attached to the presence of the Holy Spirit in human history. In his phenomenal text, *The Color of God*, Major J. Jones defines Black theology as the "inquiring of how the Holy Spirit relates to the Black human condition."[231] Because God is a trinity of holy responsive personal beings, one cannot fully conceptualize God and Jesus Christ without understanding the Holy Spirit. In the same way that we pursued a God-concept in terms of what makes sense to Black people about being human, Black Theology proceeds to develop its own view of the Holy Spirit.[232] Put simply, one of the main ways that the Holy Spirit has related to Black people has been in terms of keeping them

---

[231] Major J. Jones, *The Color of God*, 101.
[232] Henry H. Mitchell, *Black Belief*, 136-152. Mitchell treats the Holy Spirit more in keeping with a Baptist-Church theology than is a consistently presented in a Black-theological personalistic and relational way.

aimed in God's directions in the quest for liberation, freedom, and salvation.[233] While there is a liberating vision in all three biblical perspectives, the role of the Holy Spirit in the liberation of the oppressed is still up for theological discussion.

According to Jones,

The other main way that Holy Spirit has sanctified Black people is through an abiding, personal and relational presence. God and Jesus, fused, returned to us in the person of the Holy Spirit; now, in the unity of divine personhood, the Father and the Son abide among us in the person and the work of the Holy Spirit. Throughout the long ordeals of slavery and oppression, the nearness of God among Black people was a needed dimension of the slave's faith. Without a sense of God's nearness, the slaves could not have survived the suffering[234]

In Black theology, the Holy Spirit is not just Pentecostal. The spiritual connection is personal, relational, and sacred as she operates in all contexts under the omnipresence of God. For Jones, there must be "an understanding of the Holy Spirit in the more narrow tradition of Afro-American religion has its historical roots in more explicitly trinitarian and traditional in Christian thought."[235] In this vein of theological thought, I find it quite appropriate to connect the work of the Holy Spirit in traditional Christian thought to the work of the Holy Spirit in relational thought of personal human interactions.

Says Jones:

Because Black people have been personally familiar in their relationship to the Holy Spirit, they have been at home with the concept of the Holy Spirit as existing in relation to God as a responsive personal being. As the Holy Spirit, the third person of the Godhead, has always been a personal being, the Holy Spirit has always made God known to Black persons of faith as part of their human experience. The Holy Spirit's role in the Black human existence has been the central work of God in personal relation to the human race, namely

---

[233] Major J. Jones, *The Color of God*, 102.
[234] Ibid.
[235] Ibid.

maintaining and renewing our needed unity of being. Similarly, as the Holy Spirit is the continuing agent in God's plan for human identity, growth, and development, so also does the Holy Spirit relate to continuity of the saving work of God in Jesus Christ.[236]

Black people's relational familiarity with the Holy Spirit is deeply personal because it saves them from a certain type of non-salvific death that constantly lurks after them in the coloring of their skin. This redeeming quality experience in the Spirit not only makes Black people alive to the work of the Holy Spirit in their personal lives, but it also makes them more aware of the continuing presence God in their human and spiritual lives. Here, the relational familiarity with the Holy Spirit breeds a greater faith in Jesus Christ and a healthier self-esteem. It is in this relational familiarity that Black people, and other oppressed believers as well, realize that they are children of the one and true living God. The Holy Spirit's offer of continuing ever-fresh revelation of God's truth has been received by Black people as holy empowering to lead us into the fullness of the larger truth we needed to see us through the struggles toward full freedom and equal human dignity.[237] Here, "the inner working of God through the Holy Spirit has accomplished in Black people a parallel three-dimensional gift of grace: fullness of knowledge of God, forgiveness in Jesus Christ, and freedom in the Holy Spirit."[238]

Jones helps us to see the liberating nature of the Holy Spirit in Black theology when he writes that "Black Theology upholds both the objective otherness of God as the creator and ground of all existence (being) and the supreme personality of God as a responsive personal being divinely interested in human beings."[239] He posits that "The freest response to God, by definition, comes from the deepest recesses of human subjectivity, and it is the Holy Spirit who plumbs those depths with the liberating grace of God. It is the Spirit who creates the conditions in an individual's life and liberated by grace, they can shake off unfreedom."[240] Theologically, Jones interfuses the

---

[236] Ibid.
[237] Ibid., 104.
[238] Ibid.
[239] Ibid.
[240] Ibid., 105.

liberating work of the Spirit with the human notion of freedom.

> Streaming freely towards us in the prevenient grace of the Holy Spirit, God heads off unfreedom in every way. He is God ever before us, God ever behind us, and God ever within human beings. In a redemptive sense, the Holy Spirit just never lets a person be, but is forever tracking us down, refusing to leave us alone snug in our unfreedom, content with the lot of the well-kept slave. Redemption in the Holy Spirit is liberation to decision-making (either for or against the fellow freedoms of our brother and sister humans) and redemption for perfection—the never-ending process of becoming.

In the work of grace, the Holy Spirit intrinsically responds to the unfreedoms of Black people and other oppressed human beings. Existing as part of the Triune God, the Holy Spirit redeems us by always being present in our everyday lives. Redemption in the Holy Spirit is liberation because redemption is personal and relational in the life of those who exist without freedom. The Holy Spirit's redemptive work perfects people in their walk of faith with God and it enables believers to evolve, grow, and mature in their individual becoming. The one constant in human experiences of liberation, freedom, redemption, perfection, and becoming is the work of the Holy Spirit.

> It was the Holy Spirit of freedom and setting free that empowered even slaves to feel strong in a condition wherein otherwise they would not have felt weak and helpless. Never negating our personal responsibility or erasing the difficulties of a world of oppression, the Holy Spirit in Black life was the personal proof that God was "God with" his Black people. What we say of the Holy Spirit and the life and history of Black people one can also say of all humans, of each individual and each people in their own respective condition.[241]

Slavery was not the only human context in which the Holy Spirit intervened in the life of Black people. The liberating work of the Holy Spirit is sensed and witnessed throughout the history of Christian

---

[241] Ibid.

experience in a number of cultural glimpses, historical contexts, and oppressive conditions. In confidently "estimating the value of the Holy Spirit for the Black religious experiences, Jones helps Black theologians to see the Black concept of the Holy Spirit—rich in terms of its African roots and the spiritually experiential nature of Black Afro-American religious expression—as a corrective to this history of theological neglect."[242] I am in total agreement with Jones when he states that "A one-line account of the work of the Holy Spirit within the dark Afro-American religious experience is hardly possible."[243] At the very least, the Holy Spirit is infinite God who was relating to each oppressed spirit in just the way the poor soul needed, to make him or her whole and free and holy.[244] It is in this descriptive vein of thought that first-generation constructor Major J. Jones helps me to see how and why the Holy Spirit is liberatingly Black and present in the Black human, cultural and religious experiences.

The Holy Spirit is Black

As one who is Black in relational distinctness and personal uniqueness for the Black human experiences, the Holy Spirit is the third Person of the Holy Trinity. This means the Holy Spirit is God, co-equal with God the Father and God the Son and is of the same spiritual substance. God the Father, Son, and Holy Spirit are distinct from one another in terms of their personal relationship. The primary role and person of the Holy Spirit is that of uniting the believer with Jesus Christ and places him in the body of Christ, the church. The Spirit also unites believers with Christ in His death, enabling them to live victoriously over sin. Confusion exists today concerning the Person of the Holy Spirit. His or Her personality is denied by both liberal theologians and extreme religious cults. Some liberals will acknowledge he is portrayed as a person, but claim the Scripture is communicating a myth. Jehovah's Witnesses deny his personality, referring to him as simply an influence. Because of the comparatively little teaching about the Holy Spirit that has been done over the years, there are some good Christians who do not realize that the Holy Spirit is a Person.[245] Instead of critiquing those who do not believe that the

---

242 Ibid.
243 Ibid., 106.
244 Ibid.
245 Biblesprout.com, "Attributes of the Holy Spirit," Para. 1.

Holy Spirit is a person, I would much rather declare that

> The Holy Spirit is the Third Person of the Trinity-equal with the Father and Son in essence. Since one of the major aspects of God's nature is that he is a person, it follows that the Holy Spirit is a person. The apostle Paul noted the intellectual ability of the Holy Spirit when he asked, "What man knows the things of man save the spirit of man which is in him? Even so the thing of God knows no man, but the Spirit of God" (1 Cor. 2:11). The rational capacity of the Holy Spirit included wisdom and communication when Paul's prayer request for the Ephesians included "That the God of our Lord Jesus Christ, the Father of glory, may give unto you the spirit of wisdom and revelation in the knowledge of him" (Eph. 1:17). The emotional ability of the Holy Spirit is evident in the word of the apostle, "the love of the Holy Spirit" (Rom. 15:30). The love of the Holy Spirit implies the love of a real person.[246]

And because the Bible portrays the Holy Spirit as a person, my theology affirms that He or She (the Holy Spirit) is a Black person for the liberating experiences that are associated with being a Black human being in bondage and oppression. The Black personhood of the Holy Spirit has the power to liberate Black people all over the world. Not only does the person, power and work of the Holy Spirit liberate Black Christians, but he or she liberates all people who are suffering as victims of systemic oppression. To be dehumanized and oppressed within any color of human skin is to be Black.

God is Black

The father of liberation theology and Black theology, James H. Cone, strongly believes that God is Black.

> For Cone, such a focus on inward spirituality and universals does not serve the cause of black liberation. He states starkly that 'the black experience should not be identified with inwardness... It is not an introspection in which one contemplates' one's own ego. Blacks are not afforded the luxury of navel gazing'.[1] Cone does not see God's work as *generally* centered in the individual. Instead, he states that God is at work *specifically* in the community of the

---

[246] Ibid., Para. 2.

oppressed. In Cone's American context, which means God's presence is to be found in black bodies and their liberation. God is so identified with the oppressed, that we can say God is black. This may be a difficult concept for white people to grasp. Cone is not saying God literally has black skin. Cone is saying that black and white are categories created by whites to oppress blacks. Black and white stand for unjust power relationships: 'The focus on blackness does not mean that *only* blacks suffer as victims in a racist society, but that blackness is an ontological symbol and a visible reality which best describes what oppression means in America.'[2] "Because God is the God of the oppressed" and Black folk are oppressed, "God is black."[247]

In other words, God is Black not only because African Americans are Black, but God is Black because God culturally and spiritually identifies with Black people through freely giving them the gifts of courage, grace, hope, liberation, love, and vision through the transformative power of the Holy Spirit. "As Cone contends, we cannot have knowledge of God "as God is in se. Theologically, this seems impossible. We can know God only in relationship to the human race, or more particularly in God's liberating activity on behalf of oppressed humanity. The God of the oppressed, then, is discovered and experienced simultaneously in the midst of different struggle for justice, and one of the tasks of liberation God Talk is to make the connections between these experiences and understandings of God explicit."[248] Cone says again:

> But I still believe that "God is Black" in the sense that God's identity is found in the faces of those who are exploited and humiliated because of their color. But I also believe that "God is mother," "rice," "red," and a host of other things that give life (Holy Spirit) to those whom society condemns to death. "Black," "mother," "rice," and "red," give concreteness to God's life-giving presence (Holy Spirit) in the world and remind us that the universality of God is found in the particularity of the suffering poor. We can know God only in

---

[247] Mark Russ, "James Cone and liberal Quakerism," Para. 3.
[248] Susan B. Thistlethwaite & Mary P. Engel, *Lift Every Voice: Constructing Theologies*, 80.

an oppressed community in struggle for justice and wholeness. It is because I believe that "God is Black" that I also believe that the dominant, western, male theological tradition is much too limiting to speak about God."[249]

In her article, "James Cone looked evil in the face and refused to let it crush his hope," Andrea C. White chronicles the thought of James H. Cone. White says that "Cone identified black power as a religious concept and racialized oppression as a thoroughgoing theological crisis at the heart of the Christian message." What this means is that God is black, and to be black like God is a gift."[250] In other words, "Cone perceived with utmost clarity the God revealed in the black experience. Unconcerned with any metaphysical conundrum of the Christ event, Cone focused attention on divine justice in which divine wrath and divine love are not at odds with each other. He captured the subversive element in Christian thought that perceives love as violence against the status quo of white supremacy. Cone sees what he calls "the terrible beauty of the cross."[251] For Cone, "being a lover of the gospel is synonymous with being a freedom fighter. When done properly, theology is itself activist. Theology is a protest movement, and when it fails to contribute to social change it is complicit in the normalization of violence and colorblind ideologies that become the gateway to genocide."[252]

Cone teaches that the Black experience is a human experience grounded in the oppressive subjectification brought on by the demonic outreaches of racism, poverty, capitalism, unemployment, unequal education, and forms of physical brutality. These namely outreaches represented the systemic evils Cone witnessed in Bearden, Arkansas, New York City, New York, and other parts of the United States. This theological affirmation does not mean that God is Black for everybody. Here the implication is that God is Black because God is the God of the oppressed; and Black people are an oppressed people. Like the first and second-generation constructors of Black theology, Cone's theology did not allow the evil of racism to crush his hope for a better day and a better life for Black people in the United

---

[249] Ibid., 8.
[250] Andrea C. White, "James Cone looked evil," Para. 3.
[251] Ibid., Para. 4.
[252] Ibid., Para. 5.

States and all over the world. Again, hope in Jesus Christ is the work of the Holy Spirit as the person and power of the Holy Spirit centers on Cone's theological vision for the purposes of awareness and liberation. Cone was inspired and moved by the Holy Spirit in many facets of his theological development.

Christ Jesus is Black

Kelly Brown Douglas, in her famed text, *The Black Christ*, writes that "(J. Deotis) Roberts's version of the Black Christ began with an understanding of the incarnation. Roberts argued that in becoming incarnate, God identified with all humanity. Roberts argued that because Christ identified with all people, Christ identified with each person in his or her own historical particularity." This understanding of the universal Christ, who identified with humans in their particularities, formed the basis for Roberts's interpretation of what Black meant in relation to Christ.[253] Roberts referred to Christ as Black because he recognized the importance of Black people being able to image Christ as Black. For Roberts, imaging and imagining the Black Christ is a psycho-cultural experience. It is one that helps Black people with the psychological harm done to multiple generations of their people. This imaging and imagining the Black Christ are also one of a deep cultural significance.

As with Albert Cleage and James Cone, Roberts was also inspired to theologize Christ as Black because of the nature of Black people's oppression. Also, like Cleage and Cone, Roberts's Black Christ was not strictly based on the need for Black people to see Christ as Black. Roberts suggested that Christ's Blackness was an aspect of what it meant for God to become incarnate. Roberts concluded that like the White Christ, or Red Christ, "the Black Messiah is also the universal word made flesh."[254] Cone's theological affirmation that God is Black along with Roberts's groundbreaking claim that Jesus Christ is the Black Messiah is what led me to the conclusion that the Holy Spirit is a Black person. The theological assertions that God is Black because God identifies with the oppressed and Jesus Christ is the Black Messiah for Black people's own particularities makes my claim of the Holy Spirit being a Black person more credible. The person,

---

[253] Kelly B. Douglass, *The Black Christ*, 61.
[254] Ibid., 62.

power, and work of the Holy Spirit in a contemporary theology Black also represents a theology of Christian unity within and beyond the Black community (Ephesians 4). Not just for those non-white people of color, but a contemporary Theology Black includes the white poor. To be sure, unity, equality and grace in Jesus Christ is the work of the Holy Spirit. To be poor is to be oppressed. And to be oppressed is to be Black. In a portion of ways and to a humanistic degree, the white poor are Black too. Maybe not in their color of skin, but in being economically-deprived. Even as the white poor is convinced that they are superior to the Black elite, a significant percentage of the white poor have yet to come to the realization that their experiences are like those of African/Black descendants.

Theology Black Embodies the Spirit of Blackness

The Holy Spirit in a contemporary theology Black is the Spirit of blackness. The blackness of the Spirit is a distinct characteristic of theology Black whereby the Holy Spirit carries the existential hopes of an oppressed people. Taking up material space in the life of Black folk since birth while hoping to enable them to describe a particular type of physical interaction between the Holy Spirit and Black folk, the Holy Spirit means liberation and emancipation. If anyone knows what is going on in the world and why these things are going on in the world, it would be the Holy Spirit. This is because the Holy Spirit knows the mind of God. The Holy Spirit is both a world Spirit and the Spirit of the world. Theology Black is a liberation theology whereby the Holy Spirit touches down into the lived experiences of Black people of all races and cultures throughout the world. And other oppressed races of people too.

Lest we forget that Black theology is a theology of Black liberation. It seeks to measure the Black condition in the light of God's revelation in Jesus Christ (and the Holy Spirit who is the Spirit of Christ); so that the Black community can catch sight of how the gospel is in keeping with the achievements of Black humanity. Black theology is a theology of 'blackness.' It is the holistic affirmation of black humanity that emancipates black people from White racism, thus providing authentic freedom for both white and black people.[255] It is in this vein of thought that Black theology intentionally gives

---

[255] Allen Olatunde, "Black Theology Surviving Mean," Para. 5.

reference "to a variety of Black theologies which have as their base the liberation of the marginalized, especially the injustice done towards Blacks in American and South African contexts."[256] Theologically, there are numerous consistencies with the way Black people in the United States and Africa are treated. The human conditions of Black Americans and native Africans parallel one another in social, political, and economic dimensions.

At its core, "Black theology can be linked with African theology as it focuses it conversation on the church in Africa. The proposed African Theology is to be distinguished from the Black Theology which is found in the United States and Southern Africa."[257] In Black theology, the Black person knows that transformative closeness with the Holy Spirit of God play important roles in the Black spiritual and cultural traditions that inform black theology. Due to Black people's existence in the operative systems of white racism, they also know that a ghetto is the white way of saying that blacks are subhuman and fit only to live with rats. The black experience in the United States is police departments adding more recruits and buying more guns to provide "law and order," which means making a city safe for its white population.[258] On the one hand, the Black experience in the United States is police departments adding more recruits and buying more guns to provide "law and order," which means making a city safe for its white population.[259] On the other hand, the blackness of Africa was seen in different perspectives, and this motivates the position and low esteem of African in the world. Africans and Negroes in the world suffer inferiority because of their skin colour.[260]

The connotation is that Black theology is a theology of 'blackness' because it tells of Black people's theological truths. The revealing of these deep theological truths is the work of the Holy Spirit. It is the affirmation of Black humanity that emancipates Black people from white racism, thus providing authentic freedom for both white and Black people. Here, "the concept of blackness in the United States has been described as the degree to which one

---

[256] Wikipedia: Black Theology
[257] Allen Olatunde, "Black Theology Surviving Mean," Para. 6.
[258] James H. Cone, *A Black Theology of Liberation*, 24.
[259] Ibid.
[260] Allen Olatunde, "Black Theology Surviving Mean," Para. 13.

associates themselves with mainstream African American culture and values. I am black because God is black! God as creator is the ground of my blackness (being), the point of reference for meaning and purpose in the universe."[261] Because Black theology is a theology of blackness, the liberator Holy Spirit embodies the Spirit of blackness. In the Holy Spirit, blackness is the means of human survival in Black people's quest for liberation within the Creator God-Black human relationship. In Black theology, there is a cultural need for a more uplifting view of blackness and darkness as these Black spiritual images are developed phenomenologically. In theologizing blackness within the explicit work of the Holy Spirit, we find that blackness embodies the spiritual livelihoods of all Black people. Especially when it comes to the issues of justice that challenge the freedom of Black people all over the world.

Womanist theologians view blackness as a reciprocated outreach of God's love for Black humanity. According to Cheryl A. Kirk-Duggan, " *Womanist* sensibilities celebrate the freedom of being able to love all people and confidently embrace the manifestation of women's culture and life. To be *Womanist* invites balanced, holistic health and loving the spectrum of colors of Blackness. Loving Blackness is the capacity to love all people, for all other colors together are a part of the color black. Womanist theory is also physical, spiritual, emotional, and creative, and evokes a palette of variegated reality, yielding imaginative passion, love, hope, and change."[262] Blackness has always had an ancestral connection point that allows those endowed to access an entity that cannot be granted or taken away by one person or group. Because blackness is a spiritual experience of the Lord Jesus Christ in the person, power, and work of the Holy Spirit, I agree with Kirk-Duggan and J. Deotis Roberts that blackness is a symbol of self-affirmation and cultural excellence. I am also convinced that blackness is a spiritual symbol for the Black poor and all oppressed people's pursuit of justice (Isa. 28:6, Jn. 16:8).

President of Asbury Theological Seminary, Timothy C. Tennett, explains:

The Spirit calls us to be agents of social transformation. We

---

[261] James H. Cone, *A Black Theology of Liberation*, 75.
[262] Cheryl A. Kirk-Duggan, *Violence and Theology*, 20-21.

reject a truncated, post-Enlightenment form of the gospel that turns the whole enterprise into a privatized faith disconnected from the world we live in. The modern world is content with our being Christian as long as we keep it in our heads as nothing more than personal preference. The New Testament understands that holiness has implications that are personal as well as societal and structural. The church is helping to foster the in-breaking kingdom when we work for justice for the poor, hope for the disenfranchised, and desperately needed racial reconciliation. The church holds truth in morality and righteousness in a culture that has lost its way. There is no part of creation that we do not work to see under the lordship of Jesus Christ, as we become his co-laborers in reaching the world. Does your heart ache for all this?[263]

---

[263] Timothy C. Tennett, *The Spirit-Filled Life*, 43.

Chapter Three

The Holy Spirit, Black Theology, and Economics

There's a sweet, sweet Spirit in this place, And I know that it's the Spirit of the Lord; There are sweet expressions on each face, And I know they feel the presence of the Lord.[264]

A New Theological Framing

I distinctly remember my PhD adviser and director, Stephen G. Ray, Jr., the former President of Chicago Theological Seminary, and leading theologian at the Garrett-Evangelical Theological Seminary on the campus of Northwestern University, telling me that I could use the Holy Spirit as a way of understanding economics in Black poverty and vice-versa. The first two things I did following the enlightening moment with Dr. Ray was research the entirety of the Bible where the Holy Spirit and poverty are concerned. I then read select books on economic theory. In realizing that Christianity and American capitalism were not compatible, I began to particularize my thesis statements around the economic condition of Black Americans. I recall attending three consecutive American Academy of Religion meetings and talking to scholars in the fields of theology, ethics, and philosophy. In introducing to them the particulars of my PhD studies, our conversations would always park itself on the contours of Black theology, pneumatology, and economics. Seemingly fascinated by the blending collaboration of future theological thought, the established scholars took sides with the study of Holy Spirit while easing toward

---

[264] https://www/songlyrics.com/bill-gloria-gather/sweet-sweet-spirit-lyrics/

their conversational away from what I was equally enthusiastic about— Black theology as a Christian theology that takes seriously the study of the Holy Spirit *and* Black economics. I walked away from every single conversation feeling confident about what the Lord had laid on my heart. I grew increasingly comfortable being a theologian of the Black church, the Holy Spirit and of economic poverty. My seminary experiences with institutional racism, and my conversations with J. Deotis Roberts had already welcomed me into the academic arena known as Black liberation theology.

Ray, more so than any other systematic theologian that I had read, helped me to see how and why Black liberation theology is a Christian theology that exists as a contributing part of the history of Christian experience. Even as the Black liberation movement connects to Marxist economics, Minister Malcolm X and other non-Christian outreaches, the truth is that Black theology started in the Black Christian church. Contrary to what Black scholars believe, the goal of Black theology is not about linking the Black church with Marxism. The goal in Black theology is to empower and inspire the Black church to be inspired by the Holy Spirit in a way that leads them to do holistic ministry outside the walls of the Church.

The Bible is Black theology's main methodological resource for preaching, teaching, and reflecting. Without the Bible, there is no Black liberation theology. Liberation theology teaches that the Bible must be interpreted from the perspective of the oppressed and the poor. The purpose of this interpretative perspective is to protect people from further injustices and to bring to light the truth of their suffering. Indeed, liberation theology claims that the Bible is a cultural text that reveals God as the liberator of oppressed victims. This liberation is, in ways, seen as the essence of the salvation message. The liberation that the Bible speaks of is also the work of the Holy Spirit. The same holds true for Christian theology.

And so, with Black liberation theology being a workable form of Christian theology, I would argue that Black theology is the most important theological movement of the twentieth and twenty-first centuries. I say that because Black theology made it a point to challenge the various structures of racism in the United States. And this was after W.E.B. Du Bois reminded us of race(ism) being the greatest problem of the twentieth century. With pneumatology or the study of the Holy Spirit being the central doctrine of Christian theology, it should be easy to understand why poverty is the preeminent issue of the twenty-first century. Because if its connection to idolatry, poverty of any kind within any race or culture of people is a theological problem. Black poverty is a theological issue for a myriad of reasons. With the help of God, the cultural collaboration of Black liberation theology, pneumatology and economics will be continuously fluid in terms of flushing out a descriptive theology for the contemporary context.

One of my earliest revelations on the study of Christian theology was that the American and world economies have never been good for Black folk. There is no need for Christian theologians to think anything different. The theological proof is in the economic pudding. Ever since they arrived on American soil over five hundred years ago, Black people have always been the victim of a one-sided economy. Black people were poor slaves during the institution of slavery and a sizable number of them existed as poor people with full U.S. citizenship. A sizable number of Black Americans have never been productive nor have they prospered in the American capitalist economy. Even when Black people thought that the economy was shaping up to benefit them in a type of isolated way, they still ended being the deprived faces at the bottom of America's economic well. If the truth be told, it has never been well with the soul of Black folk where the American economy is concerned. Destruction, devastation, and death has followed a sizable number of Black Americans beyond the pale of their various poverty conditions.

To make things worse, theology and economics books have consistently failed to take Black economic oppression seriously; ignoring how Black folks' poverty condition has made them wanna holler[265] and yell and scream and throw up both of their hands (borrowing the words of Marvin Gaye in his song "Inner City Blues (Make Me Wanna Holler)" in the Black church experience on Sunday mornings and every other day of the week as well. In the same theological vein and just like their slave ancestors, a sizable number of Black Americans struggle to read, write, and interpret the Bible.

---

[265]https://genius.com/Marvin-gaye-inner-city-blues-make-me-wanna-holler-lyrics

This leads us to the fact that as a naturally religious people, a sizable number of Black people are also a poor people. Black people are not the only people who suffer from the epidemic of economic deprivation. While Black people in the United States have the highest percentage of poverty, a sizable number of white Americans are poor too. It is commonly known that the lower tier of white folk has suffered at the hands of American capitalism, classism, and racial underdevelopment. To be sure, theological reflections on the poverty of Black people go hand in hand with theological reflections on the Holy Spirit. You cannot discuss one without discussing the other—the Holy Spirit and poverty.

A New Theological Statement

With regards to how the Holy Spirit works in the life of those who are politically weak, economically poor, and socially oppressed, a new theological statement is up for consideration. Beginning with some sort of theological Trinitarian statement claiming that the work of the Spirit brings creation into the life of those who suffer from poverty; and where at once brings a sort of reality which that encounter provides a way for to survive in the midst of life or to be able to imagine the eschatological reality for the context and future, how does one describe a liberating theology that makes sense of these prescriptive claims—giving the method and practice of descriptive theology? To construct and describe this type of theology, two things must happen: 1. One must give a rich and thorough account of the work of the Spirit—an account that brings creation into the life of God. Whereas an interpretive reading of Black liberation theology gives witness in such a way that even in economic/ material deprivation, oppressed people could still imagine and live into new visions. In other words, focusing on the person and work of the Holy Spirit makes it possible to begin to talk about the Trinity in a way as recognizable as constructive theology—the liberating and reflective intersection of the Black religious experience and the Christian religious experience. 2. One must focus on the work of the Holy Spirit in a way that allows him or her to fully explore how God takes economic deprivation into God's self thereby signifying that one's poverty does not destroy him or her. In other words, poverty or the lack of economic resources is not the end of the human story.

While such theologians as John Calvin and Dwight N. Hopkins

affirm that one's experience with poverty can help to develop one's spirituality or sense of how the Spirit can work for those who have total dependency on God, ultimately, my theology claims that despite the level of oppression one is experiencing, the Spirit gives life in such a way that a visionary hope has materialized in the presence of structural evil. Through the person, power and work of the Holy Spirit, God liberates those who need help the most. Constructing and describing a Black economic pneumatology for the twenty-first century context is challenging. So much is going on in our world globally, culturally, and locally that it seems like the foolishness of evil is prevailing over the loving goodness of God. Hence, describing this type of liberating theology is a daunting task. Not because it has not been done before; but rather, the mission is challenging because pneumatology represents the most sacred of human experiences for Black people. When I use the word *sacred,* I am not referring to the institutional outreaches of the Black church experience. But rather, I am referring to the deep rivers of an invaluable connection to God in Jesus Christ by the power of the Holy Spirit; like the love that a child has for his or her parents.

What I am saying is that oppressed Black people have experienced a particular type of life in the Spirit. And those experiences with the Spirit have rendered them culturally mysterious or spiritually sensitive to talking about how God's grace and mercy have provided them with something that they could not provide for themselves. From the outside looking in, one might think that Black people are hesitant to talk about the work of the Spirit in their individual lives because they believe that both the experience itself and the Spirit belongs to them. What this means is that any type of effort put forth to describe these spiritual experiences presupposes the giving up of something very personal and very sacred–one's identification in and with the Spirit of God. Black folks are not aware of the fact that being a child of God means the Holy Spirit is working in their lives. For someone who does not consider themselves as religious, spiritual people's experience with the Holy Spirit or the Holy Ghost is described differently from those who attend church on a consistent basis. And if he or she does not have the language to properly express their spiritual experiences, then their interactions with the Spirit remain with each other. Either way, the Spirit gives life to Black folk and all other races of people too; whom otherwise do not have an existential alternative to being financially broke and economically poor.

From Description to Construction

To construct any type of liberation theology, I believe that the Holy Spirit must be hovering over the waters of one's biblical frame of thought. One of the major challenges of this project is in balancing the diverse types of sources. Just because there is an attempt to construct a Black liberation pneumatology, which does not mean that all the contributing sources must be Black or of African descent. But in the same token, the goal is not to chronicle Black people's experience with the Holy Spirit by gleaning details from the pen of white scholars and European thinkers. The goal is to remain true to the task of describing a liberating theology for those Black people who continue to suffer from the ill of poverty and other forms of human oppression. The words that come to mind are 'theological accountability'. As a Christian theologian and a Black religious thinker, I feel that my scholarship should be accountable to all races and cultures of people. Black folk included.

Here, the implication is that for the Black theologian to construct and describe theologies for their native people, their sources and norms must be Black as well. How does one balance what one includes and what one does not include? Or is this theological balancing the work of the Holy Spirit? On the one hand, white/European theologians, and Latin American theologians[266] alike

---

[266] Gustavo Gutierrez is the father of Latin American liberation theology. When speaking on the true meaning of Pentecost, Gutierrez believes that "The episode with Cornelius [in Acts 10] shows that the Jews 'were astonished that the gift of the Holy Spirit should have been poured out even on Gentiles.' ... What we have here, therefore, is a twofold process. On the one hand, there is a universalisation of the presence of God: from being localised and linked to a particular people, it gradually extends to all the peoples of the earth. On the other hand, there is an internalisation, or rather, an integration of this presence: from dwelling in places of worship, this presence is transferred to the heart of human history.... Christ is the point of convergence of both processes. In him, in his personal uniqueness, the particular is transcended and the universal becomes concrete. In him, in his Incarnation, what is personal and internal becomes visible. Ben Myers comments on Gutierrez's statement: Finally, let us emphasise that here there is no 'spiritualisation' involved. Gustavo Gutiérrez, *A Theology of Liberation: History, Politics, and Salvation* (New York: Orbis, 1973), pp. 109-110. Gutierrez is convinced that liberation and salvation are closely related. In using such language as spiritual freedom, spiritual journey and spiritual poverty, Gutierrez understands the practical purpose of people developing their own spirituality or growing in their awareness/view of God. For Gutierrez, the Holy Spirit connects to the

can be of service in terms of helping Black theologians to gain and regain value in the cultural truths they may have overlooked in their initial reflections. Through the practices of interpretation and reflection, other theologians can help Black scholars to see the promise of their cultural and religious experiences. On the other hand, Black theologians should be responsible for the primary interpretation of their cultural and religious experiences. White interpretations of the Black human experience can only do so much. White scholars cannot define what it means to be Black without experiencing the treatment of one who has Black skin. On the surface, though, they can certainly be of assistance.

Such is the case with Peter C. Hodgson. I am not saying that Hodgson's work is the main source of the project, but his theological affirmations are relevant enough to a part of the descriptive conversation. In Hodgson's text, *Winds of the Spirit: A Constructive Christian Theology,* he takes up the subject of African American theology and how certain scholars view the Black experience. Hodgson states that "Theo Witvliet takes partial exception to Cone's christocentrism. He thinks that the focus of the Black experience may be more pneumatological than Christological, and that it is "the renewing power of the Spirit in the praxis of Jesus of Nazareth with black history and culture."[267] In referencing Witvliet,[268] Hodgson sees an alternative view to James H. Cone's christocentric theology. This view, layered in the presence of the Spirit, speaks to the diversity of thought whereas the black experience is concerned. For Witvliet, "It is the Spirit which incorporates men and women into the messianic

---

development of the whole human person. Lastly, the Holy Spirit protects God's direct Revelation to human beings and the Catholic church. Gutierrez tends to use the words Spirit of Jesus instead of Holy Spirit. Gutierrez also believes in the outpouring and the indwelling of the Spirit within the believer.

[267] Peter C. Hodgson, *Winds of the Spirit*, 240.

[268] The author of *Way to the Black Messiah: The Hermeneutical Challenge of Black Theology* (1984) and *A Place in the Sun: Liberation Theology in the Third World* (1984), Theo Witvliet is a Dutch journalist and theologian. He believed that Black theology is not fully understood by mainstream scholars; nor is it studied enough by those who are concerned with the oppressive plight of Black people all over the world. Witvliet believes that the Black religious experience is more pneumatological than Christological because the person, power, and work of the Holy Spirit transcends the visual ministry of Jesus. While Witvliet understands the Holy Spirit to be the Spirit of Christ, he sees the existential connection between Black people and the Holy Spirit as one that is critical to the theology of the Black church and society.

community of the exalted Christ. If that does not happen, ...then a remarkably unhistorical element enters into the dialectical connection between incarnation and blackness."[269] In support of this point, Witvliet refers to the work of black South African theologian Takatso Mofokeng.[270]

In consideration of this theological framing, it is now appropriate to introduce important works on the current trends in the study of theology and economics. The reader should be able to describe key historical events and circumstances that have contributed to the need for a modern, theological analysis of the economy. This section will analyze various theological and philosophical approaches to the economy with critiques of the market and the institutional church. The assigned material will attempt to make the connection between the market economy and the church economy. Exploring such theologies as Black theology and the grassroots Liberation theology, the reader should be able use an economic analysis to assess the real problems with poverty and class struggle in the United States. This section will also help to create substantive dialogue between theology, economics, and the Holy Spirit in terms what it means to construct a Black liberating pneumatology that deals with poverty, politics, globalization, Christology, ecology, and scripture.

The Holy Spirit in Black Theology

Black theology has emerged out of the ongoing struggles of Black people to affirm their cultural identity and very humanity in the face of insurmountable odds. Over an extended period of centuries, more people traveled between Africa and America than originally recorded. Inherent within that Black transatlantic of forced migration and labor, was a form of biased racialized teaching that asserted the inferiority

---

[269] Peter C. Hodgson, *Winds of the Spirit*, 240.

[270] Takatso Mofokeng is a lecturer in Systematic Theology at the University of Botswana, Gaborone, Botswana, where he has over ten years' pastoral experience in rural and urban black parishes in South Africa. Mofokeng argues for the affirming of Black humanity and the raising of a new inclusive humanity. Here, the message of Jesus Christ's resurrection to this new inclusive humanity is that the God who raised Jesus is at work in their period of hanging on the cross, affirming black humanity and raising a new humanity and a new world in which human life will be possible for all. Like Rufus Burrow, Mofokeng believes that Black people must be liberated from the bondage of white hegemony and the legalities that have been legally put in place to keep them in an oppressive holding pattern; socially, politically, economically and educationally speaking.

and subhuman nature of Black people. The struggle of Black people that arise from the era of slavery continues in the overarching material poverty and marginalization of Black people across the world. This is precisely why Black theology's interaction with the Holy Spirit is so critical to the conversations of the Spirit's work in Christian history and the Spirit's role as the interlocutor of love between the study of theology and the science of economics.

At the heart of Black theology within the work of the Holy Spirit in the life of the oppressed is the concept of liberation. In using the term liberation, the word Black comes to represent God's symbolic and actual solidarity with oppressed people, the majority of whom have been consigned to the marginal spaces of the world solely on the ground of their very blackness, having been identified as "lesser " human beings. The most important person in the developed of the Black theology has been theologian James H Cone. But the conversation of Black theology and liberation does not end with Cone; especially where first generation constructors are concerned. As a colleague and contemporary of Cone, J. Deotis Roberts explores the reconciliatory activity of Black people in both the church and the community. Both comprise the Black religious experiences of a people who have always connected to the work of the Holy Spirit.

I say that because when a person receives Jesus as Lord and Savior, he or she is a new creation (2 Cor. 5:17), and the indwelling Holy Spirit begins the process of conforming him or her to the image of Christ (Rom. 12:1-2). Only through a spiritual transformation of the people's heart can racism and poverty end. According to a sizable number of religious thinkers, Black liberation theology fails because it attacks the symptoms without truly addressing the disease. Sin and fallenness is the disease; racism and poverty are just two of the symptoms. The message of the gospel is Jesus' atoning sacrifice for our sins and the salvation that is therefore available through faith in Christ. The cultural connection between the work of the Holy Spirit and Black theology needs unpacking.

In citing James Cone's pneumatological language in his cultural text, *The Spirituals and the Blues,* Peter C. Hodgson recognizes that the spirituals "may in fact balance christological and pneumatological language in exemplary fashion. They are after all "spirituals," and they are deeply rooted in the spirituality of African religions."[271] In his book, Cone examines the genesis of the spirituals in Black experience and presents a theological extrapolation of their message about God, Christ, suffering and eschatology. By examining the various messages of the blues, Cone concludes that they are "secular spirituals."[272] In his book Cone does not use the words Holy Spirit. Rather, he uses such phrases as the divine Spirit, the Spirit, the Spirit of God, the Spirit of Black humanity in bondage, God's Spirit, the Spirit of Black emotion, and the spirit. By doing so Cone shows the spiritual connection between the songs of the Black slave experience (the Spirituals) and the crusader message of the Blues as they are both representative of the creative ways Black people express their humanity in the Black religious experience.

In his text, *A Black Theology of Liberation*, Cone concludes:

The blackness of God means that the essence of the nature of God is to be found in the concept of liberation. Taking seriously the Trinitarian view of the Godhead, black theology says that as Creator, God identified with oppressed Israel, participating in the bringing into being of this people; as Redeemer, God became the Oppressed One in order that all may be free from oppression; as Holy Spirit, God continues the work of liberation. The Holy Spirit is the Spirit of the Creator and the Redeemer at work in the forces of human liberation in our society today. In America, the Holy Spirit is black persons making decisions about their togetherness, which means making preparation for an encounter with whites.[273]

For Cone, the work of the Holy Spirit in the context of Black oppression in the United States defines the spiritual essence and material substance of both God's revelation and human revolution. For liberating reasons, The Spirit of God works for the sake of oppressed Black people. But even with Cone stressing the spiritual presence of Christ in the lives of slaves and modern-day Black folk, Hodgson affirms the presence of a pneumatological Christology in Cone's writing. At the same time, Hodgson helps to transition the

---

[271] Peter C. Hodgson, *Winds of the Spirit*, 240.
[272] James H. Cone, *Spirituals and the Blues*, 97.
[273] James H. Cone, *A Black Theology of Liberation*, 64.

conversation from Christology to pneumatology to the spirit world in African Christianity. African theologian Mercy Oduyoye argues that the spirit world is a reality in Africa, and that Christianity needs to "have room for the concept of many Christs, persons in whom the Spirit of God dwells in all its fullness."[274] Emphasis will be placed on the role of combat, healing, sacrifice, and mediation of ancestors and companions. "In African Charismatic Christianity, the theology is christocentric but, with the emphasis placed on the Holy Spirit, one reads a binitarian approach to the Godhead. In this theology, Christ and the Holy Spirit take the place of the spirit powers that are in the service of God in the traditional cosmology."[275]

In his journal article, "Black theology and the Holy Spirit," Garth Baker-Fletcher begins discussion of Black spirituality and its embodiment of the Holy Spirit. Baker-Fletcher explains Pentecostalism's inward turn by recounting the aftermath of the Azuza Street revival that began in 1906. After starting under the leadership of Black pastor William J. Seymour in a racially mixed community in an exceptional manner, white Pentecostals took over and divided the racial composition of the movement. This racially driven split quickly took institutional form, which continues to this day. In taking seriously the biblical text and the history of the Black church in the United States, Fletcher-Baker presents an accurate analysis of how James H. Cone, J. Deotis Roberts, Dwight N. Hopkins, and Karen Baker-Fletcher theologize the work of the Holy Spirit in Black religious experiences.

> At the dawning of the era of slavery, captured West African peoples in the New World (of North and Latin American and the Caribbean) joined their voices in shouts, moans, and deep groaning their inner spirit. Calling on God's Spirit to manifest itself they looked for a release from captivity and bondage. What W.E.B. DuBois called the "spiritual strivings"[276] of black folk were uttered before the master in whispers, subvocalizations of agony, or in the times of gathered worship in what was called "hush harbors." The hush harbors were the secret places where enslaved black folk could experience the

---

[274] Peter C. Hodgson, *Winds of the Spirit*, 240.
[275] Ibid, 240.
[276] See Du Bois's take on spiritual strivings in Chapter 7.

Holy Spirit as an enlivening, wonderous, and overwhelming experience. Outside of the seeming omnipresence of the master's ears, these enslaved African peoples forged a relationship with God through the experience of the Holy Spirit. Following DuBois' instructive musings, these enslaved people allowed the Spirit to whip them into the utterly primal, emotional, and effervescent experience of what DuBois called "the Frenzy."[277]

In terms of those onlookers' questioning of what was going on in the church when Black folk began to experience the physical ecstasy of the Holy Spirit, much is to be considered in the mysterious substance of their emotional response to the invisible God working in their lives. Not all Black people were convinced of the authenticity of the visible/invisible connection. It seemed like the only ones that were shouting in the Holy Spirit were the ones who were economically poor and socially oppressed. Many of those who did not physically feel the power of the Holy Spirit in the church sanctuary looked down upon those who were inspired by God to display their emotional moments of liberation...even if they only lasted for a brief period. Black folks' questioning of their own people's spiritual authenticity has also inspired the need for a greater interpretation of their religious experiences with the Holy Spirit. The needful attempt to describe the uncontrollable and unstoppable force of the Holy Spirit's working presence in the Black church took on myriad depictions. W.E.B. Du Bois referred to Black people's holistic encounter with the Holy Spirit as the Frenzy. However,

> This Spirit-induced Frenzy was not always welcomed by all black folk, especially in the early nineteenth century. Eminent Christian physician Martin Delaney derided many black churches for what he believed to be their spirituality of excessive otherworldliness and crude imitation of white church moralism. Episcopal pastor Alexander Crummell sought to de-emphasize what he considered to be the overly zealous spirituality in black churches – calling instead for a this-worldly, tough-minded, and politically activist,

---

[277] Dwight N. Hopkins and Edward Antonio, *The Cambridge Companion to Black Theology*, 111.

theologically informed spirituality.[278] Presbyterian pastor
Edward Blyden posited such terms as "uplift" and "Elevation"
to describe a very rationalistic and systematic understanding
of Christian faith. Such a faith was radically black nationalist
and emphasized a "doctrine of divine providence that could
account for suffering as a preparation for a great work."[279] All
three black men were more interested in African Americans
learning how to be active social agents rather than validating
their spiritual propensities.[280]

On the other side of the in-person Black church shout, there
exists the liberating witness of the Holy Spirit. Cheryl J. Sanders, in
her book *Living the Intersection: Womanism and Afrocentrism in
Theology*, "proposes a simple framework for analyzing the validation
of womanist or Afrocentric claims based up the concept of the
"witness of the Spirit," a term drawn from the black church tradition,
which Sanders would augment to include two other criteria, the
witness of history and the witness of transformation. By the witness of
the Spirit, I mean the collective "Amen" of assent, endorsement, or
approval that is given by the people when a word or personal
expression is accepted as truth-bearing."[281] In the mind of Sanders and
the other Womanist theologians, the Spirit is the person of the Holy
Spirit. Sanders says boldly, "If we understand the witness of the Spirit
as a spiritual transaction or communication always meditated by
persons in some form of community, including family, then the
intergenerational dialogue between mothers and daughters that
undergirds the womanist definition can be interpreted as expressive
of the witness of the Spirit as well."[282] This spiritual transaction can
also be interpreted as the work of the of Holy Spirit. Like John
Wesley's witness of the Spirit (See Chapter 1 page 73), Sanders and
others theologize an intimately cultural witness of Black people's
experiences in the Black church, the Black community, and the Black
family-unit.

With the Black church, Black community and the Black family-

---

278 Gayraud S. Wilmore, *Black Religion and Black Radicalism*, 136.
279 Ibid., 140-141.
280 Dwight N. Hopkins and Edward P. Antonio, *The Cambridge Companion to Black Theology*, 111.
281 Cheryl J. Sanders, *Living the Intersection*, 160.
282 Ibid.

unit in theological mind, Cone and J. Deotis Roberts agree that the work of the Holy Spirit is one of healing and empowering. It is no secret that Black people are just as concerned with what happens between them (social) as they are with what happens inside of them (spiritual) as they are experiencing the power of the Holy Spirit. In his timeless classic, *Liberation and Reconciliation: A Black Theology*, Roberts writes that "For black Christians, the Holy Spirit is God within the life of the individual Christian and the fellowship of believers in Christ. The Holy Spirit is the giver of spiritual gifts and spiritual life. The Holy Spirit comforts, guides, and strengthens us."[283] Again, Roberts wants to affirm the Holy Spirit as one who has the power to strengthen an oppressed people See Joyce Meyer's theology of the Spirit's strengthening the believer on page 135. By way of this spiritual strengthening, Roberts declares that "The Holy Spirit cultivates and enriches the inner life of the Christian within his or her commitment to Afrocentrism."[284] Roberts also affirms Black theology as a conversation partner for African consciousness in that Afrocentrism helps people to discover their cultural heritage in Africa. For Roberts, one of the most efficient ways for the Black liberation theologian to become accustomed to the African religious experience is to engage the teachings of African pneumatology.

African Pneumatology

The growing vitality of African Independent Christianity today is not simply about the privately emotive, charismatic of the here-and-now work of the Holy Spirit. It embraces the history of the Holy Spirit at work over the millennia in Africa. African Christianity is grounded in this concrete and palpable sense of redemptive suffering in history. Here, it is in the holistic incarnation of the Son where the Spirit works in through the bodily flesh. African pneumatology, defined as the study of the Holy Spirit in African religious thought, is one of the sources that will help to construct a Black economic pneumatology. In referring to African pneumatology as "A Real-Life Pneumatology,"[285] Veli Matti Karkkainen describes the African Instituted Churches' (AIC) approach to the Spirit. The Africans' theological take on the Holy Spirit include contemporary

---

[283] J. Deotis Roberts, *Liberation and Reconciliation*, 64.
[284] Ibid., 64-65.
[285] Veli Matti Karkkainen, *The Holy Spirit in Ecumenical*, 170.

Pentecostalism. According to Karkkainen, this dynamic pneumatology has arisen out of a painful struggle with the more traditional theologies of the Western missionary churches.[286] Even with the struggle for religious and sociopolitical supremacy, the role of the Holy Spirit in the lives of Africans transcends the religious context of the African Institute Church. African pneumatologies describe the work of the Holy Spirit in four major roles.

1. The Spirit is the Savior of humankind.
2. The Spirit is Healer and Protector.
3. AIC Christians speak of the Spirit of justice and liberation in the context of community.
4. The Holy Spirit in AIC theology and spirituality involves earth-keeping.[287]

In sum, these four major roles of the Holy Spirit in the AIC churches affirmed the work of the Holy Spirit as one of salvation and one that liberates Africans from infrastructural bondage and economic despair. The Holy Spirit's function as healer and life-giver encompassed everything relating to human well-being, including the healing and protection of crops.[288] Interestingly, the cosmic dimension of the Spirit's work is not set over against the Spirit's role in personal salvation.[289] It can be biblically argued that the Holy Spirit saves because of Spirit's work of grace (Eph 2:8). Baptizing the African cosmology has, in turn, brought about the emphasis on the miraculous in African pneumatology and soteriology. The Holy Spirit and Salvation in African Christian Theology further argues that such stress on the miraculous blocks other ways by which the Holy Spirit might be understood in African soteriological discourse.[290]

The distinctive feature of African worldview is also the context for pneumatology and bacteriology. One of the key differences between the Western and African worldviews is the latter's focus on the spirit, the invisible reality, and spirituality. Distinguished African theologian John Mbiti[291] describes the spiritual world this way: "The

---

[286] Ibid. 170.
[287] Ibid., 170-171.
[288] Ibid., 171.
[289] Ibid.
[290] "The Holy Spirit and Salvation in African Christian Theology" (PDF)
[291] John S. Mbiti is the father of modern African theology. In his observing of and reflecting

universe is composed of visible and invisible parts. It is believed that
besides God and human beings, there are other beings who populate
the universe. These are the spirits. There are several types of spirits.
God is their Creator, just as he is the Creator of all things. The spirits
have a status between God and men and are not identical with
either."[292] Here, Karkkainen reminds us that the spiritual world is real
for the African. He (the African) is open to active communion with
spiritual forces as he faces the riddles of life. He needs the assurance
of solidarity with his human as well as his spiritual communities
which, in his traditional world view, are held together by ancestral
spirits.[293] In the Christian context, our solidarity with our human and
spiritual communities inheres in the Living Christ as mediated by the
Holy Spirit. That is to say that Christ, through the Holy Spirit upholds
and guides his Church which is the community.[294] To be sure about
what it means to describe Black theology's take on the Holy Spirit in
Africa and the United States, the Spirit of Christ is the Holy Spirit.

The Holy Spirit is awakening an enormous body of believers in
Africa who have found their way into Scripture, but not yet found
their way into the stories of early African saints and martyrs and
leaders. They no longer need to keep their light under the bushel.
They will soon be able to let it shine before the nations.[295] The song
of the Black church, "This Little Light of Mine," comes to mind in
that the liberating light that needs to shine in Africa is the same one
needed in the United States. Certainly, the Holy Spirit is awakening
an enormous body of believers in Africa who have found their way

---

on African traditional religions, Mbiti believed that salvation was the primary work of the
Holy Spirit. In affirming the special revelation of God in the New Testament as Trinity
through Christ and the Holy Spirit, as well as the inner life of the Trinitarian God Himself,
Mbiti was aware that pneumatology was new to the African adept of traditional religion.
Nevertheless, Mbiti was certain that African Christianity consists of both the Holy Spirit
who is a contributing part of the Supreme Being; and there are ancestor spirits. Both the
Spirit and the spirits make up the spirit world in African thought systems and religious
practices. In this vein of theological thought, African Christianity falls under the Gospel of
Jesus Christ and is equally undergirded by African culture and African religion. Traditional
Africans believe the ancestors, or the living-dead, as John Mbiti calls them (Mbiti 1990,
83), are the spirits of people who lived faithful and productive lives here on earth, died at
a ripe old age, and received the proper funeral rites. For Mbiti, living, dying and the funeral
rite of passage are the works of the "Supreme" Holy Spirit.

[292] Osadolor Imasogie, *Guidelines for Christian Theology*, 83.
[293] Veli Matti Karkkainen, *Holy Spirit and Salvation*, 401.
[294] Ibid., 401-402.
[295] Thomas C. Oden, *How Africa Shaped the Christian Mind*, 128.

into Scripture, but not yet found their way into the stories of early African saints and martyrs and leaders. They no longer need to keep their light under a bushel. They will be able to let it shine before the nations.[296]

This little light of mine. I'm gonna let it shine.
This little light of mine. I'm gonna let it shine.
This little light of mine. I'm gonna let it shine.
Let it shine. Let it shine. Let it shine.[297]

This little light of mine, I'm gonna let it shine..." We have all hummed this catchy little tune a time or two under the auspices of the Holy Spirit. It is based on Matthew 5:16. Jesus had just finished healing thousands and giving us the gift of the eight beatitudes. Jesus wasn't talking about making sure we turned on our porch lights at night. He was talking about letting the Holy Spirit shine brightly within us. The Holy Spirit is sent to each believer to dwell within us.[298] This illuminative "glow" means the light within you is how you allow yourself to be led by the Holy Spirit. As a guiding lamp, the Holy Spirit enables you to see with your spiritual sight. This "glow" means the light within you is how you allow yourself to be led by the Holy Spirit. What Jesus was teaching His followers was to shine their light[299], especially in times of darkness. This spiritual enabling is especially true for how the Holy Spirit works to liberate the African Independent Churches. In the words of Oden, "We leave it to the Spirit to inspire laypeople to find ways of making applicable to their vocations and political orders what the early African Christian texts and sources have to say to the contemporary crises and hopes of Africa."[300]

To a large degree, African religionists prioritize the Spirit over the Son. Within the theological boundaries of religion, culture and customs, Africans think a certain way about the power and work of the Holy Spirit. Regarding the Spirit's continued presence in the life

---

[296] Ibid., 124.
[297] https://genius.com/Aretha-franklin-this-little-light-of-mine-lyrics
[298] Heather Riggleman, "What Does it Mean to Let Your Light Shine?" Para. 7-8.
[299] Ibid., Para. 9.
[300] Thomas C. Oden, *How Africa Shaped the Christian Mind*, 154.

of Black people, Africans see the nutritional work of the Holy Spirit as physical and salvific. According to Major J. Jones, "A concept of the "Spirit of God" was a more highly developed theological commonplace among African religions than was any corresponding "divine Son" concept. This was so for many reasons. Africans are chiefly monotheistic and therefore lacking the tendency to imagine that God has a special son or daughter other than all his earthly children. The proper dwelling of God on earth, therefore, is each individual human's subjective inner being—a theological construct that contributes greatly to a sense of personal dignity."[301] For African religionists, the Holy Spirit lovingly gives Black people their culturo-spiritual sense of personal dignity. This symbiotic relationship is relational and interpersonal in theological nature.

James H. Cone

In James Cone's revolutionary text, *Black Theology & Black Power*, he affirms that the Holy Spirit is the Spirit of Black power. Cone uses the Black context in America during the 1960s as a theological backdrop to indicate that the true power of the Holy Spirit is in the equality of the Triune God. Cone never uses the words 'God in three persons' nor does he refer to the Holy Spirit as a person. However, in referencing God as Trinity, Cone believes that "God's manifestation as Spirit is indispensable for a total picture of the Christian God."[302] Cone also agrees that in the biblical tradition or contemporary theology, God as Spirit implies God as Father and God as Son. In essence, "the Holy Spirit is nothing but the Spirit of God and Christ working out his will in the lives of human beings."[303] For the purpose of demonstrating God's unconditional love for humanity, Cone affirms the Holy Spirit as "the power of God at work in the world affecting in the life of God's people for God's intended purposes."[304] Here, Cone views God's love as the initiator of the God-human fellowship in that there is no way from human to God independent of agape. Because of God's act of love to human beings, we can now have fellowship with him.[305]

---

[301] Major J. Jones, *The Color of God*, 117.
[302] James H. Cone, *Black Theology & Black Power*, 57.
[303] Ibid. 57.
[304] Ibid.
[305] Ibid., 50.

In speaking on violence and atonement, Cheryl A. Kirk-Duggan says "Further, in the power of Holy Spirit, through the risen Christ, people experience freedom from oppression, suffering, and abuse."[306] The *imago*, in a person's bodily form. Epitomizes human nature as a lucid creature with the capacity to fellowship with her or his Creator. God's likeness in humanity represents the ultimate perfecting (moving toward wholeness, holiness, completion) of humanity by the Holy Spirit. The Holy Spirit perfects an individual and makes her or him in the "image" and "likeness" of God."[307] Further, God's righteousness means God creates freedom, does justice, vindicates the poor, loves, and acts on behalf of humanity, but does not condone evil. One reconciles Black power with the loving gospel of Jesus Christ. God's love affirms Black people and moves them to confront the white neighbor. Justice tempers love to make human relationships meaningful. Black power wants to meet the needs of the oppressed in love as the work of the Holy Spirit.[308]

The task of Black theology presses for a new comprehension of Black dignity among Black people towards dissolving white racism: transformational theodicy."[309] The same holds true for theology Black in the twenty-first century; that Black power, as the power of the Holy Spirit, is meeting the needs of the poor in love as the work of the Spirit. What this means is that love, in and of itself, is the liberating work of the Holy Spirit.

For Cone, God's Spirit is not just a subjective feeling of piety or inspiration in the hearts of men but, rather an "active power, that is to say, it is the personal activity of God's will, achieving a moral and religious object."[310] Even as "the Spirit becomes the power of Christ himself at work in the life of the believer,"[311] Cone notes that "The work of the Spirit is not always a conscious activity on the part of the persons through whom God works."[312] While the work of the Holy Spirit is not always conscious, the work is always present visibly and

---

[306] Cheryl A. Kirk-Duggan, *Violence and Theology*, 72.
[307] Ibid., 74-75.
[308] Ibid.

[309] Ibid., 78.
[310] James H. Cone, *Black Theology and Black Power*, 57.
[311] Ibid., 58.
[312] Ibid., 59.

invisibly.

> The mistake of the modern church is to identify the work of God's Spirit in the believer either with private moments of ecstasy or with individual purifications from sin, particularly from a short list of ritual pollutants, such as alcohol and tobacco. This is a hopelessly impoverished view. The working of God's Spirit in the life of the believer means an involvement in the world where men are suffering. When the Spirit of God gets hold of a man, he is made a new creature, a creature prepared to move head-on into the evils of this world, ready to die for God. This is why the Holy Spirit is the power of God, for it means a continuation of God's work for which Christ died.[313]

By way of showing that the work of Holy Spirit is one that is purposed in the Holy Trinity for the sake of God and creation alike, Cone confirms that "The greatest proof that the Spirit is one with the Father and the Son is that He is said to have the same relationship with God as the Spirit within us has to us, so is the life of God."[314] That is to say that as an equal person of the Holy Trinity, the Holy Spirit operates in human beings, the Christian church and in all of creation.

In *A Black Theology of Liberation*, Cone contextualizes the Black situation in America as a matter of life and death. For Cone, it is in the situation of survival that Black theology seeks to speak the word of God. That is to say that the God who was revealed in the life of oppressed Israel and who came to us in the incarnate Christ and is present today as the Holy Spirit, has made a decision about the Black condition. God has chosen to make the Black condition God's condition.[315] This implies that God's revelation means Black liberation in an American context of Scripture. God in Black Theology is Black for the sake of liberating the oppressed. Cone expounds:

> The blackness of God means that the essence of the nature of God is to be found in the concept of liberation. Taking seriously the Trinitarian view of the Godhead, black theology

---

[313] Ibid., 58.
[314] Robert L. Wilken, *Spirit of Early Christian Thought*, 105.
[315] James H. Cone, *A Black Theology of Liberation*, 64.

says that as Creator, God identified with oppressed Israel, participating in the bringing into being of this people; as Redeemer, God became the Oppressed One in order that all may be free from oppression; as Holy Spirit, God continues the work of liberation. The Holy Spirit is the Spirit of the Creator and the Redeemer at work in the forces of human liberation in our society today. In America, the Holy Spirit is black persons making decisions about their togetherness, which means making preparation for an encounter with whites.[316]

For Cone, the work of the Holy Spirit in the context of Black oppression defines the spiritual essence and material substance of God's revelation and human revolution. For liberating reasons, the Spirit of God works for the sake of oppressed Black people. Cone's concern for the Black poor can be traced throughout his theology of God, Jesus Christ, and the Holy Spirit.

In referring to the social context of theology as one of both divine liberation and Black suffering, Cone fully understands the consequences and repercussions of Black poverty. While Cone does not use the language of economic poverty or economic deprivation, the working poor, the lower class, the underclass and underdevelopment, Cone does theologize the Black experience as one that is racially inclusive to one's experience of generational poverty. Poverty is one of the main reasons Cone references Marxism. With the understanding that Marxism is not applicable in a theological critique of race, Cone undertakes Marxism as a way of expounding on the socioeconomic misfortune of African Americans.

J. Deotis Roberts

J. Deotis Roberts' pneumatological insights begin and end with the Bible. And I do not know if that is a theological concern or not. But Roberts believes that "The Bible is a source book for theology, but it must be interpreted under the guidance of the Holy Spirit, who leads us into truth. As we read the Bible, it is the Spirit that broods over the chaos of our minds and spirits to teach, illumine, and guide."[317] This statement represents the foundation of how Roberts

---

[316] Ibid., 64.
[317] J. Deotis Roberts, *A Black Political Theology*, 37.

theologizes the Holy Spirit. In his interdisciplinary text, *Black Theology in Dialogue,* Roberts affirms that "Human liberation is at stake when one considers the unique contribution of black church theology to the doctrine of the Holy Spirit."[318] More so than any black theologian of his generation, Roberts sees the contextual need for the Black theologian to actively engage and openly discuss the Holy Spirit.

In asking the question: What is the connection between charismata and personal and social transformation?[319], Roberts posits that black theologians must consider how the nature, presence, and power of the Holy Spirit are to be understood in a meaningful way in the black church tradition.[320] In taking an exploratory look at the role of the Holy Spirit in Black theology, Roberts understands that the work of the Spirit is not confined to the church building. Put another way, Roberts understands the cultural dynamics of how the Holy Spirit works in both sacred institutions and secular environments. Still focusing on the work of the Holy Spirit, Roberts writes that "The roots of black theology are found in black spirituals, gospels, and blues, in our poetry and prose, in our art, sermons, and folklore. We have a wealth of spiritual riches that we can feast upon and even share with others who are spiritually barren in a secular culture."[321]

Roberts is certain that "a liberating Pneumatological Christology and a liberating Christological Pneumatology (together) are needed to accurately gauge the Trinitarian promise and revelation of God in Jesus Christ; as it in concert with the goal of coming to a sound doctrine of the Holy Spirit."[322] Whereas Roberts interlocks Pneumatology and Christology for the sake of better understanding the working relationship between Jesus Christ and the Holy Spirit, he also stresses that another way viewing Jesus Christ as liberator is through the prism of the Holy Spirit. In other words, to speak of the work of the Holy Spirit is to speak of both the work of Jesus Christ on the cross and his resurrection from the dead. Whereas the Holy Spirit or Spirit of Christ enabled, inspired, and empowered Jesus

---

[318] J. Deotis Roberts, *Black Theology in Dialogue*, 54.
[319] Ibid., 53.
[320] Ibid., 54.
[321] J. Deotis Roberts, *A Black Political Theology*, 147.
[322] Ibid.

Christ to suffer, bleed and die on the cross, the same (Holy) Spirit (of Christ) enabled, inspired, and empowered Jesus Christ to be resurrected from the grave. In other words, the Holy Spirit embodies the Spirit of Christ for the sake of human liberation because the Holy Spirit is the Spirit of Christ.

In his timeless classic, *Liberation and Reconciliation: A Black Theology,* Roberts writes that "For black Christians, the Holy Spirit is God within the life of the individual Christian and the fellowship of believers in Christ. The Holy Spirit is the giver of spiritual life. The Holy Spirit comforts, guides, and strengthens us."[323] Again, Roberts wants to affirm the Holy Spirit as one who has the power to strengthen an oppressed people. Still, in the Black church tradition, the Spirit is not merely a dove but wind and fire also. That is to say that the Comforter is also a Strengthener. The Holy Spirit has both presence and power. The presence of the Spirit of God is always a "moralized" presence and power[324] meaning that the Spirit empowers believers to analyze something in terms of morality, preaching, lecturing, advocating, and urging. As a Spirit-filled community, the church, according to Roberts, owes its nature and mission to the presence and work of the Spirit. Not only was the church born through an outpouring of the Spirit, but its nature, message and mission are dependent upon the Spirit's presence and power.[325] In Roberts' cultural text, *Africentric Christianity: A Theological Appraisal for Ministry,* he echoes the same theological sentiment regarding the work of the Holy Spirit as the one who leads God's people into all truth.

Without the presence and power of the Spirit in the life and witness of the Black church, the church becomes a mere organization or institution[326] that is unable to sustain and hospitalize the spiritually sick. According to Roberts, the Holy Spirit works for the purposes of reconciliation and liberation. Both are works of the Holy Spirit. There are several ways to identify the Spirit of God because the Spirit of God works for both the strengthening empowerment of the human being and for a great life and witness in the church's presence and

---

[323] J. Deotis Roberts, *Liberation and Reconciliation*, 64.
[324] Ibid., 66-67.
[325] Ibid., 67.
[326] Ibid.

power. In agreeing that the Holy Spirit has been neglected in recent Black theology, Roberts proclaims that it is quite possible for the Black worship experience to be filled with the Spirit and educated blacks still suffer from the Spirit's presence. For Roberts, the spirits must be tested to discern whether they are of God.[327]

Nonetheless, Roberts's primary motive for discussing the relationship between the Holy Spirit and Black theology is his concern that Black people are turning away from a concern for the social, economic, and political aspects of liberation in their religious life. On occasions and within different contexts, Roberts identifies poor African Americans as the Black poor. For Roberts, poverty is a major form of human oppression—one that Black theologians must make it a point to address: "Where there is a structure of evil, there is a need for a gestalt of righteousness. This is a society with white beneficiaries and black victims. The rich get richer, and the poor get poorer. Black in this society often get exist closer to Third World societies than to those who live across town in the South or those who live in the outer city in the North."[328] And because of the debilitating presence of poverty in the lives of Black folk, they are forced to live from day to day on the edges of mere human survival. For Roberts, it is not sufficient that theologians and church leaders contrast this oppressive reality with the economic deprivation in a Third World country. Roberts believes the economic plight of Black people is critical and getting worse. In this theological vein economic oppression makes way for liberation theologies of classism, sexism and for the church.

Culturally, Roberts believes that racism is alive and well in that racism is linked to the lack of economic opportunities amongst minorities. Within the theological framework of economic deprivation as the oppressive culture of Black people, Roberts pays close attention to the feminization of poverty where Black single mothers and fathers are parenting homes with disproportionate numbers of dependent children. For Roberts, Black poverty is an intergenerational situation that leads into a future of human despair and economic hopelessness. On the one hand, Black theology must be more interdisciplinary and get involved in social analysis, value

---

[327] Ibid.
[328] Ibid., 157.

clarifications and strategies leading to economic development designed to improve the plight of Black people. On the other hand, blacks must be more educated on how political power and economic means are synonymous with one another. Overall, Roberts believes that Black theology, as a theological ethic, must fully address Black poverty.

The primary reason Roberts takes church ministry seriously is because he believes that Black church ministry equals spirituality and liberation. Once the theological connection is made between Black liberation theology and the Black church, Roberts desires for Black theology to address the fact of poverty in the Black community. For the Black poor, Jesus means freedom and the Holy Spirit means liberation. For Roberts, the ministry of Jesus and the inspiration of the Holy Spirit informs Black church economics and politics in such a way that they should be willing to make a positive difference in the lives of those oppressed. Against the background of such an understanding of the Gospel, Roberts believes that the Holy Spirit must inspire Black theologians to deal with economic factor. Theologically, the economic factor (poverty) implies personal crises, social sin, and internal family issues such as motherhood and fatherhood. Roberts' theological passion for the Black church is synonymous with his belief in developing the Black family. Roberts' understanding of poverty as a structural evil leads him to the conclusion that the Black church, the Black family, Black businesses, Black schools, and the Black community share in the same sufferings of economic deprivation and desperately need the liberating work of the Holy Spirit.

Dwight N. Hopkins

As a leading, second-generation constructor of Black theology, Dwight N. Hopkins grounds his theological discussion on the anthropological implications of culture within the notion of human labor and in the context of poor Black people living in the United States. For Hopkins, this sector of the American community and the American population find itself located in a specific political economy. Most racial group(s) identified as Black fall within the working class or live in structural poverty. By working class, Hopkins is referring to those Black folk who do not monopolize and own wealth in the way that the top 10 percent of the U.S. population monopolizes and privately owns and influences the overwhelming majority of private wealth and retains exclusive purchase.[329] Here, culture is greatly determined by the economic interactions and positioning among people. More specifically, one's ownership of power over distribution [330] Like Cone and Roberts, Hopkins is theologically aware of how economic poverty destroys the various fabrics of Black peoples' lives. Unlike the first- and second-generation Black theologians, Hopkins intentionally unpacks the debilitating consequences of being Black and poor in the United States.

In many of Hopkins's published works, he describes poverty as a material and visible consequence of one's culture, labor, race and gender. Most notably, Hopkins affirms the presence of God amongst the Black poor. Hopkins expounds on the Spirit and the Poor: "From strong indications within African American religious traditions, God tabernacles especially among the African American poor and affirms the positive cultural and political traditions and practices of this sector of community. The creative and rich realities of the black poor and their contributions, real and potential, to the rest of humanity, especially to the rest of working and poor people in the United States (and the world's poor), exhibit exactly the God-poor encounter.[331] Hopkins's take on the Spirit and the poor not only represents a contemporary model of theological anthropology as found in the Black folktales, but it also reveals a critical part of Hopkins' theology of God in creation.

In his book, *DOWN, UP, AND OVER: Slave Religion and Black Theology*, Hopkins views the Holy Spirit as the present wisdom and patience of God. In citing narratives from ex-slaves, Hopkins affirms that God has a special and timely way of helping oppressed people when they need it the most. In the same tone as heard in the words of the Gospel song, 'On Time God', Hopkins writes that "Ultimately, divine patience is the Spirit working for us to be fully human, spiritually and materially, and to enable those ensnared within the oppressive clutches of death and social disease to struggle for liberation and to practice freedom."[332] Because God in

---

[329] Dwight N. Hopkins, *Being Human*, 61.
[330] Ibid., 62.
[331] Ibid., 166.
[332] Dwight N. Hopkins, *DOWN, UP, AND OVER*, 188.

Jesus Christ saves, delivers and heals, "the Holy Spirit is the greatest of all blessings for oppressed black folk, whether free or unfreeze, north or south. And the spirit for us denotes specifically patience (in God's own time and not forever) described as equal rights, privileges, liberty and independence."[333]

For Hopkins, the Holy Spirit is the deliverer from black oppression. By way of focusing on what he terms as the Spirit of liberation,[334] Hopkins connects the plight of the poor to the purpose of the Spirit. Hopkins explores:

> God, through the Spirit for us elects the poor not to sacralize poverty, but because poverty is demonic. In fact, sometimes the poor oppose the will of God for liberation, the normative yardstick for all humanity. God chooses the poor: because the ethics, ontology, and epistemology of God is total liberation by which human beings can reach the highest divine creativity; because the majority of black folk in the United States do not own the wealth, lack affirmation of their racial cultural identity, are controlled on a daily basis by demands outside of themselves, and suffer abuse for using their own language; and because of the universal implications of freeing the poor from all humanity.[335]

Hopkins's take on the Spirit of liberation is one that affirms God working with oppressed black folk and other peoples underneath the heel of victimization through the interplay of God's glory and unity, righteousness and omnipresence, constancy and eternity, omnipotence and mercy, grace and holiness, and wisdom and patience.[336] Because God works in the life of oppressed black people, the Spirit is rendered as the activity itself. According to Hopkins, the work or activity of the Spirit is described as total liberation. What this means is that the role of the liberating Spirit is both material and spiritual. To further the role of this Spirit as a vivifying agent in the

---

[333] Ibid.

[334] Hopkins uses the term Spirit of liberation in the following texts: *Introducing Black Liberation Theology, Cut Loose Your Stammering Tongue, Shoes That Fit Our Feet, Head and Heart and Being Human.* Whether or not he is referring to the Holy Spirit or Holy Ghost is up for discussion and interpretation.

[335] Dwight N. Hopkins, *DOWN, UP, AND OVER,* 189.

[336] Ibid.

co-constitution of a full material and spiritual humanity in the new Commonwealth requires further inquiry into the Spirit of liberation with us: that is to say, the reality of Jesus with us today.[337] Hopkins's message of freedom and liberation is not just for those oppressed slaves of the earlier centuries, but it also counts for the modern-day oppressions of darker-skinned human beings.

In their co-edited masterpiece, *Cut Loose Your Stammering Tongue: Black Theology in the Slave Narratives*, Hopkins and George C. L. Cummings postulate that there is substantive meaning in the experiences of the Holy Spirit as told in the slave narratives. Through the testimonies of the slaves as embedded in the context which the spiritual encounters occurred; Cummings succeeds at showing how the Spirit (of God) worked in the religious life of oppressed slaves. Like various theologians of the past, Hopkins affirms spirituality as the wisdom of experiencing poverty. For Hopkins, the Spirit of liberation is the Holy Spirit. And within his discussion on Black poverty, Hopkins stresses that the spirit of liberation speaks to and is present with all the oppressed. Because Jesus Christ represents the good news of the Gospel to all oppressed peoples, Hopkins affirms the Black Messiah for pneumatological reasons.

Hopkins theologizes the Holy Spirit as one "who manifests total liberation in macro-, micro-, linguistic, and racial-cultural identity realities in the dynamic of co-constitution of the self for a full spiritual and material humanity (goal or telos)."[338] Chapters 4 through 6 in Part 2 of *DOWN, UP, AND OVER* present three theological truths about God's Spirit. 1. In theology, God is the Spirit of total liberation for us.[339] 2. In Christology, Jesus is the fulfillment of God's promise to be the Spirit of total liberation with us.[340] 3. In theological anthropology, the human purpose is God's Spirit of total liberation in us.[341] In the final analysis, Hopkins affirms that "a constructive black theology of liberation accompanies the co-constitution of a new self and a new Common Wealth, on earth as it is in heaven."[342] Of the

---

[337] Ibid.
[338] Dwight N. Hopkins, *DOWN, UP, AND OVER*, 155.
[339] Ibid.
[340] Ibid.
[341] Ibid.
[342] Ibid.

three deposits of God's Spirit of total liberation, I am most attracted to what Hopkins says about the Spirit of God in realm of theology. For me, this realm of constructive theology makes room for and is inclusive to a descriptive Black liberation theology for the contemporary context.

In describing the acts of God and the ethics that is associated with what God does, Hopkins explains that

> The primal hope act of God is the exodus story. It signifies that paradigmatic expression of covenantal partnership of co-constitution of the oppressed self into a new liberated self. Divine intent works with marginalized humanity through liberation to exit out of physical restraints of Egyptian bondage (or whatever it exists today) and into material free space undergirded by a spiritual belief in the power of Yahweh and the human community. The Spirit of total liberation or holistic freedom of Yahweh is never in itself but is always an empowering "ruach" (breath) for poor humanity. The finger of God is for us, and the divine Spirit breathes on us for us.[343]

By way of theological introduction, notice first that Hopkins does not refer to God's Spirit as the Holy Spirit. But just because he does not call God's Spirit the Holy Spirit, does not mean that Hopkins is not referring to the liberating work of the Holy Spirit. In referencing God's Spirit in the exodus story, Hopkins uses the language of 'divine intent' to describe God's intentional acts of liberation in the life of humanity. The words 'spiritual belief,' 'power of Yahweh,' and 'holistic freedom' implicates the presence and work of God's Spirit in the Old Testament. Lastly, Hopkins digs deeper into his theological philosophy of total liberation. In presenting God's Spirit as an empowering "ruach" for poor people, Hopkins shows how total liberation could be defined as God's Spirit breathing *on* humanity as God's finger is *for* humanity. Lastly, Hopkins's language of divine Spirit brings together the liberating acts (God on us) and ethics (God for us) of God's Spirit. All of which can easily be identified as the liberating work of the Holy Spirit in the New Testament. Hopkins's theological work naturally flows into the new book's thesis argument

---

[343] Ibid.

that the Holy Spirit is the liberator of Black people and other groups, races, and cultures of oppressed people.

James H. Evans, Jr.

James H. Evans, Jr., another one of James Cone's pupils, is also a leading Black theologian of the second generation. In his comprehensive survey text, *Black Theology: A Critical Assessment and Annotated Bibliography*, Evans gives a historical take on the role of the Holy Spirit in Black liberation theology. Because the God of black theology is revealed as the One who delivered Israel out of house of bondage, liberated the African slaves and sides with the oppressed today; and the Christ of black theology is one that died the death of a slave and rose again to witness the power of God over the forces of oppression[344], the Holy Spirit in black theology is not simply that force which compels us to lead pious lives. The Holy Spirit is the presence of God in the world. The Holy Spirit is the spiritual expression of the black power movement and the political expression of Afro-American faith.[345] For Evans, there must be a dialogical and theological union between the community of faith and the spirit of freedom.

In his magnum opus, *We Have Been Believers: An African American Systematic Theology*, Evans uses Emil Brunner's concept of ecclesia. Brunner sees that "The social form of the Ecclesia was a necessary consequence of their faith.... This means that the social character of the Ecclesia resulted from the spiritual character as an association of men through the Holy Spirit through the love of Christ. And that itself was the structural law of this social entity. There was no other law, nor was there need for any. The Ecclesia was a spiritual brotherhood, free from law."[346] Evans affirms Brunner's notion of the Ecclesia by stressing that if a community of faith considers themselves to be spiritually minded, they must relate to other communities of faith in the expression of agape. As Brunner puts it, "the brotherhood can have laws and institutions, but it can never regard these as belonging to its essence. But, above all, it can never understand itself as an institution.... And this non-institutional character is much more evident still in the Ecclesia of the New Testament whose life-element

---

344 James H. Evans, Jr., *Black Theology: Critical Assessment*, 4.
345 Ibid.   .
346 James H. Evans, Jr., *We Have Been Believers*, 127.

is the Holy Spirit."[347] For Evans, the Holy Spirit is the existential dynamism of faith. Using the words of Albert Cleage, Evans posits that "The church is animated and sustained by the power of the Holy Spirit."[348]

In reading Evans's critical essay "The Holy Spirit in African American Theology" in *The Oxford Handbook of African American Theology,* I paid close attention to his presentation of the three theological models. Of the three models, Evans's take the Holy Spirit as the spirit of liberation in black religious belief and practice has served as a leading guide for the writing of this new book. Evans is correct in affirming that liberation, as an act of God, human beings, and a theological model for Black religionists, leads to both the spirit of radicalism and spirit of survival.

In his classic text *Black Religion and Black Radicalism*, Gayraud S. Wilmore argues that the Western (and modern) distinction between the human spirit and the Holy Spirit did not apply to the experience of enslaved Africans in America and elsewhere. Due in part to the fact that the Holy Spirit resides in the human spirit of the believer, the liberating work of the Spirit is both culturally productive and spiritually redemptive. Especially for those enslaved Africans who were just beginning to experience the Spirit of truth as the slave master used the Bible to justify slavery. When the Holy Spirit touch downed into the human spirit of the African slaves, culture and true salvation came to them as a form of liberation. They realized that despite their religious background, they too were born of the Spirit.

Evans shares a powerful story:

Howard Thurman, for example, through his embrace of the deep manifestation of the Holy Spirit in the human heart as well as the cosmos, was able to connect with that deep manifestation as it was expressed in the tradition of Christianity, but also in other religious traditions such as Hinduism. After an afternoon of conversing with a Hindu scholar, Thurman reflected on this experience and the breakthrough has occurred. "It was if we had stepped out of social, political, cultural frames of reference, and allowed two

---

[347] Ibid.
[348] Ibid., 136.

human spirits to unite on a ground of reality that was unmarked by differences. This was a watershed experience in my life." The Holy Spirit is associated with radical freedom in John 3:8, where Jesus states, "The wind blows wherever it pleases. You will hear its sound, but you cannot tell where it comes from or where it is going. So, it is with everyone born of the Spirit."[349]

Evans views the Holy Spirit as redeemer and liberator of the Black oppressed. But that is not the entire description of the Spirit's work. Appropriately, Evans describes the work of the Holy Spirit as one that has healing power, reaching power and spanning power. Evans posits that "The Holy Spirit is not just the name for that creative principle which undergirds black life. It is also the name for healing and redemptive power that limited the spatial reach and the temporal span of human suffering. That is, the idea that love is stronger than death, and that weeping at midnight is no match for joy in the morning, connects the Holy Spirit with the notion of liberation."[350] In describing the liberating work of the Holy Spirit in the life of those who suffer, Evans makes a major theological move when he affirms the Spirit as love. The Holy Spirit is the love that lives inside believers. With the idea that the Spirit's love is greater than Satan's plan of death for human beings, Evans confirms the power of the Spirit as one that saves, heals, and liberates. The Spirit not only gives life to the dying, but Spirit also provides joy for those that weep, grieve, and mourn.

For Evans, "The Holy Spirit in African American experience is not confined to the ethical or ritual aspects of life. The Holy Spirit points to the aesthetic aspect of life. That is, the Holy Spirit's continual affirmation of the value of black life is at the heart of the economy. Of its outward expression."[351] Historically, Black people have not prospered from the outward expressions of the American and world economies. While the inward expressions come across as a dream or a vision with good intentions, neither type of expression materializes a visible outcome that is designed to holistically benefit the Black human being. Sadly, a sizable number of Black people

---

[349] Katie G. Canon and Anthony B. Pinn, *The Oxford Handbook of African American Theology*, 166.
[350] Ibid., 166-167.
[351] Ibid., 171-172.

throughout the world still live in poverty, suffer as the result of poverty, and die in poverty. What this means is that in the realms of the cultural, social, political, and economic, a major function of the Spirit is to provide a sustaining purpose that works toward and for the survival of the oppressed. Subsequently, the biblical insight that liberation and Spirit go hand in hand has prompted contemporary historians and theologians to interpret the history of human struggle against systemic oppression as the authentic history of the Holy Spirit's presence and work on earth. Because the work of the Holy Spirit is associated with freedom and unpredictability, the Holy Ghost is a critical part of the Black church ministry in the United States and the world abroad.

Will Coleman

In Will Coleman's essay, "Coming through "Ligion": Metaphor in Non-Christian and Christian Experiences with the Spirit(s) in African American Slave Narratives," he explains the African American encounter with both spirits and the Spirit. Coleman is convinced that slave narratives are legitimate examples of Black liberation theology. But Coleman also warns against how we are to describe the actual experiences in terms of using the word *spirit* vis a vis the *Spirit*. For Coleman, for Black theology "to drink from the deep fountain of the total African American religious experience"[352], it must take into consideration the Christian and the non-Christian experience of the Spirit. Coleman recognizes that in some cases it may difficult to delineate the "theology" of the African American slaves, since traditional, Eurocentric, Christian theology is by definition critical reflection upon the God who is revealed in the Scriptures, especially through the incarnation of Jesus Christ and the work of the Holy Spirit."[353] As the result of the slave telling the story of an experience with both a spirit and the Spirit, it may be even more of a misnomer to speak of "doctrines" within certain religious slave narratives, especially those that are not explicitly Christian.[354] Despite the slight difference in feature and wording, the slaves' experience with both a spirit and the Spirit must be considered as an authentic

---

[352] Will Coleman, *Tribal Talk: Black Theology*, 48.
[353] Ibid.
[354] Ibid., 49.

experience with God. Theologically, Coleman[355] believes that both the Christian and the non-Christian experience of the spirit/Spirit stands for the slave's existential moments with the Holy Spirit.

The Holy Spirit in Womanist Theology

Womanist theology locates themes of God's liberation, justice, and freedom in the stories of the Bible, but roots that liberation in the self-empowerment of Black women. As Vanderbilt ethicist Stacey M. Floyd-Thomas writes that "Womanism is a paradigm shift wherein Black women no longer look to others for their liberation, but instead look to themselves." A womanist theologian knows the history of Black women in white America and is very clear that we have never expected liberation to come at the hands of our enslavers or even well-meaning non-Black people. Instead, our liberation must come from our own hands and is fortified in the knowledge that God will provide all we need to live the life they intended.[356]

In her enthusiastic *Sojourners* article, "The Liberating Theology that Transformed My Understanding of God," Lauren W. Reliford explains how Womanist theology has helped to inform her on who God is in the life of Black women. In the Womanist view of liberation within the sphere of Black women's self-empowerment as they look to themselves and to God in Jesus Christ by the power of the Holy Spirit for guidance and protection, Reliford finds a deep truth. She testifies:

The more I grow and learn about womanism and womanist theology, the easier it becomes to believe that I am worthy just because I exist; God created me as a Black woman for a reason and that reason is as valid and beautiful as the next. Womanist theology gave me the radical permission to accept that I deserve to be healed, empowered, protected, and free.

---

[355] I believe that Will Coleman's text, *Tribal Talk: Black Theology, Hermeneutics, and African/American Ways of "Telling the Story,"* represents the best scholarly treatment of the African slaves' experience with both the spirit and the Holy Spirit. I am a huge fan of Coleman's groundbreaking work in *Tribal Talk*. While there are several examples of black theologians (Womanist theologians included) attempting to do constructive work around pneumatology, Will Coleman, Dwight N. Hopkins, and George Cummings' witness of the Spirit in the slave context has proven to be quite useful for my theological development/interpretations.
[356] Lauren W. Reliford, "The Liberating Theology that Transformed My Understanding of God," Para. 6.

The Holy Spirit resides in me. This affirmation of my being in the face of constant dehumanization is something that I never expected to have living in the U.S. as a Black woman and, in true womanist fashion, is a blessing I want to help other women receive.[357]

In affirming what Womanists believe--that God is Spirit; I will expect Alice Walker's groundbreaking statement and argue that the reason Womanists love the Spirit is because they believe and understand that the Holy Spirit resides on the inside of them. And within this theological understanding, Womanists carry with them an intimate and personal perspective of the Spirit. In loving the Holy Spirit that resides inside of them, Womanists have reason to love themselves as the Spirit works inside of the Black woman for God's liberation of them and for their own liberation of themselves.

As an excellent form of Black liberation theology, Womanist theology is one of the sources that can help to describe a contemporary Black pneumatology. In terms of theologizing cultural texts and identifying the theological method, the word *Womanist* implies women of color or Black women. Its primary concern is that of caring for and nurturing the Black family unit while strengthening their own cultural identity. As stated earlier, one of the most poignant statements made about the relationship between the womanist and the Holy Spirit was by the famed African American author and poet, Alice Walker. Amid struggling to make sense of what it meant to be Black woman in an American context, Walker writes that "Womanists love the Spirit."[358] This one statement eloquently and controversially defines the longstanding relationship between women of color and the Spirit of God.

In response to Walker's statement of loves (music, dance, the moon, the Spirit, love, food, roundness, struggle, the folk, herself), Cheryl Townsend-Gilkes writes that "Walker emphasizes those things that make possible what has come to be called "the beloved community."[359] Townsend-Gilkes goes on to write that,

As one reflects upon these loves, it becomes clear that those

---

[357] Ibid., Para. 11.
[358] Womanist: Encyclopedia II- Womanists- Introduction, www.experiencefestival.com/a/Womanist_-_Introduction/id/...
[359] Emilie M. Townes, *Troubling in My Soul*, 239.

loves oppose directly and central hatred of this age. We live in a society that hates poor and people and yet Walker calls us to love "the Spirit." In a society that in its hatred of poor people and fat people has allowed the ethic that "a woman can be neither too rich nor too thin" to rain down life-threatening terrors on women. Walker exalts "food and roundness." And most importantly, in a society that pulls its various cultural hatreds together in such a way as to destroy and victimize Black women, Walker passionately emphasizes the importance of self-love. "Loves herself. *Regardless.*[360]

In her essay, "Womanist Theology: Black Women's Voices," Delores S. Williams states that "Walker's mention of the black womanist's love of the spirit is a true reflection of the great respect Afro-American women has always shown for the presence and work of the spirit. The importance of this emphasis upon the spirit is that it allows Christian womanist theologians, in their use of the Bible, to identify and reflect upon those biblical stories in which poor oppressed women had a special encounter with divine emissaries of God, like the spirit."[361] For such womanist pioneers as Walker, Williams, Katie Canon and others, the inspiring reality of loving the self or developing self-esteem in the midst of racial and sexual degradation, suggests that womanist theology could eventually speak of God in a well-developed theology of the spirit.[362] According to Williams, "The sources for this theology are many. Womanist Theology has grounds for shaping a theology of the spirit informed by black women's political action."[363] Throughout the course of history and in one way or another, many phenomenal black women have expressed what it means to experience the Spirit of God; however, Alice Walker's poetic musing stands as the mission statement for the powerful interaction between Womanist theology and the Holy Spirit.[364]

In pioneering feminist, Rosemary Radford Reuther's work, *Gender, Ethnicity & Religion: Views from the Other Side*, Patricia-

---

[360] Ibid.
[361] Delores S. Williams "Womanist Theology: Black Women's Voices" www.religion-online.org/showarticle.asp? title=445
[362] Ibid.
[363] Ibid.
[364] Ibid.

Anne Johnson declares that "Pneumatology is still an unchartered realm of womanist theology. Emilie M. Townes and Delores S. Williams agree that the roles of the spirit, the Holy Spirit and the human spirit, need to be clarified not only in womanist theology, but in all constructive liberationist efforts to understand how to live in God."[365] In Johnson's essay, "Womanist Theology as Counter-Narrative", she feeds off the interpretation of Townes and Williams and says that, "To live in the spirit of God requires that womanists commit themselves to the search for wholeness—physical and spiritual, concrete and theoretical. As gatherers of knowledge, womanists are dangerous to all forms of hegemony."[366] Johnson's statement along with Townes and Williams' take on Womanist pneumatology defines the Womanist interaction with the Holy Spirit. For Womanist theologians, the category of pneumatology constitutes the reality of understanding the role of the Holy Spirit in the various lives of Black women.

Linda Thomas's journal article, "The Holy Spirit and Black Women: A Womanist Perspective," gives a quality description of how the Spirit is present in the suffering and struggle of Black women and how it works for their liberation, abetting them to resist evil[367] and move towards freedom. According to Thomas, "black women have particular insight into the power of the Spirit because their historical radical marginality puts them in the center of myriad realities in which is deeply rooted, unacknowledged, and unconventional wisdom dwells."[368] Thomas's poignant analysis spotlights how Black women use their extraordinary wisdom, knowledge, and understanding to survive the evil realities associated with dehumanization and marginalization. In presenting the Holy Spirit as one who inspires the wisdom tradition. Says Thomas, "On the one hand, insight into the Spirit comes through the enduring ways that black women have called on Jesus and the Holy Spirit to be ever present in their lives. On the other hand, insight comes from African understandings of the Spirit as God present in creation, giving and nourishing all life."[369]

---

[365] Rosemary R. Ruether, *Gender, Ethnicity & Religion*, 206.
[366] Ibid.
[367] See page 190 where I talk about resisting evil as a common part of both the fruit of the Spirit and gifts of the Spirit.
[368] Rosemary R. Ruether, *Gender, Ethnicity & Religion*, 73.
[369] Ibid., 74.

They (Black women) are aware of biblical texts telling them about the presence of the Spirit: that God's Spirit rekindled dry bones into a living body (Ezekiel 37); that God's Spirit descended when Jesus was baptized by John the Baptist (Matthew 3:16; Mark 1:10; Luke 3:22); that Jesus declares the Spirit was upon him (Luke 4:16– 18); that Jesus promises the disciples that the Holy Spirit will come (John 14:15– 25); that Jesus tells them that the Spirit will give them power (Acts 1:8); and that at Pentecost, the Spirit came and the church was birthed (Acts 2).[370]

The biblical images of the presence and work of Jesus Christ and the Holy Spirit remind Black women of God's blessed interaction with those who are in need. What is so phenomenal about Thomas's scriptural references is that they all point to a form of spiritual growth that can only come through faith in God, Jesus Christ, and the Holy Spirit. The Bible teaches that the Holy Spirit comes to those who believe (1 Cor 12:13; Eph 1:13-14).

In her text, *Dancing with God: The Trinity from a Womanist Perspective*, Karen Baker-Fletcher theologizes the Holy Spirit in the presence of systemic evil. She first introduces the Holy Spirit as the *ruach*, which means in Hebrew "breath, "wind," or "spirit."[371] She describes the Holy Spirit as "the very power of life, which is God."[372] She then says that "Experience is a form of knowing. We human beings experience God through mind, body, and spirit."[373] Afterward, Baker-Fletcher affirms that, "The Holy Spirit, who is love, unites God the lover and the Son, the beloved. All three love one another relationally, in the distinctiveness of their personalities. God is communitarian within God's own nature."[374] In the economic Trinity, which is God's revelation and response to the world, the world experiences itself as beloved in Christ and in the power of the Holy Spirit.[375] Through this love, Baker-Fletcher believes "that it is important (for the world) to understand the role of the Holy Spirit as

---

[370] Ibid.
[371] Karen Baker-Fletcher, *Dancing with God*, 16.
[372] Ibid.
[373] Ibid., 18.
[374] Ibid.
[375] Ibid.

the power of encouragement in Christ."[376] In her understanding of the Holy Spirit as the Spirit of Truth, Baker-Fletcher concludes here that "A dipolar theology cannot adequately lead us into conscious, full relationship with God who is in Christ, because Christ reveals God the Father—who is a feminist or womanist view may be understood as God the Parent—and God the Holy Spirit. When we talk about the source of the strength to "take heart" or "to be of good courage," we are talking about God, who is three dynamic relations (hypostases) in one nature."[377]

Baker-Fletcher interacts with the doctrine of the Holy Spirit for the purpose of providing a theological response to the presence of evil. What Baker-Fletcher does with the doctrine of the Holy Spirit is a faith-filled proclamation or theological response to the presence of evil. Baker-Fletcher explains that "The scope of this book is to consider the work of God in a world of crucifixion in general, with attention to the activity of the three relations or "persons" of the Trinity with emphasis on the Holy Spirit as "Encouraging Spirit" who empowers the liberating activity of dancing with God."[378] For Black people in Africa and in the United States, dancing is an act of culture and of the Spirit. Even as their dancing takes place in sacred institutions and secular environments, Black people's bodily movements are guided by their connection with the Holy Spirit. They move according to the direction and guidance of the Spirit.

Patricia L. Hunter continues this pneumatological dance with God in Emilie M. Townes' book, *A Troubling in My Soul: Womanist Perspectives on Evil and Suffering*. Hunter speaks to the ways the Holy Spirit sustains women as members of a historically patriarchal, Christian Black church. In Hunter's essay, "Women's Power—Women' Passion: And God Said, "That's Good," she gives her premise on why spirituality and sexuality, as a package, are the primary theological concern of the Black church. Through Hunter's focus on the language of God in the African American religious experience, it is better understood what Delores S. Williams was alluding to when she wrote that "Regardless of one's hopes about intentionality and Womanist theological method, questions must be

---

[376] Ibid., 19.
[377] Ibid.
[378] Ibid., 23.

raised about the God-content of the theology."[379] For Hunter, a Womanist theological method intentionally engages God in Jesus Christ with hopes of affirming a certain type of lifestyle for women of color. This lifestyle is one that helps maintain physical, sexual, emotional, and spiritual health.[380] It is in the same vein that Hunter explicates the role of the Holy Spirit.

> The Holy Spirit's ability to give meaning and direction to our lives amid our rage is what sustains us. It is by God's amazing grace that we can turn our endless rage into a holy rage. With our holy rage we maintain our connections to the church, sometimes closely, other times tangentially. Our holy rage, in concert with our faith, enables us to believe in the power of the Holy Spirit to transform the church to be a place of justice and safety for women.[381]

This holy rage or holistic concern for Black women which Hunter speaks of is what led Emilie Townes to the stirring revelation that *A Troubling in My Soul* needed a sister text. As a result, Townes' book, *Embracing the Spirit: Womanist Perspective on Hope, Salvation and Transformation,* gives even more credence to the fact that Black women are remarkably familiar with the Holy Spirit. They must be for reasons of race, gender, class, sexuality, and the Black Church. Whether it be Diana L. Hayes confessing that the Holy Spirit revived her soul,[382] Karen Baker-Fletcher affirming that Jesus is the human embodiment of the Spirit[383] and that the world is of the Spirit is ever present due to the fact that God, the resurrected Jesus and the Holy Spirit are all Spirit[384], Emilie Townes' speaking of the pouring out of God's spirit showering us and allowing us to do so much more[385], C. Michelle Venable-Ridley's saying that, "dey calls 'em spirituals, case the Holy Spirit done revealed 'em to 'em[386] or Cheryl Townsend-Gilkes reminding us that "God is a Spirit and they that worship [It]

---

[379] Delores S. Williams "Womanist Theology: Black Women's Voices" www.religion-online.org/showarticle.asp? title=445

[380] Emilie M. Townes, *A Troubling in My Soul*, 195.

[381] Ibid., 196-197.

[382] Ibid., 26.

[383] Ibid., 124.

[384] Ibid., 130.

[385] Ibid., 193.

[386] Ibid., 226.

must worship [It] in Spirit and in truth."[387] Either way, the relationship between the Womanist theologian and the work of the Holy Spirit represents a critical part of describing a Black pneumatology for the contemporary context.

Townsend-Gilkes' scriptural belief that God must be worshiped in Spirit and in truth references the words of Saint Gregory of Nazianzus. In his book, *On God and Christ*, St. Gregory writes that "it is the Spirit in whom we worship and through whom we pray. "God," it says, "is Spirit, and they who worship him must worship him in Spirit and in Truth."[388] Both Townsend-Gilkes and Gregory of Nazianzus affirm a Trinitarian God. Because theologians name the Holy Spirit as the Spirit of Truth, the only way to worship God the Spirit (the Father) is in Spirit and Truth (Jn 4:23). The Apostle John records Jesus saying that he is the way, the truth, and the light (Jn 14:6). In the likeness of womanist theologians, Gregory lifts the importance of praying to God in mind and in spirit. Both Gregory and the Womanist theologians see praying in the Spirit as an act of worshiping the Spirit of God in the presence of the Spirit.

In her book, *Hope In The Holler: A Womanist Theology*, A. Elaine Brown Crawford uses the slave narratives to show how the empowering presence of the Holy Spirit (pneumatology) empowered autonomy and independent behavior that resisted the hegemony that infringed upon slave culture.[389] Like many of the second generation Black theologians, Crawford presumes that the testimony of the slave narratives was the *pneumatos* (God's Spirit), a liberating presence which created and sustained the will of an enslaved people against those people and institutions that perpetrated the exploitation African American chattel."[390] Using the character of Old Elizabeth, Crawford suggests that the Holy Spirit played a critical role in both biblical and real life stories of women who endured many trials and tribulations only to be empowered and delivered by the overshadowing of the Lord's Spirit.[391] According to Crawford, slave women were led by the Spirit to seek justice[392] and stand in prophetic critique of the race, class

---

[387] Ibid., 281.
[388] St Gregory of Nazianzus, *On God and Christ*, 125.
[389] A. Elaine Brown Crawford, *Hope in The Holler*, 38.
[390] Ibid., 39.
[391] Ibid.
[392] Ibid., 40.

and gender oppression in their lives and community.[393] For Crawford, protest was an integral part of the spirituals because protest was the slave women's way of affirming their religious experience as being authentic.

In lieu of Crawford and James Cone's *Spirituals and the Blues*, Cheryl A. Kirk-Duggan writes that "Some spirituals viewed God and Jesus as synonyms; in others, Jesus becomes a composite of Christ and Moses; still others Jesus and the Holy Spirit are coterminous. Scholars argue both for an explicit Trinity and a disregard of the same because of the omission of the term Holy Spirit in many of the spirituals."[394] The spirituals celebrated freedom: "Moses the human liberator; Christ the holy spirit Jesus, comforter and redeemer of sin; and transcendent God revealing God's real person in situations of liberation: God the Creator-Revelator (Maker), God the Freedom-Fighter (Christ Moses), God the Redeemer-Comforter (Holy Spirit Jesus)—God the Revelator, Freedom fighter, Liberator....the godhead [is] one."[395]

Monica N. Coleman uses the concept of ancestral immortality as a way of understanding the visions, dreams, and charismatic embodiments of the Holy Spirit.[396] In her book, *Making a Way Out of No Way: a Womanist Theology*, Coleman stresses that ancestral immortality and possession by African ancestors are critical to the religious experiences of Black women. Because ancestral immortality and possession help to describe the past as more than a memory[397], these experiences with God have a greater contextual meaning. In every case the person claims ignorance of his or her actions during the possession.[398]Coleman explains that

> The Gospel of John describes the Holy Spirit as the ancestral spirit of Jesus. Jesus speaks to the disciples and tells them, "Nevertheless I tell you the truth: it is your advantage that I go away, for if I do not go away, the Comforter will not come to you; but if I go, I will send him to you" (John 16:7). In the way

[393] Ibid., 39.
[394] Emilie M. Townes, *A Troubling in My Soul*, 162.
[395] Ibid., 163.
[396] Monica N. Coleman, *A Way Out of No Way*, 102.
[397] Ibid., 102.
[398] Ibid.

of that I have used the term *ancestor,* the Holy Spirit can be understood as an ancestor. Thus, a postmodern theology can also explain what some Christians call "getting happy," "feeling the spirit," "speaking in tongues," and/or "holy dancing."[399]

Coleman's explanation of experiencing the physicality of the Holy Spirit speaks to Jurgen Moltmann's take on the human experience of the Holy Spirit. In his book, *The Trinity and the Kingdom: The Doctrine of God,* Jurgen Moltmann claims that the experience of the Holy Spirit is always physical because the power of the experience represents the beginning of the resurrection of the body of Jesus Christ.[400] For Moltmann, experiencing the Holy Trinity implies being touched by the power of the Holy Spirit—every time. The physical touch itself is one of liberation, resurrection and then hope.

In her descriptive text, *The Sanctified Church,* famed novelist Zora Neale Hurston explains the connection between possession and shouting. Hurston writes that "There can be little doubt that shouting is a survival of the African "possession" by the gods. In Africa it is sacred to the priesthood or acolytes, in America it has become generalized. The implication is the same, however, it is a sign of special favor from the spirit that it chooses to drive out the individual consciousness temporarily and use the body for its expression."[401] For Hurston, shouting is a community thing[402] that is also described as absolutely individualistic.[403] It is no secret that Black people shout in the Black church. The Black shouting is the result of an emotional connection between the suffering servant and the liberating inspiration of the Holy Spirit's moving in the worship experience. Shouting in the Black church gives sensual and visible credence to the presence of God in the life of the Black believer. If one can feel the liberating presence of the Holy Spirit in the life of their worship experience, then through faith, the shouting only accentuates the guiding presence of the Spirit in Black people's everyday life.

Fredrick L. Ware describes the Black church shouting as

---

[399] Ibid., 102.
[400] Jurgen Moltmann, *The Trinity and Kingdom*, 125.
[401] Ibid., 125.
[402] Ibid.
[403] Ibid.

emotional, energetic, exhausting, and intellectual for the Christian believer.

> In African American spirituality, emotion and intellect are interrelated and necessary for apprehension of the truth. Indeed, African American worship involves spontaneous, free, and enthusiastic expression, involving hand-clapping, foot-stomping, shouting, dancing, rousing sermons, soul-stirring music, passionate testimony, fervent prayer, call and response, tongue-speaking, prophecy, miracles, conversion, shaking, and even falling out under the power of the Holy Spirit. I response to the Spirit, persons shout (speak spontaneously and sometimes loudly) "Amen," "Glory be to God," "Thank you, Jesus," and "Hallelujah."[404]

It is not only in realm of shouting aloud publicly in worship that Black believers experience the presence of the Holy Ghost. But the spirituality of Black believers is also displayed in their culturally celestial dancing during the experiences of Black church worship. Indeed, the spirituality of Black believers is multifaceted and extends beyond vocal expressions in worship. Their dancing, often rooted in cultural traditions, serves as a powerful form of connection to the divine. Even in rhythmic dancing, Black believers' connection to the Holy Spirit helps them to deal with their experiences with racism and oppression. For a sizable number of Black churches, this is what it means to feel the Spirit. According to Ware, "Sometimes their (Black believers) shouts are in the holy dance that the Spirit moves them to perform."[405]

Every time I feel the Spirit moving in my heart I will dance.

Every time I feel the Spirit moving in my heart I will dance.[406]

Like shouting in church, dancing in church is a cultural response to the Spirit moving in the heart of the Black believer. Dancing in the Spirit is a physical response to a spiritual empowerment and indwelling that helps the Black believer to connect with God in their rhythmic bodily movements. Not only is God active and present with the Black believer's body in physical texture, but God is also active

---

[404] Fredrick L. Ware, *African American Theology*, 127-128.
[405] Ibid., 128.
[406] https://genius.com/Little-richard-every-time-i-feel-the-spirit-lyrics

and present in the (human) spirit of the Black church worship experience. Dancing in the Black church experience is an intricate mixture of music, worship, and the physical inspiration of the Holy Spirit. Nevertheless, this kind of worship engages persons on the level of emotions but should not be taken to mean more emotionalism. African American spirituality can be as intense intellectually as it is emotional.[407]

As a worship practice of the Black church, dancing in the Spirit is one of the spiritual roots of Black culture. In her famed text, *Guide My Feet*, Marian Wright Edelman says that during "the week revival meetings when great Black preachers visited and lifted us beyond our daily small-town routines, work grinds, and struggles. We children watched in wonder, and often, with uncontrollable giggles, as the Holy Spirit lifted some of the old church folks from their pews as they erupted in joyful shouts and dances to God with intricate rhythmic steps the envy of Bojangles and Gregory Hines."[408] I describe the spirit of Black church worship and dancing this way: The Holy Spirit is a dynamically-liberating power that can be experienced through synergetic movements, positive energy, creative excitement, deep love, community service, spiritual forgiveness or humble surrender.

My theology affirms that Black culture is creatively birthed (in other words, it happens) when the Holy Spirit connects with the Black human spirit for creative forms of material production. This is also true of worship in the Black church. Scripture instructs all believers to worship God in Spirit and in truth. The interpretation is that believers must worship God *as* Spirit and *in* Spirit. The spoken doctrine of the Black church states that believers are to worship God for who God is and praise God for things God has done for them and others as well. When at its highest spiritual level, the Black church's acts of praise and worship confirm the presence of the Spirit. Within the worshiping of God as Spirit, there is an implicit worship response to God's gifts of grace in past, present, and future tenses. That when life becomes a living hell, Black people can lean and depend on the Holy Spirit to get them through difficult circumstances and painful moments.

---

[407] Ibid.
[408] Marian W. Edelman, *Guide My Feet*, xx.

Lisa Allen's relevant text, *A Womanist Theology of Worship: Liturgy, Justice, and Communal Righteousness,* explores the complicated legacy and history of Black worship from slavery to the contemporary context. In chronicling the life and times of Black church worship in Africa and the United States, Allen offers an approach that describes the transformative power at holistic biblical worship. With excellency in research and writing, Allen demonstrates the gifts and graces of a Black liberation theologian as she accurately describes what the Holy Spirit means to the authentic worship of Black women, and all Black people for that matter. In speaking on the development early Black theology through the liberating presence of the Holy Spirit, Allen offers a promising declaration: Though enslaved persons, particularly those who were African-born and first-generation Americans, may not Trinitarian concepts of God nor believed that only three gods—Father, Son, and Holy Spirit—were sufficient to carry out the Creator's plans, they would have understood the character and nature of the Holy Spirit.[409]

Like the way the Spirit works in the contemporary Black church worship experience, Allen poses that "The work of the Spirit in Black antebellum worship was intensify and enhance the worship and the more-hoped-for conversion experiences of the enslaved, as well as provide a liberative sense of joy, amid unbearable sorrow."[410] Inclusive to John Mbiti's teachings on African spirit possession and the work of the Spirit in Black church worship proper, Allen concludes her analysis of the Holy Spirit this way: "Though definitely not identical to the African understanding of spirit possession, the indwelling of the Spirit in Black antebellum worship was just as efficacious and transformative for the participant and would find its way into all liturgical practices of the invisible institution, and beyond."[411] Theologically, the work of the Holy Spirit transcends context, transforms individuals, grows institutions, and liberates the oppressed. What makes the liberating work of the Spirit so transformative is that God is present in both sacred institutions and secular environments.

---

[409] Lisa Allen, *A Womanist Theology of Worship*, 24.
[410] Ibid., 25.
[411] Ibid.

Chapter Four

The Holy Spirit in Theology and the Economy of God's Love

Speak to my heart Holy Spirit. Message of love to encourage me. Lifting my heart from the snare how You love, love me, and care for me. Speak to my heart now, oh Lord.[412]

I refer to the expression "economy of God" as a biblical designation that refers to God's plan for distributing economic and spiritual resources. In comprehensible terms, God loves creation in such a way that God is committed to providing humanity with the goods, products, resources, and services needed to live a decent life. This love of God comes in the form of provisions. It includes the assumption that the resources will make it to those for whom need them the most; to those intended. The theological implication is that "God is love" and the freely given grace of God's love is captured by viewing God as "the Giver" or giver of life. Practicing righteousness in God's economy of love involves loving God and loving our neighbors as ourselves (Matthew 22:39). The work of the Holy Spirit enables, inspires, and reminds believers to love God and their fellow men, women, and children. I connect the Holy Spirit with the act and presence of love because love is part of the fruit of the Spirit (Galatians 5:22-23). So that only through the Holy Spirit can believers genuinely love God and their neighbor as the Word of God commands us to (Mark 12:29-31). The Holy Spirit inspires believers

---

[412] https://www.azlyrics.com/lyrics/donniemcclurkin/speaktomyheart.html

to love God, others and themselves in the way God loves humanity.

Within the spiritual perspectives of believers receiving "God's mercy, God's grace, and God's Love, Jesus is telling us what the Reign of God is like by helping us to understand the economy of God's Love. And we come to understand that this economy is not transactional. It's not about earning or being deserving in order to be the beneficiaries of God's Love."[413] In discovering the peace of Christ, "believers experience the liberation of God's Love."[414] According to Michelle Meech, believers "live into the Reign of God that has been right there just waiting for us all along."[415] And as the Holy Spirit moves upon the face of the human spirit and calls more people to the vineyard (Matt 20:1-4), the economy of God's love vows to take care of those who put in the work needed to take care of their families. This vow of God's love includes giving the worker what is decent and right. This is how God's economy works. This is how the Reign of God has always worked.[416] The first shall be last and the last shall be first (Matt. 19:30). This is the economy of God's love.[417]

The economy of God's love is the spiritual fulfillment of all economies in the world working biblically and collaboratively for the benefit of all God's people; and not just a select few. If only a select few prosper and benefit from an unbalanced economic system, then that is not indicative of God's love. Nor is it representative of the Holy Spirit's work in human creation. While the economy of God's unconditional love originates in the work of the Holy Spirit, the painful truth of the present theological matter is that the U.S. economy has never been good for Black people. Put another way, a sizable amount of Black Americans has never felt the love of an economic system or practice. Nor have Black people experienced the love of their white counterpart as they continue to be viewed as expendable and inferior.

The U.S. economy was not good for Black people during Reconstruction, the early twentieth century, the Great Depression, World Wars I and II, Civil Rights, Post-Civil Rights, the Agricultural

---

[413] "The Economy of God's Love – The Rev. Michelle Meech" Para. 1.
[414] Ibid., Para. 25.
[415] Ibid.
[416] Ibid., Para. 27.
[417] Ibid., Para. 30.

Age, the Industrial and Post-Industrial ages, and the early parts of the twenty-first century. Heck, the U.S. economy has never been profitable for Black folk. The only reason a sizable number of Black people have survived in the United States is because of the person, power, and work of the Holy Spirit. That if it had not been for the LORD who was working on behalf of Black folk, there is no telling the number of Black people would be dead, incarcerated or the victim of a heinous act of systemic evil. A sizable number of prominent Black Americans have died while living in poverty.

Historically speaking, Black people have never had economic and financial resources in abundance. But what they have had is an abundance of God, Jesus Christ, and the Holy Spirit. So, which bode the questions: How do economics and the search for a new just economic order fit with the goals of Black theology? Does Black theology focus solely on exposing and ending racism or does it also speak out against economic injustice?[418] What does this new just economic order look like? Is it socialist or does it remain capitalistic? How does the Holy Spirit impact Black theology in doing the constructive work of alleviating racism while speaking out against economic injustice? Because the local, national and world economies do not function as economies of God's love to all races and cultures of people, the questions are legitimate.

God's Love for the Poor Interlocks Theology and Economics

One of the major claims of this new theology book is that the Holy Spirit is God's love present in all of creation. The Holy Spirit is

---

[418] In his intense article, "Black Theology's Call for Economic Justice," Aaron Kreider asks the question: "How do economics and the search for a new just economic order fit in with the goals of black theology? Does black theology focus solely on exposing and ending racism or does it also speak out against economic injustice? If one examines the history of blacks in America, the setting from which black theology emerged, the terminology that it uses, and the later writings of James Cone and Cornel West, then it becomes clear that inherent in black theology is a call for a new economic system that would reduce the harmful effects of capitalism." By way of giving some background information, Kreier expounds by saying that, "Black theology is a popular theology, designed not for an intellectual ruling elite but instead for tens of millions of working-class blacks in the United States. It emerges from their experiences of hundreds of years of white racism and economic exploitation, two forms of discrimination that are inseparable and which still exist in our time." Kreider believes that Black theology must find a way to do both—speak out against racism and economic injustice. For Kreider, these are the most important tenets of Black theology. I would argue that both goals are inclusive to the liberating work of the Holy Spirit.

love because the Holy Spirit exudes the love of God to and for all cultures, groups, and races of people. Particularly, the Holy Spirit is the love that lives inside us.[419] The work of the Holy Spirit serves as the interlocutor[420] between the practice of theology and study of economics. Theologian of culture Paul Tillich[421] references 1 Corinthians 13:8-12 when the Apostle Paul speaks in the famous words of our text, of things which are in part, or, as we should say today, fragmentary things, and of the things which are perfect, or complete. The fragmentary things shall vanish away; the complete things shall abide. The former are temporal; the latter are eternal. The fragmentary, temporal things are not merely material; they are the highest gifts of the Divine Spirit: prophecy, which is the interpretation of our time and history; tongues, which are our ecstatic feeling and speaking; and knowledge, which is the understanding of our existence.

In the demonstrative way of God's love for all people, "the Holy Spirit breaks down every wall of partition, pouring out His light in all the heart's empty spaces, gradually opening every door, gaining access

---

[420] The word interlocutor is defined as a person who takes part in a dialogue or conversation. The primary reason the Holy Spirit is an interlocutor between theology and economics is because the personhood of the Holy Spirit is active revealing to the world how the love of God operates in both our thinking theologically and in the economies of local, national and world functioning. The love of God in Jesus Christ by the power of the Spirit must be present in the social, political, and economic spheres of human and spiritual life. Without the love of God, the interactions between theology and economics are not productive. Put another way, the interactions do not line with the unconditional love and care that God has for all of creation. Scripture teaches not only that the Holy Spirit dwells in us, and with Him Love, but also that He sheds abroad that Love in our hearts. The reason we know that the Holy Spirit is love because the love of the Holy Spirit is in us.

[421] As one of the greatest theologians of the twentieth century, Paul Tillich is a theologian of culture par excellence. In the words of Tillich: Theologically speaking, (Holy) Spirit, love, and grace is the same reality in distinct aspects. (Holy) Spirit is the creative power; love is its creation; grace is the effective presence of love in man. (Amos Yong, *Spirit of Love: A Trinitarian Theology of Grace* (Waco, TX: Baylor University Press, 2012), 79-80. Specifically, Tillich believes that the Holy Spirit is the love of God as founded in the grace of God. Tillich is also a theologian of being in that he defines the Holy Spirit as God present to our spirit, divine concrete spirit, and the Spiritual Presence, regarding the Spirit's role in the Holy Trinity and in correlation to life in God, the spiritual plight of human beings, issues of morality, culture, and religion. See *Tillich's theology of the concrete spirit* from Part I- Standing within the theological circle published by Cambridge University Press on May 28, 2009.

to the soul's most secret chambers, even to the vaults underneath the structure of our being, until finally, either before or in death, the outpouring of His brightness is complete in all our personality, and the whole heart has become His temple."[422] Hence, "with all the depth of His divine Love He sought thee personally. It is Love in the richest, purest, tenderest sense of the word."[423] This otherworldly love of God is inclusive to how we think theologically and how we decide who benefits from the economics of American and world capitalism.

Abraham Kuyper explains the love of the Holy Spirit in three ways:

1. This task is executed only by means of Love. The Holy Spirit allows Himself to be grieved, provoked, and insulted; but He never yields. He is never weary of repeating the same thing to the ear that once was deaf. In our past or present there can be no sin, however base, of which He does not comfort us, which He does not pardon. He gives healing balm for every inward wound. He always has a word in good season for all that are weary. It is Love always filling us with shame; but at the same time ever uplifting, never despairing, unceasing in its devotion.[424]

2. It is not merely a Love for men in general, but in the most exclusive sense a personal Love for the individual; not only Love for the redeemed taken as a multitude, but a Love individual, peculiarly tinted to meet the special peculiarity of our being. It is not only a pity for all who suffer, like that of the nurse for the patients of her ward but love that cannot meet the needs of anyone else but is for me personally just what it must and cannot otherwise be.

3. The Holy Spirit prevails by loving us, by proving His Love, by breathing Love, while, at the same time, His victory carries Love into our hearts. Allow Him to enter your soul, and He will carry Love therein, which imperceptibly imparts itself to your heart and inclination. We yield, not because we are compelled by superior

---

[422] Abraham Kuyper, "The Love of the Holy Spirit in Us," Para. 14.
[423] Ibid., Para. 17.
[424] Ibid., Para. 15.

power, but being drawn by Love, we are so affected that we cannot resist it.[425]

Because human beings are affected by the love of the Spirit and cannot resist it, this does not mean that love alone disappears or goes away. Even those spiritual goods shall disappear with all the material and intellectual goods. They are all fragmentary, temporal, transitory. Love alone does not disappear; it endures forever (Ps. 136; 1 Cor. 13). For God himself is love, according to 1 John 4:8, who carries through the theological thought of Paul. According to Paul Tillich, the Holy Spirit is love. All that the Holy Spirit says, does and writes dispenses the love of God, love of Christ Jesus and the inspirational love of the Holy Spirit. In other words, love is because the Holy Spirit is. God loved the world so much that he gave us Jesus Christ. In giving the world Jesus Christ, we have been the recipient of the ghost and the comforter. Because the Holy Spirit is the Spirit of Christ, it can be argued that God so loved the world that He gave us the Holy Spirit as the ultimate form of love (Jn 3:16).

As the preeminent form of God's love, I am presenting the Holy Spirit as one who is not one-dimensional. Major J. Jones believes that "God's Holy Personhood as Spirit is stable, not intermittent. He is permanently relational, both to the Father and the Son (*ad extra*) and (*ad intra*) or to us human beings, not varying. He is intimately indwelling, not an external force or power like some angel or demon or pagan deity or the *loa* of voodoo."[426] The Holy Spirit in the holiness, relationality, and personableness of God is, as CME Bishop Joseph Johnson put it, "the one and only truth from which all other truth is derived."[427] That is to say, it is revelation; it is primordial to our thinking. It is the entrusting by God of his very self to us as the Spirit of Love and Truth. This is why the saints speak of the love of God within them as their own response to God: Spirit communicating with spirit, and spirit responding.[428] This line of spiritual communicating, interacting, and touching down between the Holy Spirit and the human spirit is what I refer to as culture.

The love of the Holy Spirit helps believers to "fall in love over

[425] Ibid., Para. 18.
[426] Major J. Jones, The Color of God, 112.
[427] Joseph A. Johnson, *Proclamation Theology* (published by the author, 1977), 6-7.
[428] Major J. Jones, *The Color of God*, 112-113.

and over again every day. (To) Love our family, our neighbors, our enemies, and ourselves. And don't stop with humans. (To) Love animals, plants, stones, even the galaxies."[429] The love of the Spirit embodies what it means "to be aroused by life involves the wonderful realization that grace is the place where it all begins and ends. Thirteenth-century mystic Mechtild of Magdeburg gives us a image to contemplate: "The Holy Spirit is our harpest and all strings which are touched in love must sound."[430] In considering the liberating work of the Spirit in the life of the oppressed, the love of God carries with it the formidable element of transformation. To experience the life-changing power of the Holy Spirit is to be transformed in a way that transcends what is going on in our everyday life. Spiritual and material transformation means experiencing and "welcoming the positive changes that are taking place in your life. Open up the windows and let in some fresh air. Wholeness and healing are waiting in the wings."[431] Theologically, wholeness and healing are works of the Holy Spirit.

But there is another consideration in our text which contradicts the words about love. In what Christians consider the love chapter 1 Corinthians 13, the Apostle Paul singles out knowledge, and points to the difference between our fragmentary, indirect, and darkened knowledge, and the full, direct, and total knowledge to come. He compares childish imaginations with the mature insights of the adult. Here, Paul speaks of something which, besides love, is perfect and eternal, namely, the seeing of the truth, face to face; the knowledge which is as full as God's knowledge of us. This confirms our original point that the Holy Spirit knows what is going on in this troubled world because the Spirit knows the mind of God. The primary function of the mind of God is unconditional love for all

(John. 3:16).

Black Theology as Christian Love

James H. Cone and other first-generation constructors intended for Black liberation theology to address the tens of millions of working-class Black people in the United States. Black Americans

---

[429] Frederic Brussat and Mary Ann Brussat, *Spiritual Literacy*, 22.
[430] Ibid., 531.
[431] Ibid., 24.

were living and dying in poverty. Subsequently, the major themes in Black theology are:

1. Liberation
2. Christian Love as action
3. Oppression and the "chosen people"
4. The Black cultural, existential, and religious experiences
5. An awareness of blackness that makes Black theology a worldly theology – one that is to be taught all over the world.

To be sure, Black theology is a Christian theology that is a fully contributing part of the history of Christian experience in the United States and throughout the world. Black theology is also a contextual theology that is to be taken seriously and seen as a liberating work of the Holy Spirit. In this vein of thinking theologically, Christian love, as the love of God and as a form of human action, also represents the work of the Spirit.

Cone's take on Christian love is explained in a couple of theological statements:

> In the New Testament, Christ expressed his love for people as the ultimate act of sacrifice: by dying on the cross and thus ensuring their eternal life. Throughout *Black Theology and Black Power,* James H. Cone reiterates the importance of this reading of Christ's love. Love is not a sentiment or merely a way of feeling; it is what one chooses to do every day. Real Christian love implies an element of risk: it demands all of one's person. In the context of the Black Power struggle, Christian love means joining the fight for the total emancipation of Black Americans. There is no ambiguity about this. In the twentieth century, Christ's fight is the fight for Black freedom.[432]

Love is the core message of Christianity, so it is a pervasive theme throughout Cone's book. While Cone does describe God's love for all people and its liberating power, this kind of love is not his main focus. Instead, Cone wants Christians to

---

[432] Isabel Bartholomew, "Themes," Para. 1.

know that living in Christ means taking direct action—perhaps even joining a violent rebellion, if necessary—in the fight for justice. Love and conflict are not necessarily at odds with each other in this reading; in fact, in the face of oppression, the only response of Christian love is to fight. Fighting for justice is an act of love, and the fight for justice is where Christians should locate Christ today.[433]

Cone references the example of the riots in response to Martin Luther King Jr.'s assassination in 1968:

A wave of uprisings, involving property destruction and looting, spread across the United States. Law enforcement responded violently to protesters. These riots, according to Cone, were a manifestation of Christian love responding to injustice. By refusing to accept conditions of oppression, the Black Power movement manifests Christian love in its actions.[434]

Cone's interpretations are helpful in that they lead younger generations of Black theologians into a fundamental way of defining theology. Theology is God-talk within the category of Christian love and the study of God, Jesus Christ, and the Holy Spirit. Economics is the science of material needs of human beings who want to be accepted and loved. Economics is part the created order and hence, part of God's general revelation (Ps. 19:1-4). Human beings are only able to engage in science of any kind because God intentionally created a universe with economic purpose and natural regularities, we call scientific laws (Gen. 1:1, 14-16, 20-25) In love, Christians therefore, should reject state-controlled economies or centrally controlled economics, which would concentrate the bulk of economic power in the hands of sinful capitalists. Instead, human beings should support an economic system that would equally disperse those economic resources while protecting the innocent from idolatry and exploitation.

As part of a cultural text, I am reminded of a statement from the movie *Black Adam* where Dewayne "The Rock" Johnson says that

---

[433] Ibid., Para. 2.
[434] Ibid., Para. 3.

"People do not need a hero. They need a protector."[435] The Holy Trinity and Black liberation come to mind. My questions are: Who is protecting the Black poor, the white poor, the Mexican poor, and the Indian poor in the United States? Does our elected officials and American capitalism protect those who are poor and financially vulnerable? Would American socialism be a better way? I know that the Bible says that the poor will always be amongst us, but do they have to be? Is it poor people's decision to be poor or it is the systems of control, idolatry and power that decide the economic fate of innocent human beings?

Meanwhile, the conversation of Black theology and economics has been a long time coming for those who struggle to understand God's ordaining of unequal capital. In love, the work of the Holy Spirit helps to nuance the conversation of theology and economics proper in the United States and the world abroad. While we read and study academic scholars in terms of what it means to do good theology in the spheres of economics and money, the world needs a liberating theology Black that talks about how the Holy Spirit loves the poor and cares about their plight. According to what is going on in our impoverished and violent societies, the world has failed to establish a theological vision of love and hope for the poor in our fallen world.

What this means is that the Christian church of the United States and the secular societies of the world has also failed to talk about God and poverty, and what it means to show the love of the Creator God for the poor and the oppressed. While we do not say this publicly with theological consistency, the truth is that God designed love to be experienced when we desperately need it the most. The unique way that God's love works in our lives has less to do with timing and more to do with the Holy Spirit. Somehow, through the work of the Spirit we uniquely experience his love when we need it most desperately. Theologically, the deep poverty of all genders, cultures and races are defined as desperate moments and situations in the life of God's people.

The Work of the Holy Spirit in Love, Hope, and Grace

Romans 5:3-5 tells us that we can rejoice in our sufferings because of what happens as a result. Trials and difficulties produce

---

[435] Jaume Collett-Serra, *Black Adam,* 2022.

perseverance, which in turn develops character, which then gives believers hope. And hope never disappears because the Holy Spirit pours the love of God into our hearts. With the biblical understanding that hope is the work of the Holy Spirit (Rom 5:5), what can be said about the grace of God? The Bible teaches that believers are *saved by grace* through their faith in Jesus Christ

(Eph. 2:8-9). Grace is the work of the Holy Spirit in that grace and the work of the Holy Spirit are one in the same. Here, the work of the Spirit of God is related to the grace of God. Does this mean that the Holy Spirit saves? I would say yes because the work of the Holy Spirit in salvation lines up with the actions of grace in terms it helps believers to walk in the grace of God.

The Holy Spirit helps believers to live daily by the grace of God by the work of the Spirit in us, upon us, and through us (Acts 2:38, 11:15-17; Tit. 3:4-7; Jn. 6:63, 20:21-22; Gal. 3:14; 1 Jn. 3:24). But what does the Holy Spirit have to do with grace? The Holy Spirit gives the believer myriad types of grace. The Spirit gives sanctifying grace as a way of giving life, sacramental grace to help us grow spiritually, and grace helps us to deal with everyday situations. The Holy Spirit also gives grace to the mind, body, and soul in a variety of other spiritual virtues.

2 Corinthians 13:14 says "May the grace of the Lord Jesus Christ, and the love of God, and the fellowship of the Holy Spirit be with you all." The Apostle Paul includes grace, love, and the fellowship of the Holy Spirit in one collaborative theological statement. When I use the word theological, I am implying the word Trinitarian or the Holy Trinity of God. I am certain that grace, love and fellowship is present in both the singular works of Triune God and the collaborative work of the Trinity. Paul says in 2 Corinthians 8:9: "For you know the grace of our Lord Jesus Christ, that though he was rich, yet for your sake he became poor, so that you through his poverty might become rich." Now Paul describes how contributing to this gift is Christlike. Jesus was rich and secure in the glory of heaven. He willingly became poor when He became a man, entering into the world of suffering and death in the flow of time on earth. He did this in order to die for the sins of humanity so that all who trust in Him can be forgiven of their sin and one day experience the wealth and

security of living in glory with God.[436] I often time hear scholars and armchair theologians claim that God takes in the poverty of poor people for the purpose of promising them something better in their later lives or when they get to Heaven. Does this mean that poverty has a spiritual dimension designed to benefit the oppressed? Or is Paul saying that Jesus simply demonstrates God's grace by willingly becoming poor so the Corinthian Christians could become rich forever? According to biblical scholars, the Corinthians had an opportunity to perform an act of grace themselves that would follow the example of Jesus' own sacrifice. But what does this supposed act of God have to do with the love of the Holy Spirit?

The point is that the Spirit, full of God's love, comes into the human heart, and the heart is meant to surrender to the Spirit's will and is influenced by the Spirit's nature. The Holy Spirit is the producer of love. "The point is that the Spirit, full of God's love, comes in the human heart, and the heart is meant to surrender to the Spirit's will and be influenced by God's nature."[437] As the combined love of God and the Holy Spirit, Christ's love compels us (2 Cor 5:14) to be more and more like Christ. Being a Christian means that "Life on the love train isn't about trying hard. It isn't about religious activity or attempts at moral reform. It's about being connected with and surrendered to God's Spirit getting into God's Word and living in God's community."[438] Miroslav Volf confirms that Martin Luther's famous little treatise *The Freedom of the Christian* reaches its peak when he concludes, "a Christian lives not in himself, but in Christ and in his neighbor. Otherwise, he or she is not a Christian. He or she lives in Christ through faith, in his neighbor through love. By faith he or she is caught up beyond himself/herself into God. By love he or she descends beneath himself or herself into his or her neighbor. Yet he remains in God and in his love."[439]

According to Volf, "Luther's salvific point is not that what people do does not matter; it matters profoundly—to God, to their neighbors, to themselves. Yet nothing they do changes the fact that God loves them and, if they trust in God, will remake them into new creatures,

---

[436] "What does 2 Corinthians 8:9 mean?," Para. 2.
[437] Chip Ingram, *Spiritual Simplicity*, 150.
[438] Ibid., 168.
[439] Martin Luther, *The Freedom of a Christian*, in vol. 31 of *Luther's Works*, 371.

freed from guilt and capable of loving others."[440] Meanwhile, God's love for the poor and us, indeed God's presence in us and our being "caught up beyond" ourselves and being placed "into God" most fundamentally defines us as human beings and as individuals.[441] The word that comes to mind is relationships. God desires for God's people to have loving relationships with their neighbors. Relationships are assignments. They are part of a vast plan for our enlightenment, the Holy Spirit's blueprint by which each individual soul is led to greater awareness and expanded love. Relationships are the Holy Spirit's laboratories in which He brings together people who have the maximal opportunity for mutual growth.[442]

LUCRETIUS (99-55 BCE)

Love is a product of habit. *De rerum natura*

VIRGIL (70-19 BCE)

Love conquers all: and let us too, surrender to love. *Eclogues*

OVID (43 BCE-17 CE)

Love's conqueror is he or she whom love conquers. *The Walled Garden of Truth*

Love is a kind of warfare. *Ars amatoria*

Hatred stirs up strife, but love covers all offenses.

Proverbs 10:12, RSV

Thy shalt love thy neighbor as thyself.

Leviticus 19:18

I may have all knowledge and understand all secrets; I may have all the faith needed to move mountains—but if I have no love, I am nothing.

1 Corinthians, 13, ii

Be kindly affectioned one to another with brotherly: in honor preferring one another.

Romans 10:12[443]

Another way of stating the theological obvious is that God in Jesus

---

[440] Miroslav Volf, *The End of Memory*, 198.

[441] Ibid., 199.

[442] Marianne Williamson, *A Return to Love*, 417.

[443] Frederic Brussat and Mary Ann Brussat, *Spiritual Literacy*, 238.

Christ by the power of the Holy Spirit has love and compassion for the poor. In the same way, God calls human beings in creation to reflect God's love and compassion. The Holy Spirit also works in us through the word of God. The Holy Spirit uses the power of Scripture to convict us, convince us and influence our way of thinking. The Holy Spirit does this to shape human beings into a more godly and spiritual people.

2 Timothy 3:16-17 summarizes that all Scripture comes from the inspiration of God and is useful to teach us what is true and to make us realize what is wrong in our lives. It corrects us when we are wrong and teaches us to do what is right. God uses it to prepare and equip his people to do every excellent work. God's greatest intention of human beings doing good ministry work is that of love. Euripides (496? - 406? BCE) says that "Love is all we have, the only way that each can help the other."[444] Love given by the Holy Spirit flourishes when we have the heart to love others the way Jesus would. In viewing love as a form of liberation, theology Black is a theology of liberating love for all races, groups, and cultures of oppressed people.

As the Holy Spirit works in the lives of Christians who are rich, middle to upper class, and poor, the work itself has one common goal: to make all human beings more like Jesus Christ. The Holy Spirit works in believers by renewing our minds to be like the mind of Christ. The Holy Spirit does this by convicting us of sin and leading us to repentance. Through repentance, the Holy Spirit wipes out what was dirty in us and allows us to bear good fruit. As we allow him to continue nourishing that fruit, we grow to resemble Jesus more. "But the fruit of the Spirit is love, joy, peace, patience, kindness, goodness, faithfulness, gentleness, self-control; against such things there is no law" (Gal. 5:22-23). In embracing love as a theological category, it is understood that poverty affects those we love. God in Jesus Christ by the power of the Holy Spirit loves the poor and the poor in spirit of all genders, cultures, and races. God showed his love in the most glorious way by sending his only begotten Son (Jn. 3:16), who became poor that we might become rich (2 Cor. 8-9).

And have we not witnessed the wealth of Jesus' presence in the eyes of those most poor by this world's measure? I have seen celestial

---

[444] *Orestes*, (408 BC) Greek tragic dramatist (484 BC - 406 BC)

light from the open tomb dancing like dappled light through dense forests of human suffering. Or who has not seen the vacant visage of sin-starving destitution in the eyes of the affluent; a wealthy figure staggering towards the grave under the immense weight of spiritual starvation?[445] One major message to the poor and the oppressed is that: Of these three: faith, love and hope, love is the greatest

(1 Cor. 13:13). God in Jesus Christ by the power of Spirit is love. Put another way, God loves the poor. And when I say that the U.S. economy has never been good for Black people, I am really saying that Black Americans have never felt loved and accepted by the white capitalistic counterpart, appreciated for the infrastructural contributions in developing the national and world economies and accepted as full-fledge human beings living on American soil.

In the poignant words of the famed singer Celine Dion, "Where is the love? That lets the sunlight in to start again. A love that sees no color lines. Life that begins with love. So spread your wings and fly. Guide your spirit safe and sheltered. A thousand dreams that we can still believe"[446] Another way of asking this critical question of huge theological proportion is in the absence of love, what is going on in the world today and why is there so much evil, hate, oppression, and suffering amongst humanity? What's going on in society that is disallowing people to love one another? Where is the biblical/spiritual love that makes people love others the way God loves them (Mk 12:29-31)?

By way of responding to the duo of questions, I am in solidarity with Thomas C. Oden when he affirms that "The Holy Spirit is incrementally teaching the faithful, to the extent that they voluntarily become able to read Scripture closely with their hearts shaped by the rule of faith and charity."[447] This illuminative teaching of the Holy Spirit is one that embodies the love of God in Jesus Christ for the purpose of demonstrating the liberating nature of unconditional love. The liberating love of God given to humanity constitutes a spiritual directive of charity. The rule of charity is the consequent life of the believer that communicates the love of God through the love of the

---

[445] Michael A. Milton, "What Does the Bible Say about Poverty?" Para. 13.

[446] Celene Dion, *Where is the Love? Let's Talk About Love*. 1997.

[447] Thomas C. Oden, *How Africa Shaped the Christian Mind*, 128.

neighbor by acts of mercy, generosity and gentleness.[448]

The Economic Conversation in Liberation Theology and Theology Black

When Black theologians think of economics, they usually think of the one-sided exchange of goods, products, services, and money. As inspired by the Holy Spirit, they should also think about what poverty looks like and feels like in the Black neighborhoods and communities of the United States, Africa, Brazil, Britain, and other parts of the world. The goal of this type of economics is personal enrichment instead of basic quality of life. There is spiritual economics as well which is the exchange of energy to enhance the potential for human creativity in context of community. Its goal is the empowerment of the physical community and development of humanity.

> Both economics, exchanged and spiritual, seek to create a condition of abundance, but the nature of that condition – even the definition of abundance itself – is different for each. In an economy of material goods, abundance is a quantitative idea: we have abundance if all our needs can be met, and we have a surplus left over. The extent of our abundance can be determined by evaluating or counting that surplus. In the economy of Spirit, abundance is a qualitative image: we have it when we have no obstructions within us to the presence of God and to the empowering and creative flow of life. Physical abundance may come through hoarding and accumulation; spiritual abundance comes through utilization and giving away.[449]

Theologically, "These two economies are sometimes seen in opposition to each other: to be spiritually rich, for example, one should embrace material poverty, or, on the other hand, to accumulate wealth one may need to compromise certain spiritual ideals and "live in the real world." However, in the development of a sustainable planetary culture, these two economies need to be seen as complimentary."[450] The economics of an exchanged (physical) life is

---

[448] Ibid.
[449] David Spangler, "The Economics of Spirit," Para. 3.
[450] Ibid., Para. 4.

based on the fundamental need of all organisms to survive and to grow, both as individuals and as a species.

Growth itself may be seen as having two aspects: the growth necessary to achieve a certain basic level of functioning required by survival itself and the growth that unfolds and fulfills the deeper potentials of the organism and leads to breakthroughs of behavior and possibilities. To spirit, which is eternal, survival is not an issue, but growth is. The function of life exists as a way of creating the conditions that allow life to unfold and express with even greater power and fulfillment – in a phrase, to manifest God more fully.

Thus Jesus said "I come that you may have more abundant life." This again is an issue of empowerment when it comes to demonstrating the love of God in Jesus Christ by the power of the Holy Spirit to the economically poor. Here there is no preferential option for the poor. The only option for a sizable number of the Black poor (and all other poor people as well) in the United States is to live in abject and deep poverty. Poverty of any kind that is present in any culture and race of people is not the work of the Holy Spirit. Living and dying in poverty is not God's intention for God's creation (Jn. 10:10).

In Latin American liberation theology, God takes sides with the poor against the rich in poor people's theological perspective. Latin Americans' faith in God, Jesus Christ, and the Holy Spirit according to the Bible, becomes their main source of physical and spiritual strength. Black theology, on the other hand, does not depict God as taking sides per se, but rather God liberates both the poor and the rich. Black theology in Africa, the main concern is their opposition to racism and liberation from apartheid, while African theology developed in the wider continent where the main concern was indigenization of the Christian message. Placed up against the doctrinal backdrop of the various liberation theologies, theology Black affirms the liberating work of the Holy Spirit. The Holy Spirit is the Spirit of blackness in that this Black person of color helps Black people of color to know the importance of cultural excellence, self-awareness and self-love.

Blackness of the Spirit is a distinct characteristic of theology Black whereby the Holy Spirit liberates Black people (and other groups, races, and cultures of people too) from the internalization of oppression proper and takes them to a higher place of where they can see that God created them for a good purpose. By faith, the Spirit of blackness gives hope to the hopeless and helps Black people to see how color, as the absence of purity, aiding them in connecting and identifying with the Blackness and color of the Holy Spirit. In affirming a blackness that symbolically references skin color and oppression than can be applied to all persons of color who have a history of oppression, I believe that theology Black as a form of Black theology begins with "life experiences" of economic oppression and contextually formulates theology in thereof."[451]

By way of hoping to describe a type of interaction between the Holy Spirit and Black folk in all realms and spheres, theology Black describes the narrative of the Holy Spirit working hard for the liberation of the oppressed. If anyone knows what is going on in this troubled and fallen world, it would be the Holy Spirit. This is because the Holy Spirit knows the mind of God. Theology Black is a liberation theology that touches down into the lived experiences of Black people all over the world. I harken back to the words of one of my greatest teachers and mentors Dwight N. Hopkins: "Jesus says my mission is to eradicate poverty and to bring about freedom and liberation for the oppressed, and most Christian pastors in America skip over that part of the book."[452] Put another way, Jesus' mission of eradicating poverty and bring about freedom and liberation for the oppressed were acts of unconditional love and supreme emancipation. When discussing the resourceful collaboration between theology and economics, the first word that should come to mind is love. The unconditional love of God in Jesus Christ by the power of the Holy Spirit is the true interlocutor between theology and economics.

A Theological Framing for the Black Church and the Economically Poor

The Presiding Prelate of Second Episcopal District of the Christian Methodist Episcopal Church Bishop Denise Anders-Modest says that

Every church should have a working theology of the Holy

---

[451] James H. Cone, *A Black Theology Liberation*, 18.
[452] Barbara B. Hagerty, "Closer Look Black Liberation," Para. 4.

Spirit. The CME Church or any church for that matter cannot be the church that God intends without the Holy Spirit operating with a guiding vision. For the church to be the church, the Holy Spirit operating and working in the inner confines of what the church believes. As members of the body of Christ, we must know without a doubt what the Spirit is saying in this contemporary age of Christendom. I need the Holy Spirit. We all need the Holy Spirit. The church cannot make it without the Holy Ghost.[453]

There is a fine line between the church having a working theology of the Holy Spirit and the church doing what the Holy Spirit tells them to do for the good of the people. These are not distinct realities. Here, it is my fervent prayer that the Black church recognizes how the Holy Spirit works in the collaborative relationship between theology and economics. In consideration of the theological framing at the beginning of Chapter 3, and what we have presented at the beginning of this chapter, it is now appropriate to introduce important works on the broader study of theology and economics. By way of faith, it must be assumed that the Holy Spirit has inspired the Black Church and economists to think about and write about the connecting vision between liberation theology and economics. The reader will be able to describe key historical events and circumstances that have contributed to the need for a modern, theological analysis of the economy. With the liberating work of the Holy Spirit as the main conversation, this chapter analyzes various theological and philosophical approaches to the economy with critiques of the market and the institutional church.

I am an ordained pastor of twenty-two years in the Christian Methodist Episcopal Church tradition. My experiences with pastoring economically poor churches have helped to inform me on the metaphysical relationship between pneumatology and economics. I am certain that the Holy Spirit plays a significant role in how the church does theology and economics effectively for the purposes of liberation and ministry. And in terms of reflecting theologically on the lack of economics in the Black community, context plays a leading

---

[453] Bishop Denise Anders-Modest, The 2023 Bishop's Mid-Winter Conference in Paducah, Kentucky at the Saint James CME Church.

role. But further, the various economic nuances of the Black church serve as a circumstantial microcosm of the larger economic situation in the Black community. Economically, there is a historical reason white mainline churches look differently in landscape, building size, texture, and scope. The white church's financial status in giving and raising funds for the purpose of building their local economies is more stable that than of the Black church.

Regarding the Black church's role in ministering to the poor and helping to figure out strategies to help alleviate poverty, Wylin D. Wilson makes an important statement about poverty as an economic context, theology, and justice fifty years after the War on Poverty:

Conversations about poverty in America can be heated. Individuals who want to point to poverty amelioration by both governmental and civil society argue that not only are Americans among the most prosperous people in the world but that even the most impoverished Americans are still better off than impoverished in developing countries. However, individuals who call attention to poverty's structural causes are not swayed by this argument that America's poor are somehow "better off."[454]

Speaking as a theologian of color, I find it difficult to understand how poor people of any racial, cultural, or geographical context can be better off than other poor groups of people who do not reside in the same location. Poverty of any kind amongst people of any race, culture and status represents a theological problem. Poverty defines the condition of human beings who are economically and materially poor. People all over the world live and die in poverty. The reason discussions on poverty are heated is because the conversations have become taboo. Nobody wants to be poor and live in poverty, whether they reside in an urban city or a rural town. Answering the question of what is going on with rural and urban poverty, Wilson says that "Americans has been battling these regional poverty trends for decades now. We are fifty years removed from President Lyndon B. Johnson's declaration of "Unconditional War" on Poverty and unemployment in the United States."[455]

---

[454] Wylin D. Wilson, *Economic Ethics and the Black Church*, 2.
[455] Ibid.

Speaking on the Christian church's responsibility to the poor, Wilson says that

The voices of the most economically vulnerable members of society are often absent or ignored" by the Christian church. The persons that set the agendas, those who have the power to shape our social lives together, do not seem to value the contributions, experiences, and opinions of the poor for those agendas. It seems as if when society sees the poor, it is seeing the surface, shrouded by prejudices. Or does anyone see beyond the surface, which results in real engagement in the lives of impoverished individuals? Does anyone listen to the stories, of "the least of these"? Not only does society seem not to *really* see or hear, but the actual praxis of religious institutions often likewise turns a deaf ear and blind eye to economically vulnerable individuals. Is the proclaimed acuity of seeing the poor driving churches to do justice? Even though there are biblical and theological injunctions to care for the poor members of society, do churches' interpretations of these injunctions result in the actual deeds of justice?[456]

My answer to this all-important question is no. The church's interpretation of these economic concerns does result in actual deeds. But the deeds themselves do not result in justice being done at any level in the life of those families who live in economic/material poverty. Even though "the Church broadly and the Black Church specifically have a wide spectrum of theological and normative perspectives and attitudes towards the poor and the "underclass" in urban and rural persistently impoverished communities in America,[457] these perspectives and attitudes have not produced nearly enough of what is needed, ministry and resource-wise, to help alleviate and decrease the number of people who are poverty-stricken. If the goal of the Black church is not liberation, then what is it? If they are not actively participating in helping Black people to deal with their economic deprivations and human oppressions, then from what local church perspective are they doing effective ministry from?

Does reading economics or having a working knowledge of

---

[456] Ibid. 5-6.
[457] Ibid. 6.

Black economic issues make leaders of the Black church more effective theologians? Not that the goal of being a great pastor of the Black church is that of being a theologian, but my question is: Could one's ability to read and understand economics be a gift of the Holy Spirit? It certainly supplies a hermeneutical lens that helps Black church leaders to discern the economic signs of the times in terms of understanding what is going on in the church and society. One could argue that reading and understanding economics helps ministers to critically analyze the global contexts of ministry and mission. It has been proven that reading economics also helps us in the critical areas of evangelism and stewardship.

Because we live in a globalized world clouded with various outreaches of gentrification, the study of economics cannot be rationalized as one that is only meant for trained economists. Whether we view globalization[458] as cultural, technological, political, social, environmental, or purely economic, the truth remains that Black Americans are living in harsh economic times. Their relatives, fellow church members and their close friends are employed to a degree and still living a low quality of life. That is to say that almost any issue of Black sociopolitical relevance has financial or economic dimension attached to it.

Most theologians and ethicists do not know that economics is about the allocation of scarce resources, not just "money" or time, food, transportation, or ways of communicating power and privilege. As a science, economics teaches us that we can never have an infinite amount of material resources. Even as free market capitalism aids the rich in getting richer and ensures that the poverty-stricken remains poor, the conversation of theology and economics remains taboo in sacred institutions and secular environments. For a multitude of reasons and in diverse ways, one could argue that reading economics can, in fact, make us better theologians. But without the unconditional love of the Holy Spirit leading and guiding theologians and economists, the collaboration would be more capitalistic than

---

[458] When I use the word globalization, I am referring to economic globalization. Here, I am affirming that the theory and praxis of economic globalization can both inspire economic growth in Black and brown inner-city neighborhoods and communities and help to reduce the number of Americans that live in poverty. All of whom, in some way, form, or fashion, have probably felt the power of the Holy Spirit in their lives.

theological. In other words, the interactions would do more harm than good.

If theologians and religious leaders do not have an elementary background in economics, how are we able to discuss the critical issues that are related to economics? I believe that having a working knowledge of economics is important for moral engagement with such issues as poverty, homelessness, and hunger. It should not take a rocket scientist to figure out that economics is, or should be, about people. Not one group of people, but groups, races, and cultures of people. Theologians and religious leaders alike often talk about or discuss moral issues without even mentioning the economic underpinnings to carefully consider the context of the issues. As human beings who know it takes money to survive from one week to the next, we also do not see that there are multiple forms of capital—ideas, human capital; as well as finance, technology, globalization, and other material things. Growing up in the South as a man of African American descent, I especially know what it means to suffer inhumanely at the hands of late capitalism and still be expected to live the life of a decent wage-earning, human being.

Theologically, our hope is that through the work of the Holy Spirit, the God of Black liberation will bring justice to an imbalanced economy and set the economic order as it should be following creation whereby God equally created human beings in God's image. The forthcoming Reign of God will show that the only real theology is the person and deity of Jesus Christ as founded in the liberating work of the Holy Spirit. I believe God will eventually show the entire world that the economy belongs to God anyway. If the earth is the Lord's and the fullness thereof (Ps. 24:1), then the local and world economies belong to God as well.

Michael Novak

The second level of Michael Novak's philosophy of theological economics is committed to sorting out the necessary concepts. The necessary concepts are defined as economic concepts. According to Novak, the basic disciplines of the philosophy of theological economics are: 1. The study of basic economic concepts; 2. The study of comparative economic systems; 3. The study of particular problems within economic systems. To better explain his philosophy, Novak states that

To conduct such inquiries, a broad range of considerations forces the inquirer to stretch his or her mind to reach a high degree of philosophical clarity with thirty or forty concepts that may not at first be clear in his/her head. These concepts are the varying sweep and breadth, and the draw upon different disciplines for their clarification. Simply to set them in an outline is to suggest the breadth and depth that an adequate philosophy of economics must reach. In digging deeper into more fundamental questions, the inquirer will certainly need to be clear what he or she means by such basic terms as time, family, individual, insight, happiness, equality of opportunity, political liberty, objections against socialism, and error.[459]

Because Novak shares with Max Weber a doctrine of unintended consequences whereby he believes that "we are all capitalist now,"[460] D. Stephen Long states that

Novak's use of Weber, coupled with his strategy for theology's relevance, results in an irresolvable contradiction. On the one hand we are told that capitalism needs theology because of the anthropology it provides, where the person is free to act based on his or her choices. And on the other hand, we are told that we have no choice. We are all now capitalists. At the point in his argument, Novak's 'spirit' contradicts itself, and we discover that the 'new complex of social attitudes and habits' Weber identified cannot be so easily appropriated for theological purposes.[461]

In other words, there are some economic issues within the capitalistic system that cannot be appropriated theologically or by a move of God's Spirit. Long believes that people make the choices and do the things they do because they are self-willed and not God led.

Kathryn Tanner

In her splendid text, *Economy of Grace*, Kathryn Tanner creatively deals with and processes the subjective question of what Christianity has to do with economics. More like D. Stephen Long's *Divine Economy* than M. Douglass Meeks' *Economy of God*,

---

[459] Ibid., 82.
[460] D. Stephen Long, *Divine Economy*, 14.
[461] Ibid., 15.

Tanner views the economy theologically by referencing foundational themes developed in earlier works (*Jesus, Humanity, and the Trinity*, 2001, and *Theories of Culture*, 1997). Her understanding of God as unconditional gift giver (lover of creation), existing in what she terms as noncompetitive and mutually beneficial relations, presupposes that God Almighty has the power to impact both our present cultural values and the way view economics in present day society. Tanner argues that this view of God as economist must be set in dialogue with the sometimes-corrupt global capitalism for our communal understanding of market intervention, property rights, usury, scarcity, and exchange practices to be transformed by the work of the Holy Spirit.

Almost dreaming of alternatives to the present economic system, Tanner critically analyzes the seldom used values of God's Kingdom from the premise that the very nature of God has holistic implications to bear on economic arrangements for our current socio-economic and political orders. In other words, the economy does not belong to our economists; nor does the economy belong to the people who either profit or suffer from its activity, but rather the economy belongs to God for God's reasons and God's rationale. With this 'God the economist' philosophy, Tanner introduces the concept of theology and economics as a biproduct of what she terms as a "general economy."[462] One of the more striking views of Tanner's theological economics is her declaration that money means grace and grace means money. For Tanner, money and grace are formally related with one another because they both are gifts from God (unmerited favor). What is so amazing about Tanner's theological view of money as grace is that she can unpack and appropriate her position amidst depressive economic activity (lack of money and financial resources in each society). She believes and understands that capitalism is deeply flawed and sinful. In other words, Tanner's hope for economic change is that of reforming the system instead of trying to overthrow what has done so much harm. It seems like she believes that God's grace is sufficient only for the workers of capitalism. I could be wrong.

The second part of the book gives credence to Tanner's unique ability to imagine practical alternatives to the present economic

---

[462] Kathryn Tanner, *Economy of Grace*, 18.

system. In her own respective, yet progressive way, Tanner explores alternatives to the prevailing logic of the market economy by noting that "such economies are problematically marked by the obligation to give and receive and by competition for status through conspicuous destruction"[463] In other words, political covenants and corporate alliances (local and national economic structures) have made it very difficult for the economy to function in a way that lends itself to a more universal distribution of funds. In response to this problem, Tanner attempts use theology (her view of God) to purify gift exchange by pointing out that the over functioning of a capitalistic economy can have psychological effects on those who need money, jobs, and other means of financial resources. Tanner's idea of a theological economy is a philosophy that is centered on the concept of gift.

Philosophically, Tanner believes that both gift-based reciprocity and John Locke's common right theory of possessing (private) property is deficient in the areas of distribution (capitalistic/money exchange) and exclusive poverty. Tanner finds while the rich continue to get richer, the poor continue to blindly be the victim of capitalism— lacking financial resources, land and property, credit, job opportunities, and inherited gifts. Tanner faintly converses with John Calvin while reemphasizing central themes in her doctrine of God. Her gift-based view of theological economics consistently stands in opposition of various critiques of capitalism offered by Locke and other economic theorists.

Lastly, Tanner constructively puts a theological economy to work by confessing that the challenging part of the task is to figure out a philosophical method that will create economic interdependence (amongst all people) and foster welfare and unconditional gift giving within the community. While I do not believe that Tanner is calling for a radical and revolutionary redistribution of economic wealth, I do recognize her methodology in terms of how she uses capitalism against itself. In focusing on the communal use of goods and possession within any given economy, Tanner believes that the will for change must come from Christian church. In other words, she calls for the church to be actively involved in both governmental and

---

[463] Ibid., 21.

non-governmental organizations. Tanner believes that the work of the Holy Spirit includes the church being actively involved in the whole of society.

In this vein of thinking theologically, I agree with Kent Van Til when he states that "The search for grace is noncompetitive, for wealth, competitive. Grace is distributed by God regardless of our status."[464] According to Tanner, "The whole Christian story, from top to bottom, can be viewed as an account of the production of value and the distribution of goods, following this peculiar noncompetitive shape."[465] Van Til's statement reminds me of the infamous scene in Second Corinthians where three times God refuses to remove the thorn (the sinful humanity that must lend itself to a greater dependence upon the grace of God) from the flesh of the Apostle Paul.

Making Good Theological Connections

What I am finding is that God's grace is not only sufficient to us as human beings, but it is also sufficient in terms of money and economic resources. I believe that the economists must learn how to be more obedient to the Word of God while subscribing to a more balanced distribution of goods. A more balanced distribution of goods is a real characteristic of God's economy meeting the needs of the poor. When the needs of the poor go unmet, families and individuals experience crucifixion in the economic deprivations of their human lives.

In theologizing the unconditional love of the Holy Spirit through the work done in uplifting God's creation, there is even more that could be said about the love of God as the interlocutor between theology and economics. Lying at the core of Black folks' biblical faith, the Holy Spirit spoke to me through the crucifixion and resurrection of Jesus Christ. Even as the Triune God has defeated the evil of late capitalism and racial discrimination through the resurrecting of the body of Jesus Christ, Black Americans still suffer holistically at the hands of economic poverty. Theologically, the human realities of suffering imply the absence of God's love as demonstrated by God's people. Human suffering is created by the

---

[464] Kent Van Til, "Christian Social Thought" Para. 2, p. 352.
[465] Kathryn Tanner, *Economy of Grace*, 27.

practice of capitalism which leads to the depravity of economic resources in America's Black neighborhoods and communities.

Out of a theological concern for the economic condition of Black Americans, James Cone poses that "men were not created for separations and color is not the essence of a person's humanity."[466]

Cone views God's Creation as a gift—a spiritual deepness that resides on the inside of people to live life to the fullest. That is to say that God is power to the powerless and hope to the hopeless. According to Cone, the experiential realities of being Black and poor means having no place for recreation. The reason so many people correlate being poor with being Black is because the Black race in the United States has the largest percentage of people who are living in poverty. God created us Black people as a way of preserving the integrity of God's creative power. In other words, God created human beings for a specific purpose under heaven and that purpose exists within the will of an all-knowing God. This is the purpose is life itself. God created human beings as a way of giving His creation the gift of life as a means of grace. Here, I say again that grace is the work of the Holy Spirit.

If Kathryn Tanner's argument is correct, then what are her theological assessments of the economic deprivation found in Black and brown communities? Does a community deprived of money, employment opportunity and economic resources imply a community deprived of God? Does Tanner believe that the world's economics belong to God? If so, then why are there so many poor Black folk in the inner-city neighborhoods? As full-fledged human beings, are Black people not worthy of receiving the same amount of God's grace, in the form of money, as other races and cultures of people? What is going on with theology and economics in the United States? In Marvin Gaye's prophetic ballad, "What's Going On," he says "You know we've got to find a way. To bring some loving here today oh ohhh."[467] The love that Gaye is referring to begins and ends with the liberating work of the Holy Spirit in the life of all groups, races, and cultures of oppressed people.

M. Douglas Meeks

---

[466] James H. Cone, *Black Theology, Black Power*, 17.
[467] Marvin Gaye, "What's Going On," *What's Going On*. 1971.

In his postmodern text, *God the Economist: The Doctrine of God and Political Economy,* M. Douglas Meeks teaches that "Economy means literally "the law or the management of the household. The term household includes the production, distribution, and consumption of the necessities of life. When we use the word household, we do not mean the modern notion of a family unit, but rather the site of the economy; of human livelihood ...we will refer to whole economics as a household."[468] In taking into great consideration the mission of the church of Jesus Christ, Meeks concludes that if the church is to be concerned with the poor, works of charity and spiritual unity within the Body of Christ will help us engage the problems that need the most theological attention. D.

Stephen Long's *Divine Economy: Theology and the Market* claims states that Meeks "assumes that the doctrine of the Trinity provides adequate resources for a theological economics."[469] In other words, Meeks' philosophy of theological economics is rooted what the Bible says about the Triune God (the existence of God the Father, God the Son, and God the Holy Spirit all within the same Godhead). Meeks' astute philosophy asserts that there is a connection between the Triune God and the problems human beings face in their everyday, economic life.

As a Master of Divinity student at the Louisville Presbyterian Theological Seminary (2006-2009), I recall having phone conversations with Meeks regarding the American economy within the conversations of theology and economics. I would call his office in Nashville, Tennessee and share with him the conversation of theology and economics. Upon asking me about the theological direction of my work, he would always tell me that the Holy Trinity will provide resources for all of God's people. Because all people are residents of God's house and God's economy, God has made resourceful provision for all his people. Meeks would also share with me that there is more work to be done in the collaborative areas of theology and economics. Meeks states that

> Several clusters of problems will appear prominently in our juxtaposition of God and economy. They involve implications

---

[468] M. Douglas Meeks, *God the Economist,* 3.
[469] D. Stephen Long, *Divine Economy,* 30.

of setting a critical view of the Triune God over against God concepts that are still influencing basic economic assumptions in our society. The doctrine of the Trinity is the Christian way of demythologizing God concepts that stress utopian and ideological uses of economic assumptions. Trinitarian views of God's freedom and power will be set over against claims made about liberty and justice in the modern market society assumptions about property, work, and consumption.[470]

For Meeks, simple things such as working for a living wage in our cities appropriates a justice response—a response that communicates God's biblical justice operating in a society where the gap between the rich and the poor is increasing on all economic levels. Meeks is attempting to communicate that God the economist is inspiring us through Scripture to reconceptualize God and economy through our faith and action in God's economy and the church. He states that "the Holy Spirit can be understood only through the cross, which is the center of the Christian proclamation."[471] In other words, because of the work of the Triune God on the cross, "the work of the Holy Spirit symbolizes our access to God's economy."[472] Meeks goes on to write that "The Holy Spirit is God working economically so that God's creatures and the whole creation may live and live abundantly.

This is the reason the Holy Spirit identifies with God's righteousness, which appears paradigmatically in God's raising of Jesus from the dead (Romans 1:4) and is called the "spirit that gives life" (1Corinthians 15:45). God the Holy Spirit makes present God's righteousness, which is God's power for life against death."[473] Through this immensely powerful statement, Meeks is affirming that once the church catches hold of God's vision of economy, then and only then can we more effectively address the market logic of our present economy. Then and only then can we try to strategically participate in the struggle for more jobs, better wages, and higher salaries. A key part of Meeks' theology of economics focuses on the works of the Holy Spirit. I agree with Shirley Guthrie when he posits that "The Holy Spirit is the presence and work of the living God here and now

---

470 M. Douglas Meeks, *God the Economist*, 9.
471 Ibid., 170.
472 Ibid.
473 Ibid., 171.

in our individual lives, in the church, and in the world."[474]

Now that we have set up a theological foundation for identifying the works of the Holy Spirit, the question is: How do the works of the Holy Spirit demonstrate or lead human beings to presumptions that lend itself to a particular way of understanding economics? One way to answer this question is through the economic reality of scarcity. People often think economics means studying supply and demand, the stock market, money, and banking. In fact, there are many ways one could define economics, but economists accept the definition given here because it includes the link between *scarcity* and *choices*.[475] This point is pivotal to the theologians' understanding of scarcity because when addressing the question of what to produce, "the problem of scarcity imposes a restriction on the ability to produce everything we want during a given period, so the choice to produce "more" of a good requires producing "less" of another good."[476]

After deciding which products to make, the second question for society to decide is how to mix technology and scarce resources in order to produce these goods.[477] In doing so Irving Tucker declares that "education plays an important role in answering the How question. Education improves the ability of workers to perform their work. Because the quality and quantity of education vary among nations, this is one reason economies differ in their capacity to apply resources and technology to answer the How question."[478] Once the What and Whom questions resolve, the third question is For Whom. The For Whom question means that society must have a method to decide who will be "rich and famous" and who will be "poor and unknown." In other words, more needs to be said about income distribution and poverty.[479] The *What, How* and *For Whom* questions of economic scarcity leads to theory.

Even though economic theory is unchristian because we cannot theorize the power of the Holy Spirit, Meeks posits that "Theory is critical to the extent that it explicates its foundation not in terms of

---

[474] Shirley C. Guthrie, *Christian Doctrine*, 292.
[475] Irvin B. Tucker, *Survey of Economics*, 6.
[476] Ibid., 30.
[477] Ibid.
[478] Ibid.
[479] Ibid.

axioms, principles, ideal types, social analyses and so on, but in transformative praxis. The difference in this method is that it begins with the intent of conversion and is controlled by this intent. The norm of theology is given in conversion through the power of the Holy Spirit.[480] Meeks adds that "To speak of the truth of faith one must speak of how faith transforms human action. Transformation lived out in praxis is the condition for understanding to take place."[481] To be theologically correct, transformation is the work of the Holy Spirit.

In identifying the role of the Holy Spirit and helping those called to this new field of study (theology and economics), Meeks states that "On the basis of these premises and their partial realization God sends disciples or economists into the world. Those who hear and respond find the beginning of their redemption by entering into God's economic work for the creation. They are made by just by God's grace and are thus relieved of the compulsion to produce their salvation through their own work. They are sanctified and empowered by God the Holy Spirit to enter into God's economic work of distributing the gifts of life, a work for which they would not be prepared in any other way."[482] In his own subtle way, Meeks draws near to the thesis question of how the works of the Holy Spirit and scarcity can be used as a way of understanding economics. He shares that

> The question of economics, Will everyone in the household get what it takes to live? Is referenced not to scarcity but to the righteousness of God which makes possible the sharing of the household's store? In any case the work of God which makes possible the sharing of the household's store. In any case the work of God the Holy Spirit is to subvert any *oikonomia* based on scarcity. The reason for this is that scarcity as a starting point will always produce an *oikos* in which some are excluded from the means of life.[483]

Meeks is saying that one way of understanding the relationship between theology and economics is through the purpose of the

---

[480] M. Douglas Meeks, *God the Economist*, 42.
[481] Ibid.
[482] Ibid., 44.
[483] Ibid., 94.

work(s) of the Holy Spirit. For Meeks, the purpose of the works of the Holy Spirit is to eliminate or completely do away with any form of scarcity that prohibits every household from being a part of the community of economics.

Meeks's postmodern take on the restricted relationship between theology and economics is that within the Holy Trinity (God the Father, God the Son, and God the Holy Spirit) there exist enough economic resources for every person in the world to have their basic needs met. To no fault of his own, Meeks's premise is not complete enough. Mainly because Meeks does not understand the notions of contextualization and social locations in terms appropriating the Trinity's ability to aptly supply the world's need. While Meeks's doctrine of theology and economics is biblical, it is neither theologically liberating nor is it contextually relevant enough to travel anywhere outside those places in which he has lived. In other words, Meeks' theology is not a lived theology.

For one to even assume that the doctrine of the Trinity provides adequate resources for theological economics is an average assessment as best—especially when young Black, inner-city kids are dying daily at the hands of gun violence, nihilism, starvation, lack of healthcare and self-hate; all resulting from the evil of economic poverty. Whether the doctrine of the Trinity *provides* adequate resources or not, theologians and economists alike understand there are millions of people worldwide that cannot survive as human beings because they do not *receive* adequate economic resources to supply their basic, human needs. Something is liberating about the truth of an economic analysis (John 8:32). What Meeks fails to see is that the problem with economics is not found in Trinitarian theology; rather, the main issue is how idolatry, evil and sin are ensconced in the reality of our living in a fallen world by way of utilizing the various forms of holistic oppression for the economic gain of the capitalist/racist system—a system that prohibits human liberation and ensures forms of deprivation.

According to Meeks, the Holy Trinity provides the world's population with enough economic resources to cover their basic needs. On my read and watch of the growing economic deprivation in Black and brown inner-city communities, I do not agree with Meeks' theological assessment. While I understand his take on the resourceful activity of the Holy Trinity, my problem lies in the fact that human beings are not following through on God's intentions for the Black poor. The employment opportunities, goods, services, and resources are still scarce in Black and brown neighborhoods in the United States and the world abroad. What I know to be true is that the political practices of racism and capitalism as economic systems have done great harm to Black people. Black folk have been economically crucified, deprived, and underdeveloped by the capitalist United States. J. Deotis Roberts responds with inequality and equality in mind.

> For the present, however, "black" says a great deal that needs saying. We are not considered, nor are we treated, as most hyphenated Americans. In a country that promises freedom, equality, and justice for all, we are a huge minority that has not been melted. There is something profoundly meaningful in taking a term filled with shame and placing upon it a halo of glory. This has great ethical and theological import. There is even something Christ like in taking something shameful in the eyes of the white oppressor and investing it with pride and dignity. The cross, despised by Jews and Romans alike, is a symbol of God's matchless love. "Black," therefore, in the reconception of black theology, is a meaningful symbol of our new self-understanding as persons in black skin who are equal in nature and grace with all humans."[484]

Roberts's words are helpful in unpacking the term theology Black within how the Holy Spirit works in the life of Black believers and believers of other religions, groups, races, and cultures of people. Concomitantly, theology Black comes in the reconception of Black theology as a theological symbol of Black people's new self-identification as persons of Black skin who are closely related to the person of the Holy Spirit. Just as God and Jesus Christ are Black, so too is the person of the Holy Spirit Black for purpose of liberating Black people from the systemic evils and oppressions of racism, poverty, and capitalism. So too is the Holy Ghost Black for the cultural, existential, and religious experiences of Black folk and all other oppressed groups, races, and cultures of people. Let Christian

---

[484] J. Deotis Roberts, *A Black Political Theology*, 24.

theologians and other types of religious leaders not forget that the work of the Holy Spirit has economic, material, and spiritual implications.

Shirley C. Guthrie

In his revised edition of *Christian Doctrine*, Shirley C. Guthrie identifies the works of the Holy Spirit as being a supremely unique work. As a minister of the Presbyterian USA Church, Guthrie identifies the works of the Holy Spirit as the work found in the ministry of Jesus Christ.

> We have said that the Spirit is the Spirit of God the Creator, the Lord of Israel, and the Spirit of Jesus Christ. But the Spirit is not just the agent or instrument of God the Father and the God the Son. According to the New Testament, the Spirit does something that is the Spirit's own unique work. It can be summarized with the word *new*. The Holy Spirit brings new creature life that is stronger than sickness and even death itself; brings new wisdom and guidance from God; calls, holds together, and sends out a new reconciled and reconciling community called the church; works in the world to create a whole new humanity and a whole new creation. When the Spirit breaks in, old ways of thinking and living begin to take over. Old, boring, oppressive, and dead social structures and institutions are transformed into new, liberating ones. It may not happen all at once, but when the Holy Spirit comes there is the dawn of a new day, hope for a new and different future, and courage and strength to move toward it.[485]

Guthrie elaborates on the prophetic when he unpacks the social implications of experiencing the works of the Holy Spirit. He proclaims that

> People who like things the way they are, who benefit from the status quo, who therefore value stability, permanence, and order above all else—they are suspicious and afraid of the Holy Spirit, and too much talk about the Spirit makes them nervous and defensive. But people who suffer and see no way out of suffering, who are enslaved and oppressed by their own or others' sinfulness and injustice—they yearn for the coming

---

[485] Shirley C. Guthrie, *Christian Doctrine*, 292.

of the Holy Spirit and cannot talk enough about it. For the Spirit is not just the Lord and Giver of Life but the Lord and Giver of new life—to individuals, to churches, to the natural environment, to political, social, and economic structures.[486]

Guthrie also confirms what the Bible says about the works of the Holy Spirit. He adds that

In addition to the Spirit being at work in God's creation and preservation of the world and human life in it (Gen 1:2; 2:7; Ps 104:30) and being the source of all human culture, art, creativity, and wisdom (Exo 31:1-6; 35:31; Job 32:8; Dan 1:17), the Spirit is the Spirit of the God who is on the side all who are helpless, poor, wretched, and oppressed because they have been forgotten or excluded by the rich and powerful (Ps 103:6 and Ps 146). The Spirit of the Lord is therefore present in (or "upon") leaders and prophets who demand and promise political, economic, and social justice for the victims of injustice (Isa 11:1-5; 42:1-4; 61:1-4).[487]

Now let us come back full circle. Postmodern economic theologians M. Douglas Meeks and D. Stephen Long are of the opinion that the Holy Spirit has the distributive power to provide enough resources to take care of the entire world economically and otherwise. While I do believe that true distribution lies in the hands of God, it is obvious that a sizable percentage of today's population do not receive adequate resources to survive one week to the next. Here, I believe that the theologizing of the Holy Spirit as gift and love encompasses this concurrent distribution of resources to those deprived of the same. Whether or not the resources arrive at the places where they are supposed to is another question altogether. But certainly Augustine, Calvin, Luther, and Meeks are on to something beneficial. The Holy Spirit as gift and love holds far-reaching implications for the contemporary context. The teaching that the Holy Spirit gives life; especially in those hopeless and nihilistic situations, is invaluable. This teaching is biblical, and it is accepted as the primary work of the Spirit. Gift and love represent practical forms of life that the Holy Spirit brings and gives, along with creation, faith,

---

[486] Ibid., 296.
[487] Ibid., 293.

grace, healing, justification, revivification, sanctification, and revivification. These are just spiritual possibilities.

But how does pneumatology contribute to the conversation of theology and economics? How is the Holy Spirit working in cities, towns, and rural areas where Black people are not employed in the industrial plants for the purpose of labor production? How about those who are unemployed? Concomitantly, being poor in the context of blackness means being unemployed, working for low wages, being exploited while working for low wages, owning no property and being without the necessities needed to survive from one month to the next—all of which negatively affects the Black body. Being poor also presupposes a lack of formal education and training. Does being poor mean that one is spiritual? Sadly, the lack of educational development usually stymies one's ability to find a decent-paying job or career. Again, the result of unemployment and working long hours for low wages are biproducts of economic poverty. How can the Holy Spirit give life to and liberate those who suffer from economic poverty? In his anecdotal text, *Doing Justice in Our Cities: Lessons in Public Policy from America's Heartland*, Warren R. Copeland provides a poignant reflection:

> My deepest faith is that in my actions and that of my fellow citizens make some difference. I have faith that God has entrusted us with the power to make history. As someone who meddles in social science, I have the capacity to make convincing arguments for the continuation of the status quo into the future, for an unbroken causal link between the past and the future. In fact, I spend a lot of time in my courses trying to help my students see that history does significantly shape the choices before us if we try to deal with racism or sexism or poverty or cities. It is easy to argue for historical determination. However, my faith is that the future is not totally determined. My faith is that inspired by the Spirit of Love, we can act in each moment so that the future is marked by real freedom and real diversity. In fact, I am convinced that action inspired by the Spirit of Love is a significant act of faith, even if there is little immediate evidence of success.[488]

---

[488] Warren R. Copeland. *Doing Justice in Our Cities,* 126.

Chapter Five

The Holy Spirit in Scripture, Who at Sundry Times Liberates and Gives Life

The Holy Ghost saved me. The Holy Ghost set me free. The Holy Ghost changed my life. The Holy Ghost brought me out. I found nothing but the Holy Ghost.[489]

> How can the same Scripture function in such contradictory ways? Theological reflections on the relationship between Scripture and the Holy Spirit suggest a way into this conundrum. Frederick Douglass, though not a Calvinist like Henry Highland Garnet, saw clearly the truth of John Calvin's insistence that "without the Spirit, the Word can do nothing."[490] Or rather, without the Spirit, the Word can do demonic things: the Gospel stories depict the devil himself twisting Scriptures to his purposes (Matt. 4:5-6; Luke 4:9-12). The Bible becomes a "Talking Book" as life is breathed into it. When the breath that enlivens Scripture is the Holy Spirit, the results are life-giving. However, when other spirits breathe through Scripture, the Bible can become a "poison book."
> –Amy Platinga Pauw[491]

One of the greatest and most liberating messages of the Bible is that the Holy Spirit gives life. It is the Spirit who gives life; the flesh profits

---

[489] https://www.lyricsondemand.com/r/revmitonbrunsonlyrics.html

[490] John Calvin, Institutes of the Christian Religion 3.2.33; ed. John T. McNeil, trans. Ford Lewis Battles, LCC (Philadelphia, PA: Westminster Press, 1960).

[491] David H. Jensen, *The Lord and Giver of Life*, 26.

nothing; the words that I have spoken to you are spirit and are life. The earth was formless and void, and darkness was over the surface of the deep, and the Spirit of God was moving over the surface of the waters. The Holy Spirit gives life explicitly and implicitly. The word implicit means implied but not plainly expressed. It also means essentially or very intricately connected with; always to be found in. The word explicit means said clearly and in detail, leaving no room for confusion or doubt. The Spirit gives life in that She enables us to reach God's goal for us, to be transformed into the glorious image of God's own Son (2 Cor. 3:18; also see Rom. 8:28–30).

Until the day that we see Christ, the Spirit intercedes with God on our behalf, ensuring our continued forgiveness and preserving the promise of God (Rom. 8:26–27). The letter kills, but the Spirit gives life (2 Cor. 3:6). The liberating law of the life-giving Spirit has freed human beings of all genders, cultures, and races from the enslaving law of death-giving sin. The term law in verse 2 does not refer primarily to any written code, but mainly to the authority or power of the Holy Spirit. The law of the Holy Spirit is the authority and power of the Holy Spirit; the law of sin is the authority and power of sin.

Another way the Holy Spirit gives life explicitly and implicitly is through the fruit of the Spirit. In focusing his pneumonic argument on the appropriations of the Holy Spirit in the lives of believers,[492] Timothy C. Tennett posits that

> The fruit of the Spirit should also be manifest in our community in an ever-increasing way. We live in a culture that has become degraded and crude. We live in a culture that is shockingly deficient in love, joy, peace, patience, kindness, goodness, gentleness, faithfulness, and self-control. Therefore, to bear this fruit is to shine like bright lights in a culture filled with hatred, sadness, warfare, profanity, anxiety, impatience, crudeness, faithlessness, and being out of control—the anti-fruits of the Spirit, or the fruits of the flesh. We want to see the end of all bondages to sin in our community, whether it be pornography or gaming addictions or opioid use, or drunkenness, or hating your body, or shaming, or any other signs of brokenness that would creep

---

[492] Timothy C. Tennett, *The Spirit-Filled Life*, 162.

into our community.[493]

One may wonder: How is the fruit of the Spirit liberating? The fruit of the Spirit liberates by showing people that God's way of life, teachings, (Holy) Spirit and truth are what liberates us from the bondages of sin, evil and death. The fruit of the Spirit shows that God in Jesus Christ by the power of the Holy Spirit knew what they were doing when the Holy Trinity inspired men to write the words of the Bible. The fruit of the Holy Spirit also gives the blueprint for what it means for human beings to be more committed to God and want to help others get to know Jesus Christ better. Just like the fruit that ordinary people eat to make their bodies healthier, the fruit of the Holy Spirit strengthens both our physical and our spiritual (mental) bodies.

To a large degree, the fruit of the Spirit are the gifts of the Spirit in that the fruit and the gifts of the Spirit come from the Holy Spirit. The gifts of the Spirit are simply God's way of empowering faithful Christians to do what He has called us to do. 2 Pet. 1:3 says "His divine power has given us everything we need for life and godliness through our knowledge of him who called us by his own glory and goodness." The gifts of the Spirit are simply God empowering faithful Christians to do what He has called us to do. 2 Pet 1:3 says, "His divine power has given us everything we need for life and godliness through our knowledge of him who called us by his own glory and goodness." Jesus Christ is our life source. In addition to Jesus being our life source, Tennett says that

> *The Spirit is the source of all life.* The source of God's life, in you and me, in everybody. This image of God is one of the marks that unites all of humanity. It is the Spirit of God who gives life to us marks us as bearers of the image of God. Another way of saying this is that it is the Holy Spirit who makes us distinct from the animals. This is why Jesus, in John 20:22, breathed on the disciples and said, "receive the Holy Spirit." It was meant to be a recollection of the first creation, even as Jesus inaugurated the new creation which now breaking in upon the people of God.[494]

---

[493] Ibid., 167.
[494] Ibid., 11.

It is in Jesus Christ that we live and move and have our being. He supplies all we need. He provides us daily with the requirements for life and what we need to truly live a life of sharing his love with others. Jesus Christ has done all we need to receive forgiveness, made new and have a loving relationship with God and with the Holy Spirit. Another reason that Jesus Christ is our life source is because the Holy Spirit is the Spirit of Christ (Rom. 8:9-10). Even as there is a knowledgeable gap between the person and work of Jesus Christ and the Holy Spirit (not that their ministries are competing with one another), the gifts of wisdom, knowledge, and discernment still abides in unusual ways.

In Acts 1:4, Jesus says "Wait for the gift my Father promised, *which you have heard me speak about.* Baptism of the Holy Spirit means there are spiritual gifts that the disciples and other believers will receive. But based on the Scriptures (Isaiah 11:2-3) and the Christian church's teaching we know that there are seven gifts of the Holy Spirit: wisdom, understanding, knowledge, counsel (right judgment), fortitude (courage), piety (reverence), and fear of the Lord (wonder and awe)."[495] We also know that there are nine gifts of the Holy Spirit that are somewhat different than the seven gifts of the Holy Spirit.

1. The Word of Knowledge—This gift of the Holy Spirit is having knowledge about something that you have no ability or means of knowing based on your human intelligence.
2. The Word of Wisdom—This gift of the Holy Spirit works with the word of knowledge. It gives you the ability and understanding of how to apply the word of knowledge.
3. The Gift of Prophecy—This gift of the Holy Spirit is one that the scripture says, *"to especially desire."* This gift is a direct Word from the Lord that is to be given to someone else to edify and build them up.
4. The Gift of Faith—This gift of the Holy Spirit grows as we walk with the Lord. You are saved by faith. The gift of faith is knowing full well that you cannot accomplish something on your own, but that Lord has empowered you to move into

---

[495] Jared Dees, *The 7 Gifts of the Holy Spirit Lesson Plan & Worksheet."* Para. 1.

new levels to do miracles and wonders in His name.

5. The Gifts of Healings—There are various kinds of healings that the Spirit will do. Notice that the scripture says *"gifts,"* plural. These gifts equip you in several ways to access healing for yourself or be an anointed vessel that will heal others.

6. The Working of Miracles—This gift of the Holy Spirit is depicted throughout the Bible, from Moses parting the Red Sea to Jesus feeding five thousand people. God is the same yesterday, today, and forever. Therefore, The Holy Spirit is still in the business of working miracles. Like the word of knowledge, this spiritual gift is manifested not by human efforts, but by the Holy Spirit. The work is unexplainable by nature. The work edifies and delivers others.

7. The Discerning of Spirits—This gift of the Holy Spirit equips the discerner to see evil spirits that are working in someone's life. The Holy Spirit pulls back the curtains, exposing the evil spirits so that the person can experience a breakthrough from their bondage.

8. Different Kinds of Tongues—This gift of the Holy Spirit is simply a supernatural ability to speak and pray in a tongue that you do not naturally know. This can be spoken forth in prayer direct to God, or in an assembly where God anoints another Believer, with the gift of interpretation, to interpret the word spoken in the native tongue of the congregation (1 Cor 14:2, 13-14).

9. The Interpretation of Tongues—This gift of the Holy Spirit is to interpret the tongue that was spoken. This can either be for yourself (see 1 Cor 14:13-14) or for the Church (see 1 Cor 14:27-28).[496]

The three common gifts between the 7 and 9 gifts of the Holy Spirit are *wisdom, knowledge, and discerning evil spirits* (See Linda E. Thomas's article on Womanist theology and the Holy Spirit in Chapter 3) as a way of understanding the ways and means in which the Holy Spirit gives life in the realms of the implicit and the explicit. While it may seem that the 7 gifts and 9 gifts of the Holy Spirit are different from one another in scope, the truth is that all the gifts are

---

[496] "What Are the 9 Gifts of the Holy Spirit?," Para. 12.

liberating in nature. In the Old and New Testaments, the Bible says even more about the ways and means the Holy Spirit gives life to God's creations.

Gen 1:2 says that the earth was formless and void, and darkness was over the surface of the deep, and the Spirit of God was moving over the surface of the waters. This completes the picture of a world awaiting God's light-giving, order-making, and life-creating word. The impressive land, for ancient people, fearful picture of the original state of the visible creation is relieved by the majestic announcement that the mighty Spirit of God hovers over creation. The announcement anticipates God's creative words that follow. *Spirit of God.* God was active in creation, and his creative power continues today. *Hovering over.* Like an eagle that hovers over its young when they are learning to fly.[497]

Gen 2:7 says that then the Lord God formed man of dust from the ground, and breathed into his nostrils the breath of life, and man became a living being. The word form comes from the Hebrew verb commonly referred to as the work of the potter, who fashions vessels from clay and "create" people and animals. *Breath of life.* Humans and animals alike have the breath of life in them. In being created in the image of God, humans are living creatures by way of God breathing the Spirit as the breath of life into the nostrils of people; thereby making them living beings.[498]

Job 32:8 says but it is a spirit in man, And the breath of the Almighty gives them understanding.

Job 33:4 says the Spirit of God has made me; the breath of the Almighty gives me life.

Ps. 104:30 says you send forth your Spirit, they are created, and you renew the face of the ground.

Ps. 51:11 David says to God: Do not cast me from your presence or take your Holy Spirit from me. By his Spirit, God effected his purposes in creation and redemption. David was aware that the Spirit equipped and qualified David for his royal office. The Spirit also

---

[497] *Zondervan New International Study Bible*, 6.
[498] Ibid., 9.

equipped his servants for their appointed tasks, inspired his prophets and directed their ministries. It is by the Spirit that God gives his people a "new heart and new spirit" to live by his will.

Eze. 37- Ezekiel summarizes that the hand of the LORD was upon him, and the LORD brought me out by the Spirit of the LORD and set him down in the middle of the valley, and it was full of dead dry bones. In the presence of Ezekiel, the bones came to life because the Spirit breathed life into them by way of putting God's Spirit within them.

The Holy Spirit worked in five principal areas in the Old Testament:

- Creation of human beings and the holistic sustaining of the universe
- History of redemption, particularly with the nation of Israel
- The lives of individuals
- Inspiring holiness in Old Testament believers
- Helping God's people anticipate the ministry of the Messiah

The primary Old Testament word for the Holy Spirit is ruach, used approximately 388 times. The Spirit inspired holiness in Old Testament believers and Scripture promised that someday God would put His Spirit in His people in a way that would cause them to live according to His statutes. The Holy Spirit worked in the hearts of people to enlighten, convict, and lead people to believe the content of the message as it existed in Old Testament times.

The New Testament speaks of what it means to drink from the waters of life, the Holy Spirit. John 7:38-39 *the Spirit*. Explaining the "living water" (v. 38). had not been given. In the way he would be given at Pentecost (Acts 2:1,4). *glorified*. Here probably refers to Jesus' crucifixion, resurrection, and exaltation. The fullness of the Spirit's work depends on Jesus' prior work of salvation.

In Rom 8:1-17, Paul states that because we are now under the law of the Holy Spirit, the Spirit gives us life by way of freeing us from the law of sin that brings death. The Spirit also gives life and peace to the mind that is ruled by the Spirit. Even though we will live as Christ lives in us and our bodies will die because of sin, the Spirit gives us life. The Spirit gives us life. The life that the Spirit gives us makes us right with God. Particularly, the Spirit of the God who raised Jesus from the dead gives us life by way of the Spirit living in us and giving life to our bodies. Here, the Spirit gives us life so that we can live after we have made a commitment to stop sinning and repent.

Jn 6:63 says that the Spirit gives life, the flesh counts for nothing. The words I have spoken to you—they are full of the Spirit and life. *Spirit and life.* They are the Spirit at work producing life.

In speaking on how grace is the liberating work of the Holy Spirit, 2 Corinthians 13:14 says "The grace of the Lord Jesus Christ, and the love of God, and the communion of the Holy Ghost, be with you all. Amen." Titus 3:5 declares that "he saved us, not because of righteous things we had done, but because of his mercy. He saved us through the washing of rebirth and renewal by the Holy Spirit." Ephesians 2:8-9 says that "For it is by grace you have been saved, through faith—and this is not from yourselves, it is the gift of God." The first thing I notice from the trinity of biblical texts is that the grace of Jesus Christ resides in in the love of God and the communion of the Holy Spirit. The second I notice is that Jesus Christ saved us because of His mercy, which is a form of grace. Jesus Christ also saved us through the washing of rebirth and renewal by the Holy Spirit. The last thing I notice is that we grace (of God?) saves believers through their faith (in Jesus Christ?).

Here, the Apostle Paul tells the Ephesian church that this saving grace did not come from they themselves or even the church. But rather, the saving grace of God in Jesus Christ by the power of Holy Spirit is a gift of God. When I think of the word gift, I think of the gift(s) of the Holy Spirit given to those who believe. Upon meditating on all three verses again, I can theologize salvation as the work of the Holy Spirit in understanding how and why the Holy Spirit saves. If grace saves us and grace is the work of the Holy Spirit, then one can argue that the Holy Spirit saves. To be sure, this redeeming quality work of the Holy Spirit in salvation is a liberating work.

There are biblical passages from the New Testament that speak to the liberating work of the Holy Spirit.

- Jn. 6:8 says the Holy Spirit convicts us of sin.
- Jn. 14:15-17 says the Holy Spirit dwells in us.
- Jn. 14:26 says the Holy Spirit teaches us the things of faith by reminding us of God's word.

- Jn. 16:7 says the Holy Spirit comforts us.
- Jn. 16:13 says the Holy Spirit guides us into all truth.
- Acts 9:8 says the Holy Spirit empowers us.
- Rom. 8:26 says the Holy Spirit helps us in the time of trouble.
- 1 Cor. 12:4-17 says the Holy Spirit equips us with spiritual gifts.
- Eph. 1:13 says the Holy Spirit seals us.
- Eph. 1:17 says the Holy Spirit gives us wisdom and discernment.
- Eph. 3:16 says the Holy Spirit strengthens us.
- Eph. 5:8 says the Holy Spirit fills us.
- Gal. 5:22-23 says the Holy Spirit bears fruit through us.
- 2 Tim. 1:7 says the Holy Spirit grants us the power of faith, love, and self-control.

According to the Bible, the work of the Holy Spirit liberates in a multitude of situational contexts and descriptive ways. Liberation is more than a singular act of God. Liberation is also found in those actions and experiences that led up to liberation—as revealed in the contextual work of the Holy Spirit.

Memory as the Implicit Work of the Holy Spirit

The question now is: Can the people of God remember all of what the Holy Spirit has done for them? Pope Francis recently preached: "The Holy Spirit is God active in us, God who helps us remember, who awakens our memory. Jesus himself explains this to the Apostles before Pentecost: 'the Spirit that God will send in my name will remind you of everything I have said.' In speaking on what he terms "the lessons of the passion memory," Miroslav Volf suggests that "Through the death of Christ God aims to liberate us from exclusive concern for ourselves and to empower us through the indwelling of the Holy Spirit to reach out in grace toward others, even those who have wronged us."[499] The first thing I notice in Volf's biblical proclamation of liberation is that the Holy trinity works as one through God's actions, Jesus' death and the Holy Spirit reaching out

---

[499] Miroslav Volf, *The End of Memory*, 120.

in grace toward others. Theologically, I affirm that in liberation of the oppressed, all three persons in the Godhead reach out in the grace of God to those who believe they are saved by grace through their faith in Jesus Christ. To be sure, grace is the work of the Holy Spirit. But what does that have to do with what and how we remember life experiences, visible images and bodies of knowledge and information?

The King James Version of John 14:26 gives a different interpretation: But the Comforter, which is the Holy Ghost, whom the Father will send in my name, he shall teach you all things, and bring all things to your remembrance, whatsoever I have said unto you. Both the Spirit of God and the Holy Ghost is the Holy Spirit (2 Cor. 12:10-12; 2 Cor. 3:17-18). The terms "Holy Spirit" and "Holy Ghost" mean the same thing; both refer to the third Person of the Trinity (the Father, the Son, and the Holy Spirit). The phrase "Holy Ghost" is simply an older term that dates back hundreds of years. It can be found in older versions of the English Bible (such as the King James Version). Because the word "ghost" has a different meaning today than it did hundreds of years ago, modern translations of the Bible always use "Holy Spirit." The biblical text declares that God the Father will send the Comforter Holy Ghost (NIV uses the word Advocate) to Jesus's disciples to help them with their memory of what Jesus taught them.

Still referencing John 14:26, Rick Warren uses the Good News translation to affirm that "God speaks through the Holy Spirit. He gives you thoughts. He gives you suggestions. He puts impressions or notions in your mind. When the Devil talks to you, he tempts you. But when God talks to you in your mind, he inspires you."[500] Jesus says in John 14:26, *"The Helper, the Holy Spirit, whom the Father will send in my name, will teach you everything and make you remember all that I have told you"* (GNT). For Warren, this means that if you are a Christian, then the Holy Spirit is your teacher and counselor.[501] Notice that John 14:26 (GNT) says the Holy Spirit will *"make you remember."* The Holy Spirit speaks directly to your mind. Here, the theological connotation is that the Holy Spirit brings God's truth to mind. In doing so, God relies on you to put God's

[500] Rick Warren, "The Holy Spirit Brings God's Truth to Mind," Para. 2.
[501] Ibid.

Word in your mind. When you read, study, and fill your mind with God's Word, you are storing up truth inside of you—truth the Holy Spirit will bring to mind at just the right time.[502] With regards to the liberating work of the Holy Spirit in the life of believers, memory and remembering are spiritual practices for those who allow the Spirit to teach and counsel them. In the German language, the word *Geist* means ghost, spirit (Holy Spirit), mind, or intellect. Possibly suggesting that the work of the Holy Spirit extends far down into the enterprising statuses of our mind.

As a Black man who has lived in the Jim Crow South, I am sure that there are an ample number of unforgettable things... harmful things that have happened to a sizable number of those in my race of people—things that they could never forget. I am also sure that there are things that Black people living in the Jim Crow South and other parts of the United States would love to forget. But the unbearable pain and intergenerational harm reaped upon Black people over the course of five hundred plus years can never be unremembered. Here, I am solidarity with Black British theologian Robert Beckford when he suggests that memory is problematic because of the history of violence and wrongdoing in and throughout the world. Those destructive images remain etched in the minds of those who continue to live and die in oppression. However fresh as God's morning air, memory can be a form of spiritual power and cultural liberation.

Compassion as the Explicit Work of the Holy Spirit

According to biblical commentators, the Holy Spirit is the Spirit of compassion and the compassionate Spirit. For it is the Holy Spirit that creates and develops compassion in the hearts, souls, and minds of those who believe in Jesus Christ as Lord, Savior, Redeemer, and Forgiver. Ephesians 4:32 says "Be kind to one another, tenderhearted, forgiving one another, as God in Christ forgave you." In connection to this liberating text, the Bible proves that God loves the entire world and not just parts of it. If people of all genders, cultures and races of people are not willing to follow the move of the Holy Spirit and show compassion to others, then they are not doing what thus sayeth the Lord. The only way to get rid of the old selfish nature is a supernatural grafting of a new nature: an act of

---

[502] Ibid.

the Holy Spirit. Compassion is the liberating work of the Holy Spirit.

Compassion means allowing the Holy Spirit to "open your heart, soul, and mind to the pain and suffering in the world. Reach out to others and discover rewards and obligations of deep feeling."[503] Compassion also means being kind in displaying the love of God to those who have never experienced that level of agape love. Here, there is a certain type of spiritual allowance involved in being a compassionate believer. Compassion means letting "Spirit flow through you in little acts of kindness, brief words of encouragement and manifold expressions of courtesy. These deeds will add to the planet's fund for good will."[504] Within the theological conversation on the compassion of God, the Christian mystic Mechtild of Magdeburg describes the Holy Spirit as "a compassionate outpouring of the Creator and the Son."

Of course, one of the best-known parables of Jesus focuses on the compassion demonstrated by the Good Samaritan who helps the injured man on the road to Jericho. Ryokan, the Zen monk who writes such wonderful poetry, put forward his own image of compassion: "Oh, that my monk's robes were wide enough to gather up all the people in this floating world."[505] And Protestant Jim Wallis, founding editor of *Sojouners* magazine, writes: "At times I think the truest image of God today is a black inner-city grandmother in the U.S. or a mother of a disappeared in Argentina or the woman who wake up early to make tortillas in refugee camps. They all weep for their children and in their compassionate tears arises the political action that changes the world. The mothers show us that it is the experience of touching the pain of others that is the key to change."[506]

According to Joyce Meyer, "In John 15:26 (AMPC), Jesus told His disciples, *"When the Comforter (Counselor, Helper, Advocate, Intercessor, Strengthener, Standby) comes...the Spirit of Truth Who comes (proceeds) from the Father, He [Himself] will testify regarding Me."* It's so amazing to realize that the Holy Spirit is always with us and He's the Strengthener we need to get through every problem we

[503] Frederic Brussat and Mary Ann Brussat, *Spiritual Literacy*, 20.
[504] Ibid., 22.
[505] Ibid., 90.
[506] Ibid., 90-91. Facebook, Compassion Is, October 10, 2013.

have to face."[507] In theologizing the Spirit as one who gives strength to those in need, Meyer uses scripture to reference the Spirit that comes from the God the Father *and* from his or her own phenomenal splendor. In the transcendent splendor of the Holy Spirit, there are numerous ways to describe what the Spirit does in the life of those who believe. Meyer believes that "There's a huge difference between a Christian who just tries to make it on their own and one who really relies on the Holy Spirit to enable them to do whatever they need to do. Jesus sent the Holy Spirit to take His place here in the earth. He can be everywhere, all the time, and because He lives in us as born-again believers, Jesus will never leave us or forsake us."[508] This is the liberating work of the Holy Spirit.

The Holy Spirit and Forgiveness

As a good Trinitarian, I tend to think when God the Father and Jesus Christ are mentioned in the same verse of scripture, the Holy Spirit is somewhere in the midst. Of course, the Holy Spirit was with Jesus as he suffered, bled and died on that old rugged cross. Of course, the Holy Spirit played a leading role in the resurrection of the body and life everlasting. But how many of you know that the Holy Spirit is the gift of forgiveness? He comes because of Jesus' resurrection pouring out love into our hearts through forgiveness. He does not empower us to live in the law, but rather in Christ's forgiveness. Our sins are forgiven, and we can forgive sins too. The free gift is forgiveness, because Jesus is empowered by the Holy Spirit. Again, one of the central aspects of the Holy Spirit's role is forgiveness.

According to Steve Ditmar,

The Holy Spirit is the gift of forgiveness. He comes because of Jesus' resurrection pouring out love into our hearts through forgiveness. He does not empower us to live in the law, but rather in Christ's forgiveness. Our sins are forgiven, and we can forgive sins too. The free gift is forgiveness, because Jesus is empowered by the Holy Spirit. But what happens if we separate forgiveness and the Holy Spirit? Then the law returns with work, debts and its curse. No longer forgiven, we

---

[507] Joyce Meyer, "The Holy Spirit, Our Strengthener," Para. 3.
[508] Ibid., Para. 2.

seek to live right and demand that others do the same. Holy Spirit cannot be bought or sold. He is the free gift of Jesus, promised by the Father, and sent because we are forgiven. When we forgive sins, we empower the Holy Spirit to unlock hearts and save souls. The first heart He unlocks is always mine.[509]

Overall, forgiveness is a central theme in Christian faith, and the Holy Spirit plays a vital role in facilitating this spiritual process. The Holy Spirit is who makes forgiveness a spiritual decision.

Other Interpretations of How the Holy Spirit Gives Life

Blackness embodies the spiritual livelihood of Black people. In theology Black, the powerful work of the Holy Spirit helps those oppressed and struggling to escape from political powerlessness and institutional subjectification. The Holy Spirit is a revolutionary power that helps people fight against their oppressors. Here, the relationship between oppressed Black people and the work of the Holy Spirit is uniquely personal. I refer to oppressed Black people who reside in the United States of America as African Americans. The relationship between African Americans and the presence of the Holy Spirit is deeply personal and yet religious in nature; but not always occurring within the confines of a church building. Because the Holy Spirit does not operate in one context, God works in the lives of African Americans in myriad ways and for distinct reasons.

The Holy Spirit works in sacred institutions and secular environments. For the African slaves and their descendants, the Spirit let loose in the world, disrupting structures that divided persons from one another, making all children of freedom. For the Black southerners brutalized by the laws of Jim Crow, the Spirit led them northward in hopes of finding decent paying jobs and educational opportunities. Historians refer to this geographical transition as the great migration. Being that a sizable number of Black families were able to live a higher quality of life in the northern parts of the United States, the argument is that the great migration resulted from the move and work of the Holy Spirit in the lives of Black southerners.

For those who remained in the South, the Spirit inspired prophetic leadership in Martin Luther King, Jr., and political

---

[509] Steve Dittmar, "The Holy Spirit and Forgiveness," Para. 3.

advancement in the signing of the Civil Rights Bill. For those who suffered economically under the one-sided leadership of Presidents Richard Nixon, Jimmy Carter and Ronald Reagan, the Holy Spirit birthed a Black cultural movement known as Hip-Hop, which gave rise to new and exciting ways of expressing what it meant to be Black and live in economically underdeveloped and impoverished ghettos of the inner cities. Even for those who thought they would never live long enough to witness a human being of African American descent become the elected President of the United States of America, the Spirit politically moved in the culture of a united people who believed in the power of change and transformation. Again, the Spirit of God works for the human sake of African Americans in myriad ways, for varied reasons and by way of enhancing their culture. In the words of Veli Matti Karkkainen, "Talk about the Spirit must be contextual and culture specific. The Spirit of God is no general spirit hovering above the cosmos but a Person of the Triune God who indwells believers and creation in specific and tangible ways."[510]

In referencing the presence and work of the *Ruach* in Old Testament Scripture, William C. Placher affirms that "From the start, then, the Spirit can be helpful and life-giving but also unpredictable, uncontrollable and potentially terrifying."[511] To say that the Spirit explicitly gives life to those who suffer is another way of saying that the Spirit is not theologically predictable in that God works in realms beyond human comprehension. The Spirit is the dynamic principle of life which the Apostle John speaks of in his Gospel. John postulates that "The spirit blows (pneuma pnei) where it wills...; so, it is with everyone who is born of the Spirit (pneumatos in Jn 3:8)." Spirit means that God is a vital, acting God. God grants life and vitality to creation. The human ruach/pneuma is God's inspiring breath by which life is given in creation and re-creation. God is in action in human life. God cares about what happens to human beings. God loves human beings so much that God gave us his begotten Son, Jesus Christ. The pneuma of God is God acting in creation, providence, and redemption.[512] J. Deotis Roberts's conceptualizing of a redeeming, Black pneumatology includes an intimate examination of

---

[510] Veli Matti Karkkainen, *Pneumatology: The Holy Spirit,* 9. Also see pgs. 18-19
[511] William C. Placher, *The Triune God,* 86.
[512] J. Deotis Roberts, *Black Theology in Dialogue,* 55.

the Holy Spirit working in the lives of oppressed people within *and* beyond the worship experiences of the African American church. The Spirit not only gives life to the Christian church, but she also gives life to Creation and the individual believer. What this reality implies is that for the oppressed slave or the poor African American residing in the United States, an intimate encounter with the Holy Spirit can be existential, cultural, religious, personal, or all the above.

Sundry Times of Liberation in Slave Religion

In theology Black, the Holy Spirit gives life in all phases of the African American religious experiences. For those who came to the United States by force for the sole reason of helping the white slave master prosper economically, an embracing of the Spirit of God represented a critical part of Black people's existence. For those African slaves who believed that the Lord would "make a way somehow," their faith was tested in the dehumanizing crucible of institutional slavery. Meanwhile, White masters introduced Christianity to slaves in strange bits and strategic pieces. Even though slaves were not allowed to worship God or pray to God publicly or even read the Bible for themselves, the Holy Spirit inspired them to meet, organize, and worship their God in the context of sneaking away from the living quarters when they felt that their masters would not be looking for them. As the result of the dire need for the oppressed slave to identify with the God of their daily dreams and nightly visions, the invisible institution formed, and the Black Church was born out of slavery. For the Black church, being born out of slavery means being born in the Holy Spirit and in utter poverty.

The combination of institutional slavery and other authentic experiences with God comprised the birth of the African American religious experience. Whether the slaves could express what they were feeling or not, it became quite clear that they were having spiritual experiences with the God of their Bible. That is to say that the African slaves holistically embraced the Spirit as the giver of life and was, thereby, able to establish a communicative relationship with the God whom they believed would liberate them from the bondage of indentured servitude. It is important to note that the African slaves did not exist as human beings; they were sub-human, the political property of white slave masters and their job description entailed doing and being what the slave masters wanted them to do and be.

Because the African slaves did not have a "life;" meaning that the eyes of the white oppressor did not allow them to exist as human beings, their faith in God as exemplified by their embracing of the Holy Spirit signaled their belief that a greater life existed beyond the realm of their present-day status. In William Hayden's self-written account of the slave's experience with the Spirit of God, he depicts God as creator, friend, protector, and liberator. As a slave, Hayden writes:

> Yes, gentle reader, God has sustained me in every way vicissitude in which I have been placed, and I feel well assured that He will continue to sustain, until He gathers me home, to rest with Him in endless happiness. What, but His mighty arm could have shielded me from many dangers through which I was compelled to pass, when in the possession of wealthy, influential and relentless slave-traders and slaveholders? What but His power could have snatched me from destruction, when angered men raved at me, and stood with firearms pointed at my bared bosom? and who but He could have given me power to brave my oppressors, and declare my rights, when the thong and the scourge were about to be applied to me at Natchez? None, -no, I feel that it was He alone, that thwarted them in their proposed cruelty and saved His weak and dependent creature from their savage and infamous designs. His holy name be praised-for, he has said that throughout all time. He will protect and encourage all his children, if they will but put their trust in Him.[513]

For Hayden, the slave reality of having faith in God was critical to both the bodily survival and mental exploration. While the slave's body was worked, beaten, raped, and whipped, the slave's mind could remain strong if he or she kept their thoughts on God. When the slave decided to keep his or her mind on God, their spirits were strengthened in the fact that God had prepared a greater place or better place for those who were steadfast in the faith. For the slave, a mind stayed on God resulted in a heart that believed in Jesus Christ as Lord and Savior. This spiritual belief provided a temporary escape from the dehumanizing treatment of the white slave master. Instead of focusing his or her mind on the character of the oppressive master, the slave focused his or her mind on the character of their liberator

---

513 William Hayden, *"Narrative of William Hayden,"* 201.

God. Hayden explains:

> My liberation from bondage was promised to me by my spiritual guide in the days of my youth when the chains of slavery were first riveted upon me—and the means and influences by which this happy event was to be consummated. Yes—even the year in which I was to become a free man, was made manifest to me, whilst toiling in servitude, and abject misery for the malignant gratification of my fellow man—and it was this knowledge which supported me throughout nearly forty years of unjustifiable bondage. My heart was cheered with the best conviction that I was, at that period, to become my own master, and acknowledge the right of none to command or drive me in the commission of earthly acts, save the almighty Father of the human family. And my freedom was brought around in the exact manner which the Spirit had set apart for it.[514]

Hayden believed that God's freedom meant more to him to than his master's bondage because the Holy Spirit revealed to him his identity—a free man. Here, the interpretation is that the Holy Spirit was Hayden's spiritual guide. Even amid earthly bondage, Hayden affirms God as liberator through the life-giving power of the Spirit. Hayden states that "Reader—this little narrative, which will in its pages show you more conclusively the power of which this Spirit has exerted over me during life, and the implicit obedience which I have ever yielded to its dictates—is another object brought forth at its commands. For this purpose, I was endowed with an education suitable for the object allotted me—and for this purpose, I have now placed myself before the public as an author of a strange race."[515]

In his useful text, *Shoes That Fit Our Feet: Sources for a Constructive Black Theology*, Dwight N. Hopkins creatively reveals some of the resources for Black theology within the African American religious tradition and Black culture. Beginning with the slave narratives, Hopkins describes how African slaves encountered the gospel of their masters' faith and transformed it into a gospel of liberation in the contexts of blackness and dehumanization. With

514 Ibid.
515 Ibid.

intentions of focusing on slave religion as the plumb line for black church theology,[516] Hopkins contextualizes the Black religious experience into both the theological and cultural reality of the slaves' interaction with God, Jesus Christ, and themselves (humanity). In doing so, Hopkins affirms that "Specifically, the black Christian church has been the most stable institution in its persistent effort toward political and cultural liberation in the African- American community. Because of its central role and its explicit attention to religious matters, the black church has to be a primary source for a constructive black theology."[517] Here, Hopkins take an in depth look at the Invisible Institution.

Without assuming every time Hopkins mentions the word *God* he is referring to the liberating role of pneumatology in African American religious experience, I will argue that the work of Holy Spirit played a leading role in helping the slaves to form the invisible institution. In Hopkins claiming that "God's self-revelation took place in the specific textures of an African American slave story"[518], he is implying that there is a real substance of spirituality working in the slaves' experience with God. It is a religious substance that can be considered as both spiritual and personal. Hopkins expounds:

> In slave religious culture, the liberating Spirit made one "jist turn loose lack." The Spirit fed the people and instructed them how to communicate with God using their own indigenous resources. "We used to steal off to de woods and have church, like des spirit moved us—sing and pray to our own liking and soul satisfaction," states Susan Rhodes. Her testimony exemplifies the slaves' need to be filled with the Spirit to *their* liking and soul's satisfaction. When they claimed their relation to God through the Spirit's pouring into their unique expressions, Rhodes resumes, "we sure did have good meetings, honey...like God said.[519]

For Hopkins, the Spirit not only inspired the slaves to have more religious experiences with God, but the Spirit also enhanced the culture of Black people in that the oppressed slaves were forced to

---

516 Dwight N. Hopkins and George C. L. Cummings, *Shoes That Fit Our Feet*, 6.
517 Ibid.
518 Ibid., 14.
519 Ibid., 19

create ways to identify with and be in relationship with their God. Thus, the Invisible Institution symbolized both a cultural statement of slave theology as well as a liberated space in which slaves controlled the political power to develop their theology.[520] What makes Hopkins's text so provocative is that he uses Trinitarian language in the constructing of Black theology as the Black religious experience. Like most Black theologians, Hopkins does not explicitly refer to the work of the Holy Spirit in the African American religious experience. But he does mention the cultural realities of God's liberation as ensconced in the overwhelming presence of the Spirit. It is as if Hopkins intentionally stays away from referring to the Holy Spirit as the One who liberates both the children of Israel and the African slaves.

I have heard that the relationship between Black people (African slaves) in the United States and the Holy Spirit is a *precious* one. Listening to liberation theologian Nancy E. Bedford recall a conversation she had with James H. Evans Jr.; I am assuming that Evans was implying that the way Black people interact with the Holy Spirit (and vice-verse) is too precious or too personal to describe or put into words. In other words, the relationship between Black people and the Spirit transcends what the Bible says about the work of the Holy Spirit. For me, without the work of the Holy Spirit, there are no shoes (to borrow Hopkins's words). Without the work of the Holy Spirit, there is no life, no culture, no church, no survival, and no future. In other words, the Holy Spirit (spirit, Spirit, Holy Ghost, ghost) *is the maker and producer* of shoes that will fit the feet of Black people, poor people, and other races and cultures of oppressed people.

In the book, *Cut Loose Your Stammering Tongue: Black Theology in the Slave Narratives,* co-editor, George C. L. Cummings decides that "The ultimate aim is the discernment of the Spirit of Christ the liberator, who constitutes the basis of the community's ongoing struggle for liberation and the empowerment of the black oppressed so they might better understand themselves, sustain their hope, and continue the struggle to transform their circumstances."[521]

---

[520] Ibid.
[521] Dwight N. Hopkins and George C. L. Cummings, *Cut Loose Your Stammering Tongue,* 33.

Here, Cummings implies that the experiences of the Spirit as told in the slave narratives have both theological and religious meaning. From the testimonies of the slaves which they describe their spiritual encounter with God, Cummings succeeds at showing how the Spirit worked in the religious life of oppressed Africans living on American soil. I will give one example. Cummings writes in completion:

John White from Oklahoma gave a testimony that connected slave experiences of the Spirit of the Lord with creative opportunities to escape:

The slaves would pray for them to get out of bondage. Some of them say the Lord told them to run away. Get to the North. Cross the Red River. Over there would be folks to guide them to free states.

Their encounter/visions with the Spirit enabled slaves to have the courage and hope to translate their experiences of hope into concrete actions of escaping to freedom. To the North was freedom and crossing the river, as did the Israelites crossing the river, as did the Israelites crossing the Red Sea, would bring them to freedom. The religious imagination played a powerful role in creating new horizons of possibility that linked experiences of the Spirit with the struggle for earthly freedom. Another slave from Texas named Joe Oliver gave a testimony that resonates with John White's:

Dey singing' an' shoutin' till break of day. Some goin' into trances an' some speakin' in what dey called strange tongues, dis wuz a good chance for de slaves to run away, for wen' de would rise up from dey trance some would run like de debbil wuz after him, an jes keep runnin' until he run clear off. So de w'ite folks den puts de trusty niggers to guard de door or de way dey leaves if hit in de arbor, but hit is hard to make de trusty catch dem for dey think hit de Holy Ghost dat is makin' dem run, so dey is afraid to stop dem, claimin dey can't stop de Holy Ghost.[522]

Here, Cummings demonstrates the ways in which the life of an African American slave is filled with supernatural experiences of the Spirit—some of which were not entirely religious experiences.

---

[522]   Ibid., 37.

Whether the Spirit is giving utterance to pray, providing hope and courage, showing visions of freedom and new possibilities, inspiring an authentic, spirit-filled worship experience or helping the slaves to respect the power and substance of God the Holy Spirit, ultimately, the sole purpose of the slave narratives is to describe a life-changing, existential experience with the Spirit of God.

Whereas Black pneumatology communicates a viable form of Black theology in the slave narratives, the goal of Black theology in the slave narratives is to show how the slaves' experience with the Holy Spirit helped to define their religious beliefs. In doing so, the slave narratives bring to light a specific kind of experience with God— one which can be deemed as personal. The slave masters who allowed their slaves to create their own songs in the presence of the Spirit were taking the risk of allowing them the right to be empowered artistically with a sense of uncontrollable spiritual autonomy. A collaborative consciousness of collective unity in Jesus and the Spirit of God is what kept the slaves' hopeful mind on the possibilities of what constituted their undying belief in the notion of being a liberated community. In believing that Jesus Christ meant freedom and the Holy Spirit meant liberation, the slave knew that their worship experiences meant both risky business and a profitable business. Because the slave master attempted to control the directional power of the Holy Spirit in the life of the slave, the slave's personal relationship with God is what moved the slave into their own Black spirituality of belief and liberation.

Within the context of community in song and worship, the slave Spirituals contained enough Holy Spirit to convert a multitude of slaves. The converts' intense urge for the joy of their personal salvation was a primary sign of having been truly converted. The joy of salvation drove the newly saved slave to engage others in the experiential knowledge of God's saving power. Transformation by the Spirit of God in the wilderness required that the transformed become radically engaged in the life of the community.[523] What this meant was:

> The diversity and complexity of the testimonies in the slave narratives are a witness to the complexity of any attempt to interpret their meaning theologically. First, the testimonies to the

---

[523] Ibid., 99.

power of the Spirit in the slave community are themselves ambiguous in relationship to the specifically Christian content of those experiences. This intuition only confirms the point of view articulated by Gayraud Wilmore, for example, that the content of the religious experiences of African American slaves was only more or less Christian.[524]

In their most painful moments, slave women understood sanctification as the liberating work of the Holy Spirit (1 Pet. 1:2; 2 Thes. 2:13). According to numerous slave narratives, the Sanctification Myth describes how women spiritually identified themselves as one who has been called by God, Jesus Christ, and the Holy Spirit to do the Kingdom work of ministry. Ex-slave women such as Zilpha Elaw remained and revisited slave territories where they preached the gospel of Jesus Christ in hopes of liberating their enslaved ancestors. For the slave women preachers, being sanctified meant being set apart for a chosen purpose of God in Jesus Christ by the power of the Holy Spirit. Sanctification was identified as the work of the Holy Spirit—a transformative work that was constructively done inside the body, mind, and spirit of the called woman slave preacher.

Not Spiritual Theory, But A Contextual Pneumatology

Stephen Ray reminded me that it is impossible to theorize the action and work of the Holy Spirit. Theorizing the Spirit is not the goal or objective of being a Christian theologian. The human mind is not capable of predicting or exacting the person, power, and work of the Holy Spirit. As one who knows the thoughts of God, the Holy Spirit's thoughts are not the thoughts of human beings. And vice versa. The only way the Black Christian church can begin to ascertain the work of the Holy Spirit in real time is through in-person worship, spirituality development, and community transformation. Put another way, when the believer authentically worships the LORD for who the LORD is and praises God for the things God has done, the Holy Spirit is disposed into the wiggle room boundaries to show up and show out in the life of the Black church. Not in theory but in worship where the act of worship itself is genuine only when the Holy Spirit is

---

[524] Ibid. 99. Sallie McFague, *Speaking in Parables: A Study in Metaphor and Theology* (Philadelphia: Fortress Press, 1975), 3-4, 80-83, 175-178; idem *Metaphorical Theology Models of God in Religious Language* (Philadelphia: Fortress Press, 1982), 14-15, 103-144).

visibly present in the playground of believing hearts. I personally believe that the Black church must become more of a spiritually-thinking institution and less of an emotion-based environment. It was the Pentecostal churchgoers who consistently states that when I think of the goodness of Jesus, and all that he has done for me, my soul cries out in praise and worship. Here, I believe Black churchgoers can first think about the redeeming quality of God in Christ by the power of the Holy Spirit in the lives and then worship God in Spirit and in truth.

However, within the vision of Black people's worship of God being enfleshed in God and in the oppressed communities of God, therein lies the need for a contemporary theology Black in the twenty-first century. While the Holy Spirit works to liberate oppressed Black people, non-white people and the white poor, there is a deeper meaning of the word Black. The words Spirit, spiritual, spirituality, liberation and hope come to mind. For me, Black people's affirming and believing that the Holy Spirit is a Black person for the Black religious, cultural, and existential experiences represents that meaningful symbol of their new self-understanding as persons with Black skin.

Hopefully, my reflections are helpful in unpacking the term theology Black within how the Holy Spirit works in the life of all believers. Concomitantly, theology Black is created in the spiritual preconception of Black theology as a theological symbol of their new self-identification as persons in Black skin who are closely related to the personhood of the Holy Spirit. Just as God is Black, Christ Jesus is Black, so too is the person of the Holy Spirit Black for the purpose of liberating Black people and all other groups, races, and cultures of oppressed people.

Theology Black Continued

As a form of Christian theology, theology Black is also Black liberation theology. Any liberating theology of the Holy Spirit is a form of theology Black because the Holy Spirit brings life and light to those who believe. The way the Holy Spirit works in theology Black, it brings a liberating light to the life of oppressed Black folks. This liberating work does not come as a light that replaces the darkness of the Black dark. But the Holy Spirit comes as light that confirms the spiritual Godliness of all Black people. What this spiritual blackness means theologically and economically is that to talk about the economic dimension of the Holy Spirit is to intentionally discuss the material and spiritual implications of an economy that belongs to God. Theology Black is also a contextual pneumatology that is singularly focused on the liberating work of the Holy Spirit in the oppressive conditions of Black people and other groups, races, and cultures of people. Both conversations, Black theology and Black economics, critique the demonic ungodliness of poverty that is associated with all races and cultures of people. Political pundits say that to be Black is to be poor. What they are really trying to say is that anyone who is poor is Black—regardless of their skin color. In other words, to be poor is to be Black and (economically) oppressed.

While I got the microphone, I want to again remind the readers that the American economy has been good for a sizable number of people, but not for all people. The American and world economies have not been good for a sizeable number of Black folks. I say that because when we hear words like 'economic impact,' 'economic support,' 'economic increase,' 'economic prosperity,' 'economic uplift,' 'economic parity,' 'economic equality,' and 'economic potential,' these words are never meant for the economic betterment of Black people. Normally, the American economy and the world economy bypasses Black people keeping them in a debilitating, economic condition. Is this the liberating work of the Holy Spirit? I think not. Is economic oppression the goal of the person, power, and work of the Holy Spirit? I do not think so.

When economic goods, resources and services are not reaching the communities and neighborhoods, something is terribly wrong. And God is not involved. Human hands and sinful minds have decided that certain groups of people are to grow in their own prospering and others will remain deprived and dehumanized. While the economy has not been good for Black people, the Holy Spirit has been good for and to Black people. This is precisely why Black people and other oppressed groups, races, and cultures of people must believe that the Holy Spirit means liberation, and not religious emotionalism.

The Holy Spirit and Liberation in the Black Church

The Black church must also believe that the Holy Spirit means liberation. In his important text, *Black Theology in Dialogue*, J.

Deotis Roberts writes that "A theological discussion that takes contextualization seriously must consider the unique contribution of black church theology to the doctrine of the Holy Spirit."[525] And we believe in the Holy Spirit, the Lord and Giver of Life, who proceedeth from the Father and the Son, who with the Father and the Son together is worshipped and glorified, who spoke by the prophets. And we believe one holy catholic and apostolic church. (Nicene/Constantinopolitan Creed)[526] For Roberts, the theological focus of the inherent study is on the relationship between the doctrine of the Holy Spirit and human liberation. The power of the Holy Spirit connects the charismata and personal and social transformation.[527] Roberts believes that when blacks turn away from a concern for the social, economic, and political aspects of liberation in their religious life, something unusual has been happening."[528] This unusual something can be identified as a broken connection; almost like broken bones in the human body where the Black church fails to make the existential connection between the power and presence of the Holy Spirit and social transformation.

Throughout history, many African Americans have experienced those "It's over. God is no longer with us"[529] moments. The truth is that the Holy Spirit is present in the Black church and all other Christian and world religions as well. In the Bible, God promises through the Son and the Spirit that God will never leave us nor forsake us. God will be us from generation to generation, until the end of the age. The very presence of God in our lives represents the liberating work of the Holy Spirit within the Holy Trinity.

Along the same lines as Roberts, Robert Beckford's famed book, *Dread and Pentecost: A Political Theology for the Black Church in Britain*, presents a quality argument for the Black church ministry in Britain to regain its historical, prophetic voice amidst the all too familiar outreaches of white supremacy. Writing as a Black liberation theologian with Pentecostal roots, Beckford references the Rastafari, the Caribbean's first liberation theology, as a solid example of what it

---

[525] J, Deotis Roberts, *Black Theology in Dialogue*, 53.
[526] Ibid.
[527] Ibid.
[528] Ibid.
[529] Eli Wiesel, *Night*, 76.

means for the Black church to have a liberating presence in the community of the British oppressed. Beckford peruses the doctrinal tenets of Black theology, Womanist theology and post-colonial theologies of liberation—all of which are relevant to his theological exploration of the future of Black British Pentecostalism. "In wanting to describe the Black Church as a 'shelter' or 'rescue', a place of radical transformation, driven by the Spirit and a family,"[530] Beckford makes his contribution to the conversation of the Holy Spirit in Black theology:

> Third, the Black Church must also be characterized as a centre driven by the Spirit. This third-person ecclesiology emphasizes the birth of the Church with the outpouring of the Spirit at Pentecost (Acts 2). Communion with the Holy Spirit forms a major part of the worship traditions of the Black Church – worship is subject to the 'moving' of the Spirit. The constant use of terms such as 'getting the Spirit,' 'sensitivity to the Spirit' and the filling of the Spirit' all bear witness to the centrality of the Spirit. The Spirit renews, directs and inspires the Church. However, a critical issue concerns the focus of the theology of the Spirit or pneumatology. As James Cone has argued in the African American context, the pneumatology of the Black Church cannot be simply geared towards keeping the status quo. This is especially important in contemporary Britain where racialized subordination and White supremacist ideology are still prevalent. In opposition, pneumatology must be concerned with radical holistic change. What I am suggesting here is that talk of the Spirit cannot be divorced from social change, critical analysis, or tough decisions in the quest racial justice. Therefore, I will later suggest that in order to be responsive to the holistic impulse of the Spirit, the Black Church must take seriously political theology in the form of a 'dread' theology of the Holy Spirit.[531]

This statement represents one of Beckford's three theological hallmarks of the Black church. Beckford gives theological credit to J.

---

[530] Robert Beckford, *Dread and Pentecost*, 5.

[531] Ibid., 6.

Deotis Roberts for his description of the Black church as family. Beckford says that "Also the Black Church is a family in the sense that each member is considered a brother or sister upon becoming a Christian. All have the potential to join the potential to join the family or household of God, although profession of catholicity does not always result in a multi-cultural church or Church. The Black Church is a family in the sense that all those that enter the Church as members are called to the Black Church is also the 'body of Christ.'"[532]

In her summary review of James H. Cone's *A Black Theology of Liberation*, Monique Duson writes that

> Cone sees a particular role for each member of the Godhead to play in the drama of liberation. "Black theology says that as Creator, God identified with oppressed Israel, participating in the bringing into being of this people; as Redeemer, God became the Oppressed One in order that all may be free from oppression; as Holy Spirit, God continues the work of liberation." (Note: Although this quote may sound like the heresy of modalism, in other talks Cone is clear that he does not subscribe to a modelist viewpoint.) In fact, Cone would say that a God who is not continuously working on behalf of the oppressed ought to be rejected (pg. 72). Cone writes, "Black theology will accept only a love of God which participates in the destruction of the White oppressor" (pg. 74).[533]

In the theological mind of Cone, this encounter represents the spiritual battle between good and evil. It is not a battle between flesh and blood. It is a spiritual battle of powers and principalities in high places that have been able to material evil in the physical world. This is precisely why the work of the Holy Spirit is critical to those oppressed by powers and principalities. The Spirit works spiritually and contextually in the lives of those who believe in Jesus Christ. The Holy Spirit does, in fact, continues the work of liberation.

1 Corinthians 12:3 records that "No one can say 'Jesus is Lord,' except by the Holy Spirit." Theologically, the connotation is that Jesus has risen from the dead (or has been resurrected from the grave) by

---

[532] Ibid.
[533] Monique Duson, "4 Reasons Why Black Liberation Theology," Para. 10.

the power of the Holy Spirit. What this means is that the people of God should never doubt the power of God when the Holy Spirit does not do the very things, we want him or her to do. God knows how to act on behalf of God's people. William Placher cites Michael Welker's text *God the Spirit* when he writes that "The Spirit does not act by magic, rushing down in the midst of battle; rather, somehow thanks to the Spirit, the people emerge from "insecurity, fear, paralysis and mere complaint" to find that they can face the threat and triumph."[534] The Holy Spirit works in both the spiritual body and the physical body.

Sister Kelly, an ex-slave and washerwoman, echoes earlier strains in the tradition that correlates Spirit with the life of the body. Speaking of a secret gathering of the slave church, she told of sensing the presence of God in every extremity: "I tell you it a wonderful feeling when you feel the spirit of the Lord God Almighty in the tips of your fingers, and the bottom of yo' heart." Christian spirituality, in Kelly's account, does not merely animate the body, but penetrates the body so that our lives are open to the divine embrace. The Spirit is as palpable as breath on skin, tingle on toes, lips upon lips. Living from the Spirit, we taste her presence every moment.[535] The Spirit liberates by way of giving life to the Black body and other groups, races, and cultures of human bodies too.

African Slaves Needed the Holy Spirit for Personal Reasons

Black folk needed the Holy Spirit. The economic (negative) theologizing of the African slave says so. At some point, the thought process becomes liberating memories and moments of human transformation. The Spirit has the authority (power) and vitality to possess the oppressed and guide not only their thought but also their feet to a fuller spiritual and material humanity (Ps 119:105).[536] Inspiration produces and is accomplished by certainty in one becoming a new self when one risks opening the old self to the Spirit's inspiration.[537] Even though many African slaves rejected Christianity

---

[535] Dwight N. Hopkins and George C. L. Cummings, *Cut Loose Your Stammering Tongue*, Summary of pages 74-92 of Chapter 4 in Cheryl J. Sanders's account of what she refers to as the liberation ethics as expressed in ex-slave interviews.

[536] Dwight N. Hopkins, *UP, DOWN, AND OVER*, 272.

[537] Ibid.

based on such dehumanizing mistreatment on behalf of the white slave master, the act of theologizing while being theologized was necessary and needed. I say that because Christian slaveholders went to great lengths to construct a theological anthropology that gave theological respectability to slavery. The Christian master's strategy which cultivated a dualism of soul and body attempted to justify the institution. By conceptually separating the body and soul of slaves in this theological construct, slaveholders justified abusive behavior to slaves' souls had intrinsic value. Whether viewed as capitalistic, Christian, or psychologically therapeutic, Cornel West bluntly affirms in his *Reader*, that "This racialization of American slavery was rooted in economic calculations and psychocultural anxieties that targeted black bodies."[538] E. Franklin Frazier gives clarity:

> And somewhere between capitalism and Christianity, the slave was torn away from his or her family, dehumanized to the point of animalism, raped by the slave master and others for reasons of lust and greed and forced to use all the strength of his or her body, dismembered from mind and soul, as a way of participating in a plantation system—one that tended to supplant other forms of economic exploitation.[539] The punishment for slaves who opposed the poor living and working conditions were cruel disciplines in the form of brutal beating, whipping, wearing of shackles or head irons, giving of identifications marks with hot irons, mutilation, and death.[540]

In the theological mind of Dwight N. Hopkins, the critical words are "spiritual inspiration."[541] Economically exploited and consistently beaten to an inch of their lives, or even worse, the Black slave desperately needed the inspiration of the Holy Spirit. I am sure that there were slaves who asked God in prayer to cleanse the thoughts of their waning hearts by the powerful inspiration of the Holy Spirit. While many of the African slaves were experiencing pure hell in being forced to economically prosper the white slave master, Hopkins shares that "The Spirit of liberation implanted in humanity at creation and fostered by nature in each generation can enable the oppressed

---

[538] Cornel West, *The Cornel West Reader*, 51.
[539] E. Franklin Frazier, *The Negro in The United States*, 30.
[540] Ibid.
[541] Dwight N. Hopkins, *UP, DOWN, AND OVER*, 270.

to achieve unimagined feats if the oppressed will take the risk and allow the fullness of the inspiration to blossom forth."[542] The theological interpretation is that the Holy Spirit was with the Black slaves as they suffered unimaginable pain and sorrow. Even as this demonstration of abusive behavior to the body[543] of the slave made it feasible to introduce Christianity to the soul of the slave, their experiencing the liberating power of the Holy Spirit in their private and public lives, to borrow the language of today's R&B/Hip-hop culture, it hit differently.

On the one hand, knowing that the harm done to their bodies was not representative of God's love, African slaves allowed their souls to separate for reasons of conversion. Often this decision became reality because the slave did not think much of herself/ himself. The African slaves felt that their bodies deserved the brutal treatment of a white slave master. On the other hand, the combination of being physically, psychologically, and religiously enslaved was provoking enough to inspire a response. While African slaves had varying responses to the exploitation and oppression of chattel slavery, slave narratives clearly communicate the fact that a sizable number of slaves faced these traumatic realities. Even those who claim to have not been personally subjected to the dehumanizing viciousness of the slave holding community testify to witnessing brutality directed at other slaves.[544] Being subjected to and witnessing in person the physical perils of slavery can do great to psyche and spirit of human beings. But this is why the African slaves desperately needed the liberation of the Holy Spirit. "Yet precisely,"[545] says Hopkins, "by opening oneself to and delighting in the grace of the Spirit of liberation, poor and working people can, indeed, undertake the frightening but rewarding path to a newness of life."[546] But the Spirit inspires and makes them to be free women and men—liberated in substance while structurally dominated in form.[547]

---

[542] Ibid.

[543] M. Shawn Copeland's text, *Enfleshing Freedom: Body, Race and Being,* gives the best scholarly treatment of how the Black body is theologized for the sake of the oppressor's earthly hopes and dreams.

[544] David E. Goatley, *Were You There?*, 17.

[545] Dwight N. Hopkins, *DOWN, UP, AND OVER*, 270.

[546] Ibid.

[547] Ibid., 271.

In my reading I encountered a fascinating slave narrative in Henry Louis Gates Jr. and William L. Andrews's book, *Pioneers of the Black Atlantic: Five Slave Narratives from the Enlightenment 1772-1815.* Even more so than my own account of what it means to live in oppression, this slave narrative covers the whole of defining what it means to be theologized economically as part of the overall experience of being theologized within one's humanity. The slave narrative is entitled: "The Life, History, and Unparalleled Sufferings of John Jea, the African Preacher, Compiled and Written by Himself." Through the active spheres of the Holy Spirit, Jea authors his own story:

> Our labor was extremely hard, being obliged to work in the summer from two o'clock in the morning, till about ten at night, and in the winter from four in the morning, til ten at night. The horses usually rested about five hours in the day, while we were at work; thus did the beasts enjoyed greater privileges than we did. We dared not murmur, for if we did we were corrected with a weapon an inch-and-a-half thick, and that without mercy, striking us in the most tender parts, and if we complained of this usage, they then took four large poles, placed them in the ground, tied us up to them, and flogged us in a manner too dreadful to behold; and when taken down, if we offered to lift up our hand or foot against our master or mistress, they used us in a most cruel manner; and often they treated the slaves in such a manner as caused their death, shooting them, with a gun, or beating their brains out with some weapon, in order to appease their wrath, and thought no more of it than if they had been brutes: this was the general treatment which slaves experienced. After our master had been treating us in this cruel manner, we were obliged to thank him for the punishment he had been inflicting on us, quoting that Scripture which saith, "Bless the rod, and him that hath appointed it." But though he was a professor of religion, he forgot *that* passage which saith, "God is love, and whoso dwelleth in love dwelleth in God, and God in him." And, again, we are commanded to love our enemies; but it appeared evident that his wretched heart was hardened; which led us to look up to him as our god, for we did not know him who is able to deliver and save all who call upon him in truth

and sincerity. Conscience, that faithful monitor, (which either excuses or accuses) causes to groan, cry, or sigh, in a manner which cannot be uttered.[548]

This narrative painfully brings together the aspects of Black people being negatively theologized by the white slave owner. From the slaves' testimonies of working long hours in hazardous conditions for no pay; to being physically and psychologically abused to the point of death; to experiencing the debilitating feelings of fear and helplessness; to the perplexing, self-reflecting conversation of God and the Bible, John Jea reminds us that historically, it was commonplace for Black people to theologize their experiences and at the same time be theologized in a variety of experiential ways. But does the experience of being theologized negatively always have to lend itself to the outcome of someone being 'religious' enough to endure the harm? In reading and re-reading John Jea's testimony, I find myself confused and perplexed about the religious burden of this Black Americans male's plight. Was John Jea a 'naturally religious' man or did his experiences with slavery transform him into a religious man? Did Jea's religion inspire him to subconsciously quote scripture amid brutal oppression? Was being religious about one's circumstances the only way to survive the terror of slavery? Did the nature of Black religion bring about the burden for Black people or was the Black religious experience a theological reflection of what white people desired for Black people to be? Curtis J. Evans answers:

> Persisting assumptions about black innate religiosity and the rancorous disputes about the role and function of black churches had their origins in these early discourses about black religion. "Black religion," whether conceptualized variously by whites and blacks as an amorphous spirituality, primitive religion, emotionalism, or actual black churches under the rubric of "the Negro Church," groaned under the burden of a multiplicity of interpreters' demands ranging from uplift of the race to bringing an ambiguous quality of "spiritual softness" to a materialistic and racist white culture.[549]

During the rigorous defense of my comprehensive exams at

---

[548] Henry Louis Gates Jr. and William L. Andrews, *Pioneers Of The Black Atlantic*, 369-370.
[549] Curtis J. Evans, *The Burden of Black Religion*, 5.

Garrett-Evangelical Theological Seminary, I stated to my exam committee that I did not think that the Black people were a naturally religious people. Even though I got my theological tail handed to me by the experts in the blazing-hot room of the upstairs portion of the GETS library, I still did not fully believe that Black folk were a naturally religious people. I either felt in my heart that Black people's Christianity was forced upon them for the sake of the slave master's economic gain and their own survivalist livelihood, or Black people are a naturally spiritual people more so than a naturally religious people. What I came to understand was that Black religion and Black spirituality are indispensable parts of the Black religious experiences. To be sure, Black men and women have always been poor and working people. Hopkins summarizes "In a word, the Spirit works with poor and working people to compel to against exploitative systems."[550] This spiritual working which Hopkins refers to is the liberating work of the Holy Spirit in the life of oppressed people.

Evans's masterpiece, *The Burden of Black Religion,* represents the most intriguing argument within the historical discussion of Black people's theologizing within the Black religious experiences. If Evans's book teaches us anything, it is that religion has always been a critical part of the enduring history of American thought on race relations and the transcendent role that race plays in how Black people have been negatively theologized since chattel slavery. In tracing ideas about African American religion from the Antebellum period throughout the 1950s, Evans argues that there has always been this deep-rooted notion that blacks were somehow "naturally" religious[551] or created with the purpose of being a religious people.

When Black people came to America as African slaves, they brought their religious affinities with them. Whether their spiritualities were in Christianity, Islam, Buddhism, or other forms of African religion, a sizable number of the African slaves were already in the process of theologizing their God within their cultural experiences. Because Black people were already reflecting upon God in their daily rituals, their religion came naturally as the result of the dehumanizing treatment of slavery. In other words, by way of responding to slavery's oppression with a spirituality of Black religion,

---

[550] Dwight N. Hopkins, *DOWN, UP, AND OVER,* 271.
[551] Ibid., back flap.

Black religion and slave religion were synonymous. At first, this assumed natural impulse toward religion served as a signal trait of Black people's humanity--potentially their unique contribution to American culture.[552] Whether the impulse was one of genuine spirituality or cultural giftedness, the abolitionists capitalized on what they perceived to be true and connected the intricacies of Black religion to the Black capacity for human freedom. As a Black liberation theologian of poverty and the Spirit, I would argue that the work of the Holy Spirit was one that produced both a genuine spirituality and a cultural giftedness. That is to say that while it did not always look that way, the liberating power of the Holy Spirit worked for the good of the African slave.

Within an abbreviated period, however, these introductory steps toward an equality-based, multiracial democracy were reversed as mainstream white America began to place cultural emphasis on worldly concepts over religious piety. These new priorities worked against Black people as the idea of an innate Black religiosity was used to justify and preserve Black oppression. These inequalities served as the structural ways in which Black people were theologized by their white counterpart. Later, social scientists—both Black and white— sought to reverse the damage caused by these racist ideas and in the process proved that blacks were in fact fully capable of incorporation into white American culture.[553]

Theologically, Evans's thoughtful work reveals how interpretations of Black religion played a crucial role in shaping the broader views within African Americans' human existence.

Overall, Evans succeeds in demonstrating how the history of Black people has real life consequences for their present-day contexts. In offering a fresh and innovative perspective of how religion has shaped the African American narrative, for good and bad, Evans helps us to continue the conversation of how Black people theologized while being negatively theologized in their own humanity. Here, Evans teaches us that the cultural history of Black people helps to identify the critical places where race and Black religion intersect.

---

[552] Ibid.
[553] Ibid.

The true burden of Black religion exists in Black people's ability to theologize the divine nature of God in Jesus Christ by way of the Holy Spirit and at the same time be theologized by those whose only intention was to keep them oppressed and unsettled. It is the Holy Spirit that makes Black folk a naturally religious people.

Being Theologized in the Economic Acts of Slavery and Lynching

The economic acts of institutional slavery, American capitalism, lynching, church bombings and church burnings are all intricate parts of the overarching conversation of theology and economics in the United States. While considered as forms of idolatry and structural evil, all these actions and systems carry economic implications with it. In other words, they all affect Black people and other races of people in the economic facets of their lives. These outreaches destroyed and killed human beings. While it is no secret that the Holy Spirit gave life to and played a powerful role in the abolishment of slavery and the creation of the Black church, the Spirit also gave life to Black people in their crucifying experiences with racism and oppression. Despite the forms of deadly brutality founded in the irreversible harm that was done to the mind, body and spirit of Black slaves, the fact remains that "the Spirit inspires and makes them to be free women and men—liberated in substance while structurally dominated in form."[554]

In his critical text, *Down by the Riverside: Readings in African American Religion*, editor Larry G. Murphy[555] writes that "Religion has, indeed, been a determinative dynamic in the unfolding life of the African American community in the United States."[556] Theologically, part of the reason why religion has been such a major force in the life of Black people is because Black religion has always carried with it economic and material implications. These implications, for one reason or another, stringently connects to one's view of God in Jesus Christ by the power of the Holy Spirit. Often, these economic and

---

[554] Dwight N. Hopkins, *UP, DOWN, AND UNDER*, 271.

[555] Rev. Larry G. Murphy, Ph.D., is an ordained Elder in the AME Church and is a leading historian in the fields of Christianity proper, Black religious history and Black church history. Dr. Murphy also served on my Comprehensive Exam committee and my Dissertation committee. During my PhD tenure at Garrett-Northwestern, Dr. Murphy was the professor of my *History of Black Religious Experiences* course.

[556] Larry G. Murphy, *Down by the Riverside*, 1.

material implications also carry an idolatrous love for money. Nonetheless, for the sake of *business,* African slaves were torn away from their native lands because white, Christian men in the United States had hopes and dreams of economic prosperity by way of cheap, slave labor. Because human beings of African descent came to America as property, they were purchased for a negotiated price and forced to leave their homeland for the economic gain of the white slave master. The dehumanization of the African slave on American soil was part of the social-psychological game that was played in hope of convincing the African slave of their inhumanity. Analogous to the concept of "freaking horses"[557], the white slave master figured that if he could conquer the mind of the African slave, then the dream of economic riches would soon follow.

The economic implications of slavery in the United States served as a relevant microcosm of the broader stripping of African American human and religious rights. Even today, Black people are still being theologized economically for reasons of capitalistic idolatry and systemic evil. The sizable minority of Black people living on American soil in 2024 are dirt poor and unable to pay their monthly bills. The annual poverty line statistics only tell a small part of the larger, Black economic narrative. Black on Black crime is still a relevant issue in the Black community. Famed community developer, John M. Perkins, claims that "poverty has the power to move beyond one's physical condition to claim one's whole mind. For all genders, cultures, and races of poor people, "poverty means thinking for the moment. It is the inability to think about the future because of the total demand to think about survival in the present.... A little can't help much."[558]

But a little bit of the Holy Spirit can help to liberate those who suffer from economic/material poverty. Just as W.E.B. Du Bois affirmed racism as the preeminent issue of the twentieth century, economic deprivation is the most prominent issue facing Black people in the twenty-first century. Because Black religious experiences are more pneumatological than Christological, the Holy Spirit has the authority and vitality to possess the oppressed and guide

---

[557] 'Freaking' describes what the trainer does to the horse to get maximum performance in a competitive environment.

[558] John M. Perkins, *Restoring At-Risk Communities*, 51.

poor people's feet to a greater spiritual and material humanity. Moreover, once the least in society opens to the Spirit within, it will become impossible any longer to turn away from one's call to do God's will of liberation in whatever form it assumes. In viewing the Holy Spirit as the Spirit of liberation, love, and emancipation, I am in solidarity with Hopkins when he affirms that

> Inspiration produces and is accompanied by certainty in one becoming a new self when one risks opening the old self to the Spirit's inspiration. Thus, the oppressed must dare to allow the emancipatory sacred presence to work with and on them. A definite result is acquiring rock-like confidence that this Spirit will make a way out of no way. One can only benefit from firmness of belief when one releases the fears of the self's weaknesses and of sinful structures to enable the Spirit to do its job. After that, confidence goes with the oppressed on their journey toward full humanity.[559]

Yet while resisting pretenses of human creativity, the Spirit is forever showing forth the creativity of God in fashioning new hearts in believers.[560]

---

[559] Dwight N. Hopkins, *DOWN, UP, AND UNDER*, 272.
[560] Thomas C. Oden, *How Africa Shaped the Christian Mind*, 130.

Chapter Six

The Spirit Resists/Contests the Demonic and Births Sociocultural Movements

Speak to my heart, Holy Spirit Give me the words that will bring new life Words on the wings of a morning, the dark night will fade away If You speak to my heart now.[561]

Throughout the history of Christian experience, not much has been written about the role of the Holy Spirit in the presence of racial discrimination--amidst the harm that has destroyed persons, families, neighborhoods, and communities of color. Theologically, I do not believe that the Holy Spirit is working in the demonic evil that is associated with racism and capitalism. But I am certain that the Holy Spirit resists and contests the demonic spirits that are hell bent on creating more widespread poverty, inciting more political violence, uncovering more outreaches of human trafficking, killing more innocent people, incarcerating more Black and Latino people, stripping off more functionable layers of public-school education, destroying more smaller countries, keeping more minorities lumped into underdeveloped ghettoes, and increasing the gap of wealth between the "superior" haves and the "inferior" have nots by way of spreading the croaking terror of not being able to afford healthcare due to hegemonic demonism.

While I have pondered whether blaspheme of the Holy Spirit is the only unpardonable sin (Matt 12:22-45), I have also wondered about organized sin and systemic evil is as it relates to the demonic

---

[561] https://www.azlyrics.com/lyrics/donniemcclurkin/speaktomyheart.html

showcase of racism on earth. Again, the Bible teaches that blaspheme of the Holy Spirit is the only unpardonable sin. The concept of "blasphemy against the Spirit" is mentioned in Mark 3:22–30 and Matthew 12:22–32. Jesus has just performed a miracle. A demon-possessed man was brought to Jesus, and the Lord cast the demon out, healing the man of blindness and muteness. The eyewitnesses to this exorcism began to wonder if Jesus was indeed the Messiah they had been waiting for. A group of Pharisees, hearing the talk of the Messiah, quickly quashed any budding faith in the crowd: "It is only by Beelzebul, the prince of demons, that this fellow drives out demons," they said. (Matt. 12:24).

What is the Christian church saying about the sin and evil that is associated with demonic racism and the destructive idolatries that flow from them? Does the power of the Holy Spirit work against all outreaches of sin and evil? As the work of the Holy Spirit, does God's redeeming quality of grace work in the lives of those who have consistently participated in the destroying and killing of innocent Black people? In his article, "Powers and Principalities: King and the Holy Spirit," Eugene F. Rivers argues that forces such as white supremacy are "spiritual forces of evil"[562] (Eph. 6:12, NIV) that can only be reckoned with by those spiritual weapons given to us by the Holy Spirit.

> Rivers' statement about the role of the Holy Spirit in King's work resonates with profound consequences. When we recognize the fullness of the Holy Spirit's power, we discover that the same Spirit who inspires our worship services also empowers movements such as Black Lives Matter; and the same Spirit who responds to our private prayers is the one spurring on those who fight for clean water and an end to sex trafficking.[563]

Whether or not the Holy Spirit inspires our political and cultural activism is of urgent importance today. The virulence of white supremacist discourse and action demands that the church reclaim the power of the Spirit to discern the most effective response.[564] In her article, "The Holy Spirit and Social Justice," Jill M. Johnson states

---

[562] Eugene F. Rivers III, "Powers and Principalities: King and the Holy Spirit," Para. 5.
[563] Jill M. Johnson, "The Holy Spirit and Social Justice," Para. 5.
[564] Eugene F. Rivers III, "Powers and Principalities: King and the Holy Spirit," Para. 6.

that "Any movement that addresses racism or other social ills today won't look the same as it did half a century ago. Secular activist groups such as Black Lives Matter use different tactics and methods of communication than those used by MLK and other 1960s-era civil rights workers. If we've grown accustomed to old-school activism, these differences can make us feel uncomfortable."[565] Put another way, the liberating work of the Holy Spirit in the life of any justice-minded movement gives room for different tactics and methods of communication to create various levels of productive comfort for the group. Amidst different methodologies and strategies, the Holy Spirit is the One that enables the movement to go forward.

Rivers argues that the work of these newer movements "highlights the moral and political failure of the black church to speak prophetically against the use of excessive force against black people, especially in the inner city."[566] However, Rivers also warns that these secular movements won't achieve long-term success if they're not Spirit-led. They must build on the foundations laid by King and others, who leveraged biblical understanding and intercessory prayer when standing up for the poor and marginalized.[567] Here, the instructional translation is that God's people should always listen and pay attention to the Holy Spirit moving inside of them. Oppressed Black people and other cultures and races of people must find a way to listen to what their children, relatives, and friends have to say; and let the liberating Spirit work through the generational cultures of their people. And then act courageously in the same Spirit of love.

With the notion of grassroots movements in mind, my theology affirms that the Holy Spirit is the Spirit of liberation and love. The Holy Spirit is also the Spirit of justice. In his best-selling book, *The Spirit of Justice: True Stories of Faith, Race, and Resistance*, historian Jemar Tisby speaks on the liberating work of the Holy Spirit in these two statements:

> For those who claim the Christian faith, one might understand the spirit of justice as the Holy Spirit. The indwelling Spirit empowers the believer to do the work of loving God and loving neighbor. This struggle for justice

---

[565] Jill M. Johnson, "The Holy Spirit and Social Justice," Para. 7.
[566] Ibid., Para. 8.
[567] Ibid.

encompasses both material and spiritual dimensions. As the apostle Paul once wrote once wrote long ago, "For our struggle is not against flesh and blood, but against the rulers, against the authorities, against the powers of the dark world and against spiritual forces of evil in the heavenly realms" (Ephesians 6:12).[568]

For followers of Jesus, the Spirit of justice grants them spiritual gifts to equip them for their work of redemption in the world. The Spirit supplies believers with spiritual armor to fight injustice (Ephesians 6:10-20). The Spirit enlivens and motivates the pursuit of all forms of justice because God hates injustice and seeks to correct oppression (Isaiah 1:17). The Spirit of injustice is always at work to inspire followers of Christ to undertake acts of liberation and bear witness to the good news of their Savior.[569]

As believers pray in the Spirit to the Lord for help, they should understand that the Spirit that resists evil is also the Spirit that contests suffering. In describing how the Holy Spirit is the Holy Liberator that contests the suffering of God's people, Andrea Hollingsworth "explores ways in which the Holy Spirit fights to free those threatened and bound by suffering, especially that caused by forces of injustice."[570] According to Hollingsworth,

> Christianity has long proclaimed the biblical principle that, wherever we see creation and renewed life, there we recognize and celebrate the work of the Holy Spirit of God (Psalm 104:30). But ushering in new life often involves opposing powers that obstruct renewal. Theologian Elizabeth Johnson reminds us that, "in the biblical prophetic tradition the Spirit's presence is consistently linked with the power to denounce social wrongdoing... and bring about justice for the poor[.]"[23] Indeed, a key aspect of the Spirit's life-giving presence is to contest injustice and liberate those languishing under the pain of oppression.[571]

Creation and renewed life are the works of the Holy Spirit. Along the

---

[568] Jemar Tisby, The Spirit of Justice, 5.
[569] Ibid., 5-6.
[570] Andrea Hollingsworth, "Groans Too Deep: The Holy Spirit and Suffering," Para. 25.
[571] Ibid.

same lines, becoming a new creation is the result of the Holy Spirit's working inside the believer. The Bible says that becoming a new creation is what happens when you receive salvation. Your old spirit man dies, and a new spirit comes alive. The new spirit is created in righteousness and true holiness. (Eph. 4:24). You become one spirit with God (1 Cor. 6:17). While the Holy Spirit works to liberate people from the bondage of systemic oppression, the Spirit also collaborates with believers on a personal level. In keeping with the themes of groans too deep and human suffering, Romans 8:26-27 teaches us that the Holy Spirit helps us in our weaknesses and intercedes for us by way of praying for us with groans too deep words. That is, in God's infinite wisdom, knowledge, and power, the Holy Spirit meets believers at the apex deepness of their human suffering and prays for them with inexpressible groans—groans that defy and transcend the painful difficulties of their situation.

If there were ever a group of people that needed the Holy Spirit to pray for them with groans too deep to express in words, it would the African slaves. Set up by their own ancestors and kidnapped by white colonizers, African slaves forcibly came to a place they did not want to be. In critique of how African slaves were unjustly uprooted from their native land, Howard Thurman poses the question: What might have happened if Jesus, so perfect a flower from the brooding spirit of God in the soul of Israel, had been permitted to remain where his roots would have been fed by the distilled elements accumulated from Israel's wrestling with God?[572] With theological brilliance, Thurman uses this analysis to speak specifically to Jesus' socioeconomic context. He states that "Jesus was a poor Jew."[573]

> The economic predicament with which he was identified the birth placed him initially with the great mass of men on earth. If we dare take the position that in Jesus, there was at work some racial destiny. It would be safe to say that in his poverty he was more truly Son of man than he would have been if the incident of family or birth had made him a rich son of Israel. It is not a point to be labored, for again and again men have transcended circumstance of birth and training, but it is an

---

[572] Howard Thurman, *Jesus and the Disinherited*, 16.
[573] Ibid., 17.

observation not without merit.[574]

In the spirit of resistance and contesting the systemic evils in the United States, James H. Cone confesses that

> People often ask me whether I am still angry as when I wrote *Black Theology and Black Power.* When I hear that question, I smile to contain my rage: I remain just as angry because America, when viewed from the perspective of the black poor, is no closer to Martin Luther King, Jr.'s dream of a just society than when he was killed." "What became clear to me is that, if you adopt a certain form, then form is going to push you into certain content because the form is not just the form, the form itself is content. There is content in form and in your choice of form.[575]

This powerful statement gives theological credence to the multitude of reasons I wrote my PhD dissertation and my first theology book on why Black poverty in the United States is a theological problem. In April 2023, *Inner City Blues: Black Theology and Black Poverty in the United States* was published nationally and internationally. Even though the new book focuses on the theological methodology of Cone's contemporary, J. Deotis Roberts, I am humbly thankful that I was able to find a statement from Cone that described his raging displeasure with Black poverty in the United States. In *Inner-City Blues,* I stated that Cone was aware that there was a considerable number of white Americans who lived in poverty.

Anthony G. Reddie was certain Cone knew that poverty had a certain skin color, implying that Cone was aware how economic poverty was prevalent in a sizable number of Black neighborhoods and communities. Even as Roberts is my theologian of choice from the first-generation of Black constructors, Cone's words still hold theological weight for me; especially where the important conversation of the Holy Spirit and Black poverty in the United States is concerned. Without the academic courage and vision of Cone, there is no Black theology for Black Americans and the Black church. This is precisely why *What's Going On?* is a more academically-

---

[574] Ibid.
[575] Corey D. B. Walker, "Love and a Theology of Blackness: A Meditation on James H. Cone," Para. 1.

ladened follow-up to *Inner-City Blues*. The Holy Spirit has "spoken clearly to me"[576] throughout the course of my published writings.

According to Linda E. Thomas and Dwight N. Hopkins, the world must take a serious look at spiritual poverty. Both theologians expound on the notion of spiritual poverty:

> After structural poverty, we look at spiritual poverty. This concept has often ridiculed or condemned by progressive or justice-minded, religious people of African descent. Such reactions are understandable because both white Christian preachers during American slavery and white missionaries to Africa and the diaspora have reinterpreted and hence manipulated the notion of spirituality as an opiate of poor and working-class communities. Generally, missionaries in the early United States and those abroad told black people to rely on a spiritual Jesus and not to worry about material white supremacy, economic inequality, and gender discrimination. Here, spirituality serves as a drug because it does not focus oppressed people on the structures of capitalism and heinous forms of human poverty. However, we would suggest that the idea of spiritual poverty offers a very important heuristic even for justice-minded and progressive Christians.[577]

Hopkins defines Black theology as "how God, or the spirit of freedom works with the oppressed black community for their full humanity."[578] Hopkins also defines Black liberation as "a specific God-talk, God-walk, an intellectual discipline and a way of life."[579] These definitions are important to the fact that Hopkins takes the Black experience seriously. For Hopkins, the Black experience is a critical resource used by the Black theologian to develop one's method. I define Hopkins' theological method as Eco-cultural theological anthropology for the Black experience. Eco meaning ecological and cultural as having earthly and spiritual implications for the relationship between theology and culture. For Hopkins, the spirit of

---

[576] The title of my PhD dissertation is '*Cause De Spirit Spoke to Me: Robertsian Conversations on Black Liberation Theology Amidst Economic Deprivation*. For me, writing theology books is also the work of the Holy Spirit.
[577] Peter Paris, *Religion and Poverty*, 130.
[578] Dwight N. Hopkins, *Introducing Black Theology*, 46.
[579] Dwight N. Hopkins, *Being Human*, 8.

freedom is the Holy Spirit collaborating with the oppressed Black community for their full humanity. My question now is: Where is the Spirit of hope in all the evil outreaches that continue to go on throughout the world? What's going on in our society?

The Holy Spirit in Sociocultural Movements, the Bible, and Cultural Texts

While most of the theological attention on the work of the Holy Spirit has been given to the new spirituality of the individual believer and the spiritual affections of the local church community, what has not been affirmed publicly is how the Holy Spirit works in social movements—movements that are designed to bring material awareness to the social, political, and economic injustices that continue to fuel and perpetuate human oppression. Just as the 'on the ground' work of the Holy Spirit in social movements was underestimated, "the deeply spiritual foundation of the Civil Rights movement is often under-emphasized. The movement that sought political and legal equality for Black Americans was grounded in faith. The devout Christian commitment of virtually all its leaders, from Martin Luther King, Jr. to Fannie Lou Hamer to John Lewis, inspired them to work for the dignity and equality of all. Rosemarie Freeney Harding (1930–2004), the wife of civil rights leader Vincent Harding (1931-2014), recalls the transformational power of the Holy Spirit working in the movement during that time."[580]

> One of the most exciting things for me about being in the freedom movement was discovering other people who were compelled by the (Holy) Spirit at the heart of our organizing work, and who were also interested in the mysticism[2] that can be nurtured in social justice activism. We experienced something extraordinary in the freedom movement, something that hinted at a tremendous potential for love and community and transformation that exists here in this scarred, spectacular country. For many of us, that "something" touched us in the deepest part of our selves and challenged us in ways both personal and political.[581]

As a Black liberation theologian and activist, I would argue that the

---

[580] "Spirituality Civil Rights Movement", Para. 1.

[581] Ibid., Para. 2.

greatest challenge faced by those who were deeply involved in the Civil Rights Movement was that of enfleshing a type of radical love that would yield substantive results. King often spoke of God's love as a radical 'on the ground' love that went beyond the particularizing of local contexts into the more expansive 'world house' love among all believers, cultures, faiths, and human beings. This is precisely why I theologize the love of God in the world as the conversational interlocutor between theology and economics, between oppression and liberation, between Black theology and white theology, and between the Black church and the White church.

According to Harding,

> There was an energy moving in those times. Something other than just sit-ins and voter registration and Freedom Schools. Something represented by these signal efforts but broader. As I traveled around the country in the sixties, it seemed to me that the nation—from the largest community to the smallest— was permeated with hope; the idea that people can bring about transformation; that what we do matters. To be sure, it can be affirmed that the energy was the Holy Spirit's energy working in the bodies, minds and spirits of the Body of Christ and other religions as well. With hope and transformation being the work of the Holy Spirit, it is easy to see how "living and working in their presence hastened changes in your own thoughts, your reactions, your priorities, even if you weren't always cognizant of the shift. Being constantly in the presence of people who believed and acted from the understanding that love and forgiveness were essential tools for social justice; being surrounded by people like that fed those commitments in me, in many of us. And it infused the nation. To some degree for those who were willing to believe that love and forgiveness were also works of the Holy Spirit, their "participation in the Movement gave the people "a craving for spiritual depth.[582]

Sometimes not knowing what was right or wrong in a situation, they had to be quiet about it. Had to go somewhere and just meditate

---

[582] Ibid., Para. 5.

about it. Pray on it.[583] Here, the Holy Spirit instructed the people of God to be quiet, meditate and pray about what to do and say next. This is what it meant to be led by the Holy Spirit with involvement in social movements—movements that transcended individual aspiration. According to Rick Herrick, "This spiritual dynamic is turbocharged through participation in a social movement centered around bringing love, peace, and justice to the world. In such movements when thousands of people relate to each other as Thous, Divine love is magnified and is encountered as a loving impulse that spreads throughout the community. A spirit of love, the sense of the essential goodness of life, erotic and compassionate energy descend upon the participants within the movement. Christians know this transforming and healing energy as the Holy Spirit."[584]

> Gabel speaks from an intimate knowledge of this process. He has been there. Participation in the social movements of the sixties changed his life. Because of these experiences his goal in life has been to build a new world around this loving impulse. By ending our sense of separation and fear, we can learn to see and think about the world differently. Movement toward peace, economic and social justice, environmental health all follows from the creation of loving individuals living within a socially connected community. If you are looking to meet the Holy Spirit, participate in a social movement. In doing so, you will be joining with God to make the world a better place.[585]

Oscar Merlo is certain that experiencing the inspiration of the Holy Spirit means getting involved in social movements. It was

> The kind of thing that in retrospect made sense, but I think nobody could have predicted it. As we look back through history, we can see how the Holy Spirit moved amidst chaotic social times. More unpredictable is to see how the JPM (Jesus People Movement) received wide secular coverage without the power of today's social media mechanisms. These historical takeaways affirm that secular media and society sees the good of the gospel being lived out through a community

---

[583] Ibid.
[584] Rick Herrick, "Meeting the Holy Spirit," Para. 3.
[585] Ibid., Para. 4.

of love. A love in action that characterizes the church must be shown as we face complex times in American contemporary history.[586]

Merlo demonstrates why the people believed that getting involved in sociopolitical movements presupposes doing the work of Jesus. Because the Holy Spirit is the Spirit of Christ, to be inspired by the Spirit to get involved in movements is the embodiment of people doing what Jesus wants them to do. Six decades ago, America was experiencing a moral and spiritual decadency like the condition of our times. However, in Southern California, the Holy Spirit empowered a generation, and a spiritual awakening took place on par with the 1906 Azusa Street Revival. It was amazing how hippies, homeless people and the marginalized were being transformed by the Word of God into preachers, worship leaders and agents of redemption.[587] To be sure, the 1906 Azuza Street Revival was the work of the Holy Spirit in the life of the Christian church and individual believers alike.

Speaking on Black church preachers as agents of communal redemption and world change, the article "Powers and Principalities: King and the Holy Spirit," by the Reverend Eugene F. Rivers III, traces King's theological formation and unpacks King's insistence that the civil rights movement be grounded in Christian principles of nonviolence, love, and unconditional forgiveness. Rivers writes, "It was the Holy Spirit, which he allowed to work in and through him, that made Martin Luther King Jr. the most influential voice of conscience and religious freedom in the United States in the twentieth century."[588] Rivers' statement about the role of the Holy Spirit in King's work resonates with profound consequences. When we recognize the fullness of the Holy Spirit's power, we discover that the same Spirit who inspires our worship services also empowers movements such as Black Lives Matter; and the same Spirit who responds to our private prayers is the one spurring on those who fight for clean water, normal temperatures in global warming, higher wages, better salaries, infrastructural development in inner-city communities and neighborhoods; and an end to all forms of human trafficking and

---

[586] Oscar Merlo, "The Jesus People Movement," Para. 5.
[587] Ibid., Para. 1.
[588] Jill M. Johnson, "Holy Spirit and Social Justice," Para. 4.

oppression.[589]

The Creative Work of the Holy Spirit in Black Culture

The transcendent work of the Holy Spirit in the life of believers is liberating and creative. In Black theology, the Holy Spirit connects with the human spirit of Black people for the visible creation of Black culture. Black culture is a productive culture born, constructed, and created by the power of the Holy Spirit throughout the world. Black culture is the material result of the Holy Spirit working in sociocultural movements and sociopolitical contexts. Often, the creation of Black culture took place in the worst of socioeconomic situations. For example, the Black political uprising of the late 1960s and early 1970s saw the creation of the Congressional Black Caucus. In addition to the increase in political leadership, musicians, professional athletes, and more Black-owned businesses were created for the much-needed improvement of Black America. The development of Black culture in the United States came in a diversity of forms. One of those forms was a cultural text. Examples of Black cultural texts are the Bible, books, poetry, music, videos, social media, plays, churches, educational institutions, movies, opera, museums, sports, political movements, food, fashion, sitcoms, church sermons, dancing, speeches, art, trades, and other forms of human creation.

I would argue that anything that Black people have invented for the development of the United States and the world abroad, the presence and work of the Holy Spirit inspired them to do so. Put another way, God has blessed Black people to develop and further their cultural existence in the places they reside. Africa, Britain, Jamaica, Brazil, Puerto Rico, the Caribbean, and the Dominican Republic included. Theologically, let us not forget that the Holy Spirit works in sacred institutions, secular environments and in other religions outside of Christianity.

The study of the Holy Spirit in Black theology informs the world that the Holy Spirit holds a loving, creative, and productive presence in the downtrodden ghettoes of the United States and the world abroad. In attempting to describe how the Holy Spirit works in the poorest of Black neighborhoods and communities, one of the greatest sociocultural movements of the twentieth century is that of Hip-Hop

---

[589] Ibid., Para. 5.

music. As a form of cultural text, cultural development, and cultural movement, the culture of Hip-Hop filled with an existential sense of hope, spiritual giftedness, trained artistry, and creative imaginations. All of which come from the Holy Spirit. The point I am attempting to make is that Holy Spirit helped to create the culture of Hip-Hop in the geographic context of economic deprivation and other forms of internalized oppression.

Willie Hudson's book, *The Holy Ghost Got A New Dance: An Examination of Black Theology and Holy Hip-Hop in Inner-City*, centers on the vision of how the merger of Black theology and Holy Hip-Hop will go a long way in expanding the people's faith in God and inner-city ministry. This cultural expansion has spiritual implications in that the Black theology/Holy Hip Hop collaboration helps to bring about freedom, self-awareness, education, and jobs to the myriad faces of systemic oppression. While not every layer and texture of Hip-Hop culture is holy, it does not mean that the movement is without a spiritual presence. Hip-Hop may not be one of the Black church's favorite conversations, but the growing culture of the movement has given disenfranchised Black people a sense of spiritual hope and cultural identity.

I am certain that a sizable number of the rappers, poets, artists, dancers, and business owners have faith in God. In other words, they know where their help comes from. The unfamiliar dance that Hudson is referring to is two new dances—a holy ghost filled dance in the streets and a new type of cultural dance in the Black church. Both of which are inspired by the power of the Holy Spirit. Theologically, I do not consider Black theology and Holy Hip-Hop as a double-edged sword. I view them as collaborative partners in the ministry of the Holy Spirit. According to Hudson,

> The Holy Ghost dance is an indication of God's presence taking over the flesh and mind lending itself to the power of God's Spirit inwardly (See my definition of culture and Black culture in Chapter 2). It is an outward action of surrender to the goodness of God in the lives of believers. Worship surrenders our spirit to God because of who He is, and praise is our surrender to God for He has and continues to do in our lives. There must be a balance of praise and worship; and if the balance is imperfect in any way, God is not glorified.

However, to many who witness this dance, there is a degree of skepticism that this form of worship is fleshly and contrived. It is an "old" form of worship started by the older generation of church. Furthermore, when young people of the millennial generation witness the "Holy Ghost Dance" red flags of distrust and fakeness become evident. Young millennials must be taught that dancing with the Spirit is a form of worship even though evil tries to corrupt it with ungodly fleshly expressions. [590]

Since Hip-Hop lyricists and rappers intentionally reference God, Jesus Christ, and the Holy Spirit in their music, the Hip-Hop cultural movement of the late twentieth century is a contributing part of the history of Christian experience. Just like the sermons preachers preach, and the music gospel singers sing, the Holy Spirit inspires Hip-Hop artists to lay down the tracks for their new songs. This spiritual inspiration may very well be their personal form of worship. We would be surprised to know that there are a host of Hip-Hop rappers who pray to God before they write and record their music. In terms of using God-language in their songs, such rappers as Tupac Shakur, D.M.X., KRS ONE, Nasir Jones, Kanye West, Kendrick Lamar, Drake, J. Cole, Big Sean, Chance the Rapper, Fat Joe, Logic, Frank Ocean, Lecrae, Pusha T, Big K.R.I.T., and Remy Ma have all referenced God, Jesus Christ, and the Holy Spirit in their music. In the realms of Black culture, religion, and spirituality, the Holy Spirit leads, guides, and inspires. In sectors of the United States and the world abroad, Hip-Hop artists have more influence than preachers and pastors. They have greater followings as well. Just because an overwhelming majority of rappers and poets were born and raised in impoverished neighborhoods, does not mean they have not felt the power of the Holy Spirit in their lives. Because they have. People can feel and hear the Spirit in their music.

Queensbridge, New York rapper Nasir Jones talks about his experience with God as he continues to produce relevant music for the culture of Hip-Hop at age 50. Moreover, Nas recently took to Twitter on Saturday (July 22) to thank the inspiration behind this five-album run. "I'm happy to be around making new music because I love it," he said. "Having the best year of my life. I caught the Holy

---

[590] Willie Hudson, *THE HOLY GHOST GOT A NEW DANCE*, 131.

Spirit and I'm grateful to be giving it all to the world. *Magic 2*." Considering the impressive and dominant nature of the past few years for them, no wonder there are spiritual forces at play here.[591] One person who's not bothered by this Machiavellian symbiosis of success and access is Dej Loaf herself. Over the phone she's soft-spoken yet brimming with confidence: "My range is ridiculous, man. I know what the people want to hear, and I've got it all." She perceives a divine element in her muse: when she's on a roll with songwriting she calls it "catching the holy ghost." Makes sense; in 2014 I wouldn't put it past the Lord to browse Datpiff for new prophets.[592] Both Nas and Loaf are believers in Jesus Christ who have felt the transformational power of the Holy Spirit in their everyday life.

Rap music is often seen as a Black secular response to the pressing social issues of the time. Poverty included. Rap music is not known for its spirituality, spiritual commitments, and spiritual foundations. But that does not mean the culture itself is not in touch with the Spirit of God. Many rappers and contributors of Hip-Hip experience a divine spiritual element in their cultural muse. Which is no different than Black churchgoers catching or feeling the Holy Ghost during their worship experiences. The Spirit is present in both sacred institutions and secular environments. In a substantive way, however, Hip-Hop represents a sociocultural movement of an oppressed people who have suffered socially, politically, and economically while lumped in underdeveloped inner-city neighborhoods.

As the result of their victimization, lyricists and rappers are inspired by the Holy Spirit to express their authentic selves through their gifts and grace for music and other forms of material culture. The unique development of Hip-Hop culture over the last 50 plus years comes in the form of a sociocultural movement that resists, contests, and responds to holistic trauma that is associated with the internalization of human oppression. The exuberant culture known as Hip-Hop moves the needle forward in Black people's search for freedom and liberation. I believe the Holy Spirit has her or his inspirational hands all over the movement of Hip-Hop and the

---

[591] Gabriel Bras, "Nas Attributes His Run To "The Holy Ghost," Para. 2.
[592] Ezra Marcus, "DeJ Loaf Is Feeling Herself," Para. 2.

multiple genres that accompany it.

Yet, like spirituals, the rhythm and blues, and gospel music, rap has deep connections to African American religious traditions. Anthony B. Pinn's book, *Noise and Spirit: The Religious and Spiritual Sensibilities of Rap Music,* explores the diverse religious dimensions of rap stemming from Islam (including the Nation of Islam and Five Percent Nation), Rastafarianism, and Humanism, as well as Christianity. Thriving even under slavery, sharecropping, imprisonment, and the urban housing project, the "spirit" finds crafty inlets into daily life, starting with the spirituals and extending to blues, jazz, soul, and finally hip-hop. The presence of spiritually informed behavior is evident in the performance practice of many black popular music forms, right up from the blues men and women to the b-boys and b-girls.[593] In other words, Black popular music has always been a spiritual art form.[594] This is because Black music has always had a spiritual tradition. Disappointingly, the spiritual dimension of Black popular music is unresearched. Using the terms religious and spiritual interchangeably in her groundbreaking analysis, Christina Zanfagna poses that

> The literature on hip-hop and spirituality, although gradually increasing, is minimal. Sustained critical analysis has yet to be done. Scholars who touch upon the topic generally mention it in passing as a peripheral concern. The first sources to embark on this important subject matter are Michael Eric Dyson's *Between God and Gangsta Rap* (1996) and two issues of the *Black Sacred Music* journal (1991, 1994). Dyson's book title is misleading; he writes about his personal rise from the Detroit ghetto to public intellectual, his existence between God and gangsta rap, the pulpit and streets. *Noise and Spirit: The Religious and Spiritual Sensibilities of Rap Music*, edited by Anthony Pinn, is the only book solely dedicated to this subject (2003). Robin Sylvan's *Traces of The Spirit: The Religious Dimension of Popular Music* (2002) and Teresa Reed's *The Holy Profane: Religion in Black Popular Music* (2003) each devote a chapter to religious concerns in rap music. While they offer

---

[593] Christina Zanfagna, "Under the Blasphemous W(RAP)," Para. 3.
[594] Ibid., Para. 2.

interesting insights, their studies never move beyond lyrical analysis to the music itself.[595]

Even in what several pundits would perceive as a secular or nonreligious culture, speaking of Hip-Hop, the fact remains that without the person, power and work of the Holy Spirit/Spirit/spirit, the realities of being spiritual or sensing the spiritual under the sacred gazes of one's spirituality are not possible. It is the Holy Spirit that makes Hip-Hop spiritual while inspiring believers to express the unexplainable depths of what the Spirit is saying and doing to them in the development of their spiritualities.

In this poetic cultural text, poet Adrienne Rich reflects on the presence of the Spirit in Black neighborhoods:

> Bad air in the tunnels
>
> voice of the ghetto
>
> *god loves you*[596]

The Holy Spirit is Present in Secular Music Too

As a believer and a follower of the historical book of Acts, I have felt the power of the Holy Spirit as I listened to secular music. God is present in secular music. As one who believes that the Holy Spirit works in sacred institutions and secular environments, I am certain that I have felt the comforting presence of God when I listen to rhythm and blues, love ballads, and socially conscious music as well. Look no further than the one who inspired the title of this new book, Marvin Gaye. Gaye was a legendary American singer known for his soulful and spiritually uplifting music. One of his notable songs that reflects themes of spiritual awakening and unity is "Wholy Holy." This soulful track was released in 1971 as part of Gaye's landmark album "What's Going On." The message of this song is contextualized in the lyrics. The lyrics convey themes of spiritual reflection, unity, and the pursuit of a higher purpose. Gaye's emotive lead vocals, combined with gospel-infused background vocals and choir arrangements, create a soul-stirring experience.[597]

In terms of legacy, "Wholy Holy" remains a revered piece

---

[595] Ibid., Para. 5.
[596] Adrienne Rich, *The Dream of Common Language*, 39.
[597] Microsoft Bing—Marvin Gaye on the Holy Spirit

among fans of soul and gospel music, contributing to Marvin Gaye's legacy as an artist who used his platform to address social and spiritual matters through his art. Interestingly, Marvin Gaye's songs often blend unbounded sexuality with references to the Holy Spirit, reflecting the tension between the flesh and the spirit. His music resonates with listeners on a deep level, touching both earthly desires and spiritual longing.[598] It is spiritually fascinating how artists like Gaye can explore such complex themes through their work.

Gaye is not the only secular balladeer who carried a spiritual zeal inside their music. Even as Michael Jackson, the King of Pop, was a Jehovah Witness, he understood that his gifts for dancing, singing, and writing music were God-given. In the words of Jackson:

"It's terrific to see people smile, laugh or cry with joy. Music, peace and love: that's what I'd wish for!"

"What can I do but bring forth the talent that God gave me? That's all I want to do; to share the love and gift of entertainment. That's all I want to do. I don't want to hurt anybody."

"I love my children so much. They have changed me and my outlook on life. I just wish people would leave me alone to get on with my life. I'm just a person who wants to be honest and do good, make people happy and give them the greatest sense of escapism through the talent God has given me. That's where my heart is, that's all I want to do. Just let me share and give, put a smile on people's faces and make their hearts feel happy." (1999)[599]

When Jackson mentions the words God, love, gift, joy, and heart, I begin to make intimate connections to the person, power, and presence of the Holy Spirit. Just by observing the energetic movements in Jackson's bodily movements, one could tell that he was inspired by the power of the Holy Spirit. In other words, Jackson believed in someone much greater than himself. Jackon's contemporary, Prince Rogers Nelson was raised as a Seventh-Day Adventist but eventually converted into a Jehovah's Witness later in his life. It may not seem apparent from his performances, but religion and spirituality have been influential to his career and personal life.

---

[598] Ibid.
[599] "Michael Jackson—In His Own Words"
www.michaeljacksonlegacy.org/michael/michael-jackson-in-his-own-words

Like all other individuals struggling with their faith, Prince had to seek answers and the truth. In a 1999 interview with a Dutch TV program, he described his life destination as "complete oneness with the spirit of God and knowledge of the truth."[600] The Spirit of God is the Holy Spirit.

Luther Vandross, not to be confused with the German theologian Martin Luther, wrote a song that ministered to my spirit when I was going through a difficult time. The title of the song is "Little Miracles Happen Everyday" (1993). Because I view the miracles of God in my life as the work of the Holy Spirit (1 Cor 12:7-10), I was instantly drawn to Vandross's cultural musings.[601] Vandross begins the testimonial song this way:

[Verse 1]
One thing I would love to do
Is talk to someone
Wish I knew who
Sometimes the people who know the least say the most
Makes you wonder who you can trust
What's gonna happen

The first thing I know
God is love
The next thing would be

---

[600] Elisa Meyer, "Prince: Reflecting on his Life, Religion, & Spirituality," Para. 2.

[601] My theology affirms the working of miracles as a spiritual gift distributed by the Holy Spirit in the life of believers. While God in Jesus Christ by the power of the Holy Spirit is the ultimate miracle-worker, the Holy Spirit works inside the believer to visibly manifest such law-defying feats. These deep-seeded feats demonstrate God's power and presence in the world. In explaining the meaningful role of the Holy Spirit in the life of Christ, Mark Jones states that, "Every other act upon Christ's human nature was from the Holy Spirit. Christ performed his miracles through the power of the Holy Spirit, not immediately by his own divine power. In other words, the divine nature acted not *immediately* by virtue of "the hypostatic union" (the joining of two natures in Christ's singular person) but *mediately* by means of the Holy Spirit. The conventional way of understanding Christ's miracles has typically been to argue that Christ performs miracles by virtue of his own divine nature. But on Owen's (and others') model, the Holy Spirit is *the* immediate author of Christ's graces. This manner of understanding the relation of the Spirit to Christ's human nature preserves his true humanness and answers a host of biblical questions that arise from a close reading of various texts." In this statement, Jones is speaking on the topic of "Savior by the Spirit". Mark Jones, "Why Jesus Needed the Holy Spirit," *desiring God* March 12, 2019. Para. 5.

He loves me
Sometimes I'm tired of waiting for a thing or someone
Then I stop and see what He's done
And I know everything will come

[Chorus]
And it may be today
Anything can change, nothing stays the same
And maybe today
What's tomorrow for?
No one knows for sure
Through it all come what may
Little miracles happen every day

In 1981, the great Patti Labelle wrote a song entitled "The Spirit's in It". Known for the fiery earth-shattering, first soprano tones in her classically trained voice, LaBelle talks about the Spirit of God with these words:

I know it is in you
And it won't leave you alone
I'm talking about the Spirit
The Spirit's in it
And you can't fight it no more
The Spirit's in it
And it won't let you go forth
So, stop - stop a moment
I got a better idea
Let's talk it over
Let's get together sometime

The Spirit's in it
There's no place you can go
The Spirit's in it
Now you can't say you don't know
So, wait - wait a second
Let me suggest to you
We can do better, do better
In time

We can do better in time

The Spirit's in it
And you can't find it no more
The Spirit's in it
It done open an' shut the door

So, listen to me people
Get control of yourself
Let's get together
And work things out

The Spirit's in it
There's no need in you hidin'
The Spirit's in it
Can't you hear it
Testify, yeah

Labelle believes that the Holy Spirit is present in the situations of humanity—actively working in their lives for good purposes that lead them to being more faithful to God while enjoying the cultural blessings of God.

Theologically, Bob Marley's spiritual journey is fascinating on many fronts. While he is best known for his reggae music and Rastafarian faith, his connection to the Holy Spirit runs deep. Before his death in May 1981, Marley publicly confessed Jesus Christ as his personal LORD and SAVIOR. In terms of Marley's spiritual development in rural Jamaica,

His faith was steeped in multifaceted spirituality. The communal rhythms of bush agriculture, African stories, and Black church hymns shaped his worldview. The presence of "duppies" (spirits of the dead) added an otherworldly dimension to his surroundings. Marley's maternal grandfather, Omeriah, was a myalman (medicine man) who practiced healing. His work was seen as a divine calling. His mother, Cedella, embraced Pentecostalism, where the Holy Spirit's power descended on devotees. Harvest season produce was even tied to the altar in gratitude. Even as a child,

Marley displayed a preacher's Holy Ghost fire. His interest in reading was linked to his extensive knowledge of the Bible. The Wailers once performed in a cemetery at night to overcome stage fright, turning it into a ceremonial concert for the "duppies."[602]

Marley's music was the material result of his personal relationship with God. Under the inspirational power of the Holy Spirit, Marley's music became a worldwide revival, uniting nations, races, cultures, and groups of people through its powerful, common good messages. In terms of the Spirit helping him to practice what he sung about, Marley's faith was central to his entire lifestyle ("livity"). His Rastafarian beliefs infused his music with themes of equality, justice, and spiritual awakening.[603] All of which constituted the liberating work of the Holy Spirit in the life of the oppressed throughout the late 1900s. At the very least, believers can sense that Marley is experiencing the presence and power of the Holy Spirit when he was performing his transforming music live on stage with other members of his band.

Just like it is no secret what the LORD can do (Lk. 8:17) referring to the far-reaching work of the Holy Spirit), it is no secret that Aretha Franklin, the iconic Queen of Soul (sacred and secular combined), had a deep connection to gospel music and spirituality. These are insights related to her relationship with the Holy Spirit. The daughter of a prominent Baptist minister, Franklin recorded the powerful gospel track "Wholy Holy" in 1972 as part of her album *Amazing Grace*[1]. The song features James Cleveland and The Southern California Community Choir. *Amazing Grace* remains the best-selling gospel album of all time and earned Aretha a Grammy in 1973 for Best Soul Gospel Performance. In the biopic *Respect*, Aretha's character acknowledges how the Holy Spirit saved her career and life. Despite personal struggles, she found solace in gospel music and its transformative power[2]. As a child of God who often felt the power of the Holy Spirit in her personal life, Franklin also found spiritual solace in secular music. This is because she believed that God was the author of gifts, graces, and musical talents.

---

[602] Microsoft Bing—Bob Marley on the Holy Spirit
[603] Ibid.

Aretha's album *Spirit in the Dark* (1970) reflects her spiritual journey. The title track captures the essence of her soulful performances and connection to something greater.[604] Franklin believes that the moving action of getting the Spirit is inspired by the abiding presence of the Holy Spirit. This getting the Spirit can take place in both sacred institutions and secular environments. I am certain that the Spirit in which Franklin is referring to with God being present in the dark is the Holy Spirit, the third person of the Holy Trinity (See my reflections on the Holy Spirit working in dark people, places, and spaces in Chapter 2). The point of these theological reflections is that gospel singers are not the only Black vocalists who feel the Holy Spirit in their lives. Here, the critical importance of having a spiritual journey is also a major emphasis of those who sung popular music in the presence of various audiences, both sacred and secular.

Historical Context of "What's Going On" and the Work of the Holy Spirit

Like such liberation theologians as Martin Luther King, Jr., Malcolm X, James H. Cone and J. Deotis Roberts, and Delores S. Williams, God anointed the voice of Bob Marley and Marvin Gaye through musical songs to bring justice to the nations and bring awareness to the plight of the poor. When Marvin Gaye's groundbreaking album, "What's Going On," released in 1971, the U. S. unemployment rate was at a high 6% (10% unemployment amongst Black folk). And Black people were protesting police brutality and Americans of all colors were angry over the Vietnam War. In lieu of the horrible assassinations of Martin Luther King Jr. and Presidential candidate Robert F. Kennedy three years earlier, economic poverty was widespread over the course of all races and cultures of people. After witnessing a scuffle between police and demonstrators at an Anti-Vietnam War protest, Gaye felt convicted and bothered in his spirit and troubled at what he was seeing on the American landscape.

And as a result, Gaye began to write about what was going on in the United States of America. By all accounts, the song "What's Going On" illustrates the challenges in society during the 1960s--" spirituality, brotherhood, oneness of man"--and speaks to what Gaye

---

[604] Microsoft Bing—Aretha Franklin on the Holy Spirit

thinks are the solutions."[605] Instead of focusing on describing the problems, Gaye wanted to produce a solutional interpretation, a soothing Balm in Gilead, if you will, in his music that would serve as a descriptive response to what was going on in the poverty-stricken neighborhoods of the United States.

Concomitantly, the song, "Mercy Mercy Me (The Ecology)" is an honest and direct truth-telling about how human beings can negatively impact their own environment. According to a sizable number of listeners and discerners, the rhythmic sound of "Mercy, Mercy Me" has an "inherent spiritual dimension"[606] that embraces a diversity of traditions from European cultures to Black churches. Identified as a beautiful piece of musical and cultural creation, the album's spiritual dimension carries theological implications for the contemporary context. Nothing or nobody's music within God's creation is spiritual without the powerful influence of the Holy Spirit. The Bible says the Holy Spirit is the power source to our spiritual life. It is like the electricity to a light bulb that exists in darkness. Without electricity, the light bulb is powerless and useless. In the same way, without the Holy Spirit guiding our lives, a Christian will have no power to live the kind of life God calls us to live (Gal. 5:16-18).

How are we to know what is going on in the world and in society if we are not spiritual? The act of being spiritual by way of one's developing spirituality is only possible through the Holy Spirit. The Apostle John wrote that "He teaches you about all [spiritual] things" (1 John 2:27). John's response was what the readers were taught under the Spirit's ministry through the apostles not only was adequate but was the only reliable truth. The teaching ministry of the Holy Spirit (what is commonly called illumination) does not involve revelation of new truth or the explanation of all difficult passages of Scripture to our satisfaction. Rather, it is the development of the capacity to appreciate and appropriate God's truth already revealed—making the Bible meaningful in thought and daily living. The Spirit's ministry included all things necessary to know for salvation and Christian living.[607]

---

[605] Tonya Mosley and Samantha Ralphelson, "50 Years Later, Why Marvin Gaye's Seminal Album 'What's Going On' Endures," Para. 10.
[606] Ibid., Para. 17.
[607] *Zondervan New International Study Bible*, 1947.

The Apostle Paul says "And hope does not disappoint us, because God's love has been poured into our hearts by the Holy Spirit, whom He has given us." (Rom. 5:5). Paul teaches us that the believer's hope is not to be equated with unfounded optimism. On the contrary, "it is the blessed assurance of our future destiny and is based on God's love, which is revealed to us in the death of Christ. Here, Paul has moved from faith to hope to love. When we first believed in Christ, the Holy Spirit poured out his love in our hearts, and his love for us continues to dwell in us. All true believers have the gift of the Spirit."[608]

Especially regarding how the Spirit inspires today's theologians and religious leaders to interpret what is going on within our troubled society, could it be that Paul Ricoeur was correct in his hermeneutical assessment of how people read the biblical text? Or could the late Marvin Gaye have experienced the power of the Holy Spirit in his distanciation moments between the years of 1968 and 1971? Either way, the nation gave witness to hatred, suffering and injustice in such a way that it placed a critical spotlight on racism, poverty, and drug abuse. Operating with the notion that Black music (and all music for that matter) is theological, Gaye's introspective lyrics are given credit for promoting awareness of ecological issues before the public outcry that these structural evils had become prominent. Could Gaye's musical genius point to the fact that he was troubled by the way people read the Bible in and out of church? Could Gaye have been spiritually moved by the way white people interpreted the experiences of Black people from the position of oppressor? I would say yes.

The questions of what it means to be human, who is human and who is not human layers in the conversation of who is superior and who is inferior. In adding to those complicated questions, the humanistic notions of educational advancement, cultural empowerment, and economic self-sufficiency, one can see how it would be difficult for an awakened people to not be troubled about the lack of love that defines what is going on in certain parts of the country. To this theological dilemma, Paul Ricœur's take on biblical hermeneutics and distanciation as founded in the work of the Holy Spirit is helpful. Ironically, a sizable amount of Christians believes that if they pray, the Holy Spirit will give them the proper

---

[608] Ibid., 1745.

interpretation.

It is true that the Holy Spirit is available to help ("Helper;" Jn 14: 16, 26; 15: 26) believers ascertain the correct meaning of the Bible's statements, commands, and questions. When Jesus says, "And I will ask the Father, and he will give you another Counselor to be with you forever—the Spirit of Truth," he is introducing the first of a series of important passages about the Holy Spirit. Another counselor is a gift of the Father; another besides Jesus. Or "Helper" or "Advocate." It is a legal term, but with a broader meaning than "counsel for the defense" (see 1 Jn 2:1). The word originally referred to any person who helped someone in trouble with the law. The Spirit will always stand by Christ's people.[609] Along the same lines, Jn 14:26 reads that, "But the Counselor, the Holy Spirit, whom the Father will send in my name, will teach you all things and will remind you of everything I have said to you." Jesus teaches that both the Father and the Son are involved in the sending (see Jn 15:26). The Spirit's reminding believers of everything that Jesus Christ has taught is crucial for the life of the Christian church—and for the writing of the New Testament.[610] In John 15:26, Jesus says: 'When the Counselor comes, whom I will send to you from the Father, the Spirit of truth who goes out from the Father, he will testify, for you have been with me from the beginning." The fact that the Holy Spirit goes out from the Father refers to the Spirit's being sent to do the Father's work on earth rather than to his eternal relationship with the Father. In the word becoming flesh, John teaches that Jesus came as a witness to testify concerning the light, so that through him all men might believe (Jn 1:7).[611]

As trained theologians, Bible scholars, religious leaders, and lay people, let us not forget that the Holy Spirit is a major part of the hermeneutic process because He is "the Spirit of truth" who Jesus said, "will guide...into all truth (Jn 16:13). Let us not forget who is doing the teaching and the training. We are not told whether the Spirit hears from the Father or the Son, but it obviously does not matter, for the verse stresses the close relationship among the three. The words *yet to come* means the whole Christian way or revelation (presented and preserved in the apostolic writings), still future at the

---

[609] Ibid., 1653.
[610] Ibid., 1654.
[611] Ibid., 1621.

time Jesus spoke.[612] And as Paul wrote, "We have...the Spirit who is from God, that we understand what God has freely given us." (1 Cor 2:12). Paul believed that the Spirit of the world connects to the wisdom of the age. The spirit of human wisdom as alienated from God represents the attitude of sinful nature. Wisdom from the Spirit is needed in both the Christian Church and the public society. 1 Cor 2:13 says "in words taught by the Spirit." The message Paul proclaimed was expressed in words given by the Holy Spirit. Thus, spiritual truth was aptly combined with Spirit-taught words.[613]

Lewis O. Brogdon says that

Scripture has long been regarded as a pneumatic text in which one encounters the living voice of God. The word pneumatic comes from the Greek word pneuma which means a current of air or a breeze. It is often translated as spirit in the New Testament (John 4:24; 2 Corinthians 7:1; Colossians 2:5). Interestingly, it can also be translated as the wind and conveys the idea of movement or a force that animates or moves material objects. Therefore, when I say that this multivolume book has pneumatic features, I mean the Holy Spirit works with, in, among, and around the biblical text to enable the reader to understand its contents and see its full import. African Americans from slavery to contemporary Pentecostal and Neo-Charismatic ministers speak of receiving revelations and insight into the meaning of the Bible. The belief in the Bible's pneumatic voice is not exclusively Pentecostal and Neo-Charismatic. But rather, Christian history provides abundant examples of the ways in which God's breath and presence are encountered, both in the words of the text and beyond or as a result of reading or hearing the words of the text.[614]

Brogdon's contribution to the discussion of the Spirit's role is biblical hermeneutics is critical because Paul Ricoeur believed that hermeneutics functioned as a mode of discovery. He called this idea heuristics.[615] Heuristics is the process of relating to general strategies

---

[612] Ibid., 1656.
[613] Ibid., 1771.
[614] Lewis O. Brogdon, *Interpreting Problematic Texts*, 14-15.
[615] Morny Joy, British Society for Phenomenology. "Paul Ricoeur and a Hermeneutics of

or methods for solving problems while hermeneutic explains, interprets, illustrates, or elucidates what could be. Both initiatives, hermeneutics, and heuristics are inspired by the work of the Holy Spirit.

As I bring this chapter to a close, I ask the important questions: What's going on in the world and in the United States of America? What's going on with the Holy Spirit in theology Black, economics, and race? What's going in the Christian church? In 1971, ironically, the American people were learning through the Pentagon papers how the U.S. government had lied to them about the Vietnam War. The people's displacement, disillusionment and disregard led them to the feeling of being used. Terribly like the way the Black American slave felt used in their developing and modernizing the infrastructural economy of the United States in the 16th and 17th centuries, the American soldiers and their respective families did not feel appreciated for their services. They too felt they were treated as if they were less than human. The liberating work of the Holy Spirit showed the American soldiers what was going on. What is going on in the fallen world and in the rich and powerful United States? In the prayerful words of Marian Wright Edelman, "Is America's economy open to us? For the many children who have to stay poor on the bottom so too few can stay rich on the top?"[616]

Spirit Lecture

The title of this lecture is: "The Work of the Holy Spirit in the Presence of Evil." This revised lecture was delivered at the Garrett-Evangelical Theological Seminary on the campus of Northwestern University in Evanston, Illinois.

God is thus neither the "eternal present" nor the "absolute future" for the community of faith. It came to see, from its historical experience, that what God's action does is to create an explosiveness that is both present and negates the present. Because God acts, "every situation is pregnant with ultimate possibility; every moment is made explosive by the presence of an infinite. "We know", says Paul (Rom 8:22), that the whole creation is groaning in travail until now. And

Human Capability and Fragility" britishphenomenology.com/208Paper4.aspx
[616] Marian W. Edelman, *Guide My Feet*, 97.

not only the creation, but we ourselves, who have the first fruits of the Spirit, groan inwardly as we wait for adoption as sons, the redemption of our bodies. For in this hope, we are saved.[617]

When engaging in theological discourse about the work of God in the presence of evil, it has become commonplace to reference theodicy and affirm that in God having control over the actions of Satan, God allows evil for reasons of goodness and order. In other words, talking about evil in light of the presence of God automatically presumes that God has a purpose for allowing evil to penetrate the creation. In the Christian tradition, believers often refer to this as God bringing good out of evil.[618] To this assertion, I would affirm that Christian theology does not take sin and evil seriously. By that, I mean that those who attempt to define the parameters by which theology exist do not seriously consider nor recognize the structural similarities in the way that evil works in context. The truth is that if there are not similarities, then we cannot talk about evil; we can only talk about an instance, and how everything within that must be treated as if it occurs *sui generis* or as if evil is unique in its own characteristics. These are all instances of structural reality or a larger reality, whether we want to view this larger reality as personified, spiritual, or through a social scientific lens.

Stephen Ray's notion of the surpluses of evil asserts that there are consequences of evil which are surplus or that go beyond the scope of the original act; over which the original perpetrators and victims have no control. Once we see evil systematically operating in a space where the perpetrators and victims have no control, the question of God arises.[619] Thus, the purpose for constructing this study is to begin discussing the myriad ways the Holy Spirit can be interpreted as an active worker on behalf of humanity and in the presence of structural evil. Before looking at the ways the Holy Spirit works in the presence of evil, we must definitively qualify what we mean by the word *evil*.

What Is Evil?

The New International Version of the Life Application Study

---

[617] Ruben Alves, *A theology of human hope*, 96.
[618] Karen Baker-Fletcher, *Dancing with God*, 93.
[619] Notes from Dr. Stephen G. Ray's Sin and Evil class, Garrett- Evangelical Theological Seminary, Spring 2010.

Bible defines evil as morally bad or wrong; something that causes harm or distress. In our PhD *Sin and Evil* class, the introductory definitions of evil revolved around the idea of something or someone that does bodily harm to another. Other definitions juxtaposed evil as the opposite of good or anything that goes against what Scripture says about God. Stephen Ray defines evil as 'simply anything that causes unnecessary suffering'.[620] In expounding on his theological definition of evil, Ray cites such entities as nature, structures, systems, food, individuals and groups of individuals to elucidate the fact that the only person(s) who can truly define the parameters of evil are the one(s) who are experiencing evil. For Ray, the victims of unnecessary suffering are the only ones who are qualified to establish the basis for defining and describing evil.

Fourth Century theologian, Saint Augustine, believes that evil is the removal of good. In expounding on what he calls the fallenness of humanity, Augustine uses the language of 'good' and 'goodness' to imply that the goal of humanity should always be to seek good—even for the sake of evil. For Augustine, the fallen nature of humanity is what leads to the flaw or the propensity to sin or participate in acts of evil. In other words, being drawn to God for the sake of seeking the good has its limitations. By stating that evil is the removal of good, Augustine implies that in this universe even that which called evil, well ordered, and kept in its place, sets the good in higher relief, so that good things are more pleasing and praiseworthy than the evil ones. It must be noted, however, that Augustine is not saying that evil does not contain elements of pleasure, purpose, and praiseworthiness, but only in contrast with 'good' can we see how evil is representative of a removal of good in the world. Augustine believes that God is so supremely good and omnipotent that God, among God's works, can bring good even out of evil. Bruce Harbert translates Augustine's teaching on evil this way:

> For what else is that which is called evil but a removal of good? ... The flesh itself is the substance, a good thing to which those evil things, those removals of the good, known to health, occur. In the same way all evils that affect the mind are removals of the natural good: when they are cured, they are not moved to somewhere else, but when they are no longer in

---

[620] Ibid.

the mind once it has been restored to health, they will be nowhere.[621]

Kathryn Tanner puts it this way: Since God created all that is (other than God), Augustine further concluded, as a way of refuting the Manicheans, that nothing that exists, insofar as it exists, is evil. Evil is always an absence or distortion, the lack of some good that might have been.[622]

In her groundbreaking work, *Dancing with God*, feminist theologian, Karen Baker-Fletcher, asks that critical questions of 'What does it mean to live in the courage of Christ in a world of persecution, crucifixion, hatred, and evil? What does it mean to overcome evil when we are still living in a world of "crucifixion"?[623] Upon asking these critical questions, Baker-Fletcher refers to womanist Whiteheadian theologian, Monica Coleman, for her working definition of evil. In defining evil, Coleman notes that

"For Whitehead, evil occurs in two ways. First, it occurs in human freedom in various contexts and situations. Second, evil is "the loss of actuality...That is, when an actual entity becomes a new thing, it ceases to be. It is gone. Actual entities are constantly becoming, but they are also 'perpetually perishing.'"[624] This prompts Baker-Fletcher to define evil as death. Baker-Fletcher affirms that "Evil, in a relational theology, is the opposite of life. The nihilistic presence of evil is an ongoing problem in existence, but God overcomes it."[625] For Baker-Fletcher, the Whiteheadian definitions of evil are complimentary because the decisions human beings make says something about our perspectives on life and death. Baker-Fletcher concludes that whether "we choose to participate in God's activity for the well-being of creation or contribute to the problem of evil,"[626] the human reality of contributing to the problem of evil constitutes sin.

In his acclaimed text, *Black Theology in Dialogue*, J. Deotis Roberts concludes that "evil exists in various realms. These realms are personal, collective, structural, natural, and moral. Given the

---

[621] John E. Rotelle, *The Augustine Catechism*, 40.
[622] William C. Placher, *Essentials of Christian Theology*, 99.
[623] Karen Baker-Fletcher, *Dancing with God*, 93.
[624] Ibid.
[625] Ibid.
[626] Ibid.

variety of realms that evil exist (hides), Roberts asserts that "sin and evil involve about more than the abuse of sex in personal life. But when we take a look at sinful social structures, we are overwhelmed by the complexity of evil.[627] For Roberts, the goal of evil is to increase the personal suffering of the victims of oppression[628]—in a way that affects the whole community and brings shame upon it.[629] Whether Roberts is expounding on what he terms as the unfinished agenda of Black theology, an unfinished agenda for praxis, the results of the intrinsic nature of evil in African religious discourse or the question of God, evil and suffering in the story of Job, he always finds a way to return to his original premise that as agents of good (as well as evil), the only way for human beings to confront evil[630] is through faith in God.

In her book, *Life Abundant: Rethinking Theology and Economy for a Planet in Peril*, Sallie McFague mimics Roberts by affirming that "Evil, both in its natural and moral forms—earthquakes and selfishness—are certainly part of existence in the neo-classical economic paradigm, but neither is insurmountable."[631] For McFague, the greater evil is not the worst of natural disasters, but the ordinary poverty, illiteracy, illnesses, and despair at the high percentage of the human population experience everyday.[632] Moreover, McFague sees evil as a myriad of forces, actions and attitudes that works in opposition to God. But how does evil work? When asking the question of how does evil actually works, it is appropriate to begin the discussion of referencing the instances of evil. When we speak of the instances of evil, we are not talking about propositional truths of Christianity. Propositional truths of Christianity keep us more focused on who we wake up next to instead of the people starving around the corner from us.[633] The impulse toward life is the impulse

---

[627] J. Deotis Roberts, *Black Theology in Dialogue*, 95.

[628] Ibid., 115.

[629] Ibid., 22. Here, Roberts is speaking from the perspective of African Traditional Religion and how evil negatively affects the livelihood of the oppressed people there in Akan.

[630] Ibid., 115. When I use the words confront evil, I am referring to what Roberts terms as "God enabling these people to find meaning at a survival level." This confronting evil as a way of finding meaning within human oppressions is the work of the Holy Spirit.

[631] Sallie McFague, *Life Abundant*, 152.

[632] Ibid., 154.

[633] Notes from Dr. Stephen G. Ray's Sin and Evil class, Garrett- Evangelical Theological Seminary, Spring 2010.

away from evil.

According to Terrence Des Pres, the impulse away from evil is an impulse away from self-preservation--in a very interpersonal manner and toward a cooperative freedom. In other words, evil works in the reality of sin. Once the notion of sin enters the conversation or the environment, the human tendency is to turn our attention to the heart of the sinner; thereby, ignoring and turning away from the broken flesh. The broken flesh represents the concrete consequences of the hands of evil. This active unfolding of sin and evil is one of the primary ways evil works—by changing the subject. In his book, *The Survivor*, Des Pres' argues that we cannot turn away from the broken flesh toward the ethereal and spiritual. Des Pres' main point is that evil is not something abstract and "out there" in another realm, but rather it emerges from and exists within material and concrete bodies, relationships, and civilizations.

Another way that evil works is by hiding. One of the places that evil hides is in the everyday, mundane shortcomings of human beings. But because the human heart is a manufacturer of idols, it predisposes us to want to affiliate ourselves with a cause larger than ourselves – groups, gangs, politicians, and sports teams; for the sake belonging to something or someone and out of the human need for love and attention. Radical evil also hides itself in everyday, mundane things. The reason we term this radical evil is because we are not able to recognize it for what it is until it is too late. This is what makes this form of evil difficult to see.

In his book, *The Hitler Salute: On the Meaning of a Gesture*, Tilman Allert argues that by sacralizing the universe, the Germans lost their ability to appeal to anything beyond what is present. In other words, the lynch mob does not arise until multiple instances of evil on the level of the mundane have been normalized and accepted. By paying attention to what is taking place on the level of the mundane, the banal, one can hope to recognize or preclude the manifestation of radical evil on a larger scale—the materialization of evil lurking and working in the shadows of the presence of a mesmerizing evil. As a way of leading future theologians and scholars into his analysis of mesmerization as the transitional implication between power and principality, and in following Augustine's take on evil, Ray confirms that evil is present and working in the sin of what he terms as the materialization of "the effaced Imago Dei."[634] For Ray, evil is working within the human reality of the heart, mind, and hands of sinners. By way of discussing ideology and gestures, we have visited the place where mesmerization begins (ideology) and where it ends (a gesture). Once a gesture or an idea permeates all of society, it automatically fulfills the role of mesmerization.

Once the evil process mesmerization begins, the next stage is the materialization of ideology. This is primarily because materialization is the goal of the journey of evil. When we make the journey from power to principality (when something that exists in the realm of the extra personal begins to secrete material being or have material affects) the idea has taken on material being. So that by the time we get to the gesture (per se), evil has become mundane as it conducts itself as a normal part of everyday life and everyday material relations between people. That is to say that at the same time mesmerization is taking place, the process of materialization is occurring as well. The powers of evil are thereby taking on material beings (principalities, e.g., bureaucracy). What makes our reasoning or outlook on evil so dangerous is that as creatures of the future, we tend to focus solely on the process of mesmerization and ignore the process of materialization in the present. The materialization of evil is another way that evil works. In other words, when evil is efficient and sophisticated, we tend to admire it.

The Holy Spirit Is Working

In his work, *Christian Doctrine*, Shirley Guthrie posits that the Holy Spirit works by way of spirituality. He states that "Christian spirituality recognizes the presence and work of the Holy Spirit in bad as well as in good times."[635] Guthrie goes on to say that "True spirituality is that of Christians who know that "in the suffering of this present age" (between the times), the Spirit does not always save us from our weakness but helps "in our weakness" to give us the comfort, help, courage, and strength to endure and entrust our lives to God, knowing that "neither death, nor life, nor angels, nor rulers, nor things to come, nor powers, nor height , nor depth, nor anything

---

[634] Notes from Dr. Stephen G. Ray's Sin and Evil class, Garrett- Evangelical Theological Seminary, Spring 2010.

[635] Shirley C. Guthrie, *Christian Doctrine*, 301.

else in all creation, will be able to separate us from the love of God in Christ Jesus our Lord" (Rom 8:18, 38)."[636]

In his contemporary account of the works of the Holy Spirit, Veli Matti Karkkainen, writes that "Jesus' own understanding of his mission in terms of the Spirit was different; this difference becomes clear especially in his role as an exorcist and in his consciousness of inspiration. According to the Synoptics, his success as an exorcist was undeniable. "But if I drive out demons by the Spirit of God, then the kingdom of God has come upon you" (Mt.12:28)."[637] While this text does represent one way of seeing how the Holy Spirit works in the presence of evil, it is important that we stay away from spiritualizing evil. The reason we want to avoid spiritualizing evil is because the process of spiritualization is part of the mesmerization process. The time, effort and focus we put in attempting to reduce evil to just a spiritual existence, is the time we have lost in recognizing that the materialization of evil has taken shape around us.

Stephen Ray teaches one should not say anything about God that one would not say in the presence of burning babies.[638] I believe in this theological affirmation because burning babies are the result of the materialization of evil. When talking about the work of the Holy Spirit in the presence of evil, I first want to lift the fact that the Holy Spirit works on the whole of God's creation. Further, the Holy Spirit is the love and greeting that passes from the Father to the Son to humanity. A source of comfort, guidance, survival, truth and healing, the Holy Spirit makes himself visible within the realm of the intersubjective and the interhuman. In other words, as the Holy Spirit is constantly moving amongst humanity, we find that there is a powerful connection between the Holy Spirit and human spirit.

What this means is that human relationality is the image of God. According to George S. Hendry, "The problem of the relation between the Holy Spirit and the human spirit is one that has been neglected in the mainstream of Christian theology. Throughout the greater part of its history, Christian theology has been chiefly concerned with the doctrine of the Holy Spirit, the Spirit "who

---

[636] Ibid., 302.
[637] Veli Matti Karkkainen, *Pneumatology: Holy Spirit*, 29.
[638] Notes from Dr. Stephen G. Ray's Sin and Evil class, Garrett- Evangelical Theological Seminary, Spring 2010.

proceeds from the Father and the Son," and in this it has been faithful to the emphasis of the New Testament; it has shown little interest in the question of how the spirit that is in man, and in this too it has followed the example of the New Testament. Hendry goes on to affirm that the real question is 'how is the divine Spirit related to human beings?"[639] My response to this important question would be that the divine Spirit is related to human beings through the liberating *work* of the Holy Spirit.

In the Holy Spirit embodying the greeting and the love passed between the Father and the Son; the intersubjective and the interhuman is the space of the divine, something redemptive is happening. Where the divine materializes and becomes present (Levinas), the Imago Dei is effaced through the replacement of that which binds the life of God together to that which is something other than God. This is main reason why Sister M. Aquinas refers to the God the Holy Spirit as the sanctifier.[640] For Aquinas, even in the presence of evil God has the power to sanctify (what God does in us) us for the sake of comfort, healing, and goodness. The reason why Aquinas affirms that God the Holy Spirit works in the presence of evil is because the Spirit, according to theologian Hans Kung," works *when* and *where* he wills."[641] In separating the work of the Holy Spirit from the operation of the church, Kung affirms that the power of the Holy Spirit can work anywhere God chooses—including in the presence of evil.

What is going on today in this fallen world? Does a purely materialist conception of the world occlude, in Christian conversation, the possibility of the movement of the Holy Spirit? Des Pres happily says yes because he does not ascribe belief to any theistic religion. How does a theologian, who has certain commitments that go beyond a strict materialist conception of the world, speak of God and the Holy Spirit in such circumstances? This notion of materialist conception represents the reason J. Deotis Roberts believes that Black theology (and any other theology for that matter) must take seriously the doctrine of the Holy Spirit. Roberts concludes that human liberation is at stake when the theologian takes seriously the

---

[639] George S. Hendry, *The Holy Spirit*, 96.
[640] The Sanctifier is the title of Sister M. Aquinas' book on the doctrine of the Holy Spirit.
[641] Michael Ryan, *The Contemporary Explosion*, 45-46.

study of pneumatology.

The Holy Spirit works in the presence of evil. The Holy Spirit works in the following ways:

1. Through one's own spirituality or faith
2. As the result of one's own recognition of the possibility of materialized evil
3. By way of the connection between the Holy Spirit and the human spirit
4. Through the *works* of the Holy Spirit
5. Through the power of the Holy Spirit
6. For the sake of the liberation of human beings
7. Through the individual's sacrificial decision (one's calling) to stand for justice and righteousness

Theologically, one of the important things that this study has taught me is that it takes sermons (preaching) and lectures (teaching) to get at the heart of what is going on in the United States and the world abroad. One thing we know for sure about what is going on in present-day society is that evil is working in a multitude of ways. Nevertheless, the task of describing theology is not an emotional one. But rather, it is one that requires commitment and passion. The present task requires energy, constructive collaboration, knowledge, and a deep understanding of how the Holy Spirit works in creation, the Christian Church, human beings, and society. What thing I am sure of is that it was the Spirit of God that inspired these scholars to construct theological reflections on the issues of race and poverty in the United States. I say that because theological writing is a spiritual gift (1 Cor. 12:11) that results from the Holy Spirit filling us with hope until we overflow (Rom. 15:13) with descriptive words and creative narratives. The Holy Spirit also empowers the Christian theologian to write the vision on the tablets of their inner-most, spiritual convictions (Hab. 2:2, Acts 1:8).

Darvin Anton Adams

Chapter Seven

Distinguishing J. Deotis Roberts from Jurgen Moltmann and More Spirit-Talk

Father, father, father. We don't need to escalate. You see, war is not the answer. For only love can conquer hate. You know we've got to find a way. To bring some loving' here today.[642]

　　In 1971, the year in which Marvin Gaye released *What's Going On*, the American people were learning through the Pentagon papers how the United States government had lied to them about the Vietnam War. The people's displacement, displeasure, disillusionment, and disregard led them to think they were taken advantage of. Sadly, the nation claimed to not have enough resources to offer those who were deployed from active duty and sent home from Vietnam. Educational opportunities and decent jobs were far and few between. Benefits were at a stronghold minimum. Like the way the Black American slave felt used in their developing and modernizing the infrastructural United States in the 16th and 17th centuries, the American soldiers and their respective families did not feel appreciated for their services. When I mention the African/Black American slave, I am referring to the instances of African Chattel Slavery and Wage Theft. With institutional slavery at the capitalistic forefront of keeping Black folk in poverty, the empirical foundation of the racial wealth divide has deep roots in our national history. The economic contours of American slavery also paved the way for a

---

[642] https://genius.com/Marvin-gaye-whats-going-on-lyrics

racially exclusive land redistribution.

It baffles me how Black folks were good enough to be taken from their homeland of Africa and work for the economic prospering of the white slave master; but were not good enough to be citizens of the very place they resided, worked, and modernized. In addition to not having access to educational tools or any form of economic self-sufficiency, Black people have always existed without full and respectable citizenship. Citizenship has always been one of the major foundations of the racial wealth divide in the United States. Around the time of President Lincoln signed the Emancipation Proclamation into law (1865), racially discriminatory immigration policy was already the norm. Citizenship and immigration go hand in hand where the plight of nonwhite Americans is concerned.

Still reflecting on what was going on in 1971 when Marvin Gaye released his transcendent album, *What's Going On*, the Civil Rights Movement of the 1950s and 1960s was on a down-slide and Black folk were catching pure hell from employers and corrupt law enforcement officers. The rise and fall of the Black Panther Party mixed with the deaths of NAACP icon Medgar Evers, President John F. Kennedy, Minister Malcolm X, Dr. Martin Luther King Jr., Presidential candidate Robert F. Kennedy, Chairman Fred Hampton, and other courageous human beings made for a difficult time. Especially in the Jim Crow South where Black folk were consistently suffering, bleeding, and dying at the hands of racial discrimination. The United States was a spiritual, social, political, and economic mess that seemed on her way to an eternal damnation. This demonic vision sounds terribly like what is going on in the United States today. Here we are 53 years later, the nation and world remain in a terrible human crisis. With wars and rumors of wars super numerated around nuclear capacity, one-sided racialized politics, territorial vengeance, and economic hegemony, one would think that the evil of systemic oppression is winning out in the most critical of moments. As a product of the Black church and a trained theologian, I still believe in the power and work of the Holy Spirit.

In answering the question of what is going on, New Testament scholar Lewis Brogdon believes that the United States is losing its soul. In a recent *Courier Journal* article, Brogdon explains the contours of why America is losing its soul and why everyone in our country should be having this exact conversation. In addition to an overarching political dysfunction, Brogdon claims that

> There are also gross economic inequalities and poverty that affect millions of lives. Then there is persistent violence at every level of human and social interaction from domestic violence and rape to mass shootings. In the face of such big and complex social problems, the empty quest of materialism and pleasure seeks to fill or give meaning to the rampant nihilism we have unleashed on ourselves and each other. All of this is happening amid the devastating loss of life. For over a year, major news networks tracked the number of Americans contracting and dying from the coronavirus. The numbers are staggering. 561,000 Americans have died—more than the deaths from World War I and II.[643]

Brogdon's poignant reflections suggest that important conversations about the moral and spiritual corrosion of our country must take place. Because of the compounding forms of structural evil and mounting oppression, the United States is on the brink of an eternal burning. Brogdon is sure that our country has reached a state of national and spiritual emergency.

In response to Brogdon's groundbreaking analysis, my question is: Where is the spirit of hope in fighting against what is going on with the countless evils that are present in churches, in politics, in the nation and in the world? Jurgen Moltmann's important text, *The Spirit of Hope: Theology for a World in Peril*, helps to answer the probing questions with regards to what Christian hope looks like in the face of those ideologies and structural evils that deny hope to God's creation. Predictably, Moltmann recommends that we learn from the past and look to our future with faith in God for the theological blueprint to deal with the structural inequities of the present day. In discussing what he terms as the social conditions of misery[644] within the culture of human life, Moltmann hypothesizes that,

A general impairment of life also exists in miserable social

---

[643] Lewis Brogdon, "Is America in danger losing its Soul? The conversation everyone needs to have in 2012" The Courier Journal June 3, 2021.

[644] Jurgen Moltmann, *Spirit of Hope*, 6.

conditions. For more than 40 years, we have heard repeatedly and everywhere the charge that, despite all political efforts, the social gap between the rich and the poor is widening. It is not just in the powerful countries of the two-thirds of the world that a small, rich sector of the population rules over the masses of the poor. In the democracies of the developed world, the financial asset gap between financiers on the one hand, and low-income workers, welfare recipients, the unemployed, and those not able to work, on the other hand, takes on obscene proportions. Yet democracy is grounded not only in the freedom of citizens but also in their equality. Without social justice in life opportunities and the comparability of life circumstances, the commonweal dies and with it what holds society together falls apart, Trust is lost.[645]

While Moltmann understands the unaccounted-for-connection between social inequality and economic inequality, his argument of how the visible compounding of social justice evils working at the same time can lead to the death of culture and life as we know it is solid. I have yet to read Moltmann's theological take on the oppressive plight of native Africans and Black Americans and how the idolatry of racism has destroyed and killed off millions of Black folks in the United States. Here, the problem lies within the realities of experience and theological discourse. The problem also lies in our definition of hope. According to the Bible, hope is the work of the Holy Spirit (Romans 15:13; Galatians 5:5). While Moltmann is a renowned theologian of the Spirit, he is not a Black liberation theologian nor is he a liberation theologian. He is a Christian theologian of the highest quality.

In the words of George C.L. Cummings, "Black theology asserts the priority of the black experience of enslavement and a struggle for liberation as the starting point of black theological discourse. Close scrutiny of the slave narratives shows that they can provide the raw material for an interpretation of the Spirit and eschatology in the slave narratives"[646] Along the same lines, I believe the Holy Spirit provides

---

[645] Ibid.
[646] Dwight N. Hopkins and George C. L. Cummings, *Cut Loose Your Stammering Tongue*, 42.

the raw materials for the liberation of the oppressed. The work of the Holy Spirit is the raw material that enhances our understanding of where the Black poor exist in the United States. Poverty in the Black community is a form of enslavement that must be addressed by Black theologians, Black religious leaders, and Black politicians. The idolatry that is associated with economic deprivation in the Black inner-city neighborhoods brings about a deliberate "harm that deadens the human conscience to the needs of the poor."[647] Thus far, theologians of European and American descent have had little to say about the economic plight of Black people. Roberts imagines that

> The perspective of Black theology is being sharpened by the "liberation theology" of Latin America, which is different from the theology of hope as set forth by Moltmann and Pannenberg. The assumptions of European and American theologians about how God relates to human different from those of Rubem Alves of Brazil and Gustavo Gutierrez of Peru. Moltmann and Pannenberg are speaking out of affluent and serene ivory towers, even though they try hard to be sensitive to poverty and oppression. Likewise, there is a difference between hope and liberation in Carl Braaten, Fredrick Herzog, and Rosemary Reuther. While the latter two can take up and lay down the burden of oppression at will. The black theologian, on the other hand, knows what it means to bear the "mark of Cain" for a lifetime. There is even a very important experiential difference between those black theologians who speak from the ivory towers of white academic centers in the North and those who identify with the poverty and insecurity of struggling black academic institutions in the South. How ironical it is that those black scholars in religion who have set themselves up as kingmakers and the chief spokesmen of black religious experience are part of the "brain drain" and choose not to suffer the afflictions of their people.[648]

For material reasons of Black theological hope, the Holy Spirit led me to distinguish the work of J. Deotis Roberts from that of Jurgen Moltmann. On the evening of April 4, 1968, J. Deotis Roberts was in

---

[647] Stephen G. Ray Jr., *Do No Harm*, xi.
[648] J. Deotis Roberts, *Black Political Theology*, 26-27.

Durham, North Carolina attending a conference at Duke University. He was listening to German theologian Jürgen Moltmann present a paper on the theology of hope. Roberts, a soft-spoken Baptist minister and a theology professor at Howard University in Washington. He had spent years wrestling with philosophical questions about God, existence and meaning. Listening to Moltmann, Roberts began to wonder what Moltmann's theology — what any theology — had to say to "a hopeless people" living in an age of blatant nihilism and human suffering.[649] Part of what bothered Roberts regarding Moltmann is the fact that Moltmann hardly ever talked about the maltreatment of Black people in the United States and Africa. It seemed as if Moltmann had something theological to say to every group of hopeless people but those skinned in Black and shades of brown. Moltmann failed to discuss the commonalities between the massacred Africans, Germans, and Jews in Germany and the alienated, lynched, murdered Black human beings in Africa and the United States. Did Moltmann believe that Black people in Africa and the United States deserve subhuman treatment? To be certain, something about Moltmann's theology rubbed the younger Roberts the wrong way. If there was a late century theologian who knew what was going on in the world, it was Jurgen Moltmann, correct?

In critiquing the economic and geographical contexts of Pannenberg[650] and Moltmann's reflections, Roberts is certain that

> The so-called theology of hope has a good psychological ring for a hopeless people. It does not, however, ring true to the

---

[649] Harrison Smith, "J. Deotis Roberts, a pioneer of Black Theology, dies at 95" The Washington Post August 16, 2022.

[650] Wolfhart Pannenberg's theology of hope is an integral part of his take on history as a form of revelation within the resurrection of Christ. A German systematic theologian, Pannenberg's theological emphasis focuses on the future or the eschaton as the point of transcendence in God. For Pannenberg, the term "hope" capsulizes the thorough-going eschatological orientation of his theological program. Like Moltmann, Pannenberg's theology of hope affirms that hope, as the vision of eschatology, has a living future because the future hope of the world rests in God. In that Pannenberg's entire systematic theology focuses on the eschaton, it characterizes a theology of hope. Pannenberg's theology of hope places priority on what he terms as the eschatological consummation in the Kingdom of God as found in the truth of faith, ultimate faith, and the truth of God. For an exhaustive account of Pannenberg's theology of hope, see Stanley J. Grenz's text, Reason for Hope: The Systematic Theology of Wolfhart Pannenberg (Grand Rapids, MI: Wm. B. Eerdsman Publishing Co., 2005).

black experience. Like many other "transport" theological movements, it belongs to another "situation." Insofar as it speaks directly to the Marxist-Christian dialogue, it will find "domestication" in white America difficult also. The "political" and "revolutionary" aspects of the theology of hope are addressed primarily to the Third World as it confronts a postcolonial period of development. This latter aspect of the theology of hope may be examined with profit by the interpreter of the Christian faith to black people who belong essentially to the oppressed of humankind."[651]

In other words, the theologies of hope created by non-Black theologians have not been inclusive in mentioning the economic deprivation of Black folk in the United States.

The economic oppression of Black Americans provides an important reason to distinguish Roberts' theology of hope from Jurgen Moltmann's theology of hope; especially where the theologizing of Black poverty is concerned. Both Christian theologies differ in scope and tenor. Roberts believes that Black liberation theology in the United States is a theology of hope. What this means for Roberts is that

> There is a need for a theology growing out of the experience of the black American. Whereas today there is much excitement over the revolutionary theology in general, and a theology of hope in particular, the unique problems of the black experience are not properly treated. Most theologies of hope, liberation, and revolution center in the Marxist-Christian dialogue in Europe, in liberation struggles in southern Africa, or in the political upheavals in Latin America. While black Americans share the aspirations of others in the Third World, they are constantly reminded of Dr. King's prophecy: "All Africa will be free before black Americans are free.[652]

---

[651] J. Deotis Roberts, *Liberation and Reconciliation*, 83.

[652] Deotis Roberts, *A Black Political Theology*, 15-16. Like Derrick Bell's argument in *Faces at the Bottom of the Well*, Dr. King believed that the oppression caused by racial discrimination in the United States would be a permanent fixture in the life of Black Americans. Because the liberation of Black folk is underemphasized in the both the Black church and American society, King grew in his uncertainty of Black people's social,

Roberts's point is that

> A people cannot make it without meaning, especially if they are an oppressed people seeking liberation. The mission of black theology is to interpret this experience so that young and old may be able to appreciate the deep religious roots of black culture. Those who study black history, and the black arts must also study the history of the black church and the meaning of black religion. This study will indicate that our suffering has not bred that bitterness and despair which is more deadly to the self than it is to those who have caused the suffering. What we need is meaning and hope if we are making the proper protest against injustice to experience the liberation we seek.[653]

Roberts's theology of hope is founded on the fact that Black people "are a hopeless people who have majored in hope. If we have a mission to our people, it is to provide a theological understanding of this hope."[654] Roberts writes that "When social and economic conditions are extremely bad, most people will just give up. At best they will seek survival at its lowest level."[655] This statement speaks to the hope that poor Black people live with daily. According to Roberts, "This is the stuff out of which black theology emerges. Without our strong religious experience, we would have been crushed by the circumstances of black suffering under the heels of white oppression. We have had to deal with the ultimate issues of life and death. Ours has been a faith for survival."[656] Roberts goes on to say that

> Ours has been hope against hope. Indeed, for us faith has been the substance of things hoped for. It has been based upon unseen evidence. We have overcome when there were no grounds of hope. The black faithful know what it means to reach out into the

---

political, and economic freedom. With a hope for the present day, King stressed the need for Black Americans to have civil and human rights. King's statement of Africa's freedom coming to fruition before the liberation of Black people in the United States represented his growing pessimism toward the blatant mistreatment of Black folk by way of white power, white privilege, and white resentment. King's critique of white power working against the powerlessness of Black humanity included both the United States and Africa.

[653] Ibid., 59-60.
[654] Ibid., Back Cover.
[655] Ibid., 63-64.
[656] Ibid., 64.

darkness and grasp the hand of God, to take a step at a time in the shadows and to find such trust better than light, better than a well-trodden path. Ours is a hope against hope, but it is a living hope.[657]

To affirm a present hope operating in the context of hopelessness, Roberts believes that eschatology is closely tied to ethics. For Roberts, "Both ethics and eschatology are essential to black political theology. They are interdependent and inseparable. One cannot see the present life in full focus without a look at the future life, but neither may one fully appreciate the future life apart from the present life."[658] What this means is that "Eschatology can no longer be a mere addendum to black theology. It is at the center of any theology which endeavors to bring a meaning hope to the weak and the powerless. Ethics is also pivotal to a theology that is concerned with the liberation of the oppressed in the here and now."[659]

On the other hand, Jurgen Moltmann's theology of hope encompasses the logos of Christian eschatology in such way that it "includes the return of Christ in universal glory, the judgment of the world and the consummation of the kingdom, the general resurrection of the dead and the new creation of all things. These end events were to break into this world from somewhere beyond history and put an end to the history in which all things here live and move."[660] For Moltmann, the logos of Christian eschatology is the future hope of God working in the future and throughout history for the sake of present-day circumstances. With the future hope of God as his beginning point, Moltmann believes "the Christian faith banished from its life the future hope by which it is upheld, and relegated the future to a beyond, or to eternity, whereas the biblical testimonies which it handed on are yet full to the brim with future hope of a messianic kind of world,--owing to this, hope emigrated as it were from the Church and turned in one distorted form or another against the Church."[661] Placing one's faith in Jesus Christ as the messiah of the future hope, Moltmann's theology of hope becomes an eschatological

---

[657] Ibid., 64-65.
[658] Ibid., 179.
[659] Ibid.
[660] Jurgen Moltmann, *Theology of Hope*, 15.
[661] Ibid., 15-16.

vision of future events within the past, present and future lives of God's creation.

For Moltmann, "Eschatology means the doctrine of the Christian hope, which embraces both the object hoped for and also the hope inspired by it. From first to last, and not merely in the epilogue, Christianity is eschatology, is hope, looking forward and forward moving, and therefore also revolutionizing and transforming the present."[662] Again, Moltmann views the revolutionizing and transforming of the present through the lens of a future hope that is always moving toward a biblical hope in God. For Moltmann, God is the God of hope in that God "with future as his essential nature, as made known in Exodus and in Israelite prophecy, the God whom we, therefore, cannot have in us or over us but always only before us, who encounters us in his promises for the future, and when we, therefore, cannot 'have' either, but can only await in actual hope."[663] Moltmann's eschatology proclaims Jesus Christ as the infinite hope for the future because "Christian eschatology speaks of Jesus Christ and his future by recognizing the reality of the raising of Jesus and proclaiming the future of the risen Lord."[664]

Moltmann cites Colossians 1:27 where "They all say: 'He is our hope'. In this announcing his future in the world in terms of promise, they point believers in him towards the hope of his still outstanding future. What this pointing of believers to Jesus Christ means is that "Hope's statements of promise anticipate the future. In the promises, the hidden future already announces itself and exerts its influence on the present through the hope it awakens."[665] Moltmann believes that "Hope's statements of promise, however, must stand in contradiction to the reality which can at present be experienced."[666] What this means for the believer in Jesus Christ is that these lived experiences do not line up with the reality of what is happening in one's life. For Moltmann, believers in Jesus Christ "do not seek to bear the train of reality, but to carry the torch before it."[667]

---

[662] Ibid., 16.
[663] Ibid., 17.
[664] Ibid.
[665] Ibid., 17-18.
[666] Ibid., 18.
[667] Ibid.

While Moltmann defines eschatology as the future hope of God in Christ for the people of faith, J. Deotis Roberts places an eschatological emphasis on the present-day realities of Black Americans. Roberts confesses that

> Eschatology for blacks must be both *realized* and *unrealized.* Whereas the evangelical-pietistic version of eschatology is preoccupied with the future, black theology must begin, I believe, with the present. In other words, for black Christians realized eschatology, the manifestation of the will of God in the present—abstractly as social justice and concretely as goods and services to "humanize" life—must be a first consideration for a doctrine pointing to the eventual consummation of God's purposes in creation and history. Those messianic and apocalyptic versions of eschatology centering in heaven and hell, future punishments and rewards, the resurrection of the flesh, will become less and less attractive to black people struggling to survive, even under the threat of genocide, here and now. The promise of future awards or punishments makes little impression. Heaven as a reward at some unforeseeable future time brings little hope to the hungry and mistreated black person. Hell-future makes little impression upon blacks living in hell-present of shacks, rats, roaches, hunger, unemployment, and inhumane treatment. The resurrection of the flesh is bad news for blacks who suffer so much undeserved pain in the present body.[668]

Says Roberts again: The brink of utter despair will buy this. We need a bringing together of ethics with eschatology in a way that will empower blacks for a better life now.[669] Whereas Moltmann connects the future hope of God to one's present-day faith in Jesus Christ "who has a future because of his resurrection"[670], Roberts defines faith as "the anxiety that is associated with our finitude as persons. Through this experience one knows the freedom of the Christian person. Through the reunion of the separated—God and humanity, and person to person—health and wholeness come to individuals and communities. Hence, the liberated person is also the reconciled

---

[668] J. Deotis Roberts, *Liberation and Reconciliation*, 83.
[669] J. Deotis Roberts, *Black Political Theology*, 182.
[670] Jurgen Moltmann, *Theology of Hope*, 17.

person."[671] Because "the Christian faith is a religion of hope, humans are not alone in their struggle for the good, and death is not defeat but an experience of "overcoming the world."[672] Roberts believes that "Faith is the experience of being seized by the Ultimate."[673] "Through faith Christ becomes a contemporary of the black person"[674] in the everyday life of Black people. Here, Roberts affirms that "Christ is Lord, just as much to the present Christian as he was to the disciples, if through faith he becomes our contemporary. The black Christ, the Christ of the black person's faith, is with the black person in his or her experience of oppression at the hands of the white person."[675]

Roberts's theology of hope is a "living theology. On the one hand, it can provide a Christian understanding of present reality, and on the other hand, it provides a perspective for new historical realities."[676] Here, Roberts believes that messianic hope is a pivotal concept centered in the message of redemption. For Roberts, "Christ is above all cultures at the same time that he walks in a through them for their transformation and redemption."[677] The message of redemption through Jesus Christ is an important part of the Black religious experience because it offers a liberating hope to a people who remain oppressed in the present-day reality of the here and now.

The Holy Spirit, Christian Eschatology, and the Meaning of Spirit(ual)

What role does the Holy Spirit play in Christian eschatology? The Bible teaches that "The coming of the Spirit at Pentecost represents both fulfillment and anticipation of eschatological expectations in as much as Pentecost both fulfills previous expectations regarding the coming of the Spirit and represents a promise of the future consummation of the work of God."[678] Speaking on the narrow tent known as the heavenly dwelling of God's people, the Apostle Paul writes:

---

[671] J. Deotis Roberts, *Black Political Theology,* 156.
[672] J. Deotis Roberts, *Liberation and Reconciliation,* 55.
[673] Ibid.
[674] Ibid., 74.
[675] Ibid., 75.
[676] Ibid., 32-33.
[677] J. Deotis Roberts, *Black Theology Dialogue,* 13.
[678] Andrew K. Gabriel, "The Holy Spirit and Eschatology—with Implications for Ministry and the Doctrine of Spirit Baptism," Para. 1.

For we know that if the tent that is our earthly home is destroyed, we have a building from God, a house not made with hands, eternal in the heavens. For in this tent we groan, longing to put on our heavenly dwelling, if indeed by putting it on we may not be found naked. For a while we are still in this tent, we groan, being burdened–not that we would be further clothed, so that what is mortal may be swallowed up by life. He who has prepared us for this very thing is God, who has given us the Spirit as a guarantee (2 Corinthians 5:1-5).[679]

On the other side of the pneumatological coin,

Paul's eschatological conception of the Spirit's work also comes out clearly in the great resurrection chapter, 1 Corinthians 15. In the unit, verses 42-49, the one word used to describe the future resurrection (that is, eschatological) body of the believer is "spiritual" (*pneumatikon*, vs. 44). The reference of this adjective is neither anthropological (to the body adapted to the human spirit or in which that spirit has gained ascendance or dominance) nor substantial (to the presumably immaterial pneumatic substance of the resurrected body) but to the activity of the Holy Spirit.[680] Paul's point is that the resurrection body is what it, with the eschatological qualities, because it has been so thoroughly transformed and renewed by the Holy Spirit that the single term that best describes its concretely is "spiritual".[681]

In the biblical sense, one way of parsing out the word "spiritual" is through the gifts of the Spirit given to the church. The gifts of the Spirit are given as they exist for the present time in relation to the study of eschatology. The workings of the Holy Spirit impel onward to the surface of the present-day order. These spiritual workings are inseparable from "the present form of this world [that] is passing away" (1 Corinthians 7:31 ESV). Cross referencing 1 Corinthians 7:31

---

[679] www.biblegateway.com

[680] This conclusion follows from Paul's only other use of the psychikon-pneumatikon contrast earlier in 2:14-15 as well as the fact that, apart from the (unrelated) exception in Eph. 6:12, Paul always uses the adjective pneumatikon to refer to the activity of the Holy Spirit; cf. R. B. Gaffin, Jr., *The Centrality of the Resurrection* (Grand Rapids: Baker, 1978), 85f.

[681] Richard B. Gaffin, Jr., "Holy Spirit and Eschatology," Para. 12.

with 1 Cor. 13:3, it is safe to affirm Paul's main point in the entirety of 1 Corinthians 13: without the Spirit of love, prophecy and tongues among other gifts have a temporary function that is designed to pass away (vs. 8 and 9), while those works of the Spirit, like faith, hope and love, endure (v. 13). And of these three, love is the greatest. One of the most important teachings of this book is that believers cannot be spiritual without the presence, work, and gifts of the Holy Spirit. The greatest gift of the Spirit is love. The work of the Holy Spirit is what makes up theology Black and the economy of God's love. For Gaffin, "the fruit of the Spirit as pre-eminently love"[682] is what "effects eschatological breakthroughs."[683]

To be spiritual is to be in tune with the Holy Trinity under the spiritual (Triune) hospices of the three job descriptions of the one Godhead. In the Black Church hymn, "Holy, Holy, Holy," the writer states at the end, "God in three persons. Blessed Trinity." In knowing that the eschatological functions within the economic realm of human life, Gaffin's main point is that "The Spirit is eschatological, resurrection power; he is the eschatological Spirit because his power is resurrection power."[684] The Holy Spirit played a significant role in the resurrection of the body of Jesus Christ. God the Father and Jesus the Son alone would not have been enough to resurrect the body and spirit of Jesus. It had to be collective efforts of all three persons of the Godhead. Together, the combined power of the Holy Trinity was enough to resurrect Jesus out of the grave and defeat sin, death and evil. Romans 8:11 says "But if the Spirit of him that raised up Jesus from the dead dwell in you, he that raised up Christ from the dead shall also quicken your mortal bodies by his Spirit that dwelleth in you." Here, the implication is that the Holy Spirit is the resurrection Spirit. In other words the Holy Spirit is the power of God for God's people. Our position in Christ makes resurrection power available to us (Eph 1:18-20). The power of God resurrected the body of Jesus.

In referencing the slave narratives as a source of Black theological discourse, George C.L. Cummings says that "the biblical concept of the Spirit stresses the eschatological character of the reality of God as a presence that points to a new and transformed future (2 Cor. 5:1-5;

---

[682] Ibid., Para. 43.
[683] Ibid.
[684] Ibid., Para. 46.

Eph. 1:11-15). The presence of the Spirit as a means to discovering new horizons of faith and hope has a promissory dimension."[685] By way of affirming the work of the Holy Spirit as the spiritual hope for Christian believers, Black people experience the work of the Holy Spirit as hope. This is precisely why Black theology is an important study of and within Black religion. To speak of Black theology without referencing the historical totality of Black religious experiences would be irresponsible. And vice versa with the Black religious experiences and the emergence of Black theology in the United States and the world abroad.

New Testament theologian Essau McCauley believes that Black theology offers hope because it supplies a spiritual alternative to the myriad oppressions that seem to prevail in the face of innocent human beings. McCauley posits that Black liberation theology "is only one [but a powerful] strand of Black Christians opposing slavery."[686] According to McCauley, "There was a strong emphasis on brotherhood, on one blood, and how, because we are all part of the human family, we should be together."[687] The push for human unity amongst Black people of all groups, races, and cultures is critical part of the Black theological philosophy. The strand of Black theology that McCauley is referring to is one that brings great hope for future generations of Black people in all groups, races, and cultures. Other strands of this theology developed churches that emphasized accommodation with the larger white society, and there were "holiness churches" that had a strong focus on the Holy Spirit.[688] Within the realm of Black liberation theology in modernity, the Black church affirms hope as the work of the Holy Spirit in the presence of the oppressed.

With the understanding that hope is the work of the Holy Spirit, Chip Ingram writes that "Our hope is received when the Spirit of God—through the Word of God and in the context of community—pours out his love in our hearts. No matter what we've been through, whether it's an unthinkable loss, a betrayal, a tragedy, or a

---

[685] Dwight N. Hopkins and George C. L. Cummings, *Cut Loose Your Stammering Tongue,* 45.

[686] "Black Theology Offers Hope," Para. 11.

[687] Ibid.

[688] Ibid., Para. 12.

dysfunctional relationship, we can see that there is hope."[689] The reason why the Bible says that we do not weep as one who has no hope is because the Holy Spirit is working in our weeping and the weeping is designed to give strength and heal (See Preface). Same is true when David wrote that "Weeping may endure for a night, but the joy will come in the morning (Psalm 30:5; See James H. Evans's theology of the Holy Spirit in Chapter 3)." Again, the Holy Spirit is working in the pain of our weeping moments as like a mother she allows for the mourning weeping of her children to endure for some time before the joy of the Holy Spirit comes again on the morning of God's choosing. Defenses come down and people get real, and God's Spirit begins to bring healing and restoration as truth replaces image management.[690] Here, the spiritual turning point in our deep mourning and sad grieving means surrender and vulnerability and serving others[691] while we still have the Spirit's breath in our bodies.

The Holy Spirit and Eschatology in the Slave Narratives

In discussing the Holy Spirit and Eschatology in the slave narratives, George C. Cummings affirms that the slave testimonies to the Spirit and eschatology "entail a complex web of counter-hegemonic religio-cultural traditions that constituted the basis of their hope for a transformed culture."[692] Because the work of the Holy Spirit in the lives of slaves pointed them to a present and future liberation, they were sure that these existential revelations were biblical. In their understanding that slavery was not of God, the slaves began to discover, envision, and experience the presence of God in a way that led them to their own theologizing. For those slaves who converted to Christianity by way of their faith in Jesus Christ, their encounters with the Spirit were complex because they were more spiritual. The slaves' experience with a holistic Spirit of God was one that showed them the ways they could enjoy their God-given freedom. Within the visions of faith, hope and freedom on full display, the Spirit showed the slaves what was going on and what would go on in

---

[689] Chip Ingram, *Spiritual Simplicity*, 153-154.
[690] Ibid., 186-187.
[691] Ibid, 187.
[692] Dwight N. Hopkins and George C. L. Cummings, *Cut Loose Your Stammering Tongue*, 42.

the future. Put another way, the slaves' experience with the Spirit of God was both existential and eschatological. Under the inspiration of the Holy Spirit, the slaves understood that their creator God had something much greater for them than the chains of slavery. In this theological vein, the slave narratives are an important and irreplaceable form of Black theology.

> In addition, the slave narratives testify to the persistence of hope, human dignity, and self-affirmation that bear witness to the presence of the Spirit of God. This was the pneumatos (God's Spirit), a liberating presence which created and sustained the will of an enslaved people against those people and institutions that perpetrated the exploitation African American chattel. Whereas hegemonic religion and culture defined them as less than human, counter-hegemonic traditions functioned as an oppositional force, affirming their humanity, and sustaining their hope. Several dimensions of the Spirit's presence in the slave community are evident in their testimonies.[693]

The slaves understood the ministries of hope, human dignity, and self-affirmation as the liberating work of the Spirit. In testifying about the goodness of God in presence of the Holy Spirit, they understood that the Spirit of God was their first, last and only savior from the dehumanizing experience of enslavement. If anyone could help the Black slaves in their weakness, it would be the Holy Spirit. It was the same Holy Spirit who gave the Black slaves utterance to talk about their experiences with the Spirit of God.

In the context of spiritual worship, religious life became a context of slaves expressing themselves physically in myriad ways—dancing, screaming, shouting, moaning, and groaning. The Lord allowed Black slaves to transcend the horizon of their immediate experiences and to hope for a future in which they would be free. Freedom was not an abstract concept but a concrete hope that led them to hope and work for historical freedom. The significance of their expectations of hope and justice are to be found in the promissory character of God's eschatological presence in their community.[694]

---

[693] Ibid.
[694] Ibid.

Within the person, power, and work of the Holy Spirit in the life of the Black slave, there is something eschatological about the shouting. In their personal longing to be free human beings on earth, the Holy Spirit helped slaves to understand the greater meaning of being free in Christ Jesus. Even as the notion of historical freedom did not apply to their present situation, it was still something worth hoping for and working for. Not so much in an end-times context. But as Black slave moved toward the end of their earthly lives, they were also moving closer to being a part of that great getting up morning when all God's children will be resurrected alongside their LORD, savior, and redeemer. For the Black slave, this innovative and regenerative work of the Spirit was the promise of freedom that transcended their oppression experiences.

Put another way, "The eschatological hopes and aspirations of the slave community became evident in the Spirit who guarantees the future as one of freedom and justice. There is an immanent character to the slave testimonies concerning their visions of freedom. The eschatological views linked their ardent expectations of God's future with their historical struggle for freedom."[695] Still focusing on the liberating work of the Holy Spirit in the lives of the Black slave, I envision these eschatological hopes, aspirations and views keeping the slaves' mind in a growing peace while helping them to survive the demonic onslaughts of the slave master from one day to the next. Eschatologically and theologically, the Holy Spirit was able to make a way out of no way by way of healing the broken skin that continued to land on the bloody backs and heads of the Black slave.

It is here in the imaginative pocket of spiritual awareness that "The eschatological expectations shared in the slave testimonies showed that their encounter with the Spirit of the Lord enabled them to evolve a critique of racism and racists, dream a grand vision of freedom, nurture communal relationships, fight for freedom, defend one another, affirm their humanity, and hear the melody of the future with such clarity that they literally, in faith, were compared at great cost to dance to the melody of the future by acting in the present to create it.[696] Surely, the Black slave knew that his or her historical freedom would catch up to them through the liberating work of Jesus

---

[695] Ibid., 43.
[696] Ibid.

on that ole' rugged Cross. This historical freedom could only be realized by faith through God's collaborative gifting of past, present, and future freedoms to the multiple generations of Black slaves.

Overall, the role that the Holy Spirit plays in Christian eschatology is one of spiritual perspectives. Before the slaves could be physically free, they had to experience a spiritual freedom that could only come from an intimate life encounter with the Holy Spirit. While a sizable number of Black slaves did not experience their human/physical freedom down here on earth, they had enough faith in the Bible and what the Holy Spirit revealed to them. The combination of what the Bible says about being free in Jesus Christ along with the work of the Holy Spirit is what enabled the Black slaves to have a deeper relationship with their Creator God.

The Holy Spirit and eschatology in the slave narratives represent a legitimate form of Black liberation theology. In his article, "Liberation Theologies in America," Craig L. Nessan proclaims that "Deep conviction about the work of the Holy Spirit in history through the power of the spoken word and courageous actions are embedded in church traditions with affinity for black liberation theology. Eschatological hope for liberty and justice for all, including black people, translates the expectation of heaven into worldly activism."[697]

The Holy Spirit in Black Spirituality and the Unspoken Spoken

I define *theology* as holistic discourse of the Holy Spirit's work within the study of God in religious faith, Christian practice, human experience, and cultural spirituality, which gives biblical reasoning for the liberating truth of God to become known in any context. The word 'spirituality' is a critical part of my defining theology, Black theology, and Christian theology. I believe that for one to identify the critical norms and sources of one's theology, he or she must be operating from a working definition of theology that gives meaning to one's critical approach to biblical hermeneutics, theological praxis, and research analysis. For me, cultural spirituality takes place in the presence of the Holy Spirit as she touches down on the human spirit. There is no Black spirituality without the work of the Holy Spirit. I say that because Black spirituality is a Black cultural spirituality that is developed and displayed under the anointing of the Holy Spirit.

---

[697] Craig L. Nessan, "Liberation Theologies in America," Para. 15.

Dwight N. Hopkins believes Black spirituality is about loving God's people and helping the poor. In other words, demonstrating the love of God to poor people is greater than preaching the correct biblical doctrine. Theologically, Black spirituality prioritizes goods and services to the poor over church doctrine. In the existential context of spiritual blackness, culture in Black spirituality happens when the Holy Spirit connects with the human spirit for the purpose of material production. In addition to the traditional notions of being called God-talk, I also define *theology* as Spirit-talk.

In his article, "God Over Everything: Black Spirituality and the Paradox of Religion," Julian Mitchell writes that

> Since the times of slave masters dropping bibles down to shackled Africans who couldn't read or speak the English language – black people have always developed a deeply personal definition of God and their spiritual identity. Enduring extreme persecution and exploitation, black people took the template of Christianity and customized it to reflect their own interpretation of its teachings. As a result, spirituality became the soul of our artistry, the language of our existence, and the backbone of our communities. It instilled a sense of power and purpose within a race of people who were deemed powerless.[698]

A much-needed, theological framing bodes the proverbial questions of: What does spirituality look like in the realm of Black religion proper? With the Bible declaring that we are to walk by faith and not by sight, is Black spirituality recognizable to the human eye as a Christian phenomenon? Or does Black spirituality include non-Christian experiences as well? Is Black spirituality shaped by the deep-seeded earth or is it metaphysically birthed in the Holy Spirit? Its origin encompasses both realities. Only God knows for sure.

But for a while now the Black church has placed the practice of religion up against one's individual and personal need for spiritual-spirituality development. Meanwhile, the pervasive presence of religion and spirituality in black culture has expanded the scope of this interpretive work to include a wide array of ideas and impulses.[699]

---

[698] Julian Mitchell, "God Over Everything," Para. 5.
[699] Cheryl J. Sanders, *Living the Intersection*, 11.

Here, the implication is that Black church experiences were designed "to illustrate Afrocentric values, spirituality, and culture."[700] Most pastors of the Black church define spirituality as one's personal relationship with God. In the proverbial relationship *over* religion discussion, the prevailing notion is that one's need for a developing relationship with God is greater than our religious commitments to the institutional church. This affirmation comes without our defining what spirituality looks like in the organic spectrum of blackness in the United States.

Theologically, the Black church needs Black religion and Black spirituality working cogently. The development of one's relationship within God in Christ by the power of the Holy Spirit without a conscientious religious conviction in place is nonproductive. Absolutely, we must know God in the pardon of our sin, and we must know the doctrine of the church in which we are a contributing part of. Not necessarily for a denominational claim of absolute truth, but for a substantive knowledge base of what we mean when we say that we are members of the Black church. While I do believe that our spirituality gives scope and shape to our religious convictions, I am sure that our religious affirmations give substantive merit to what it means to be spiritual. In other words, the Black religious experience makes the necessary connection between Black spirituality and Black religion. I say that because I consider the Black spirituality to be an important, contemplative practice of the Black church.

In a modern view of Black spirituality in the United States, Barbara A. Holmes and M. Shawn Copeland suggest that "black religion is characterized by its theological diversity and its broad spectrum of cultural nuances."[701] Put another way, Black religion is not composed of one single experience. Theologically and culturally, Black religion has always been composed of a myriad of experiences plural. Moreover, Holmes views the work of the Spirit as an integral part of Black religious discourses on spirituality, holiness, worship, biblical interpretation, and social activism. As stated earlier, in his essay "Toward A Common Expression of Faith: A Black North American Perspective," Gayraud Wilmore argues that the holiness of the church is evident in the spirituality of the Black church and that

---

[700] Ibid., 160.
[701] Barbara A. Holmes, *Joy Unspeakable*, 4.

spirituality is a sign of the movement of the Holy Spirit in the world.[702]

Black and Womanist theologians alike have shared what they believe to be the Holy Spirit's directional involvement in the practice and presence of Black spirituality, the consensus is that without the power and presence of the Holy Spirit working in the life of the believer, there would not be a Black religious experience or the possibility of spiritual liberation from the bondage of oppression. Here the implication is that Black spirituality is spirituality proper. In Michael Battle's book, *The Quest for Liberation and Reconciliation: Essays in Honor of J. Deotis Roberts*, Delores Carpenter writes that, "Spirituality is a belief and hope that one can be a part of the habitation of God, a sanctuary for God, a touchstone. It is the part of a human being that invites that invites Holy Spirit with a welcoming reception."[703] Put another way, spirituality connects the Holy Spirit to the human spirit for reasons of order, purpose, guidance, instruction of Scripture, reason, tradition and provision and protection from evil. Using an African spiritual, Diana L. Hayes supports Carpenter's claim by affirming that

> Spirituality is a rock to hang on to when the world is rushing out of control. It is the unseen force that gives you the courage to push when you'd much rather pull. It shows the way when it seems there is no way. It makes sense out of nonsense and encourages you to have faith –help is just around the corner. It is the balm that soothes and heals your inner wounds. With spirituality, you rest easy knowing that whatever ails you, enrages you, troubles you, or gets on your last nerve, this too shall pass. It's the map to inner peace on a road that never ends. And it ain't just about being deep. Spirituality makes you leave the pity party. It lightens you up. All of a sudden, you find that you are laughing at yourself. And with others. Even when it hurts. Simply put, feeling the spirit brings you joy. And as countless sisters who have gone before you and who are living it every day will testify; spirit is the salve needed to heal and transform.[704]

The Spirit of the unspoken spoken is the Spirit of Black

---

[702] James H. Evans, Jr., *Black Theology*, 171-172.
[703] Michael Battle, *Quest for Liberation*, 162.
[704] Emilie N. Townes, *Embracing the Spirit*, 25.

spirituality. Both identities represent the person and power of the Holy Spirit. In identifying Black theology as spirituality or a responsible, Black spirituality, it is contextually appropriate to connect the reality of liberation to the work of God the Holy Spirit. I say this because the main job description of the Holy Spirit is to give life. If we take the Spirit out of life, then we have lost both the battle and our everlasting minds. Because life is a spiritual battle between matters of spirituality and carnality, human beings need the Spirit just to survive. Just as the reality of God taking on our particularity has universal implications, so too does God take the parenthetic has contextual implications. If we view God as both universal and contextual, then the work of God the Holy Spirit is both universal and contextual. Even though human beings will never be able to fully understand each other in this fallen world, we can acknowledge that the Holy Spirit works in the ways that we comprehend biblically and in ways that we will never fully comprehend. With all due respect and deference to what the Bible says about the Holy Spirit, as believers, we can never deny the *supernatural experience* of the Holy Spirit working in our lives. Black people may struggle to give descriptive reasoning to this experience, but the experience *itself* can still be one of physical healing and theological clarity ensconced in spiritual ecstasy.

One of the connecting nuggets that I found in my research is that the Holy Spirit gave our slave ancestors their Black spirituality. In his book, *DOWN, UP, AND OVER: Slave Religion and Black Theology*, Dwight N. Hopkins theologizes the Spirit of God as deliverer and healer. In citing examples from ex-slaves, Hopkins affirms that God has a special and timely way of helping oppressed people when they need it the most. In the same tone as heard in the words of the Gospel song, On Time God, Hopkins writes that "Ultimately, divine patience is the is the Spirit for us to be fully human, spiritually and materially, and to enable those ensnared within the oppressive clutches of death and social disease to struggle for liberation and to practice freedom."[705] Because God in Jesus Christ saves, delivers and heals, "the Holy Spirit is the greatest of all blessings for oppressed black folk, whether free or unfree, north or south. And the spirit for us denotes specifically patience (in God's own time and

---

[705] Hopkins, *DOWN, UP, AND OVER*, 188.

not forever) described as equal rights, privileges, liberty and independence."[706] Theologically, Hopkins believes that caring for and ministering to the poor takes precedence over preaching and teaching correct doctrine.

For Hopkins, the Holy Spirit is the deliverer from Black oppression because one's interaction with the Holy Spirit is what funds Black spirituality. Hopkins's take on the Spirit of liberation is one that affirms God working with oppressed black folk and other peoples underneath the heel of victimization through the interplay of God's glory and unity, righteousness and omnipresence, constancy and eternity, omnipotence and mercy, grace and holiness, and wisdom and patience.[707] Because God works in the life of oppressed Black folk, the Spirit is rendered as the activity itself. Hopkins concludes that "The work or activity of the Spirit is described as total liberation. What this means is that the role of the liberating Spirit is both material and spiritual. To further the role of this Spirit as a vivifying agent in the co-constitution of a full material and spiritual humanity in the new Commonwealth requires further inquiry into the Spirit of liberation with us: that is to say, the reality of Jesus with us today."[708]

Metaphysically and spiritually speaking, I would venture to say that the Holy Spirit does more than what the Bible records. In *Jesus and the Trinity: A Key to a Deeper Religious Experience*, Walter Russell Bowie writes that "This inability to explain the ultimate metaphysical being of the Holy Spirit can leave the restless intellect unsatisfied—as indeed how could it be otherwise for our finite minds? But always a vital matter is that the reality of the very God does come as Holy Spirit to human hearts and souls in a certainty that does not depend on explanation."[709] As Ernest F. Scott has written: The belief in the Spirit has always sprung out of an experience.... In times of religious awakening ...men have felt themselves possessed with a quickening and uplifting power, which seemed to come directly out of a higher world.[710] While Bowie and Scott are not of African descent,

---

[706] Ibid.
[707] Ibid.
[708] Ibid.
[709] Walter R. Bowie, *Jesus and the Trinity*, 68.
[710] Ernest F. Scott, *Spirit New Testament*, vi.

their musings have theological implications for the discussion on Black theology and pneumatology because they keep believers pointed toward and in the direction of experiencing the Holy Spirit. The Apostle Paul writes to the Romans that "In the same way, the Spirit helps us in our weakness. We do not know what we ought to pray for, but the Spirit himself intercedes for us with groans that words cannot express (Romans 8:26). "Paul explains the groans as an experience with the Holy Spirit." Here, the experience of the Holy Spirit results in what I term as spirituality or a true relationship with God in Jesus Christ through a Trinitarian awareness of the Spirit.

For those African slaves who believed that there was a God and a Jesus Christ and a Holy Spirit but could not put it together rhetorically because of what they were being taught scripturally, perhaps they were inspired by something or somebody to believe that when the Holy Spirit was working, the Holy Trinity was present. The slaves received the gift of a Trinitarian spirituality in the reality of God the Holy Spirit helping them to see that what they were experiencing was not the end of the story. The spiritual rubber meets the stony road when the slaves stole away to worship God away from the presence of the slave master. The invisible institution was the work of the Holy Spirit where slaves had an experience with God that helped them to make the pneumatological connection between their suffering and the God they worshiped. The slaves' experiences of bondage and oppression are what confirmed their growing awareness of freedom and liberation. Once again, the work of the Holy Spirit is sacred, secular, universal, and contextual.

Another way of engaging the Spirit of the unspoken spoken in a Black theological context is by listening to and imagining what is going on behind what the scholars are writing. When we listen to the actions of the Spirit, those actions or moments not expressed in words, we see the Holy Spirit working for the good of those who love God and are called according to God's purpose (Rom. 8:28). We see God relieving the pregnant slave woman from her earthly misery as the white slave master beats her profusely. Here, the reality of death can be the result of the Spirit working. Throughout history, the Spirit of God called a sizable number of African American slaves and other oppressed Black people to their eternal rest; relieving them of more pain as the white oppressor physically persecuted them. Further, despite being economically, politically, and socially oppressed, the power of the Holy Spirit sustained Black people to the point of where they could tell the story. Despite the constant threat of death, neither the lack of education nor the economic resources to acquire material things, Black people still had the Lord on their side in the form of the Holy Spirit. Because of their experiences with the Holy Spirit, Black people were confident that God would not fail them. Even if it meant dying, the Holy Spirit assured Black people of their safe identity as children of the one and true living God. The Spirit of the Lord operated within the radical affirmation of slave autonomy and independence manifest in the slaves' willingness to defy their oppressors to serve God.

In addition to the eschatological nature that is found in the work of the Spirit, David Emmanuel Goatley affirms the pneumatological legitimacy of African American slave spirituals in the work of Lawrence W. Levine, John Lovell, Jr., Sterling Stuckey, Henry Hugh Proctor and Willis J. King. Goatley firstly affirms that "The majority of spirituals have themes related to hope, victory, and liberation."[711] Not only was the Holy Spirit present in the slave narratives, but the Spirit was also present in the culture of the music (See my definition of culture in Chapter 6). The Spirit enabled the slaves to retain freedom of thought and the spiritual and mental tenacity to deal with their dehumanizing circumstances. The Holy Spirit not only worked on the hearts of the slaves, but the Spirit also created an atmosphere that allowed the slaves to see God working in their oppressive situations. These Black religious experiences are the foundations of a modern-day Black church hermeneutic.

What this means theologically is that the person, power, and work of the Holy Spirit is the hermeneutical bridge between Jesus of Nazareth, his message concerning the power of God, with the manifestation of God as Liberator within the religious experiences that are associated with instances of Black culture and images in Black history. The theological teaching of a doctrine of the Spirit as the creative, empowering, and liberating power in the Black experience explains how the Spirit of Christ provides a hermeneutical key by

---

[711] Dwight N. Hopkins and George C. L. Cummings, *Cut Loose Your Stammering Tongue*, 132.

which oppressed races, cultures, and groups of people establish spiritual continuity between Jesus of Nazareth and the liberating presence of Christ as the Black Messiah. Jesus of Nazareth, according to the written testimony of the early church, was the embodiment of God in the world (Col. 2:9). God and the Holy Spirit are the surrounding stories of Jesus Christ as they are Ones that resurrected Jesus out of the grave. Under the inspiration of the Holy Spirit, the story of Jesus of Nazareth as the Crucified One is a spiritual expression of God's heart for those crucified by enslavement and oppression. The unity of the Spirit is found in the unity of the Holy Trinity as the Spirit of Christ is present in the experiences of Black enslaved people.

From the perspective of spiritual unity, Frederic and Mary Ann Brussat affirm that "In this age of global spirituality, respect differences but affirms commonalities. Work together with those who are trying to make the world a better place."[712] Spiritual unity is the undenominational and inter-religious result of God's love flowing from heart to heart and breast to breast. Spiritual unity is also the work of the Holy Spirit. Spiritual unity is the biproduct of spirituality and spiritual literacy. Meanwhile, "Spirituality is alive and well in many religious congregations where individuals have expressed the desire to deepen their relationships to God. Programs in spiritual formation are attracting those interested in exploring their own traditions and learning about other approaches to life in the Spirit."[713]

Even deeper, "Spiritual literacy is about paying attention. All kinds wonderful and important things are going on directly in front of us, but we miss most of them because we are not awake."[714] Being spiritually awake can be the difference between experiencing joy and experiencing dispiritedness in life. Theologically, I say that because joy is a spiritual practice that governs equally to all believers by the transformational love of the Holy Spirit. Jesus's work on the cross gives material and spiritual credence to the experience of joy in the life of the believer. The Spirit was with Jesus as he suffered, bled, and died for the sins of the entire world. As greatest form of liberation, the work of the Holy Spirit played a leading role in resurrecting

---

[712] Frederic Brussat and Mary Ann Brussat, *Spiritual Literacy*, 24.
[713] Ibid., 31.
[714] Ibid., 52.

Jesus's body out of the grave.

Conclusion

Thinking Spiritually in the Spiritual Darkness: Moving Toward Orthodoxy

Thankfully, it was Nancy E. Bedford, the Georgia Harkness Professor of Theology at the Garrett-Evangelical Theological Seminary, who inspired me to think deeply and spiritually about the word *explicit* in terms what it could mean to construct a Black pneumatology for the contemporary context. In addition to the biblical realities of healing and miracles, I was always thinking of such categories as the supernatural, conversion, empowerment, and ecstasy. It seems to me that when talking about the sacredness of the Holy Spirit's interaction with Black people and other races and cultures of people too, in sacred institutions and secular environments, it becomes a difficult conversation because Black people either do not have the words to describe the unique deepness of how the Spirit has literally saved or impacted their lives or Black scholars and churchgoers have to come to a conclusion that the specific ways and means which the Holy Spirit works in our lives cannot be referenced in all of what the Bible says about the work, power, and presence of the Holy Spirit. That is not to say that the constructive work cannot be done because I believe it can. As one who is committed to writing a Black descriptive theology, I often time find myself wondering about the cultural creativity and unexplainable depth of such a theological exploration within the work of the Spirit.

As both a spiritual mother and my doctoral professor, Nancy E. Bedford reminded me that

> It is true that you might have to think of an apophatic pneumatology rather than a cataphatic one. But there is still a way to put into words something of that movement of the Spirit in the Black Church and among the lives of Black folk generally. The resilience, the bonds of friendship and kinship, the persistence, the hope, the beauty—these things that one finds in the Black community (up against and in spite of the death, destruction, incarceration, violence) are typical of the work of the Spirit. I don't think the Bible tells all the story: it

opens up our stories to something new, in conjunction with the way of Jesus, yet moving further along that path. I think you are on to something important when you say this cannot be formulated—that is true! And yet it can be articulated to some extent.[715]

Theologically and culturally, I am certain that Dr. Bedford was trying to explain to me why the Holy Spirit can reveal to the world exactly what's going on and give us the blueprint of how the church is to respond to such evil catastrophes. I say that because Apophatic theology is spiritual knowledge of God obtained through negation.

Definitively, "apophatic theology is a negative spirituality type of theology. Negative theology, also known as Apophatic theology, is a theological method of describing God by negation, in which one avers only what may not be said about God. This approach, often called the via negativa, is a favorite among mystics who often insist that their experiences of divinity are beyond the realm of language and concepts. The purpose of Negative theology is to gain a glimpse of God (divinity) by articulating what God is not (apophasis), rather than what God is."[716] This "way of negation" emphasizes mystery and yet the Bible says that it is the Holy Spirit that sovereignly reveals "the deep things of God" to us, "But as it is written, Eye hath not see, nor ear heard, neither have entered into the heart of man, the things which God hath prepared for them that love him. But God hath revealed them unto us by his Spirit; for the Spirit searches all things, yea, the deep things of God. (1 Corinthians 2:9).[717]

A further problem in addition to that of us trying to theologize the specifics of the mysterious unknown with Orthodox mysticism is that the following the "way of negation" can lead to ecstasy seeking. Orthodox mystics find it acceptable to

---

[715] This is an email that Dr. Nancy E. Bedford sent me on February 17, 2016, as I was preparing for my Comprehensive Exams at Garrett-Northwestern in Chicago. In addition to teaching me a PhD course on Constructive Pneumatology for the Contemporary Context (2010), Dr. Bedford also served on my Comprehensive Exam Committee (2016) and my Dissertation Committee (2018). In theologizing the role of the Holy Spirit in the Christian life, Bedford brilliantly teaches how the power and presence of the Holy Spirit inspires believers to resist injustices, while embracing life-giving practices. Bedford views the Holy Spirit as One that helps people to follow Jesus within the theological categories of joy, resistance, and biblical activism.
[716] New World Encyclopedia, 5.
[717] 1 Corinthians 2:9-10 NIV

teach the attainment of a state of ecstasy to "penetrate the highest spiritual reality." An example of ecstasy seeking by prayer is found in the fourteenth century writings of Gregory of Sinai, a recognized saint in the Orthodox Church. Noetic prayer is an activity initiated by the cleansing power of the Spirit and the mystical rites celebrated by the intellect, Similarly, stillness is initiated by attentive waiting upon God, its intermediate stage is characterized by illuminative power and contemplation, and its final goal is ecstasy and the enraptured flight of the intellect towards God.[718]

The seeking of ecstasy or any other type of spiritual status within the pursuit of intellect towards God is not the goal of pneumatology. Because the Holy Spirit cleanses the thoughts of our hearts through the inspiration of the Holy Spirit, the goal of studying the person, power and work of the Holy Spirit is surrendering and waiting on God's revelation by grace through faith in Jesus Christ. Here, the work of the Holy Spirit is salvific and redemptive. Praying to God in the name of Jesus is a sacred act that is inspired by the Spirit, who is the highest spiritual reality in the universe.

The Holy Spirit in Black Orthodoxy or Not?

According to Esau McCauley, "The Black Christian tradition is not and has never been a monolith, but it is fair to say that the Black church tradition is largely orthodox in its theology in the sense that it holds to many of the things that all Christians have generally believed."[719] What this means is that an "unapologetically Black and orthodox reading of the Bible [that] can speak a relevant word to Black Christians today. I want to contend that the best instincts of the Black church tradition—its public advocacy for justice, its affirmation of the worth of Black bodies and souls, its vision of a multiethnic community of faith—can be embodied by those who stand at the center of this tradition."[720] The liberating work and power of the Holy Spirit advocates for justice in the domains of Black oppression as it is envisioned within ethnic diversity. But just because the Holy Spirit is active in the religious, cultural, and human experiences of Black people, that does not mean that the Black church tradition is

---

[718] St. Markarios of Corinth (Philokalia), St. Gregory of Sinai. "Introductory Note," 237.
[719] Esau McCauley, *Reading While Black*, 5.
[720] Ibid., 5-6.

orthodox in its theology. Or in her biblical thinking. I say that because the orthodox mind sets forth historical reasons to believe that the spiritual continuity of salvation and redemption has been sustained by the power of the Holy Spirit over exceedingly great obstacles. Orthodox history calls this providence.[721]

Before I expound briefly on the tenets of orthodoxy proper, I would like to share one simple reason Orthodoxy is not as rooted in the Black church as it should be. In his article, "Is Orthodoxy Strong in the Black Church?," Jerry L. Buckner posits that the lack of Christian orthodoxy in the Black church is due to the lack of focus on teaching Christian doctrine. According to Buckner, "The essential doctrines of the historic Christian faith such as the Trinity, the deity of Christ, the vicarious atonement of Christ, the bodily resurrection of Christ, and the second coming of Christ are not being strongly taught in most Black churches."[722] In other words, "There is no training on the essentials of the Christian faith."[723] Reasons for this critical observation range from a lack of formal training amongst the laity to the lack of theological (educational) training amongst the ordained clergy. As a seminary-trained pastor in the Christian Methodist Episcopal church tradition, I find substantive merit in both McCaulley and Buckner's theory. While not leaning toward either side, the Spirit tell me that the Black church lacks Christian orthodoxy because it has become rigidly limited in its teaching of the Christian doctrine. While the Black church remains justice-minded in the face of systemic oppression, they teach the biblical doctrines for the sole purpose of receiving an immediate economic/material gain.

Orthodoxy in the classical Christian sense is right remembering in accord with the apostles' teaching. Orthodoxy understands itself as enlivened by that ongoing work of the Spirit that helps believers

---

[721] Thomas C. Oden, *How Africa Shaped the Christian Mind*, 120. While the Holy Spirit and God's providence are distinct concepts, they are both integral to Christian theology and the understanding of God's relationship with humanity. The Holy Spirit is the spiritual means by which God lovingly interacts with believers, while providence is the overarching plan that God has for all of creation. What this means is that the interacting work of the Holy Spirit in the life of believers is an inclusive part of God's plan for creation. The Holy Spirit works in all of creation: the Church, human beings, animals, nature, weather, and plants (Gen 1:2).

[722] Jerry L. Buckner, "Is Christian Orthodoxy Strong in the Black Church?," Para. 6.

[723] Ibid.

remember the New Testament witness reliably in the light of ecumenical consensual exegesis. God's own Spirit is working within out limitations, our consciousness and within our memory to correct and sustain the right collections of the truth and unity of apostolic teaching.[724] Thomas C. Oden expounds even more:

> The simple process of transmitting the religious tradition to our children it itself considered in orthodox Christianity as a work of the Holy Spirit, a gift of grace, not a good human work alone without grace. The writing of the apostles, the apostles' right remembering our remembering of the apostles rightly—these are truly human acts into which the Spirit enters and participates to inspire, encourage, and guarantee the truth of the reliable transmission of the revealed Word. The mystery of the truth of the true humanity and true divinity of the incarnate Lord is analogous to the mystery of the truth of the Spirit transmitted through history by means of written documents.[725]

The rule of faith is the baptismal confession that the faithful learn when they become baptized, the key reasoning of triune teaching: God the Father reveals himself in his Son through the Holy Spirit.[726] One who pits tradition against Scripture or faith against charity has already lost touch with the orthodox sense of balance that the Holy Spirit is encouraging by helping the believer remember Scripture rightly and read its message faithfully within ever new historical contexts.[727] The Spirit guards the truth, but this does not imply that finite witnesses to the truth are foolproof. The Spirit glorifies God the Son, according to African orthodoxy, but is not preferential toward the skin color of that attest that sonship.[728] Here, the revealing of God's truth coupled with an increasing human creativity (culture) are the liberating works of the Holy Spirit.

In the words of John R. Gresham, Jr.:

Also, the whites from Eastern Europe had nothing to do with the chattel slavery of our ancestors nor established the Jim

---

[724] Thomas C. Oden, *How Africa Shaped the Christian Mind*, 127.
[725] Ibid.
[726] Ibid., 128.
[727] Ibid.
[728] Ibid., 129.

Crow laws. Greeks and Serbs were slaves to the Ottoman Turks up until the early 1800s. Russian monks defended the humanity and rights of Native Alaskans and helped push for the liberation of serfs (semi-slaves) in their own nation. Arabs, Lebanese, and Syrians do not consider themselves to be white. As for the Egyptians and Ethiopians, they certainly aren't white. Thus, for a black American to become an Orthodox Christian is to join a universal body of believers that are not defined by Thomas Jefferson's assumed white supremacy and Finis Dake's Biblical misinterpretations of black "inferiority."[729]

The teaching point is that despite the destructive harm that white Americans has done to Black Americans, the Spirit holds a creative and transformational presence in and throughout Christian and world history. With a certain type of spiritual recognition of who has been obedient to the Spirit's directing and who has not been obedient, it is safe to say that the Holy Spirit works in Christian orthodoxy for the benefit of the Black believer. Now whether the Black church believes this or not is always up for discussion. John 3:8 says "The wind blows wherever it pleases. You hear its sound, but you cannot tell where it comes from or where it is going. So it is with everyone born of the Spirit (NIV).'" My hope is that Black liberation theology and the Black church are born of the Spirit. Our liberating actions will tell of what takes place in the future.

However, on the other hand, Black practitioners and Black scholars agree that it is extremely difficult for the Black church to weigh in on issues of Christian orthodoxy because so much of what it considered orthodoxy is nothing more than Eurocentrism packaged in a contemporary (postmodern) theological model. Put another way, it would be problematic for Black religionists to lean too heavily either on white liberal theology or white conservative theology when there are so many areas of concern within the fields of Black liberation theology and Black church theology. Defined as the study of the Holy Spirit, pneumatology in Black theology and Black religion inspires people of color fight against the social, political, and economic issues that stem from a demonically oppressive way of being theologized

---

[729] John Gresham, "To Be Black and Orthodox," Para. 3.

within and beyond their culturo-religious experiences. Here, the restraining power of the Holy Spirit works in the presence of a growing systemic evil. When the Black church declares that God can do all things but fail, one interpretation should be that the Holy Spirit gives Black believers the deep utterance needed to be justice-minded Christians and competent teachers of the Christian doctrine (Acts 2:4).

As we have attempted to unpack what it could mean for the Black church to be more rooted in Christian orthodoxy, it is important to remember these two things about Orthodox Spirituality:

1. A person can abide in Christ, accomplish His commandments and be in communion with God the Father only by the presence and power of the Holy Spirit in his life. Spiritual life is life in and by the Holy Spirit of God.[730]

2. The Holy Spirit proceeds from the Father and is sent into the world through Christ so that human persons can fulfill God's will in their lives and be like Christ. The spiritual fathers of the Orthodox Church say that the Holy Spirit makes people to be "christs," that is, the "anointed" children of God.[731]

In addition to enabling believers to abide in Christ, to be like Christ, to be "christs," and to be children of God, the Holy Spirit is who makes believers spiritual. Spiritual life is life in the Holy Spirit. One cannot be spiritual or have any type of spirituality with the inspiration of the Holy Spirit.

Meanwhile, Christians of all groups, races, and cultures are not able to speculate about the Logos after the coming of Christ, who is the divine Logos in the flesh, and who sent the Holy Spirit to the world and "teaches us all things."[732] Theologically, being spiritually obedient to the leading and guiding of the Holy Spirit should be one of the main goals of being a Christian. Making progress in the spiritual life and attaining spiritual perfection took place in our Lord's death and resurrection. These acts enable us to recognize our awareness and growth in internalizing the presence of the Holy Spirit within us. The word I am referring to is love. The purpose of being a human

---

[730] "Orthodox Spirituality: The Holy Spirit," Para. 1.
[731] Ibid., Para. 4.
[732] George C. Papademetriou, "*An Introduction to Orthodox Spirituality*," Para. 6.

being is to achieve moral perfection through the acquisition of the Holy Spirit. The truth is that the world needs an apophatic theology in place to describe what the Holy Spirit was doing in the contemporary context. On my read and watch of the United States and the world abroad, there seems to be commonalities between the existential years of 1971 and 2023. One could argue that much has not changed in terms of corrupt politics, race relations, and economic poverty in the U.S. over the course of fifty plus years.

I Ask Again: What's Going On?

The late Marvin Gaye's important, theological question of 1971, "What's Going On", is still on the table of the dark history of Christian experience in the United States 2023. The same social evils that plagued our country 52 years ago have reared its ugly head again in the form of a growing neighborhood segregation, racial discrimination, economic deprivation, police brutality, white supremacy, educational inequalities, and low-paying jobs. Even today in the early parts of 2023, Black men are being killed at the negligent hands of white and Black cops, hip-hop rappers are being murdered at a record pace, people are still dying at the hands of Covid-19, gun violence is at an all-time high with racism being alive and well, inner-city neighborhoods are still deprived and underdeveloped, the U.S. public school system is trending in the wrong direction, jails and prisons are still full of Blacks and Latinos, the cost of seemingly rises every week, the country has fallen deeper in love with white nationalism, and the minimum wage in the commonwealth of Kentucky remains at $7.50 per hour.

I harken back to Lewis Brogdon's observational claim that America is on the brink of losing it soul. One of my early responses regarding Brogdon's claim was that as a Christian theologian, I am not fully convinced that the United States has ever really had a soul to begin with, politically speaking and otherwise; bit more less exist in a position to where she is in grave danger of losing her soul. I begin to ask the question of What's Going On? Who is willing to use God-talk as a way responding to this all-important question? In the words of Marian Wright Edelman, "Why is there still, in Cold-War America, such unbearable dissonance between promise and performance, between good politics and effective public policy, between professed and practiced family values, between calls for community and rampant individualism and greed; between our capacity to prevent and alleviate child killing, poverty, and disease and our political and spiritual will to do so in the richest and most powerful nation on earth?"[733]

Within the agency of Black theolgical discourse, Riggins Earl teaches that an embodied soul experience represents a way of describing the slaves' experience with the Holy Spirit. In other words, there is communicative interaction of the Black human soul with the Spirit of God. Earl describes this spiritual experience as "Being born of the spirit of God, felt his power, tasted his love and seen the travel of his soul. Slaves likened their experience of this rite of passage to having been "struck dead...; killed dead by God and made alive." This death experience, ironically, was characterized as both a life-taking and life-giving phenomenon.[734] Even as I have never correlated death with the work of the Spirit, the Bible teaches that "the Lord gives, and the Lord takes away Job 1:21." The activities of giving and taking can be interpreted as works of the Spirit. The Spirit knows what is going on because the Spirit knows the mind of God. The Spirit also knows best for God's people in terms of her deciphering of what the outcome could mean to the situation of concern.

According to Earl, "The most dramatic moment of the conversion experience, according to the narrators of it, was when slaves were overwhelmed by the Spirit of God at some unprecedented time and place. One might be working in the field, cooking in the kitchen, or lying across the bed when such a dramatic moment of spiritual transformation."[735] The teaching point is that no one knows when, where and how the Spirit will work in their life situation. Therein lies the mystery of the Holy Spirit (John 3:8). Spiritually, it is wise to "accept the unknown as part of life. Don't try to unravel the profound mysteries of God, human nature, and the natural world. Love the ineffable."[736] The reason that the saving love of the Holy Spirit is too great to express in words because it is a liberating love

---

[733] Marian W. Edelman, *Guide My Feet*, 86.
[734] Clifton H. Johnson, *God Struck Me Down*, 59. See also Kurt Buhring's *Spirits on the Inside: Spirit(s) in Black Religion* (London, EN: Palgrave McMillan, 2022) and Riggins Earl's *Dark Symbols, Obscure Signs: God, Self, and Community in the Slave Mind.* (Knoxville, TN: University of Tennessee Press, 2003).
[735] Riggins Earl, *Dark Symbols, Obscure Signs*, 60.
[736] Frederic Brussat and Mary Ann Brussat, *Spiritual Literacy*, 24.

that goes beyond what the Bible says about the work of the Spirit.

My Experiences with the Holy Spirit

Speaking of God's liberating love, my earliest experiences with the Holy Spirit took place as a young child at my grandmother's house in Hopkinsville, Kentucky. In learning how to pray at an early age, I often time found myself meditating on the things that I was seeing in my elementary life. At times when I was praying with my eyes closed, I would feel my body moving in a spiritual wave-length kind of way. On numerous occasions I would feel as if I was floating squarely parallel in the air. Obviously, I could not hold myself up like that without someone holding me or helping to undergird me. But I sometimes felt wavy and watery in my prayers as I transitioned into meditation where I could feel someone holding my physical body up. In a vertical parallelism that felt like flowing water, my inner body lifted with my physical body. Even as these spiritually meditative experiences felt a bit weird, I understood them to be safe places for me to be in. What I come to realize was that these spiritual experiences with God was God's way of overtaking my body and mind for the purpose of God showing me that I belonged to Him. This was the work of the Holy Spirit.

My other experiences with the Holy Spirit showed me how God is a protector in the life of those who believed in God. When I was 14 years old, a group of violent teenagers violently attacked me. As I was walking through a housing project in my neighborhood, three intoxicated males jumped me. Even though I endured violence to the body and face with numerous punches and kicks, I never felt the pain of those blows. I only felt the force of the wind coming in my physical direction. I recall taking a hard punch to the face and falling to the ground. But I did not feel the power of the punch nor the contact that forced me to the ground. But I remember feeling a protective shield around my face that did not allow me to feel any physical pain. As I took fisted punches, it felt like a lined pocket of wind pressed up against my face. While on the concrete ground, I realized that one of the attackers had a gun in his pocket. I was able crawl from the middle of the crowd and run down the street away from those whose intent was to do harm. Even as it might have seemed that my life was in danger, I was able to escape unscathed and with all my faculties in place. On that dramatic night, I am certain that the Spirit protected and shielded me from all harm in real life situations.

I also feel the protective comfort of the Holy Spirit in my dreams and nightmares. Just when I have fallen off a deep cliff and I am about to violently touchdown onto the ground, the Spirit wakes me up just before I hit the ground. The Spirit also wakes me up in my dreams as I am being chased by full-grown lions and physically bitten by ferocious tigers. While I have been bitten by wild animals in my dreams, the Spirit always protects me from feeling the full pain of the attack. On the other side of spiritual dream coin, the Spirit guides me in what it seems like to be an all-out physical battle with some the greatest killers in movies like Halloween and Friday the 13th. It seems like the Spirit guides me into these physical battles and allows me to fight until the possibility of death shows forth. And then I am awakened from my sleep. It never fails that when I feel like I am going to perish in my dreams, the Spirit awakens me just in time. The Spirit also allows me to see deceased people in my dreams. Many of the deceased ancestors I see in my dreams are close family members or someone to which I was once connected. Through the work of the Holy Spirit, I have seen Dr. Martin Luther King, Jr., and Minister Malcolm X in my dreams. On occasions, both prophets have appeared to me in a fleshly image. They were either staring at me or pointing at me with instructional intentions. The Holy Spirit brings to my mind things that have happened to me in my past and things that have not yet happened but could happen in the future. In this vein of theological thought, the Spirit actively serves as strengthener, protector, reminder, and savior of my life in my conscious dreams (Acts 2:17).

As one who has driven hundreds of thousands of automobile miles on the road to and from places throughout the United States, I have physically felt the life-saving power of the Spirit. A large majority of my long-mileage trips have been for educational and ministry reasons. I recall three occasions where I was driving late at night, and I fell asleep at the wheel. In each of the three instances, the Spirit awakened me from my sleep just as I was approaching a disastrous ending. While it was unwise to be driving late at night without proper rest, I always felt comfortable traveling for what I considered to be Godly reasons. Like my dreams, the Spirit would always wake me up from my sleep-in time enough for me to correctly maneuver the wheel of car from driving over a nearby cliff or hill. These spiritually awakening moments were invigorating enough to help me drive the rest of the way with an energy to drive alertly and with greater awareness.

I was even more aware of what it would take for me to drive home safely after the Spirit of the Lord had seen fit to save my life once again. As a pastor in the Christian Methodist Episcopal Church tradition, we often drive a distance to the churches we have been appointed to. Our words for a driving or traveling preacher are commuting to Church as an itinerant preacher. One thing I have learned in the constant practice of commuting to and from churches and school via driving cars is that we need the Holy Spirit to lead, guide and protect us every step of the way. I am a living witness to what the Holy Spirit can do in the life of those who believe. As a Type-2 diabetic there were two times in my life where my blood sugar rose above 1800. Both times I was hospitalized in a diabetic coma. Both times the Holy Spirit gave me life and saved my life as the doctors were not sure if I was going to live or not.

Growing up in the Freeman Chapel Christian Methodist Episcopal Church in Hopkinsville, Kentucky, I experienced the Holy Spirit in a multitude of ways. I normally felt the power of the Holy Spirit in the worship experience. I felt the Holy Ghost as I sung in the youth choir, mass choir and fellowship choir. I felt the Holy Spirit as I was ushering, and I felt the Spirit in Sunday School. However, the times in which I felt the Holy Spirit the most was after the preached word during the invitation to Christian discipleship. For an unexplainable reason, the Spirit would always crunch down on me after the preacher and choir was standing together in solidarity by way inviting the parishioners to Jesus Christ. One song that touched deep inside my soul was "He Wants to Save You." This is a slow-paced song that is designed to spiritually tug at the heart of the unsaved and the backslidden. When we sang this song, I would always feel myself welling up on the inside. I would well up in such a way that I would lose my breath, and tears would flow from my eyes down my flushed cheeks. Even when I knew that the Spirit was coming my way as we sang this song, I still could not stop her. Normally, the Spirit would move me in such a way that I would have stopped singing altogether and sat down in my choir seat.

I had an extremely religious aunt by the name of Rosa White. She is deceased now. After church, Aunt Rosa would always wait for her teenage nephew so she could hug me and tell me that she wished that I would stop all that showing off. She would always tell me that it does not take all that crying and shit to sing songs for God during the morning worship experiences. I would try to explain to her that it does take all of that to sing and feel inspired by the power of the Holy Spirit. Obviously, she disagreed. I could not explain to my Aunt Rosa what I feel within and beyond when I feel the Holy Ghost in church. I did not have the language, nor did I have intergenerational testimony of what the Spirit had done for me over the course of multiple decades. All I had were those few sacred moments with God in the church building.

I did not know my paternal grandmother Carrie Ann White-Adams. Sadly, she passed away when I was 3 years old. Being that my Aunt Rosa was my late grandmother's close sister, she was the perfect replacement. In treating me like a grandson and helping to raise myself and my twin brother, Aunt Rosa existed as my grandmother in place of my deceased grandmother. This close ancestral replacement also represents the work of the Holy Spirit; that when one close relative is taken away from us in death God will provide us with another close relative to fill that spirito-cultural void. Here, the Holy Spirit is seen as a keeper, a replacer, and a restorer. To be sure, my experiences with the Holy Spirit are continuing, eventuating, personable, relational, and salvific (saving-grace). The words of Howard J. Rice ring true: The Holy Spirit is the source of the faith within us. No spiritual act that we can do can come from our natural powers; it must be from the inspiration of the Holy Spirit which resurrects our dead souls, opens our eyes, and enables us to have the strength to obey God. Without this divinely given inspiration we remain stubbornly closed to God.[737]

As one who has preached 1,400 plus sermons over the course of 20 years of pastoring, I have always felt the regenerative power of the Holy Spirit every single time I have stood in the pulpit of God. Again, the Holy Spirit has never failed to give me the strength and vision needed to minister effectively. Each time I opened my mouth to preach the Word of God, the Holy Spirit gave me the holistic

---

[737] Howard L. Rice, *Reformed Spirituality*, 50.

utterance to do so at a high spiritual level. James Forbes's stellar book, *The Holy Spirit and Preaching,* successfully shows how contemporary preaching can be enriched by a fresh appropriation of the power of the Holy Spirit.[738] Here, Forbes "strongly believes that an effective call to the Holy Spirit empowerment is a most valuable homiletical offering."[739] For Forbes, the anointing of the Holy Spirit is the central paradigm for a rich discussion on what it means to remain faithful to the biblical vision of God in our week to week preaching. Theologically, Forbes is "convinced that vast improvements in preaching can be expected if, in addition to traditional preparation for the preaching for the preaching ministry, more attention is given to the process by which preachers are endowed with the Holy Spirit for the work they are called to do."[740] Forbes is convicted by the fact that *the anointing makes the difference.*[741] Theologically, Forbes presents the anointing of the Holy Spirit in the life of Jesus as a practical model of spiritual formation for the ministry of preaching.[742]

Preaching faithfully under the transformative inspiration of the Holy Spirit is what builds up the Christian church. While it does not get mainstream theological airplay, faithful preaching in the Holy Spirit builds up neighborhoods, communities, and systems. This is because the Holy Spirit works in sacred institutions and secular environments. But preaching the Bible in the anointing of the Spirit takes place in the church building and in other places outside the church building. It can be argued that believers can have church in myriad places. Church does not always have to take place in a church building. The African slaves stole away from the presence of their masters and had church near the rivers, in the woods and amongst the animals of the forest. It was then that the oppressed slaves knew what it meant to know the essence of liberation---as the Spirit commissioned them and gave them utterance to do so.

In accordance with Christian history, World history and Black history, the greatest sermons and community-uniting messages have been preached in alternative venues. Subsequently, Forbes is correct

---

[738] James Forbes, *The Holy Spirit and Preaching*, 14.
[739] Ibid.
[740] Ibid, 15-16.
[741] Ibid., 16.
[742] Ibid.

in assessing the cultural art and spiritual practice of preaching the Bible as the liberating work of the Holy Spirit. Along the same theological lines, Henry Mitchell suggests that "The Black sermon is produced in a process which has already been clearly established as deeply involving the congregation. Black folk-theology of the people has always gone a step further and assumed that there was a third personal presence in the process, even the Holy Spirit. Black congregations have literally claimed the promise that "where two or three are gathered together in my name, there am I in the midst of them" (Matthew18:20)."[743]

With theological regard to the spiritual process of preaching, H. Beecher Hicks, Jr. instructs Black preachers to "be open to the action of the Holy Spirit; feel the movement of wind and fire in yourself even as it becomes manifest in those you serve."[744] To this way of thinking spiritually, Timothy Keller says that "the difference between good preaching and great preaching lies mainly in the work of the Holy Spirit in the heart of the listener as well as the preacher—and no one can—because that secret lies in the depths of God's wise plans and the power of God's Spirit. I'm talking about what many have referred to as "unction" or "anointing."[745] My collaborative translation is that great preaching in the power of the Holy Spirit is biblical preaching that attempts to liberate in a holistic sphere of awareness.

W.E.B. Du Bois and the Spiritual Darkness of Black Liberation

The spiritual darkness of Black liberation is not something to be ashamed of. But it is something Black people should celebrate as often as they can. That is, there is something theological to say about the intimate connection between the Spirit of God and the darker-skinned human being. Even though the word 'dark' carries a negative connotation in standard English vernacular (the Bible too), the pigmented dark skin of Black people is a Godly attribute that carries spiritual implications. Because Black people were created in the image of a beautiful God, then it can be affirmed that their Black darkness is beautiful as well. Due to the work of the Holy Spirit, Black people are children of God and contributing members of the body of Christ. My theology, which is a Black Christian liberation theology,

---

[743] Henry H. Mitchell, *Black Preaching*, 196-197.
[744] H. Beecher Hicks, Jr. *Preaching While Bleeding*, 93-94.
[745] Timothy Keller, *Preaching*, 11.

says that all three persons of the Holy Trinity are Black for the human, religious, and cultural experiences of Black people in the United States and the world abroad.

History teaches us that not all people have had good feelings and thoughts of Black people. If anyone knew what was going on with Black people in the early twentieth century, it was W.E.B. Du Bois. Riggins Earl is correct in his strategically placing the slaves' embodied soul experience with the Spirit of God between tasting the love of God and being slaughtered by hell's dark door. Earl's notion of hell's dark door takes my spirit back to Du Bois's *The Souls of Black Folk*. Pages 5 through 7 of *Souls* represent the greatest trinity of page-writing I have ever encountered in my theological reading life. In speaking of Black people's spiritual strivings in the late 1800s and early 1900s, Du Bois[746] narrates his reflections around the word dark. In identifying

---

[746] As one who believed in the holistic beauty of blackness, W. E. B. Du Bois was certain that the Spirit presided over the spiritual strivings of Black people. He also believed that the soul is a moving spirit. In the mind of Du Bois, spiritual strivings had a purpose: attaining freedom and liberty. Du Bois saw freedom and liberty as holistic endeavor of the oppressed race —one that included religion. For DuBois, emancipation was the goal of freedom. In his magnum opus, The Souls of Black Folk, Du Bois writes a series of theological statements: "Here at last seemed to have been discovered the mountain path to Canaan; longer than the highway of Emancipation and law, steep and rugged, but straight, leading to heights high enough to overlook life." "To the tired climbers, the horizon was ever dark, the mists were often cold, the Canaan was always dim and far away. If, however, the vistas disclosed as yet no goal, no resting–place, little but flattery and criticism, the journey at least gave leisure for reflection and self–examination; it changed the child of Emancipation to the youth with dawning self–consciousness, self–realization, self–respect. In those sombre forests of his striving his own soul rose before him, and he saw himself, —darkly as through a veil; and yet he saw in himself some faint revelation of his power, of his mission." "Nevertheless, out of the evil came something of good, —the more careful adjustment of education to real life, the clearer perception of the Negroes' social responsibilities, and the sobering realization of the meaning of progress." "So dawned the time of Sturm und Drang: storm and stress to–day rocks our little boat on the mad waters of the world–sea; there is within and without the sound of conflict, the burning of body and rending of soul; inspiration strives with doubt, and faith with vain questionings. The bright ideals of the past, —physical freedom, political power, the training of brains and the training of hands, —all these in turn have waxed and waned, until even the last grows dim and overcast." As one who was profoundly aware of how the Holy Spirit inspired what he termed "the frenzy" during the Black church experiences, Du Bois believed in the spiritual power of the slave spirituals. Du Bois was sure that in their spiritual strivings, Black people would one day be free and experience the same freedoms of their oppressors—"Freedom, too, the long–sought, we still seek, —the freedom of life and limb, the freedom to work and think, the freedom to love and aspire." The liberating work of the Holy Spirit was at strong play in the slave spirituals; it inspired the Black church worship "frenzy" of the Southern Negro revival, and it would help Black people attain their freedoms of being a

racism as the "vast social problem"[747] that has feasted on the darker-skinned folk, Du Bois confesses that "The Nation has not yet found peace from its sins; the freedman has not yet found in freedom his promised land. Whatever of good may have come in these years of change, the shadow of a deep disappointment rests upon the Negro people, --a disappointment all the more bitter because the unattained ideal was unbounded save by the simple ignorance of a lowly people."[748] Du Bois uses the word lowly to describe how Black people had already begun to experience the dark moments of their human existence. Afterward, Du Bois gives a list of people, places and things that continued to move Black people's souls backward into spiritual darkness. He mentions such structural evils as "a tantalizing will-o'-the-wisp, maddening and misleading the headless host. The holocaust of war, the terrors of the Ku-Klux-Klan, the lies of carpetbaggers, the disorganization of industry, and the contradictory advice of friends and foes, left the bewildered serf with no new watchword beyond the old cry for freedom."[749] These descriptive words were not mere forethoughts. They were the raw thoughts of a disgruntled scholar who knew what was going on.

Du Bois moves us closer into those dark moments of early twentieth century blackness when he says that, "Slowly but steadily, in the following years, a new vision began gradually to replace the dream of political power,--a powerful movement, the rise of another ideal to guide the unguided, another pillar of fire by night after a clouded day."[750] Then Du Bois showed the world, in eloquent prose, what is really going on in the United States of America. The descriptive word *dark* is birthed in the ever-glowing blades of human oppression. Says Du Bois:

> Up the new path the advance guard toiled, slowly, heavily, doggedly; only those who have watched and guided the faltering feet, the misty minds, the dull understandings, of

---

full-fledge human being. In Yolonda Pierce's interpretation of Du Bois's Souls of Black Folk, she defines soul as a "moving spirit." For Du Bois, spirit implies race and human autonomy. He fully embraced the spirit of agitation as protest as the means to progress within the Black race.

[747] W.E.B. Du Bois, *The Souls of Black Folk,* 5.
[748] Ibid.
[749] Ibid.
[750] Ibid.

dark pupils of these schools know how faithfully, how piteously, this people strove to learn. It was weary work. The cold statistician wrote down how the inches of progress here and there, noted also where here and there a foot had slipped, and someone had fallen. To the tired climbers, the horizon was ever dark, the mists were often cold, the Canaan was always dim and far away. If, however, the vistas disclosed as yet no goal, no resting-place, little but flattery and criticism, the journey at least gave leisure for reflection and self-examination; it changed the child of Emancipation to the youth with dawning self-consciousness, self-realization, self-respect. In those somber forests of his striving his own soul rose before him, and saw himself, --darkly as through a veil; and yet he saw in himself some faint revelation of his power, of his mission.[751]

By way of describing the inner and outer feeling what it meant to be the darker-skinned human being in the white-dominated land, Du Bois identifies two prominent problems wrapped in one significant package. "For the first time," says Du Bois, "he sought to analyze the burden he bore upon his back, the dead weight of social degradation partially masked behind a half-named Negro problem."[752] To accurately interpret Du Bois, the historian and sociologist, juxtaposes that the Black theologian understand how the idolatry of white racism creates material and structural poverty for a sizable amount of Black people. To be sure about what Du Bois is getting at in terms of him describing what was going on, one must be clear about the obvious fact that racism and poverty, as the half-named problems, represented the one whole existential nightmare of their human existence in the United States. If it were not for the systematic evils of racial discrimination and structural poverty, the souls of Black folk in the early twentieth century would have had a better chance of living on past their slave ancestors and contemporary brothers and sisters. Where white racism is present in Black neighborhoods and communities, there is also the economic poverty of Black folk.

Du Bois teaches us that

---

[751] Ibid.
[752] Ibid.

A people thus handicapped ought not be asked to race with the world, but rather allowed to give all its time and thought to its own social problems. But alas while sociologists gleefully count his bastards and his prostitutes, the very soul of the toiling, swearing black man is darkened by the shadow of a vast despair. Men call the shadow prejudice, and learnedly explain it as the natural defense of culture against barbarism, learning against ignorance, purity against crime, the "higher" against the "lower" races. To which the Negro cries Amen! and swears that to so much of this strange prejudice as is founded on just homage to civilization, culture, righteousness, and progress, he humbly bows and meekly does obeisance.[753]

Social, political, economic, and educational allowances have never been bestowed upon Black Americans. Nor has the very race of the original perpetrators honestly and systematically unpacked those oppressions. Prejudice not only implies racism and racial injustice, but it also condones violence being done to what racists consider the inferior group of people. Certainly, Black folk have acquiesced, in some degree, to the blatant harm that continues to threaten Black folks' ability to pay their monthly bills on time and live a halfway decent quality of life.

I am in solidarity with Du Bois when he iterates that Black Americans "must defend their own civilization, their own culture, their own righteousness, and their own progress. Even if they do not own much of anything wealth-wise, land-wise, or business-wise; or they have not acquired their forty acres and a mule, Black folk should never consider themselves as inferior to the majority race. Black folk should always conduct themselves as a people who will always have a living soul."[754] Du Bois poetizes the Black experience: "So dawned the time of Sturm and Drang: storm and stress to-day rocks our little boat on the mad waters of the world sea; there is within and without the sound of conflict, the burning of body and rending of soul; inspiration strives with doubt, and faith with vain questionings."[755] Despite the continued oppressions as founded in their material shortcomings, Black people have always been a people of the Holy Spirit. The Holy

---

[753] Ibid., 6.
[754] Ibid.
[755] Ibid.

Spirit is the one who prompts the spiritual strivings of Black Americans.

> Work, culture, liberty,--all these we need, not singly but together, not successively but together, each growing and aiding each, and all striving toward that vaster ideal that swims before the Negro people, the ideal of human brotherhood, gained through the unifying ideal of Race; the ideal of fostering and developing the traits and talents of the Negro, not in opposition to or contempt for other races, but rather in large conformity to the greater ideals of the American republic, in order that someday on American soil two world-races may give each to each those characteristics both so sadly lack. We the darker ones come even now not altogether empty-handed: there are to-day no truer exponents of the pure human spirit of the Declaration of Independence than the American Negroes; there is no true American music but the wild sweet melodies of the Negro slave; the American fairy tales and folklore are Indian and African; and, all in all, we black men seem the sole oasis of simple faith and reverence in a dusty desert of dollars and smartness.[756]

Black people's contribution to American culture was founded in the development of their own culture. While they did not receive ample monetary contributions for their laboring work, their spirits were fed as their eyes remained on the prize of human freedom. Their spiritual strivings led them into their material and spiritual hope for liberation.

The Meaning of Liberation and Life in the Spirit

Jesus means freedom and the Holy Spirit means liberation. Put another way, the ministry and work of Jesus Christ on the Cross is what gives Black people their freedom. The Holy Spirit, on the other hand, is the liberator of Black believers and all other groups, races, and cultures of oppressed people. Of course, freedom and liberation go hand in hand when discussing the oppressive plight of Black and brown-skinned people in the United States, Africa, and the world abroad. That is because the concept of freedom is engrained into the theoretical notions of liberation. And the concept of liberation is engrained into the theoretical notions of freedom. One cannot

---

[756] Ibid., 7.

experience liberation without believing in their hearts that they are free to do so. Even as freedom and liberation are the collaborative works of Jesus Christ and the Holy Spirit (Jesus Christ frees and liberates; the Holy Spirit emancipates and liberates), my argument is that freedom is the primary work of Jesus Christ and liberation is the primary work of the Holy Spirit.

James H. Cone believes that Jesus Christ alone is the ground of human liberation. Citing Luke 4:18-19, Cone interprets the text as saying that Jesus Christ is the one who sets the captives free. For me, setting the captives free is more so the work of freedom. Even as the Bible says that who the Son sets free is truly free indeed (John 8:36), this biblical freeing does not come across as the work of liberation. As much as I love and admire the father of Liberation theology, I respectfully disagree with Cone. I say that because freedom and liberation are not the same experiences and realities. I define freedom as the quality or state of being free to make decisions regarding one's human situation.

Freedom is also defined as liberation from slavery or restraint; being liberated from the power of another; independence. Liberation is the act of setting someone free from imprisonment, slavery, or oppression. When I think of Black liberation theology, I tend to focus on the liberating acts of the Holy Spirit in the life of the oppressed. Both biblical and nonbiblical. In this vein of thought, I define liberation as *ultimate freedom* and *total emancipation*. Here, the holistic liberation of the Holy Spirit is different in scope from the freedom that is given through Jesus Christ. While Jesus Christ gives believers a supreme quality or state of being free, the Holy Spirit acts and performs liberating acts that is transformative and powerful enough to set people free from oppression. Mentally, physically, and spiritually.

Within the human experiences of freedom and liberation, the resulting quality or state of being free is on a lower level than the liberating act itself. Let me explain. Theologically, it is possible to be free and not liberated. It is possible to have that quality or state of being free and never experience the act of holistic liberation. This is because the liberating acts of God's Spirit supersedes the Christian quality or state of being free. In his timeless classic, *God of the Oppressed*, Cone asks the tough questions surrounding the quiet presence of the Holy Spirit amid the history of evil that has done enormous amounts of harm to God's people. And rightfully so. I ask the same questions about how the presence of a resurrected Christ, who sits at the right hand of God, has also allowed millions of innocent people across the world to suffer and experience things so hideous that they defy description. Appropriately, William Jones's question of 'Is God a white racist?'[757] is still on the conversational agenda of Black liberation theology.

Major J. Jones explains that

> Black people did more than fix on Jesus as their Savior beyond this world. As discussed above, Jesus Christ was understood in the Black community to the Liberator—spiritual, political, and, if necessary, revolutionary. But it was in the tension between faith in Jesus as the Liberator here and faith in Jesus as the Liberator here that the Holy Spirit did powerful work among Black people. Even though he had been crucified, Jesus had never totally subjected to the powers of this world; now, in power of the Holy Spirit, neither need the Black slave be. Jesus Christ was King of kings and Lord of lords; and it was God through Jesus Christ who would eventually set things right for Black people. In the meantime, Blacks kept in personal touch with God through the Holy Ghost and at a distance from the White-folks' world, in which the Black person knew better that Jesus Christ was more powerful than any contrary force at work to negate the slave's personhood. When society and slavery, struggle and poverty all said it wasn't so, the Black person listened instead to the Holy Spirit, who told the truth that comes from God: Black people are people, and they are a people of God.[758]

Could it be that Jesus Christ is identified as the great liberator, and the Holy Spirit is the one who embodies the love of God and liberates the oppressed? While it can be argued that the Black cultural human experience is more pneumatological than Christological, what can be said about the Black religious experiences regarding the liberating work of the Spirit in the life of the believer? Major J. Jones suggests

---

[757] William R. Jones, *Is God A White Racist?: A Preamble to Black Theology* (Boston, MA: Beacon Press, 1997).
[758] Major J. Jones, *The Color of God*, 107.

that "Black theologians need to take seriously the traditional importance of the Holy Spirit for the Black church. Because the Holy Spirit has been at the heart of the Black religious experience since slavery days, to do Black Theology without the Holy Spirit is to do theology without the prayer or the worship-life or the heart of Black people."[759] What does liberation really look like if the Holy Spirit is the only one who knows what is going on in the world?

James H. Cone scholar Anthony G. Reddie describes what liberation looks like in these keynote thoughts: Just as the Incarnation – Jesus's historical presence in the world – shows that being flesh, being human and living in a particular time and space (a context) is important, so too does Pentecost. Pentecost shows that the Holy Spirit does not eradicate our differences; rather, the Spirit celebrates them.[760] Reddie explains:

> But life in Spirit (i.e. living as Christians) is about being one in Christ, in fellowship with each other. Being in community with each other and with Christ can take us beyond what it means to be linked to a particular identity – in this case, being Black. The status that is often linked to particular identities (being male, or being a Jew, for example) is exploded. The Spirit does transcend all this (Galatians 3:28). There is, therefore, a tension between these two differing ways of seeing identity. One, that in Christ, the differences around ethnicity or gender are overcome and made irrelevant; but also, the counter view, that in Christ we come to celebrate those very things as essential parts of who we are. Black theology seeks to look at how we live together as people across our differences of ethnicity and cultures, class and economic disparities.[761]

In lieu of Reddie's theological proclamations, I am now remembering my PhD advisor Stephen Ray telling me that the Holy Spirit inspires believers to live a life that is pleasing to God. Living together as people across our differences of ethnicity and cultures, class and economic disparities also includes living out a radical self-love. All these lived realities represent the theological models of the economy of God's

---

[759] Ibid., 117.
[760] Anthony G. Reddie, "Black theology: an introduction," Para. 11.
[761] Ibid., Para. 10.

love as revealed in the liberating work of the Holy Spirit. In this vein of theological thought, I posit that love is profoundly liberating in that love is a form of human and spiritual emancipation.

Along similar lines, Black feminist Sonya Renee Taylor believes that liberation is radical self-love. She reflects on an experience with other Black feminist change makers: "Sipping caipirinhas and cackling into the blue-black sky, my favorite rabble-rouser of the group, longtime activist, and artist Kai (pronounced Kai-ee), in her half teasing, wholly provocative way, queried the group, "We doing all this fighting for liberation. Any of y'all know what liberation looks like?"[762] Christian theologians believe that liberation is messy, slow, and blurry at best. There is only a handful of theologians who believe that the Jesus Christ is liberator. Even less believe that the Holy Spirit is liberator. Taylor is certain that "Liberation is the opportunity for every human, no matter their body, to have unobstructed access to their highest self; for every human to live in radical self-love."[763] As a Black theologian of poverty, pneumatology, culture, and the Black religious experiences, I am certain that the liberating work of the Holy Spirit empowers people of all groups, races, and cultures to live their best life in their own bodies and in radical self-love.

The Holy Spirit is the Holy Liberator of the oppressed. To a degree, the lack of self-esteem and self-love in one's life is the internalization of human oppression. Theologically and contextually, I am certain that the inspiration of the Holy Spirit was hovering over a concerned group of 51 Black church ministers when they met on July 31, 1966 and purchased a full page ad in The New York Times to publish their "Black Power Statement", which proposed a more aggressive approach to combating racism using the Bible for inspiration.[764] Not only were the group of ministers moved by the Spirit in their search for racial justice and human equality, but they had also been anointed by God to act on the vision of liberation that was planted in their human spirits. Concomitantly, the Holy Spirit is also the liberator of Black theology. Without the liberating work of

---

[762] Sonya R. Taylor, The Body Is Not an Apology, 115.

[763] Ibid., 116.

[764] Barbara B. Hagerty (March 18, 2008). "A Closer Look at Black Liberation Theology". NPR. Archived from the original on July 26, 2018. In my research, I found that this article was retrieved on March 12, 2019.

the Holy Spirit in the life of all groups, races, and cultures of people, there is no Black liberation theology in the United States and the world abroad. The Holy Spirit is a worldwide Spirit that inspires liberating campaigns and movements all over the globe. The current reality of the Holy Spirit in the present struggle to liberate life is the properly biblical focus of Black Theology.[765]

The Holy Spirit is the Spirit of Liberation and Emancipation

Historically speaking, Black people have never had economic and financial resources in abundance. But what they have had in their religious, cultural, and existential experiences is an abundance of God, Jesus Christ, and the Holy Spirit. There is no Black spirituality, spiritual liberation, spiritual striving, spiritual life, spiritual growth, spiritual worship, spiritual substance without the life-giving work of the Holy Spirit. The Holy Spirit is who makes believers spiritual. Not our religious deeds. But the person, power, and work of the Holy Spirit in theology Black is what liberates the oppressed from the bondage of sin, evil and death. Subsequently, love is the biblical interlocutor between the growing conversation of theology and economics. The goal of interlocking theology and economics within the Spirit of love is emancipation. The idea that the Holy Spirit brings about a liberating freedom that inspires believers to love, *be loved*, and cared for is a theological one that presupposes the unity and diversity of the Holy Spirit's dispersing of gifts for the upbuilding of God's Kingdom (Matt 6:33).

The Black church, the Black community, the Black poor, and the world abroad can also declare the Holy Spirit is the Spirit of emancipation. What this means is that the Holy Spirit emancipates or frees people from the bondage of their personal and spiritual circumstances. "Now the Lord is the Spirit, and where the Spirit of the Lord is, there is freedom. 2 Corinthians 3:17" This physical reality in creation is also a spiritual reality inside every follower of Christ. Jesus is the light of the world. When we surrender our lives to Him in faith, He invades the sin-darkness (which is the opposite of a theological blackness) of our soul with His light through the Holy Spirit who now lives in us. His light brings change, healing, and freedom. Galatians 5:1 says, "It is for freedom that Christ has set us

---

[765] Major J. Jones, *The Color of God*, 115.

free. Stand firm, then, and do not let yourselves be burdened again by a yoke of slavery." To be emancipated, liberated, and set free carry the same meaning in that something good from God in Jesus Christ by the power of the Holy Spirit is taking place in the life of the believer. By faith in God's infinite wisdom, knowledge, and power, one can believe that there is a spiritual connection between President Abraham Lincoln freeing the slaves through the Emancipation Proclamation and the liberating work of the Holy Spirit. Galatians 5:1 says, "It is for freedom that Christ has set us free. Stand firm, then, and do not let yourselves be burdened again by a yoke of slavery. There is perhaps nothing sadder than a free person continuing to live as a slave.[766]

> Historian and genealogist Antoinette Harrell has uncovered cases of African Americans still living as slaves 100 years after the issuance of the Emancipation Proclamation by Abraham Lincoln on January 1, 1863. Throughout her 20 years of research, she has unearthed some rare, painful stories in the deep south of black people who had no idea they were free all the way up to the 1960s. They were forced to work, violently tortured, and raped. While the intent of the Emancipation Proclamation was to end slavery for every African American, the reality is that it did not. It provided the means for freedom, but unless it was applied to each individual slave's life, it was of no use on a personal level.[767]

The truth of the Bible is that all Christians have the Holy Spirit within them, and the consequence of that reality is that we are spiritually alive, free from the power of sin, and recipients of divine resurrection power, both now in a spiritual sense (Rom 8:10) and later when we transcend and overcome physical death. As the Apostle Paul said in Romans 8:11, "If the Spirit of him who raised Jesus from the dead dwells in you, he who raised Christ Jesus from the dead will also give life to your mortal bodies through his Holy Spirit who dwells in you." Paul's words provide serious implications for how people are to live today based on the truth that Christians will overcome death because of the presence of the Holy Spirit within them. Because of the divine power of the Holy Spirit – a power that can raise human beings out

---

[766] "Emancipated," Para. 3.
[767] Ibid., Para. 4.

of the grave. The Holy Spirit empowers believers to live a new spiritual life—one that both provides the means for freedom in everyone's life. African American slaves understood that the power of the Holy Spirit meant freedom and liberation from sin; despite their belief that death, forced labor, torture and rape was not the end of their story.

I recently watched the movie *Emancipation* (2022) starring Will Smith where he portrayed a runaway slave with great talents and spiritual gifts. *Emancipation* is one of the greatest slave movies I have ever seen. Black movies about slavery are not only cultural texts created by the Holy Spirit, but they also represent Black theology in the form of cinematic production. The most powerful parts of *Emancipation* took place in how the runaway slave related to God through the directing work of the Holy Spirit. In telling his estranged family and anyone else who would listen that God was with them, the genius slave Peter escaped from the treacherous plantation and ran all the way to the freedom land of Baton Rouge, Louisiana. From the all-important perspectives of human survival and hearing from God, Peter was able to escape death in a multitude of ways. When I say that he escaped death on numerous occasions, I am implying that Peter was consistently delivered from the jaws of death by the person, power, and work of the Holy Spirit. Peter was a man of great faith and deep spirituality. The Holy Spirit gave life to Peter throughout his time as a slave and a soldier. The Spirit led him back to his family just as Peter said the Spirit would.

The Holy Spirit not only gave Peter the strength to endure, but he or she also communicated with him and showed him directional signs of where he was to go in escaping death at the hands of the white slave master. The most profound symbolism of the Holy Spirit in the movie was the physical presence of white doves. It seemed like the doves always flew in the direction of Peter, the child of God. On the other hand, the doves flew in the opposite direction of the white slave master and his two handlers. One in which was Black. My interpretation of the Holy Spirit working in the life of Peter is that the Spirit gave him the power to kill a large crocodile, hold his breath underwater for an extended period, heal his wounded body of bullets, sharp teeth, deep scrapes, survive the dangerous elements of the Louisiana swamp, and obediently follow the directions of the Holy

Spirit from the very moment he made the courageous decision to escape from the slave plantation.

Because of how the Holy Spirit worked in Peter's spirit, in his physical body and mind, and in the cultural atmosphere, he was sure that God was always with him. Even when Peter's life was on the line. The Holy Spirit was also working inside Peter as he was fighting in the Civil War as a recruited member of the Union Army. The Spirit led Peter to strategically play dead, help those wounded in battle and move methodically from one place of battle to another (1 Sam 17:47). I refer to these productive actions as forms of Black spirituality. Black spirituality is the spiritual medium between the Holy Spirit and human (spirit) beings that feeds the cultural identity of Black theology in the United States and the world abroad. What this means is that

> Black Theology must proceed to develop its teaching on the Spirit if it is to maintain its voice of moral authority. Our God is a God who gives persons the power to be and to become. The Holy Spirit of God and Christ is the legitimator of Black being at all levels and in all times. Just to be has never been a simple matter for Black people At times, it has taken more than merely human courage; at times, it has taken sheer tenacity inspired by the Holy Spirit, God's own personal indwelling agent. It was God, and God alone who upheld us; and God is the eternal Creator and Judge, in who's Holy Being rests the total reality of all that is. God's being is the moral law and the ultimate truth on which all human truths, laws, and morality are grounded. But God's greatest expression of love may become known. The Black Messiah was God's greatest expression of love to his oppressed human children. Now, returned to us and fused with Jesus Christ in the Holy Spirit, God binds us to himself and to our fellow human beings with cords of love and mutual respect, opening human eyes to the complete evidence of God as creator and judge, lover and liberator.[768]

As a form of Black cultural spirituality, Black theology stands firmly on the regenerative ground of the Liberator Spirit's love. Black is a symbol of God's presence in history on behalf of oppressed

---

[768] Major J. Jones, *The Color of God*, 117.

groups, races, and cultures of human beings. Where there is Black, there is oppression. But that is not the end of story for oppressed groups, races, and cultures of people. Oppression does not represent the end of Black people's fate. I believe that where there is Black, blackness or darkness, there is the liberating work of the Holy Spirit. Where the Spirit of the LORD is, there is liberty (2 Cor 3:17). In theology Black fashion by way of leaning and depending on the power of the Holy Spirit to liberate all groups, races, and cultures of people, I conclude this pneumatology book by quoting Du Bois again: "In song and exhortation swelled one refrain—Liberty; in his tears and curses to God he implored had Freedom in his right hand. At last, it came, --suddenly, fearfully, like a dream. With one wild carnival of blood and passion came the message of his own plaintive cadences: --"Shout, O children! Shout, you're free! For God has bought your liberty!"[769] Jesus paid it all. All to Him I owe. Sin has left a crimson stain. He washed me white as snow. The work of the Holy Spirit is our ultimate freedom. Our ultimate love. And the Spirit of God is our liberating all and all.

> *Sweet Holy Spirit, Sweet heavenly Black Dove,*
> *"Stay right here with us, filling us with Your love.*
> *And for these blessings we lift our hearts in praise;*
> *Without a doubt we'll know that we have been revived,*
> *When we shall leave this place."*[770]

---

[769] W.E.B. Du Bois, *The Souls of Black Folk*, 4.
[770] *Divine Hymns*, Para. 2

Darvin Anton Adams

Bibliography

Adams, Darvin A. *'Cause De Spirit Spoke to Me: Robertsian Conversations on Black Liberation Theology Amidst Economic Deprivation.* PhD Dissertation, Evanston: Garrett-Evangelical Theological Seminary/Northwestern University, April 2018.
_____ *Inner-City Blues: Black Theology and Black Poverty in the United States.* Eugene, OR: Cascade Books, 2023.
Akinwale, Fumoni. "23 Powerful Biblical Scriptures" https://whenyouneedgod.com/23-powerful-biblical-scriptures-on-healing-and-restoration/
Allen, Lisa. *A Womanist Theology of Worship: Liturgy, Justice and Communal Righteousness.* New York, NY: Orbis Books, 2022.
Allert, Tilman. *The Hitler Salute: On the Meaning of a Gesture.* New York, NY: Metropolitan Books, 2008.
Alves, Rubem A. *A theology of human hope.* New York, NY: Corpus Books, 1971.
Angell, Collin. "Paul Ricoeur and Biblical Hermeneutics: Narrative, Genre and Self" *Academia* https://www.academia.edu/79255119/Paul_Ricoeur_Biblical_Hermeneutics_Narrative_Genre_and_Self
Augustine, Saint. *On Christian Doctrine.* Mineola, NY: Dover Publications, 2009.
_____. *The Confessions.* Peabody, Massachusetts: Hendrickson Publishers, 2004.
_____. *The Confessions of Saint Augustine.* Oxford, EN: World's Classics, 2009.
_____. John E. Rotelle, ed. *The Trinity.* Hyde Park, NY: New City Press, 1991.
_____. *The Trinity: De Trinitate,* Second Edition. New York, NY: New York City Press, 2012.
"Moral Selves: Politics as a Crisis of Meaning" *Dr. Christopher Ryan Mabolic: Life, Works & Writings* January 3, 2008. https://ryanmaboloc.blogspot.com/2008/01/paul-ricoeur-on-ethics.html
Baker, Garth. "8 – Black theology and the Holy Spirit from Part II - Themes in black theology" Published online by Cambridge University Press: September 28, 2012. https://www.cambridge.org/core/books/abs/cambridge-companion-to-black-theology/black-theology-and...
Baker-Fletcher, Karen. *Dancing with God: The Trinity from a Womanist Perspective.* Nashville, TN: Chalice Press, 2007.
Barrois, Georges. ed. *The Fathers Speak: St Basil the Great, St Gregory of Nazianzus and St Gregory of Nyssa.* Crestwood, NY: St. Vladimir's Seminary Press, 1986.
Barth, Karl. *The Theology of John Calvin.* Grand Rapids, MI: Wm. B. Eerdmans Publishing Co., 1995.
Bartholomew, Isabel. "Themes" *enotes* https://www.enotes.com/topics/black-theology-black-power/themes
Basil the Great, Saint. trans. David Anderson. *On the Holy Spirit.* Crestwood, NY: St. Vladimir's Seminary Press, 1997.
Basil the Great, Saint. Verna E. F. Harrison, et al. *On the Human Condition.* Crestwood, NY: St. Vladimir's Seminary Press, 2005.
Battle, Michael. *The Quest for Liberation and Reconciliation: Essays in Honor of J. Deotis Roberts.* Louisville, KY: Westminster John Knox Press, 2005.
Bedford, Nancy E. Constructive Pneumatology for the Contemporary Context: PhD course. Garrett-Evangelical Theological Seminary. Evanston, Illinois. Spring 2010.
Beckford, Robert. *Dread and Pentecost: A Political Theology for the Black Church in Britain.* Eugene, OR: Wipf and Stock, 2011.
Bell, Derrick. *Faces at the Bottom of the Well: The Permanence of Racism.* New York, NY: Basic Books, 1993.
Biblesprout. https://www.biblesprout.com
"Black Theology Offers Hope," *Christian Reformed Church.* February 1, 2023. https://www.crcna.org/news/black-theology-offers-hope
Boff, Leonardo. *Holy Trinity, Perfect Community.* Maryknoll, NY: Orbis Books, 2000.
Bowie, Walter R. Jesus and the Trinity. Whitefish, MT: Literary Licensing, LLC, 2012
Bradley, Anthony B. "The Marxist roots of black liberation theology" *Acton Institute* April 02, 2008. https://www.acton.org/pub/commentary/2008/04/02/marxist-roots-black-liberation-

theology

Brogdon, Lewis O. *Interpreting Problematic Texts in the Bible* (Lanham, MD: William Seymore Press, 2018.

_____ "Is America in danger of losing its soul? The conversation everyone needs to have in 2021" *Courier Journal* June 3, 2021. https://www.courierjournal.com/story/opinion/2021/06/03/is-soul-of-america-in-danger-conversation-us-sho...

_____ *The Bible in the Ashes of Social Chaos: An Introduction to Problematic Texts.* Eugene, OR: Cascade Books, 2023.

Brussat, Frederic and Mary Ann Brussat. *Spiritual Literacy: Reading the Sacred in Everyday Life.* New York, NY: Scribner, 1996.

Buhler, Pierre. "Ricoeur's concept of distanciation as a challenge for theological hermeneutics" *Academia.* 2011. https//:www.academia.edu/86466609/Ricoeurs_concept_of_distanciation_as_a_challenge_for_Theological_hermene...

Buhring, Kurt. *Spirits on the Inside: Spirit(s) in Black Religion.* London, EN: Palgrave McMillan, 2022.

_____. "The Spirit in Modern Black Theology and Religion" Springer Link September 11, 2022. https://link.springer.com/chapter/10.1007/978-3-031-09887-1_6

Buckner, Jerry L. "Is Orthodoxy Strong in the Black Church?" *Contending for the Faith* June 10, 2009. https://contendingfaith.org/is-Christian-orthodoxy-strong-in-the-black-church/

Burdick, John. "What is the Color of the Holy Spirit?: Pentecostalism and Black Identity in Brazil" *Syracuse University,* 1999. https://experts.syr.edu/en/publications/what-is-the-color-of-the-holy-spirit-pentecostalism-and-black-ide/

Calvin, John. *Institutes of the Christian Life,* translated from the 1559 Latin ed. Ford Lewis Battles, 2 volumes in Library of Christian Classics, Book Three. The Way in Which We Receive the Grace of Christ (Philadelphia, PA: The Westminster Press, 1960), 3.2.33 (1:580). www.foundationrt.org/outlines/Calvin_Institutes_III.pdf

Canon, Katie G. and Anthony B. Pinn, eds. *The Oxford Handbook of African American Theology.* New York, NY: Oxford University Press, 2018.

Chung, Paul S. *The Spirit of God Transforming Life: Reformation and Theology of the Holy Spirit.* London, EN: Palgrave McMillan, 2009.

Coates, Ta-Nehisi. "The Case for Reparations" *The Atlantic* June 2014. https://www.theatlantic.com/magazine/archive/2014/06/the-case-for-reparations/361631/

Coleman, Monica A. ed. *Making A Way Out of No Way: A Womanist Theology.* Minneapolis, MN: Fortress Press, 2008.

Coleman, Will. *Tribal Talk: Black Theology, Hermeneutics, and African/American Ways of "Telling the Story."* University Park, PA: Pennsylvania State University Press, 1999.

Comblin, Jose. *The Holy Spirit and Liberation.* Eugene, OR: Wipf and Stock, 2004. "Compelling truth the truth about the bible: What is biblical illumination?"

Cone, James H. *A Black Theology of Liberation.* Maryknoll, NY: Orbis Books, 2010.

_____ *Black Theology and Black Power.* Maryknoll, NY: Orbis Books, 1997.

_____ *God of the Oppressed.* Maryknoll, NY: Orbis Books, 2015.

_____ *The Spirituals and the Blues.* Maryknoll, NY: Orbis Books, 1992.

_____ "Black Theology and Black Power" *enotes* https://www.enotes.com/topics/black-theology-black-power/themes

Copeland, M. Shawn. *Enfleshing Freedom: Body, Race, and Being.* Minneapolis, MN: Fortress Press, 2009.

Copeland. Warren R. *Doing Justice In Our Cities: Lessons in Public Policy From America's Heartland.* Louisville, KY: Westminster John Knox Press, 2009.

Crawford, A. Elaine Brown. *Hope in the Holler: A Womanist Theology.* Louisville, KY: Westminster John Knox Press, 2002.

Dees, Jared. "THE 7 GIFTS OF THE HOLY SPIRIT LESSON PLAN & WORKSHEet" *The Religion Teacher* April 19, 2012. https:www.thereligionteacher.com/gifts-of-the-holy-spirit-lesson-plan/

Departments of Christian Education of the AME Church, AME Zion Church, and the CME Church. *Advent: Prophecy and Expectation.*

De Pres, Terrence. *The Survivor.* New York, NY: Pocket Books, 1977.

Dees, Jared. "THE 7 GIFTS OF THE HOLY SPIRIT LESSON PLAN &

WORKSHEet" *The Religion Teacher.* April19, 2012. https://www.thereligionteacher.com/gifts-of-the-holy-spirit-lesson-plan/

Dion, Celine. "Where Is The Love" *Let's Talk About Love.* Song #7, 1997.

Dittmar, Steve. "The Holy Spirit and Forgiveness" *Jubilee* February 11, 2020. https://www.jubileechurch.org/secret-place/the-holy-spirit-and-forgiveness/

Divine Hymns. https://divinehymns.com/lyrics/theres-a-sweet-spirit-song-lyrics/

Douglass, Jane Dempsey. "The Lively Work of the Spirit in the Reformation" Volume 23, Number 2 Spring 2003, pg. 121. https://wordandworld.luthersem.edu/content/pdfs/23-2_Holy_Spirit/23-2_Douglass.pdf

Dowley, Tim. ed. *Introduction to the History of Christianity: Third Edition.* Minneapolis: Fortress Press, 2018.

Du Bois, W.E.B. *The Souls of Black Folk.* Columbia, SC: 2017. 80689396R00067

Duggan-Kirk, Cheryl A. *Violence and Theology.* Nashville, TN: Abingdon Press, 2006.

Duson, Monique. "4 Reasons Why Black Liberation Theology is Another Gospel" *The Center for Biblical Unity.* January 11, 2022. https://www.centerforbiblicalunity.com/post/4-reasons-why-black-liberation-theology-is-another-gospel

Dyson, Michael E. *Between God and Gangsta Rap: Bearing Witness to Black.* Walton Street, OX: Oxford University Press, 1997.

Earl, Riggins. *Dark Symbols, Obscure Signs: God, Self, and Community in the Slave Mind.* Knoxville, TN: University of Tennessee Press, 2003.

Edelman, Marian W. *Guide My Feet: Prayers and Meditations on Loving and Working for Children.* Boston, MA: Beacon Press, 1995.

"Emancipated" *Touching Lives with James Merritt.* August 24, 2022. https://www.touchinglives.org/devotionals/emancipated

Evans, Curtis J. *The Burden of Black Religion.* New York, NY: Oxford University Press, 2008.

Evans Jr., James H. *Black Theology: A Critical Assessment and Annotated Bibliography.* Westport, CT: Greenwood Publishers, 1987.

_____ *We Have Been Believers: An African-American Systematic Theology.* Minneapolis, MN: Augsburg Fortress Press, 1993.

Forbes, James A. *The Holy Spirit and Preaching.* Nashville, TN: Abingdon Press, 1989.

"foundations for holistic ministry lesson two – icreation," https//socialwork.web.baylor.edu/sites/g/files/ecbvkj326/files/2022-o2/Foundations_lesson_2.pdf

Frazier, E. Franklin. *The Negro in The United States: Revised Edition.* New York, NY: The Macmillan Company, 1957.

Fuqua, Antoine. *Emancipation.* Apple TV+, 2022.

Gabriel, Andrew K. "The Holy Spirit and Eschatology-with Implications for Ministry and the Doctrine of Spirit Baptism" *BRILL* September 10, 2016. https://brill.com/view/journals/pent/25/2/article-p203_4.xml

Gaffin Jr., Richard. *The Centrality of the Resurrection: A study in Paul's Soteriology.* Grand Rapids, MI: Baker Books, 1978.

_____ "The Holy Spirit and Eschatology" *GraceOnlineLibrary* https://graceonlinelibrary.org/eschatology/the-holy-spirit-and-eschatology-by-richard-b-gaffin-jr/

Gates Jr., Henry L. and William L. Andrews. *Pioneers Of The Black Atlantic: Five Slave Narratives from the Enlightenment,* 1772-1815. Washington, D.C.: Civitas Counterpoint, 1998.

Gaye, Marvin. *What's Going On?* Motown Records Tamla. Song #1, 1971.

George, Timothy. *Theology of the Reformers.* Nashville, TN: B&H Publishing Group, 2014.

Goatley, David E. *Were You There?: Godforsakenness in Slave Religion.* Eugene, OR: Wipf and Stock Publishers, 2021.

Grentz, Stanley J. *Reason for Hope: The Systematic Theology of Wolfhart Pannenberg.* New York, NY: Oxford University Press, 1989.

Gresham, Jr., John R. "To Be Black And Orthodox: Part of My Story" *Orthodox Christian Laity* February 4, 2016. https://ocl.org/to-be-black-and-orthodox-part-of-my-story/

Guthrie, Shirley C. *Christian Doctrine: Revised Edition.* Louisville, KY: Westminster John Knox Press, 1994.

Gutierrez, Gustavo. *A Theology of Liberation: History, Politics, and Salvation.* New York, NY: Orbis Books, 1973.

Hagerty, Barbara B. "A Closer Look at Black Liberation " *npr* March 18, 2008. https://www.npr.org/templates/story/story.php?storyId=88512189

Hauck, Kenneth C. *Rebuilding and Remembering*. St. Louis, MO: Stephen Ministries, 2021.

Hayden, William. "Narrative Of William Hayden Containing A Faithful Account Of His Travels For A Number Of Years, Whilst A Slave, In The South" Cincinnati, Ohio: Ohio Clerk's Office, 1846.

Hemati, Christi. "Paul Ricoeur and Christian Humanism: Mediation of the Finite-Infinite" A paper Submitted to the Eighth Annual Paideia College Society Student Conference Dallas, Texas April 2005. https://www.dbu/naugle/paideia/archives/spring-2005/_documents/papers/2005_christi_hemati.pdf

Hendry, George S. *The Holy Spirit in Christian Theology*. New York, NY: SCM Press ltd.;, 1957.

Herrick, Rick. "Meeting the Holy Spirit: A Review Of "The Desire for Mutual Recognition" *progressivechristianity.org* November 13, 2018. https://progressivechristianity.org/resource/meeting-the-holy-spirit-of-the-desire-for-mutual-recognition/

Heron, Alasdair I. C. *The Holy Spirit: The Holy Spirit in the Bible, the History of Christian Thought, and Recent Theology*. Louisville, KY: Westminster John Knox Press, 1983.

Hicks, Jr., H. Beecher. *Preaching While Bleeding: Is There A Prophet in the House?* Chicago, IL: Urban Ministries, Inc., 2017.

Hodgson, Peter C. *Winds of the Spirit: A Constrictive Christian Theology*. Louisville, KY: Westminster John Knox Press, 1994.

Hollingsworth, Andrea. "Groans Too Deep: The Holy Spirit and Suffering" *Biola Canter for Christian Thought* April 1, 2019.

Holmes, Barbara A. *Joy Unspeakable: Contemplative Practices of the Black Church*. Minneapolis, MN: Augsburg Fortress Press, 2004.

"Holy Spirit" in Christian Denominational Variations*." The Spiritual Life*. https://slife.org/holy-spirit-in-christian-denominational-variations/

Hopkins, Dwight N. *Being Human: Race, Culture and Religion*. Minneapolis: Fortress Press, 2005.

_____ *Down, Up, and Over: Slave Religion and Black Theology*. Minneapolis, MN: Fortress Press, 2000

_____ *Heart and Head: Black Theology in Past, Present and Future*. London, EN: Palgrave Macmillan, 2003.

_____ *Shoes That Fit Our Feet: Sources For A Constructive Black Theology*. Maryknoll, KY: Orbis Books, 1993.

Hopkins, Dwight N. and Edward P. Antonio, Eds. *The Cambridge Companion to Black Theology*. Cambridge, MA: Cambridge University Press, 2012.

Hopkins, Dwight N. and George C.L. Cummings. Eds. *Cut Loose Your Stammering Tongue: Black Theology in the Slave Narratives*. Maryknoll, NY: Orbis Books, 1991.

https://divinehymns.com/lyrics/theres-a-sweet-sweet-spirit-song-lyrics/

https://genius.com/Aretha-franklin-spirit-in-the-dark-lyrics

https://genius.com/Aretha-franklin-this-little-light-of-mine-lyrics

https://genius.com/Little-richard-every-time-i-feel-the-spirit-lyrics

https://genius.com/Luther-vandross-little-miracles-happen-every-day-lyrics

https://genius.com/Marvin-gaye-inner-city-blues-make-me-wanna-holler-lyrics

https://genius.com/Mrvin-gaye-whats-going-on-lyrics

https://genius.com/Patti-labelle-the-spirits-in-it-lyrics

https://hymnary.org/text/holy_ghost_my_comforter

https://kinginstitute.stanford.edu/king-papers/documents/suffering-and-faith

https://www.bing.com/search?q='What's+Going+on%3F+is+an+idiomatic+expression+either+used+as+an+inform...

https://www.catholic.org/prayers/prayer.php?p=331

https://www.desiringgod.org/articles/why-jesus-needed-the-holy-spirit

https://www.facebook.com/CompassionIs/posts/212820082227006/

https://www.lyrics.com

https://www.lyricsondemand.com/r/revmiltonbrunsonlyrics/theholyghostlyrics.html

https://www.songlyrics.com/bill-gloria-gather/sweet-sweet-spirit-lyrics/

https://www.songlyrics.com/new-jersey-mass-choir-/holy-spirit-lyrics/

Hudson, Willie. *THE HOLY GHOST GOT A NEW DANCE: An Examination of Black Theology And Holy Hip-Hop in Inner-City Ministry*. Eugene, OR: Resource Publications, 2016.

Hurston, Zora Neale. *The Sanctified Church*. Berkeley, CA: Turtle Island, 1981.

Imasogie, Osadolor. *Guidelines for Christian Theology in Africa*. Accra, GH: African Christian Press, 1983.

What's Going On?

Ingram, Chip. *Spiritual Simplicity: Doing Less and Loving More.* New York, NY: Howard Books, 2013.

Internet Encyclopedia of Philosophy Iep.utm.edu https://iep.utm.edu

Jasper, David. *A Short Introduction to Hermeneutics.* Louisville, KY: Westminster John Knox Press, 2004.

Jeanrond, Werner G. "Hermeneutics and Christian Praxis: Some Reflections on the History of Hermeneutics." Journal of Literature & Theology, Vol. 2, No. 2, September 1988.

Jensen, David H. ed. *Lord and Giver of Life: Perspectives on Constructive Pneumatology.* Louisville, KY: Westminster John Knox Press, 2008.

"John Wesley SERMON II: THE WITNESS OF THE SPIRIT DISCOURSE II" https://biblesnet.com/john-wesley-witness-of-the-spirit-2.pdf

Johnson, Clifton. *God Struck Me Down: Voices of Ex-Slaves.* Eugene, OR: Wipf and Stock Publishers, 2011.

Johnson, Jill M. "The Holy Spirit and Justice *"ministrymatters* May 1, 2018. https://www.ministrymatters.com/all/entry/8965/the-holy-spirit-and-social-justice

Johnson, Joseph A. *Proclamation Theology.* Jackson, MS: Fourth Episcopal District Press, 1977.

Jones, Major J. Jones, *The Color of God: The Concept of God in Afro-American Thought.* Macon, GA: Mercer University Press, 2000.

Jones, Mark. "Why Jesus Needed the Holy Spirit," *desiringGod* March 12, 2019. https://www.desiringgod.org/articles/why-jesus-needed-the-holy-spirit

Jones, William R. *Is God A White Racist?: A Preamble to Black Theology.* Boston, MA: Beacon Press, 1997.

Joy, Morny. British Society for Phenomenology. "Paul Ricoeur and a Hermeneutics of Human Capability and Fragility" britishphenomenology.com/208Paper4.aspx es,

Kardec, Alan. *The Spirits' Book.* Sheridan, WY: Kalpany LLC, 2021.

Karkkainen, Veli-Matti. *Holy Spirit and Salvation: The Sources of Christian Theology* _____. *Pneumatology: The Holy Spirit in Ecumenical, International, and Contextual Perspective.* Grand Rapids, MI: Baker Academic, 2018.

Keller, Timothy. *Preaching: Communicating in the Age of Skepticism.* London, EN: Penguin House, 2016.

Kelley, Joseph T. *Saint Augustine of Hippo: Selections from Confessions and Other Essential Writings, Annotated and Explained.* Nashville, TN :SkyLight Paths, 2010.

Kerr, Hugh T. ed. *Readings in Christian Thought.* Nashville, TN: Abingdon Press, 1990.

King Jr., Martin Luther. "Our God Is Able" *The Martin Luther King, Jr. Research and Educational Institute* https://kinginstitute.stanford.edu/king-papers/documents/our-god-is-able _____. "Pilgrimage to Nonviolence" *The Martin Luther King, Jr. Research and Educational Institute* https://kinginstitute.stanford.edu/king-papers/documents/pilgrimage-Nonviolence _____. "Prayer Pilgrimage for Freedom," 17 May 1957.

Koech, Joseph. LIBERATOR: *A Study of Luke 4:14-30 in the African Context.* 2000.

Kreider, Aaron. "Black Theology's Call for Economic Justice" February 13, 1997. www.campusactivism.org/akreider/essays/libtheo1.text

Kuyper, Abraham. *The Work of the Holy Spirit.* Grand Rapids, MI: Wm. B. Eerdmans Lightning Source, 1941.

Landry Ministries, Curt. "What Are the 9 Gifts of the Holy Spirit? Understanding Their Purpose" August 2, 2023. https://www.curtlandry.com/9-gifts-of-the-holy-spirit/

Latourette, Kenneth S. *A History of Christianity.* New York, NY: Harper & Row, 1953.

Lenker, John N. ed. et al. *Sermons by Martin Luther: Volume 3 For Pentecost* martinluthersermons.*com/*Luther_Lenker_Vol_3.*pdf*

"Lisa Allen-McLaurin on the One Word Worship Model" December 18, 2023. https://worship.calvin.edu/resources-library/lisa-allen-mcclaurin-on-the-oneword-worship-model

Long, D. Stephen. *Divine Economy: Theology and the Market.* New York, NY: Routledge, 2000.

Luther's Pentecost Sermons in *Sermons of Martin Luther, vol. 3,* pp. 272-404.

Maddox, Randy L. ed. *Rethinking Wesley's Theology for Contemporary Methodism.* Nashville, TN: Abingdon Press, 1998.

Manschreck, Clyde L. ed. *A History of Christianity: Readings in the History of the Church from the Reformation to the Present.* Hoboken, NJ :Prentice Hall, 1964.

Marcus, Ezra. "DeJ Loaf Is Feeling Herself: How A Detroit Rapper Caught The Holy Ghost" *NOISEY.* September 25, 2004. https://www.vice.com/def-loaf-is-feeling-herself-how-a-detroit-rapper-caught-the-holy-ghost/en/article/64jj36/

Martinez, Archbishop Luis M. *The Sanctifier: The Classic Work on the Holy Spirit*. Boston, MA: Pauline Books and Media, 2023.

Mbiti, John S. *African Religions and Philosophy*, Second Edition. Portsmouth, NH: Heinemann, 1990.

McCaulley, Esau. *Reading While Black: African American Biblical Interpretations as an Exercise in Hope*. Westmont, IL: Intervarsity Press, 2020.

McFague, Sallie. *Life Abundant: Rethinking Theology and Economy for a Planet in Peril*. Minneapolis, MN: Fortress Press, 2000.

_____ *Metaphorical Theology: Models of God in Religion*. London, EN: SCM Press, 1983.

_____ *Speaking in Parables: A Study in Metaphor and Theology*. Philadelphia, PA: Fortress Press, 1975.

Meeks, M. Douglass. *God The Economist: The Doctrine of God and Political Economy*. Minneapolis, MN: Fortress Press, 1989.

Merlo, Oscar. "The Jesus People Movement: 50 Plus Years Later: How the Holy Spirit's Work then Can Give Us Hope for the Future" June 17, 2020. https://www.biola.edu/blogs/talbot-magazine/2020/the-jesus-people-movement-50-plus-years-later

Meyer, Elisa. "Prince: Reflecting on his Life, Religion, & Spirituality" *World Religion News* April 22, 2016. https://www.worldreligionnews.com/religion-news/prince-reflecting-on-his-life-religion-spirituality/

Meyer, Joyce. "The Holy Spirit, Our Strengthener" *Joyce Meyer Ministries* https://joycemeyer.org/everydayanswers/ea-teachings/the-holy-spirit-our-strengthener

"Michael Jackson—In His Own Words" www.michaeljacksonlegacy.org/michael/michael-jackson-in-his-own-words

Microsoft Bing: Search engine by Microsoft

Milton, Michael A. "What does the Bible Say about Poverty?" July 25, 2019. https://www.christianity.com/wiki/christian-life/what-does-the-bible-say-about-poverty.html

Mitchell, Julian. "God Over Everything: Black Spirituality and the Paradox of Religion" October 23, 2015. *HUFFPOST* https://www.huffpost.com/entry/god-over-everything-black_b_8310172

Mitchell, Henry H. *Black Belief: Folk Beliefs of Blacks in America and West Africa*. New York, NY: Harper & Row, 1975.

_____. *Black Preaching*. New York, NY: J.B. Lippincott Company, 1970.

Modest, Denise Anders, "The Bishop's Council Meeting of the Kentucky Region Conference" Paducah, Kentucky December 4, 2023.

Moltmann, Jurgen. *Theology of Hope: On the Ground and the Implications of a Christian Eschatology*. Minneapolis, MN: Fortress Press, 1993.

_____ *The Trinity and the Kingdom*. Minneapolis, MN: Fortress Press, 1993.

"Moral Selves: Politics as a Crisis of Meaning" *Dr. Christopher Ryan Mabolic: Life, Works & Writings* January 3, 2008. https://ryanmaboloc.blogspot.com/2008/01/paul-ricoeur-on-ethics.html

Mudge, Lewis S. Introduction. *Essays on Biblical Interpretation by Paul Ricoeur*. www.religion-online.org/showchapter.asp?title=1941&C...

Murphy, Larry G. *Down by the Riverside: Readings in African American Religion*. New York, NY: NYU Press, 2000.

Nazianzus, St Gregory. *On God and Christ: The Five Theological Orations and Two Letters to Cledonius*. Yonkers, NY: St. Vladimir's Seminary Press, 2011.

Nelson, Timothy J., *Every Time I Feel the Spirit: Religious Experience and Ritual in an African American Church*. New York, NY: University Press, 2004.

Nessan, Craig L. "Liberation Theologies in America" *Oxford Research Encyclopedias* December 19, 2017. https://doi.org/10.1093/acrefore/9780199340378.013.493

Nevares, Gabriel Bras. "Nas Attributes His Incredible Five Album Run To "The Holy Spirit" *Hnhh entertainment*. July 23, 2023. https://www.hotnewhiphop.com/697727-nas-run-music-holy-spirit

Ngong, David. "The Holy Spirit and Salvation in African Christian Theology Imagining a More Hopeful Future for Africa" *Academia*. https://www.academia.edu/24659258/The_Holy_Spirit_and_Salvation_in_African_Christian_Theology_Imagining_a_...

Nothstine, Ray. "The theology of John Wesley" *Acton Institute* Volume 18, Number 2. July 20, 2010. https://www.acton.org/pub/religion-liberty/volume-18-number-2/theology-john-wesley

Novak, Michael. *The Spirit of Democratic Capitalism*. Seattle, WA: Madison Books, 1990.

Oden, Thomas C. *How Africa Shaped the Christian Mind: Rediscovering the African Seedbed of*

Western Christianity. Downers Grove, IL: IVP Books, 2007.

Olatunde, Allen T. "Black Theology: A Surviving Mean to Blackness and Darkness of Africa from Slavery" *African Missiology* April 2012. https://africanmissiology.blogspot.com/2014/03/black-theology-surviving-mean-to.html

Orestes, (408 BC) Greek tragic dramatist (484 BC - 406 BC).

"Orthodox Spirituality: The Holy Spirit" *Orthodox Church in America* https://www.oca.org./orthodox-faith/spirituality/orthodox-spirituality/the-holy-spirit

Palmer, G.E.H. *The Philokalia: The Complete Text (Vol. 1); Compiled by St. Nikodimos of the Holy Mountain and St. Markarios of Corinth.* Burnt Mill, Harlow: Faber & Faber, 1983.

Papademetriou, George C. *An Introduction to Orthodox Spirituality.* Brookline, MA: Holy Cross Orthodox Press, 1984.

_____ August 17, 2012. https://goarch.org/introduction-articles/-/asset_publisher/zg5D5ENaCTK9/content/an-introduction-to-orthod...

Paris, Peter J. *Religion and Poverty: Pan-African Perspectives.* Durham, NC: Duke University Press, 2009.

Parrella, Frederick J. "5-Tillich's Theology of the concrete spirit: From Part I- Standing within the theological circle" Published online by Cambridge University Press; May 28, 2009. https:www.cambridge.org/core/books/abs/cambridge-companion-to-paul-tillich/tillichs-theology-of-the-co...

Perkins, John M. Ed., *Restoring At-Risk Communities: Doing It Together & Doing It Right* Grand Rapids, MI: Baker Books, 1995.

Perry, Whitall N. The Spiritual Ascent: *The Compendium of the World's Wisdom.* Louisville, KY: Fons Vitae, 2000.

Pierce, Yolonda. "The Souls of Du Bois' Black Folk" *The North Star* vol. 6, no. 2, Spring 2003. https://www.princeton.edu/~jweisenf/northstar/volume6/pierce.html

Pinn, Anthony B., ed. *Noise and Spirit: The Religious and Spiritual Sensibilities of Rap Music*

Pinn, Anthony B., and Katie G. Canon. Eds. *The Oxford handbook of African American Theology.* New York, NY: Oxford University Press, 2014.

Pinn, Anthony B. and Monica R. Miller. Eds. *Religion in Hip-Hop: Mapping the New Terrain in the US.* New York, NY: Bloomsbury Academic, 2015.

Placher, William C. *The Triune God: An Essay in Postliberal Theology.* Louisville, KY: Westminster John Knox Press, 2007.

Potter, G. R. *Zwingli.* Cambridge, MA: Cambridge University Press, 1977.

Prenter, Regin. *Creator Spiritus: Luther's Concept of the Holy Spirit.* Eugene, OR: Wipf and Stock Publishers, 2001.

Prevot, Andrew. "Divine Opacity: Mystical Theology, Black Theology, and the Problem of Light-Dark Aesthetics" *SSCS* January 5, 2017. https://sscs.press.jhu.edu/blog/article-divine-opacity-mystical-theology-black-theology-and-problem-light-da...

Ray, Stephen G. *Do No Harm: Social Sin and Christian Responsibility.* Minneapolis, MA: Fortress Press, 2002.

_____ Pneumatology in African American Religious Experiences: PhD course. Garrett-Evangelical Theological Seminary. Evanston, Illinois. Spring 2012.

_____ Sin and Evil: PhD course. Garrett-Evangelical Theological Seminary. Evanston, Illinois. Spring 2010.

_____ Theology and Economics: PhD course. Garrett-Evangelical Theological Seminary. Evanston, Illinois. Fall 2009.

Reddie, Anthony G. *Black Theology.* London, EN: SCM Press, 2012.

_____ "Black theology: an introduction" *Theos* August 25, 2020. https://www.theosthinktank.co.ik/comment/2020/08/12/black-theology-an-introduction

Reed, Teresa. *The Holy Profane: Religion in Black Popular Music.* Lexington, KY: University Press of Kentucky, 2004.

Reliford, Lauren W. "The Liberating Theology that Transformed My Understanding of God" *Sojourners* March 23, 2023. https://sojo.net/articles/liberating-theology-transformed-my-understanding-god

Reynolds, Blair. *Toward A Process Pneumatology.* London, EN: Associated University Press, 1990.

Rice, Howard L. *Reformed Spirituality: An Introduction For Believers.* Louisville, KY: Westminster John Knox Press, 1991.

Rich, Adrienne. *The Dream Of A Common Language: Poems 1974-1977.* New York, NY: W.W. Norton & Company, 1978.

Ricoeur, Paul. *Freedom and Nature*, Evanston, Northwestern University Press, 1966.

_____ *Hermeneutics and the Human Sciences: Essays on language and interpretation*. Edited, Translated and introduced by John B. Thompson. Cambridge: Cambridge University Press, 1981.

_____ *Time and Narrative: Volume One*. Chicago, IL: The University of Chicago Press, 1984.

Ricoeur, Paul and Hans Gadamer. *The Conflict in Interpretation: Essays in Hermeneutics*. Evanston, IL: Northwestern University Press, 2007.

Ricoeur, Paul. "Toward a Hermeneutic of Revelation," https://www.jstor.org/stable/1508979

Riggleman, Heather. "What Does it Mean to Let Your Light Shine?" *Christianity.com* https://www.christianity.com/wiki/bible/what-does-it-mean-to-let-your-light-shine.html

Rivers III, Eugene F. "Powers and Principalities: King and the Holy Spirit" *Plough* May 16, 2018. https:www.plough.com/en/topics/justice/social-justice/powers-and-principalities

Roberts, J. Deotis. *A Black Political Theology*. Louisville, KY: Westminster John Knox Press, 2005.

_____ *Africentric Christianity: A Theological Appraisal for Ministry*. Prussia, PA: Judson Press, 2000.

_____ *Black Theology in Dialogue*. Louisville: Westminster John Knox Press, 1987.

_____ *Liberation and Reconciliation: A Black Theology*. Louisville, KY: Westminster John Knox Press, 2005.

_____ *The Prophethood of Black Believers: An African American Theology for Ministry*. Louisville, KY: Westminster John Knox Press, 1994.

Rotelle, John E. ed. *The Augustine Catechism: The Enchiridion on Faith, Hope, and Love*. Hyde Park, NY: New City Press, 1999.

Ruether, Rosemary R. ed. *Gender, Ethnicity, and Religion: Views from the Other Side*. Minneapolis, MN: Fortress Press, 2002.

Russ, Mark. "James Cone's 'A Black Theology of Liberation' and white liberal Quakerism" *Jolly Quaker* August 3, 2020. https://jollyquaker.com/2020/08/03/james-cones-a-black-theology-of-liberation-and-white-liberal-quakerism/

Russell, Walter B. *Jesus and the Trinity: A Key to a Deeper Religious Experience*,

Ryan, Michael. *The contemporary explosion of theology*. Lanham, MD: Scarecrow Press, 1975.

Sanders, Cheryl J. *Living the Intersection: Womanism and Afrocentrism in Theology*. Minneapolis, MN: Augsburg Fortress Press, 1995.

Sanders, Fred. "Pneumatology of Freedom" December 7, 2020. https://scriptoriumdaily.com/a-black-american-pneumatology-of-freedom/

Sanders, Scott R. *Writing from the Center*. Bloomington, IN: Indiana University Press, 1997.

Sanusi, Mayoma. "Healing is Essential to Liberation" *Medium* July 29, 2021. https://hria.org/2021/07/29/healingandliberation/

Savage, Barbara D. *Your Spirits Walk Beside Us: The Politics of Black Religion*. Cambridge, MA: The Belknap Press, 2008.

Schaab, Gloria L. *Liberating Pneumatologies: Spirit Set Free*. Spring Valley, NY: Herder & Herder, 2021.

Sermon 13, "On Sin in Believers." In The Sermons of John Wesley, edited by Thomas Jackson. Global Ministries of the United Methodist Church. http://www.umcmission.org/Find-Resources/ Global-Worship-and-Spiritual-Growth/John-Wesley-Sermons/ Sermon-13-On-Sin-in-Believers

Serra-Collett, Jaume. *Black Adam*. New Line Cinema, 2007.

Shults, F. LeRon and Steven J. Sandage, *Transforming Spirituality: Integrating Theology and Psychology*. Grand Rapids, MI: Baker Academic, 2006.

Smith, Barry D. "Distanciation and Textual Interpretations" Volume 43, Number 2, June 1987. https://www.erudit.org/en/journals/Hp/1987-v43-n2-lpt2128/400302ar.pdf

Smith, Harrison. "J. Deotis Roberts, a pioneer of Black Theology, dies at 95" The Washington Post August 16, 2022. https://www.washingtonpost.com/obituaries/2022/08/16/black-theology-deaths-roberts-dead/

Sobrino, Jon. *Jesus the Liberator: A Historical-Theological View*. Maryknoll, NY: Orbis Books, 1994.

Spangler, David. "The Economics of Spirit: Spiritual economics as an exchange of energy to enhance the potential for creating" *Context Institute Spring* 1983. https://www.context.org/iclib/ic02/spangler/

"Spirituality in the Civil Rights Movements" *Center for Action and Contemplation* December 2, 2020. https://cac.org/daily-meditations/spirituality-in-the-civil-rights-movement-2020-12-02/

Stanford Encyclopedia of Philosophy-Hermeneutics. plato.stanford.edu/entries/hermeneutics/

Stephens, W. P. *The Theology of Huldrych Zwingli*. Oxford, EN: Clarendon Press, 1988.

St. Markarios of Corinth (Philokalia), St. Gregory of Sinai. "Introductory Note,"

Struk, Alexander. "The Hermeneutics of Testimony: Ricoeur and a LDS Perspective" *Aporia* vol.19, no. 1, 2009. https://aporia.byu.edu/pdfs/struk-the-hermeneutics-of-testimony.pdf

Sylvan, Robin. *Traces of the Spirit: The Religious Dimensions of Popular Music.* New York, NY: NYU Press, 2002.

Tanner, Kathryn. *Economy of Grace.* Minneapolis, MN: Fortress Press, 2005.

_____*Jesus, Humanity, and the Trinity: A Systematic Theology in Brief.* Minneapolis, MN: Fortress Press, 2001.

_____ *Theories of Culture: A New Agenda For Theology.* Minneapolis, MN: Fortress Press, 1997.

Taylor, Sonya R. *The Body Is Not an Apology: The Power of Self-Love.* Oakland, CA: Barrett-Koehler, 2018.

Tennent, Timothy C. *The Spirit-Filled Life.* Franklin, TN: Seedbed Publishing, 2019.

"The Economy of God's Love – The Rev. Michelle Meech" *St. John's Episcopal Church* September 24, 2013. www.stjohnskingston.org/sermon/the-economy-of-gods-love/

"The Holy Spirit and the Movement of God's Biblical Basis"

The Road to Zero Wealth: How the Racial Wealth Divide is Hollowing Out Americans Middle Class. Washington, DC: Institute for Policy Studies (INEQUALITY.ORG) and Prosperity Now, 2017. https://inequality.org/research/zerowealth/

Thistlethwaite, Susan B. and Mary E. Potter. *Lift Every Voice: Constructing Theologies from the Underside.* New York, NY: Orbis Books, 1998.

Thomas, Frank A. *The Choice: Living Your Passion Outside Out.* Hammond, IN: Hope For Life International Books, 2013.

Thomas, Linda E. "The Holy Spirit and Black Women: A Womanist Perspective" *Springer Link* https://link.springer.com/chapter/10.1057/978113746220_5

Thurman, Howard. *Jesus and the Disinherited.* Boston, MA: Beacon Press, 1996.

Tillich, Paul. *Systematic Theology, Vol. 3: Life and the Spirit History and the Kingdom of God.* Chicago, IL: University of Chicago Press, 1963.

Tisby, Jemar. *The Spirit of Justice: True Stories of Faith, Race, and Resistance.* Grand Rapids, MI: Zondervan Reflective, 2024.

Topping, Richard R. *Revelation, Scripture and Church: Theological Hermeneutical Thought of James Barr, Paul Ricoeur and Hans Frei.* London, EN: Routledge, 2018.

Townes, Emilie N. ed. *A Troubling in my Soul: Womanist Perspectives on Evil and Suffering.* Maryknoll, NY: Orbis, 1993.

_____ *Embracing the Spirit: Womanist Perspectives on Hope, Salvation and Transformation.* Maryknoll, NY: Orbis Books, 1997.

Tucker, Irvin B. *Survey of Economics.* Boston, MA: Cengage Learning, 2018.

Volf, Miroslav. *The End of Memory: Remembering Rightly in a Violent World. Grand Rapids, MI:* William B. Eerdmans, 2006.

Van Dusen, Henry P. *Spirit, Son, and Father: Christian Faith in the Light of the Holy Spirit.* New York, NY: Scribner's Publishing, 1958.

Von Loewenich, Walther. *Luther's Theology of the Cross: Martin Luther's Theological Breakthrough.* Minneapolis, MN: Augsburg Publishing House, 1976.

Walker, Corey D. B. "Love and a Theology of Blackness: A Meditation on James H. Cone" *Black Perspectives* September 5, 2018. https://www.aaihs.org/love-and-a-theology-of-blackness-a-meditation-james-h-cone/

Wallis, Jim. *Faith Works: How Faith-based Organizations Are Changing Lives, Neighborhoods and America.* Berkeley, CA: Pagemill Press, 2000.

Ware, Fredrick L. *African American Theology: An Introduction.* Louisville, KY: Westminster John Knox Press, 2016.

Warren, Rick. "The Holy Spirit Brings God's Truth to Mind" *PastorRick.com* August 3, 2019. https://pastorrick.com/the-holy-spirit-brings-gods-truth-to-mind/

Waters Sr., Kenneth L. "Afro-Pentecostalism: Black Pentecost and Charismatic Christianity in History and Culture" *Christian Scholars Review* April 15, 2013. https://christianscholars.com/afro-pentecostalism-black-pentecostal-and-charismatic-christianity-in-history-and-cult...

Welker, Michael. God the Spirit. Eugene, OR: Wipf and Stock Publishers, 2013.

_____ *The Work of the Spirit: Pneumatology and Pentecostalism.* Grand Rapids, MI: Wm. B. Eerdmans Publishing, 2006.

Wesley, John. *A Plain Account of Christian Perfection,* quoted by M. James Sawyer, "The Witness of the Spirit in the Protestant Tradition," Bible.org.

_____ "On Sin in Believers," "Holy Spirit in Christian Denominational Variations" *The Spiritual Life* https://slife.org/holy-spirit-in-Christian-denominational=variations/
_____ "The Witness of the Spirit: Sermon 10 [text from the 1872 edition]"
_____ "The Witness of the Spirit: Sermon 11" SPIRIT DISCOURSE II
West, Cornel. *The Cornel West Reader.* New York, NY: *Civitas* Books, 1999.
"What Are the 9 Gifts of the Holy Spirit?," *Curt Landry Ministries.* August 19, 2012. https://www.curtlandry.com/9-gifts-of-the-holy-spirit/
"What does 2 Corinthians 8:9 mean" *Bibleref.com* https://www.bibleref.com/2-Corinthians/8/2-Corinthians-8-9.html
"What is Biblical Illumination" *Compelling Truth.* https://www.compellingtruth.org/biblical-illumination.html
Wiesel, Elie. *Night.* New York, NY: Hill and Wang Publishers, 2006.
Wilken, Robert L. *The Spirit of Early Christian Thought: Seeking the Face of God.* New Haven, CT: Yale University Press, 2005.
Williams, Delores S. "Womanist Theology: Black Women's Voices" *Religion Online* www.religion-online.org/showarticle.asp? title=445
Williamson, Marianne. *A Return to Love.* San Fransisco, CA: HarperOne, 1996.
Wilmore, Gayraud S. *Black Religion and Black Theology: An Interpretation of the Religious History of African Americans.* Maryknoll, NY: Orbis Books, 1988.
Wilson, Wylin D. *Economic Ethics & the Black Church.* London, EN: Palgrave McMillan, 2017.
Wikipedia: Pentecostalism https://en.wikipedia.org/wiki/Pentecostalism
Woodley, Randy. *Living in Color: Embracing God's Passion for Ethnic Diversity.* Downers Grove, IL: Intervarsity Press, 2004.
Womanist: Encyclopedia II- Womanists- Introduction, www.experiencefestival.com/a/Womanist_-_Introduction/id/... www.biblegateway.com
Yong, Amos. *Spirit of Love: A Trinitarian Theology of Grace.* Waco, TX :Baylor University Press, 2012.
Yong, Amos, and Estrelda Y. Alexander. Eds. *Afro-Pentecostalism: Black Pentecost and Charismatic Christianity in History and Culture.* New York, NY: NYU Press, 2011.
Zanfagna, Christina. "Under the Blasphemous W(RAP): Locating the "Spirit" in Hip-Hop" Pacific Review of Ethnomusicology Volume 12 (2006). https://ethnomusicologyreview.ucla.edu/journal/volume/12/piece/507
Zondervan. et al. *The Third Person of the Trinity: Explorations in Constructive Dogmatics.* Grand Rapids, MI: Zondervan Academic, 2020.
Zondervan. *NIV Study Bible.* Grand Rapids, MI: Zondervan, 2008.

Table of Names

Darvin Anton Adams

Darvin Anton Adams